Eastern Orthodox Christianity
Christianity
The Essential Texts

Bryn Geffert and Theofanis G. Stavrou

Yale UNIVERSITY PRESS

New Haven and London

Published with assistance from the Louis Stern Memorial Fund.

Yale University Press books may be purchased in quantity for educational, business, or
promotional use. For information, please e-mail sales.press@yale.edu (U.S. office) or
sales@yaleup.co.uk (U.K. office).

Set in Sabon type by Newgen North America.
Printed in the United States of America.

Library of Congress Control Number: 2015955421
ISBN 978-0-300-19678-8 (paperback : alk. paper)

A catalogue record for this book is available from the British Library.

This paper meets the requirements of ANSI/NISO Z39.48-1992 (Permanence of Paper).

10 9 8 7 6 5 4 3 2 1

Contents

PART III Modernity and Upheavals

Contents

Sources in *Eastern Orthodox Christianity: Supplemental Texts*

yalebooks.com/eoc

Preface

Before you is a peculiar history of Eastern Orthodox Christianity, a tradition itself considered peculiar (if considered at all) by many who know Christianity only in its Protestant and Roman Catholic variants, or who know Christianity not at all.

Who are "Eastern Orthodox Christians"? The term tells us at least three things about those who identify with it. Eastern Orthodox Christians consider themselves . . .

- . . . "Christians," that is, followers of Jesus of Nazareth (born ca. 7–2 BCE; died ca. 30–33 CE), whom they believe to be the "Christ" (a Greek translation of the Hebrew word "Messiah"), namely the "anointed one," the savior of humankind; and not only the son of God, but God himself.
- . . . "Orthodox," which can be translated as "right believing" or "right worshipping"; in other words, they consider themselves to believe the right things and to worship in the right ways. The degree to which other Christians may or may not believe correctly or worship properly has been (and remains) a matter of great dispute in Eastern Christendom, but virtually all Eastern Christians agree that they themselves are uniquely orthodox.
- . . . "Eastern," that is, faithful to a tradition that developed in "the East": in Egypt, Greece, Constantinople (now Istanbul), Palestine/Israel, Syria, Georgia, Armenia, and, later, in Bulgaria, Romania, Serbia, Ukraine, Belarus, and Russia. Today, Eastern Orthodox Christians can be found throughout the world; large populations live in Western Europe, the United States, Canada, Central Asia, and

Australia, but most of these communities consist of or at least derive
from immigrants from "the East."

Scholars of Eastern Orthodox Christianity frequently note its long
tradition of *apophatic* theology, that is, a theology that readily acknowledges how little we know or can know about an ineffable and
ultimately unknowable God. In other words, Eastern Orthodox theologians focus to a degree unusual in the Christian tradition on what
God is *not*. Given this tradition, we thought it appropriate to begin by
noting what this book is not. It is not . . .

- . . . *religious history*. It does not, in other words, present history
  through any particular religious, philosophical, or theoretical lens.
  We strive to portray the beliefs and history of Eastern Orthodox
  Christians with sympathy and respect, and we strive as well to avoid
  rendering any judgments—positive or negative—on those beliefs.
  While acknowledging the practical limits of pure objectivity, we
  seek objectivity nevertheless.
- . . . *a traditional, historical narrative*. This book is a collection of
  primary sources, woven together with introductions and narratives,
  which, we hope, together provide a coherent history of Eastern
  Orthodox Christianity. Hence this is a history of religion through
  the eyes of those who lived it, shaped it, wrestled with it, opposed it,
  abandoned it, fought it, and drew inspiration from it. It is history as
  told by those who experienced it.
- . . . *comprehensive*. Everybody who knows anything about Eastern
  Orthodoxy will immediately object to our decision not to include
  [name your source or topic here]. And virtually every objection
  will have merit. A complete history of Eastern Orthodoxy is impossible. We've tried instead to present a representative history, a
  history that explores important themes through illustrative topics.
  Thousands of interesting and consequential events and sources did
  not make the cut, for no other reason than—unlike the infinite God
  the Eastern Orthodox worship—space is finite. An online supplement to this volume includes additional sources, and entire subjects,
  not covered here (yalebooks.com/eoc). But it too fails the test of
  comprehensiveness.

So what *is* this book? We hope that it is . . .

- . . . *accessible*. We assume little knowledge on the reader's part about
  theology or the history of religion. Those with scant background
  in Christianity or the history of Eastern Orthodoxy should face no
  serious obstacles here. However, this is not "history lite." We include

serious and sometimes difficult readings, while doing all we can to guide readers through the more challenging passages. Our introductions place sources in their historical contexts, discuss their significance, explain unfamiliar concepts, and tie the sources to larger themes and problems. Footnotes define and explain terms, ideas, places, and objects with which readers may be unfamiliar.

- . . . *lively*. We selected sources designed to entice and engage. Three undergraduate editorial assistants reacted frankly to potential sources, fought for some, persuaded us to withdraw others, and unearthed and inserted some of their own. We shared drafts with other students who provided valuable feedback. And we surveyed professors who teach courses in Eastern Orthodox history, asking them to suggest additions. The resulting sources—more than three hundred of them—we believe, are intriguing, often absorbing, and sometimes riveting.

- . . . *diverse*. We cover a vast range of subjects, time periods, and themes. This work is big—too big for one volume—and we've thus paired it with an online supplemental volume. A list of contents for the *Supplemental Texts* appears in the front matter of this volume. Although by no means comprehensive (see the disclaimer above), we trust that this work is sufficiently far-reaching to serve as the primary or sole text for a class on the history of the Eastern church.

- . . . *multidisciplinary*. Our work contains readings in anthropology, art, film, history, law, literature, music, politics, theology, and women's studies.

- . . . *multicultural*. Although the Eastern church understands itself as the one true church and its faith as constituting the *oikoumene* (a term used in the Greco-Roman world to denote the entire inhabited earth), Eastern Christianity developed in peculiar ways in peculiar settings. This book grapples repeatedly with the tension between Orthodoxy as an ecumenical, universal confession and Orthodoxy as multiple representations of distinct cultures. We discuss the ways that ethnicity, language, geography, nationalism, emigration, political struggles, missionary excursions, and invasions shaped Orthodox Christianity around the world. We give special attention to Greece, Byzantium, and Russia, that is, the historic centers of Eastern Orthodoxy. We examine the ways Byzantine culture influenced Russian Christianity; the ways Byzantine Christianity defined itself against Islamic, Arabic, and North African religions; and Russia's increasingly nationalistic understanding of Christianity. But we also range far beyond these major centers of the faith: we consider Orthodoxy in Alaska, Armenia, Egypt, Ethiopia, Georgia, Mount Athos, Palestine, Poland, Romania, Syria, and Ukraine, asking how

these cultures received, modified, or rejected aspects of a faith and
regional identities that originated elsewhere.

- ... *multisensory*. Sight and sound play an outsize role in Orthodox
worship, a role greater than in any other variant of Christianity.
To be sure, much of this work consists of texts: biographies, poems, short stories, sermons, saints' lives, novels, treaties, treatises,
primers, laws and regulations, manifestos, polemics, field reports,
personal letters, official communiqués, pamphlets, newspaper articles, certificates, hagiographies, statements of faith, travelogues,
eyewitness accounts, instructional manuals, liturgical books, scripture, forged documents, grants, and commentaries. But a history
of Orthodoxy based on texts alone would provide an incomplete
account of its history and priorities. In the supplement we thus include reproductions of icons for sections on iconography. We gathered recordings overseen by academic musicologists that attempt
to reproduce Byzantine chants as they may have sounded at their
inception. We include recordings of Tchaikovsky's, Rachmaninov's,
and Stravinsky's church music. The section on Orthodoxy in the Soviet Union reprints antireligious propaganda, including posters and
photographs of museums and parades. Most novel and interesting,
perhaps, are portrayals of Orthodoxy in film, excerpted from twelve
movies, ranging from anti-Orthodox propaganda to pro-Orthodox
themes. These clips explore many of the themes raised elsewhere in
the work, while illustrating the profound influence of Orthodoxy on
artists and the larger cultural milieu.

Our work uses translations by others when possible, although we
regularly revised those translations to clarify meaning, to improve
awkward prose, to conform to modern style and conventions, and to
ensure consistency when consistency seemed desirable. We produced
translations of our own when no good options were available in English. Most explanatory glosses are our own, although we borrow on
occasion from the editors of work translated by others.[1]

---

1. To save space, we do not usually cite editors (other than in the main citation
to each text) responsible for explanatory information in footnoted glosses.

Acknowledgments

This book owes a great deal to many people, most of all to the undergraduates who assisted us. Kate Lichti and Margaret Barter Gipson spent a summer with Bryn Geffert at the beginning of this project choosing and editing sources. Their frank assessments of potential texts—their advocacy for striking some and adding others—did a great deal to set the book's tone. Their energy and goofiness (including their bicycle liberation project) made the summer one of the most rewarding in memory. Rachel Gucker did incredible work on the book's maps, essentially teaching herself cartography on the fly. She also suggested sources and edited many others; her editorial fingerprints can be found throughout. Daniel Rono assumed the formidable task of gathering permissions to use work under copyright. A dogged pursuer and a shrewd negotiator, Daniel immersed himself in the often surreal world of publishing mergers, rival claimants, disappearing rights-holders, and orphaned works. If any lesson can be drawn from his work, it is that U.S. copyright law desperately needs wholesale reform.

Robert Nichols, a friend and mentor to both of us for many years, offered regular advice. He first suggested the four-part structure the book eventually assumed.

St. Olaf College and Amherst College provided significant monetary support. Both institutions zealously support faculty research and, perhaps even more important, encourage and enable partnerships between faculty and undergraduates for said research.

Sarah Miller, Heather Gold, and Ash Lago at Yale University Press and our copy editor, Jessie Dolch, were great. Miller encouraged our project when we first approached her and arranged a survey of faculty and scholars in the field to ascertain interest. Gold and Lago helped us surmount many small obstacles. Dolch helped produce a final text much better than the one we submitted.

Four translators helped with sources that frustrated us: Kevin Kain tackled Old Church Slavonic in "Questions of Kirik," Andrey Kvasyuk parsed the archaic verbiage spouted by the fast-talking Petr Mamonov in *Tsar,* Jack Kollman translated legalese from the *Stoglav* Council, and Soterios Stavrou translated the Greek Holy Synod's condemnation of Nikos Kazantzakis.

We conclude by thanking our students at Amherst College and the University of Minnesota and all the figures in the field of Eastern Orthodox history who offered advice: Rosalie Beck, Peter Bouteneff, Chris Chulos, Flora Curta, Michael S. Flier, Paul Gavrilyuk, Robert H. Greene, Bruce F. Holle, Matt Miller, Bradley Nassif, Theophilus C. Prousis, Roy Robson, Vera Shevzov, Stephen J. Shoemaker, Edward Siecienski, Franklin Sciacca, Jaroslav Skira, Mark Steinberg, Christine D. Worobec, and Viktor Zhivov. We are grateful for their advice on broad themes and small particulars. Of course we, not they, are to blame for all final decisions, inclusions, exclusions, and errors.

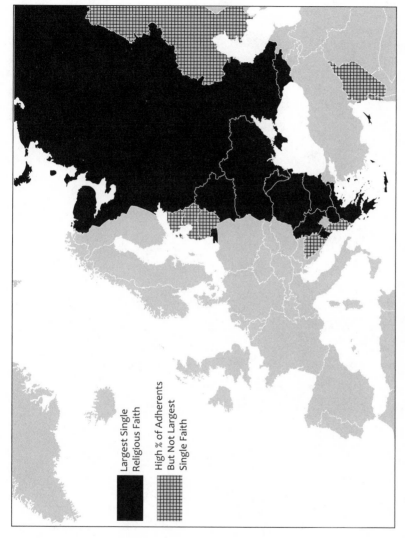

Figure 1. Concentration of Eastern Orthodoxy, 2010

Eastern Orthodox Christianity

PART I

Origins and Metamorphoses

Beginnings, Scripture, and Patristics

When did Christianity begin?

Those who acknowledge its roots in Judaism might posit Christianity's origins as far back as the 1900s BCE, that is, to the earliest days of the Hebrew patriarchs, those tribal leaders whose stories appear in the Torah—the first five books of Hebrew scripture. Those books, assembled perhaps in the 400s BCE from texts dating as far back as 900 BCE (texts derived, in turn, from older, oral traditions), constitute the scriptural basis of Judaism, the great monotheistic religion of the Middle East before the advent of Islam. The Torah and Hebrew scriptures that followed tell the story of the Israelites, who understood themselves as "God's people," people chosen by Yahweh—the one true God—to live under God's protection in return for following God's laws.

Christians who see Judaism primarily as a precursor to Christianity (a stance unacceptable to most Jews) focus on Jewish texts that predict the coming of a messiah, a great king who would free the Israelites from foreign rule and establish the kingdom of God here on earth. Passages from Isaiah—texts written, perhaps, during the 400s and 500s BCE—speak passionately about one named "Immanuel" ("God is with us"): an "anointed one" who would wrest light from darkness, peace from strife, and reign forever with "justice" and "righteousness." Of course most Jews insist that the long-awaited Messiah has yet to arrive. But small numbers of Jews, most famously the Apostle Peter and the Apostle Paul, identified this Messiah (or "Christ" in Greek) in the person of Jesus of Nazareth.

3

Hence many Christians posit the beginnings of Christianity with the birth of this itinerant teacher, born sometime between the years 7 and 2 BCE, who, over the next thirty-odd years, wandered the countryside, performed miracles, spoke in parables, proclaimed the coming of God's kingdom, referred to himself as the "Son of God" and "Son of man," and promised "eternal salvation." Numerous Gospels written during the decades following Jesus's death report his deeds and teachings. Over time, however, the church bestowed its blessing on just four of these Gospels—Matthew, Mark, Luke, and John—written between 65 CE and 110 CE. The church declared the remaining Gospels, most of which no longer survive, to be heretical, that is, contrary to God's truth.

Thus some people date Christianity's origins from the beginning of the Christian church, the institution built by those who claimed Jesus as the Christ and established which teachings about him should be accepted as valid.

Today, what most Christians—be they Eastern Orthodox, Roman Catholic, or Protestant—know about the early church, they know from these texts, which—together with various letters and sermons by Christian teachers—constitute what we call the "New Testament." The New Testament provides important insights into the formation of the church and the development of early Christian theology. Thus any understanding of Christianity requires some familiarity with Christian scripture, which most Christians regard as holy, inspired by God, and the foundation of faith. Many Protestant Christians consider these scriptures to be self-sufficient, the fullness and completeness of God's revelation, with no need of supplements or clarifications.

But here we find a deep divide between Protestant Christians on one hand and Roman Catholic and Eastern Orthodox Christians on the other. Protestant arguments in the 1500s about the self-sufficiency of scripture—that is, arguments that deemphasized, discounted, or even ignored the writings of the church fathers and later statements by theologians and councils—represented something radical and new. Martin Luther's mantra, *sola scriptura* ("by scripture alone"), proved anathema to the Roman Catholic Church in the West and the Orthodox Church in the East. Scripture alone is not sufficient, they replied. Our predecessors left us a crucial body of literature essential in defining and understanding the faith. Why, Roman Catholics and Eastern Orthodox asked, should we ignore the inspired work of godly men (with the emphasis on "men")?

The work of these men—the "church fathers" who authored "patristic" (from the Latin *pater,* or father) literature—focused on exceptionally difficult questions.

What, for example, is the "church," which the New Testament's book of Acts and Paul's epistles mention so often?[1] What powers does it have?

Who, exactly, was Jesus? A holy man? A holy man with supernatural powers? A divine man? God? If God, how can we acknowledge Jesus as such while still believing in only one God, that is, while remaining true to the monotheism of Judaism from which Christianity sprang?

And how does the Holy Spirit, mentioned throughout the New Testament, accord with the notion of one God? Does talk of a Trinity—of "God the Father," "God the Son" (Jesus), and "God the Holy Spirit"— necessarily devolve into polytheism?

Christological and Trinitarian theology, that is, theology that grapples with the nature of Jesus Christ and the nature of the Trinity, proved arduous and contentious in part because the New Testament did not anticipate all the questions later Christians posed. New Testament scripture offers nothing but silence on the composition and nature of the Trinity. In fact the word "Trinity" appears nowhere in scripture. Hence all orthodox and many unorthodox understandings of the Trinity (to note just one example) hearken back to brutal debates between patristic writers—debates we examine in the pages ahead.

For now, however, the chief point for a book about Eastern Orthodoxy is this: according to Eastern Orthodox theologians, patristic writings are as important, nearly as important, or only slightly less important than canonical scripture. Orthodox clerics like to remind their Protestant counterparts that (1) patristic writings recognized by the church tackled important questions that scripture did not, and that (2) *the church and its councils* established the canon of scripture. In other words, scripture itself did not determine which scriptures among hundreds were valid; debates within the church, inspired by the Holy Spirit, determined which scriptures were valid. To put it another way, the Eastern Orthodox insist that scripture grew out of the church; the church did not grow out of scripture.

The same is true of patristic writings, say the Eastern Orthodox. The church and its councils decided which were valid and which were

1. See section 1, "Church in Scripture," in the online supplement.

inadequate or heretical. Thus scripture and patristics bear whatever authority the church, acting under the influence of the Holy Spirit, ascribes to them.

This is a difficult notion for Protestants who understand scripture as the self-sufficient rule of faith. In fact the Orthodox sometimes accuse Protestants of "bibliolatry," suggesting that Protestants elevate the Bible to a place of sole authority that only God can occupy. Suggesting that the Bible is self-sufficient, say the Orthodox, denies God's ability to reveal himself in new ways. Revelation did not end with the Bible: it continues to this day through the work of the Holy Spirit in the church.

New Sect

In accord with the observations above, we begin our history of Eastern Christianity with a patristic letter, an effort to settle some of the vexed questions the early church faced.

Ignatius of Antioch served as the "bishop," or overseer, of churches in Antioch—a city on the Mediterranean Sea in what is now south-central Turkey. The following letter, which Ignatius wrote to Christians in Smyrna (modern-day Izmir on the west-central coast of Turkey), interests us for at least three reasons.

First, it illustrates the precarious position of Christians in what was then the Roman Empire. Ignatius wrote this letter on his way to Rome in chains, having been arrested in Antioch for his faith. He would soon die in the Roman arena, ripped apart by wild beasts as entertainment for the masses. In fact Ignatius knew the Smyrnians he addresses in this letter only because the soldiers leading him to Rome stopped en route in Smyrna.

Second, Ignatius's letter demonstrates how unsettled were fundamental points of Christian doctrine at this early time in the church's history. Who or what was Jesus? Was he God? If so, did he possess actual flesh? (Can God be flesh?) If not, did Jesus truly suffer when he was crucified?

Some Christians known as Docetists argued that Christ, as God, could not have possessed a real body. God, after all, has no body. Hence the physical Jesus whom disciples followed around the countryside was only an "apparent" body—a phantom apparition. And Jesus's crucifixion was thus an illusion. In this letter, Ignatius attacks these beliefs, suggesting that anybody subscribing to them merits only

7

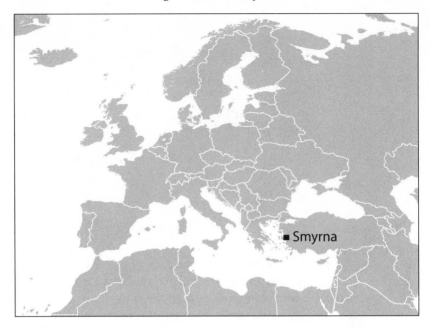

Figure 2. Smyrna

"condemnation." His arguments set the stage for more nuanced and complex arguments in the centuries to follow, arguments we engage later in our work.

Third, Ignatius's letter tackles—again, in nascent form—questions about authority in the early church. Here Ignatius lays out a sketchy yet firm case for hierarchy. The church in his estimation (and in the estimation of those whose arguments later won the day) is not a communal organization of equals. It is an organization led by and subject to decisions by leaders: bishops, presbyters, and deacons. Bishops, in fact, should function much like Christ on earth.

Ignatius's arguments are simple and direct. And although they settled almost no issue decisively, they set the stage for more arguments to come.

Letter of Ignatius to the Smyrnians (ca. 107–110)

Ignatius of Antioch, "The Epistle of Ignatius to the Smyrnaeans," *Ante-Nicene Christian Library* (Edinburgh: T & T Clark, 1867), 1:238–55.

· I ·

I glorify God, even Jesus Christ, who has given you such wisdom. For I have observed that you are perfected in an immoveable faith, as if you were nailed to the cross of our Lord Jesus Christ, both in the flesh and in the spirit, and are established in love through the blood of Christ, being fully persuaded with respect to our Lord, that he was truly of the seed of David[1] according to the flesh, and the Son of God according to the will and power of God; that he was truly born of a virgin; was baptized by John, in order that all righteousness might be fulfilled by him; and was truly, under Pontius Pilate and Herod the tetrarch, nailed [to the cross] for us in his flesh. Of this fruit we are by his divinely blessed passion, that he might set up a standard for all ages, through his resurrection,[2] to all his holy and faithful [followers], whether among Jews or Gentiles,[3] in the one body of his church.

· II ·

Now, he suffered all these things for our sakes, that we might be saved. And he suffered truly, even as also he truly raised himself up, not, as certain unbelievers maintain, that he only seemed to suffer, as they themselves only seem to be [Christians]. And as they believe, so shall it happen to them, when they shall be divested of their bodies, and be mere evil spirits.

· III ·

For I know that after his resurrection he was still possessed of flesh, and I believe that he is so now. When, for instance, he came to those who were with Peter, he said to them, "Lay hold, handle me, and see that I am not an incorporeal[4] spirit." And immediately they touched him, and believed, being convinced both by his flesh and by his spirit. For this cause also they despised death, and were found its conquerors. And after his resurrection he ate and drank with them, as being possessed of flesh, although spiritually he was united to the Father.

· IV ·

I give you these instructions, beloved, assured that you also hold the same opinions [as I do]. But I guard you beforehand from those beasts in the shape of men, whom you must not only not receive, but if it be possible not even meet; instead you must pray to God for them if by any means they may be brought to repentance, which, however, will be very difficult. Yet Jesus Christ, who is our true life, has the power of [affecting] this. But if these things were done by our Lord only in appearance, then

---

1. *seed of David*—the books of Luke and Matthew report that Jesus was a descendant of King David, whose reign is described in the Hebrew books of Samuel.

2. *resurrection*—rebirth after death.

3. *Gentiles*—non-Jews.

4. *incorporeal*—without a body.

I, too, am bound only in appearance.[5] And why have I also surrendered myself to death, to fire, to the sword, and to the wild beasts? For he who is near to the sword is near to God. He who is among the wild beasts is in the company of God, provided that he is so in the name of Jesus Christ. I undergo all these things so I may suffer together with him, who became a perfect man inwardly, thus strengthening me.

· V ·

Some ignorantly deny him—or rather have been denied by him—advocating death rather than the truth. These persons have not been persuaded by the prophets, nor by the law of Moses, nor even to this day by the Gospel, nor by the sufferings we have each endured. For they think also the same thing regarding us.[6] [. . .] Whoever does not acknowledge this has in fact altogether denied him, being enveloped in death. I have not, however, thought it good to write the names of such persons, inasmuch as they are unbelievers. Far be it from me to make any mention of them, until they repent and return to [a true belief in] Christ's passion, which is our resurrection.

· VI ·

Let no man deceive himself. The things that are in Heaven and the glorious angels and rulers—both visible and invisible—shall incur condemnation if they do not believe in the blood of Christ. [. . .] Consider those who are of a different opinion about the grace of Christ that has come to us—how opposed they are to the will of God. They have no regard for love; no care for the widow, the orphan, or the oppressed; of the bound or of the free; of the hungry or of the thirsty.

· VII ·

They [who do not believe in the physical body of Jesus] abstain from the Eucharist[7] and from prayer, because they confess not the Eucharist to

5. *bound only in appearance*—black humor: Ignatius is bound and on the way to his death in the arena.

6. *think also the same thing regarding us*—that if Christ only *appeared* to suffer (i.e., did not really suffer in an actual body), then we suffer for no good reason.

7. *Eucharist*—one of the earliest ceremonies in the Christian church, in which participants drank wine and ate bread in memory of Christ's shed blood and crucified body. See Matthew 26:26–28, in which Jesus, aware of his impending death, instructs his disciples in the ritual: "While they were eating, Jesus took a loaf of bread, and after blessing it he broke it, gave it to the disciples, and said, 'Take, eat; this is my body.' Then he took a cup, and after giving thanks he gave it to them, saying, 'Drink from it, all of you; for this is my blood of the covenant, which is poured out for many for the forgiveness of sins'" (NRSV).

be the flesh of our savior, Jesus Christ, who suffered for our sins whom the Father in his goodness raised up again. Those, therefore, who speak against this gift of God[8] incur death in the midst of their disputes. It would be better for them to treat it with respect so that they also may rise again. It is fitting, therefore, that you should stay away from such persons and not speak about them either in private or in public; instead pay heed to the prophets and above all to the Gospel, in which the passion [of Christ] has been revealed to us and the resurrection has been fully proved. Avoid all divisions as the beginning of evils.

· VIII ·

See that you all follow the bishop—even as Jesus Christ followed the Father—and the presbytery[9] as you would follow the apostles, and reverence the deacons as the institution of God. Let no man do anything connected with the church without the bishop. Only a Eucharist that is [administered] either by the bishop or by one the bishop entrusts should be deemed a proper Eucharist. Wherever the bishop appears let the multitude [of the people] be there also, for wherever Jesus Christ is, there also is the catholic church. It is not lawful either to baptize or to celebrate a love-feast[10] without the bishop; whatever a bishop approves is pleasing to God, so that everything that is done may be secure and valid.

· IX ·

Finally, it is reasonable that we should return to soberness [of conduct] and exercise repentance toward God while we still have the opportunity. It is good to reverence both God and the bishop. He who honors the bishop has been honored by God; he who does anything without the knowledge of the bishop [in reality] serves the devil. [. . .]

Governor Pliny to Emperor Trajan on "Christians" (ca. 112)

The Genuine Works of Flavius Josephus, trans. William Whiston (Worcester, MA: Isaiah Thomas, 1794), 1:66–69. Several revisions with reference to *The Letters of Pliny the Younger,* trans. Betty Radice (Baltimore: Penguin, 1963), 293–94.

Roman authorities first began to notice Christianity, the new sect born of Judaism, during the last third of the first century CE. Roman

8. *gift of God*—the Eucharist.
9. *presbytery*—a church's governing body of elders.
10. *love-feast*—Eucharist.

informers sometimes conveyed wild tales about Christian practices. Some even accused Christians of practicing cannibalism. (It seems clear that these reports arose from misunderstandings about Communion rituals in which Christians professed to eat the body and drink the blood of Christ.)[11]

The fundamental precepts of Christianity ran counter to the polytheistic paganism that served as Rome's state religion. Understandings of Jesus as the "Son of God" bumped uncomfortably against the same title—*divi filius*—claimed by Roman emperors.

Following is a somewhat puzzled query from Governor Pliny, a relatively new governor in the Roman province of Bithynia between the Mediterranean and Black Seas. Addressed to Pliny's boss, the Roman emperor Trajan, sometime around 112—that is, just two to five years after Ignatius's letter to the Smyrnians—Pliny's letter seeks advice on how to investigate and punish members of this "mad sect" who refuse to reverence the emperor's statue.

This letter is the first we have in which a Roman official acknowledges Christianity as a religious group in its own right; up until this point Roman leaders seem to have considered Christianity merely a form of Judaism.

Sir,

It is my constant method to apply to you for the resolution of all my doubts; for who can better govern my dilatory way of proceeding or instruct my ignorance?

I have never been present at the examination of Christians, and so I am unacquainted with the type of inquiry and what and how far they are to be punished; nor are my doubts small about whether a distinction should be made between the ages [of the accused], and whether tender youths ought to have the same punishment as strong men. Or whether there should be room for pardon upon repentance. Or whether one who had been a Christian but has forsaken Christianity should have an advantage [over one who has not]. Or whether the mere name [of Christianity]—without any crimes linked to it—should be punished, or whether the crimes attributed [to Christianity] should be punished.

In the meantime, I have taken the following course with those who have been brought before me as Christians. I asked them whether they were Christians. If they confessed that they were, I asked them again, and a third time, mixing threats with questions. If they persevered in their

---

11. *eat the body and drink the blood of Christ*—a reference to the Eucharist.

confession, I ordered them to be executed; for I am convinced that this stubbornness and inflexible obstinacy deserve to be punished.

There are some of this mad sect whom I noted to be Roman citizens, so they might be sent to Rome.

After some time, as is usual in such examinations, the crime spread and many more cases came before me.

A libel was sent to me, though without an author, containing many names [of persons accused]. These denied that they were Christians now or ever had been. They called upon the gods and supplicated to your image, which I had brought to me for that purpose, with frankincense and wine; they also cursed Christ. None of these things, it is said, can any Christian be compelled to do, so I saw fit to let them go.

Others of those named in the libel admitted they were Christians but then denied it again; they said they had been Christians, but then ceased to be—some three years ago, some many more; and one said he had not been for twenty years. All of these worshipped your image and the images of our gods; they also cursed Christ. However, they assured me that the totality of their fault or mistake was this: that they were accustomed on a stated day to meet together before it was light and to sing a hymn to Christ, as to a god; and to oblige themselves by a sacrament [or oath] not to do anything ill: they would commit no theft, or pilfering, or adultery; they would not break their promises or deny what was deposited with them[12] when it was required back again. It was then their custom to depart and to meet again at a common but innocent meal, although they had given up this practice after the edict I published at your command, in which I forbade any such conventicles. These examinations made me think it necessary to inquire by torture what the truth was; I tortured two servant maids, who were called deaconesses. But I still discovered nothing except they were addicted to a bad and extravagant superstition.

I have therefore put off any further examinations and have consulted you, for the affair seems to be well worth consultation, especially on account of the number of those who are in danger; for there are many of every age, of every rank, and of both sexes, who are now and hereafter likely to be called to trial and to be in danger; for this superstition has spread like a contagion, not only into cities and towns, but into country villages as well. There is yet reason to hope it may be stopped and corrected. To be sure, the temples, which were almost forsaken, are already beginning to be frequented again; and the holy solemnities, which had lapsed, have begun to be revived. The sacrifices,[13] for which very few purchasers had appeared of late, begin to sell well everywhere. Thus it is

---

12. *deny what was deposited with them*—refuse to return money loaned or invested.

13. *sacrifices*—animals used for sacrifice.

easy to suppose how great a multitude of men may be amended, if place for repentance be admitted.

Emperor Trajan replied to Pliny as follows:

My Pliny,

You have adopted the appropriate method in examining the causes of those who had been accused as Christians, for indeed no certain and general form of judging can be ordained in this case. These people are not to be sought; but if they are accused and convicted, they are to be punished, albeit with this caution: he who denies being a Christian, and makes it plain that he is not a Christian by supplicating to our gods, may be granted pardon upon his repentance, even though he had been a Christian formerly. As for libels sent anonymously, they should have no place whatsoever in any accusation, for that would be a very ill example, and not agreeable to my reign.

New Church—Constantine
and Constantinople

In light of Governor Pliny's letter, it should come as no surprise that early Christians had little to do with the Roman state, which was *the* power in most of the known world.

Christians rarely served in the Roman army, even though it offered an excellent career for ambitious young men. In fact Christians generally avoided administrative roles, which required them to venerate Roman gods and, at times, to persecute other Christians.

Most early Christians came from the lower classes. Few members of the great Roman families converted, since conversion would have ended their privileged positions with the state. Women appear to have joined the faith, at least initially, in greater numbers than men. Widows in particular found themselves drawn to Christian communities, given these communities' emphasis on providing for the impoverished.

Converting to Christianity was risky. The persecutions of Emperor Nero (54–68 CE) are legendary. It is possible that both the apostles Peter and Paul were in Rome in 64 CE when Nero began burning Christians, opening his gardens to spectacles in which Christians were slaughtered while he mingled with the crowds, dressed as a charioteer.

Subsequent emperors adopted various approaches toward Christianity, ranging from targeted slaughter to policies akin to don't-ask-don't-tell. Emperor Trajan (98–117 CE) adopted this latter approach: Christians should not be sought out, but if reported, they should be punished. Trajan was willing, however, to pardon Christians who would prove their loyalty to the empire by worshipping Roman gods.

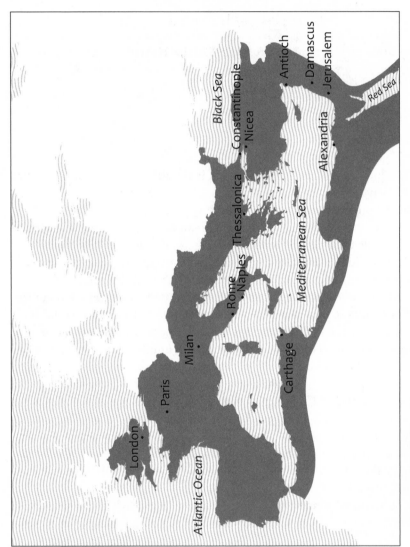

Figure 3. Roman Empire, ca. 400

The last great Roman persecution occurred in 303 CE when Roman legions surrounded the town of Phrygia in modern Turkey to enforce an imperial edict requiring citizens to offer sacrifices to the pagan gods. When Christians in the city refused, Romans troops set the town on fire, killing all its inhabitants.

Christians faced persecution from the Jewish community as well, as we know from Paul's writings.[1] Such persecutions increased notably after 70 CE, that is, after the Roman army destroyed the Jewish temple in Jerusalem: the persecution of Jews, not surprisingly, bred Jewish intolerance toward Christians. After the 70s CE Jewish leaders rarely allowed Christians to preach in synagogues.

Christian worship thus retreated into private homes, where many Christian rituals that persist today developed. By the first century candidates for baptism received lengthy instruction in the Gospels and in Christian doctrine. Communion services also began in the first century.[2]

The faith spread quickly. By 150 CE churches could be found in almost all Roman provinces between Syria and Rome. Missionaries also established churches in Egypt, in modern Algeria, and even beyond the Roman Empire into Persia and India. Christians on the Mediterranean's eastern and African shores dominated theological inquiry; many of the most prominent early patristic writers lived in Alexandria, Egypt.

The church struggled painfully to work out what it believed during these years of intermittent persecution. While it may be tempting to view the resultant arguments as battles over minor or silly points, we must remember that these points were held by people willing to die for their faith in a hostile Roman state. Questions about Christ's nature were not merely academic questions; they were questions about the man or God-man for whom friends, neighbors, and family members sacrificed themselves. Who was this Jesus who some claimed was divine? Was he fully God? Was he fully man? Was he some combination?

These questions were complicated even more by debates about *who* could decide. Who comprised the church that Jesus claimed to establish? And, for that matter, what was the church? Jesus gave few

1. See section 1, "Church in Scripture," in the online supplement.
2. See Hugh Wybrew, *The Orthodox Liturgy* (Crestwood, NY: St. Vladimir's Seminary Press, 1990). This section draws heavily on Wybrew, both in organization and in content.

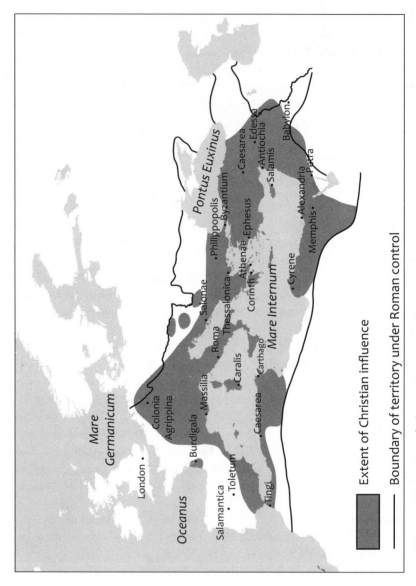

Figure 4. Expansion of Christianity, 100s and 200s

indications. Was it a collection of individual congregations? Was it some larger body? Were its boundaries mystical or concrete? Who belonged? Who was in charge?

Ignatius, the bishop of Antioch whose letter appears above, first used the term "catholic church" in that letter to express his belief in a universal body that oversees and cares for all who consider themselves Christian. The church, according to Ignatius, is not merely a loose organization of like-minded people, but a body that can exercise authority over the beliefs and practices of its members.

According to Ignatius, the church's authority lies with its leaders, namely with presbyters or ministers (those who lead congregations) and bishops (those church leaders to whom presbyters report). Ignatius described the bishop as the "supreme head" of the church who functioned "as the Lord" on earth. Only the bishop, Ignatius insisted, could perform baptisms or administer the Eucharist (Communion).[3] Only the church, governed by its leaders, should regulate the faith. The church, guided by the Holy Spirit, decides what is true and what is not. The church decides which accounts of Jesus's life are correct. The church decides which texts constitute legitimate scripture. And the church may excommunicate, that is, officially exclude from the church, anyone who refuses to heed its decisions.

Thus, in fewer than three decades after the composition of the four Gospels now in the modern canon, the church claimed the right to decide which Gospels were valid and which were not. Such questions mattered, since we know of about two dozen Gospels that circulated during the early centuries. Infancy Gospels told of miracles performed by Jesus as a child, about snakes "bursting apart" in his presence, and about Jesus fashioning live sparrows from dirt and water.

Who decided whether these accounts were valid? The church.

Questions about the validity of competing Gospels informed questions about the nature of God and the nature of Jesus. Early Christians drew varying conclusions about Jesus's identity simply on the basis of the four canonical Gospels. When accounting for all the additional, competing Gospels—Gospels that did not make the canon—possible interpretations become endless. Fierce debates about the person and nature of Jesus, Jesus's relation to God, and the nature of God raged throughout the 100s and 200s.

---

3. *Eucharist*—one of the earliest ceremonies in the Christian church, in which participants drink wine and eat bread in memory of Christ's shed blood and crucified body. See Matthew 26:26–28.

Marcion (ca. 110–160), a shipping magnate, struggled mightily to accommodate his belief in an all-powerful Christian God with the existence on earth of pain and suffering (the question of "theodicy").[4] He solved his problem by concluding that there must be two gods. The first, he surmised, was the Jewish God described in the Hebrew scriptures: a brutal, spiteful, and capricious god. This creator-god demanded that humankind observe rules no person could hope to fulfill. Fortunately, however, a higher, loving god—a god not known to the god of the Hebrew scriptures—pitied humans and sent his son to earth to redeem them. Jesus's mission: to reveal to humankind this greater god and to overthrow the malevolent Hebrew god. But the Hebrew god, infuriated by Christ's compassion, ensured Christ's execution on the cross. In doing so, however, the Hebrew god condemned himself, for such action ran contrary to his own moral law. Only the Apostle Paul,[5] argued Marcion, fully realized the distinction between the law of the Hebrew god and the grace of the true God revealed by Jesus. For Marcion, the Gospel of Luke and Paul's writings pointed the way to salvation; Marcion thus proposed his own canon of scripture, which excluded the Gospels of Mark and Matthew. Although Marcion was excommunicated in 144 for such beliefs, they enjoyed widespread support.[6]

Another diverse set of beliefs, sometimes termed "Gnosticism" (the *g* is silent), long bedeviled what would become Orthodox Christianity. Gnostics adhered to an understanding of the soul as a divine light or being—a light caught and imprisoned against its will in a physical body. Much like the ancient Zoroastrians in Persia, Gnostics saw the universe in binary terms. A good lord—a lord of light—struggled constantly with an evil spirit of darkness. Gnostic Christians viewed Christ as a key player in this cosmic fight: Christ brought "gnosis," that is, God's light and knowledge, in effect revealing the divine light captured in material bodies. Those who could grasp and accept this secret knowledge would be saved. Certainly not all Gnostics were Christian (all manner of pagan beliefs can be termed "gnostic" if we understand Gnosticism simply as a belief in some sort of divine light), but these beliefs did fit nicely into certain conceptions of Christianity.[7]

---

4. An engaging summary of heresies in the early church, from which this introduction draws, may be found in Brian Moynahan, *The Faith* (New York: Doubleday, 2002). See especially 112–14, 118.

5. See section 1, "Church in Scripture," in the online supplement.

6. Moynahan, 112–13.

7. Ibid., 113.

But in the dualistic worldview of Gnosticism (i.e., in a world in which light and truth represent the polar opposites of darkness and evil), it was difficult to explain a Christ who was both God (or divine light) *and* human (or evil matter). How could Christ be both? Christ—the embodiment of the divine light—could not exist in a corrupt, material world. According to some Gnostics, then, the crucifixion had to be an illusion. Christ could not actually have died; the divine light could not be snuffed out: death bears only upon evil matter. In one gnostic work that did not make the canon, the Apocalypse of Peter, Christ stands outside his body, laughing as it is crucified on the cross.[8]

Valentius, an Egyptian clamoring to be appointed bishop of Rome, established his own following in the mid-100s by teaching that our material world originated with the fall of Sofia, the female personification of the "divine wisdom" mentioned in Hebrew scriptures, especially in the book of Proverbs. This Sofia, or wisdom, Valentius argued, was the name for one of the powers emanating from a supreme god. Sofia created the lesser god of the Hebrew scriptures. But the power of the higher god—Christ—united itself with the human being Jesus to bring saving gnosis (knowledge) to humankind. Those who fully understood and accepted this gnosis were destined for the highest spiritual realm after death. Other Christians—Christians who failed to grasp this gnosis—could only hope to reach a lower realm through faith and good works. Everyone else was doomed to everlasting punishment. Just as it did Marcion, the church deemed Valentius a heretic. Yet his teachings persisted: Irenaeus, the Orthodox bishop of Lyons in the late 100s, felt compelled to attack both Marcion and Valentius in a major polemical work by emphasizing Christ's full humanity.[9]

Gnosticism cropped up again in the Manichaeans, a sect named after Mani, an eccentric Persian who beheld a vision in which his heavenly twin ordered him to teach the "true" message of Christ. Like Valentius and Marcion, Mani believed in an age-old conflict between darkness and light. (We use the word "manichean" today to denote any sort of philosophical dualism.) According to Mani, Satan ruled the domain of matter (evil), while God ruled the spirit world of light (good). Mani preached that Buddha, Noah, Abraham, and Jesus had all been sent to cleanse the world and make it ready for the god of light, and he apparently claimed at various times to be the reincarnated

8. *The Coptic Apocalypse of Peter*, ed. Henriette W. Havelaar (Berlin: Akademie Verlag, 1999), 101.

9. Moynahan, 114.

Buddha, Krishna, and Zoroaster. Such purification required celibacy, vegetarianism, teetotalism, and no physical work. Mani was killed in 276, but not before he made a number of missionary journeys into India, Afghanistan, and other Christian territories.[10]

Such diverse and contradictory beliefs were probably inevitable as long as Christianity remained a persecuted sect relegated to the outskirts of society. Although the church hierarchy claimed the right to establish doctrine since the early 100s, it found itself constrained in what it could dictate: it is difficult to govern a religion when its adherents are in hiding and dispersed widely throughout a sprawling empire. Uniformity of doctrine requires coordinating the activities of one's members, but the possibility of such coordination remained limited within a persecuted body.

All this changed dramatically when, in October 312, the Roman emperor Constantine claimed to witness a "heavenly sign of God." Constantine reported to his friend, the historian Eusebius, that he looked up in the sky and saw a cross of light shining above the sun, with an inscription exhorting him to "conquer by this." His entire army, Constantine said, witnessed the cross as well. Later that day, during a nap, Christ appeared to Constantine with the same sign and commanded him to build a replica of the cross and to use this replica to protect himself in battle. Constantine converted to Christianity (although without an official declaration until a decade later) on the basis of these visions.

The implications of Constantine's conversion were enormous. Christianity now claimed the head of the Roman Empire—a pagan empire—as its own. Under Constantine Christianity transformed itself from a persecuted sect, despised by the most powerful government the world had ever known, into that same government's favored religion.

Constantine and his co-emperor Licinius issued the Edict of Milan, a manifesto of religious toleration that bestowed full legal rights on Christians. Roman governors received orders to stop persecuting Christians. Christians received permission to worship as they wished. Any property seized from Christians was to be returned immediately. The imperial government gave cash subsidies to Christian ministers. Constantine proclaimed the first day of every week a day of rest, thus formally instituting a Sabbath. And in 321 he made it legal for citizens to bequeath land and money in their wills to the church. (A good por-

10. Ibid., 118.

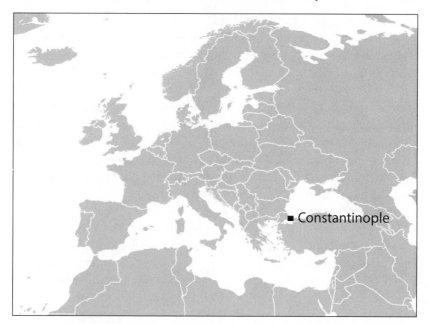

Figure 5. Constantinople

tion of Christianity's early adherents were widows without heirs, and the church's encouragement of virginity and celibacy meant that many members never married and claimed no heirs other than the church; the result—a major influx of cash.)

Constantine, ambitious and grandiose, decided to build an entirely new capital for his empire. Rome, a reminder of the empire's republican past, seemed an affront to Constantine's imperial ambitions. Its senators still resented the emperor's absolutism, not to mention his new religion, and it remained a center of paganism and practices incompatible with Constantine's new faith.

Constantine chose as the site for his new capital the passage between the Mediterranean and the Black Sea, that is, Istanbul in modern-day Turkey, a location with more strategic import than the hills of Rome. He named his city Constantinople after himself and populated the imperial court with a new aristocracy to supplant the pagan and resentful senators back in Rome.

Although Constantine tolerated some aspects of traditional paganism, he recognized Christianity as *a* religion of the empire (Emperor Theodosius would make it *the official* religion of the empire in 391), with its own de facto capital. In the centuries to come, Christianity would become and remain the official religion of almost every European country until the French Revolution at the end of the 1700s.

But if Christianity was now officially recognized within the Roman Empire, what, exactly, was official Christianity? What should "official" Christians believe? Patristic literature to date had tackled difficult subjects but without sanction from any official bodies.

In theory, tricky questions would now be easier to solve, given the faith's new status within the empire. Theologians could conduct debates in the open. The state could sponsor theological conferences. Christians could travel freely to disseminate opinions and conclusions. And, perhaps most significant, the power of the state could be used to settle intractable debates.

What were the difficult questions of the 300s? The exact nature of Jesus and the nature of the Trinity remained problematic. In Matthew 28:19 Jesus commanded his disciples, "Go therefore and make disciples of all nations, baptizing them in the name of the Father and of the Son and of the Holy Spirit" (NRSV). But Matthew also affirmed quite strongly that there is only one God. Theologians agonized over how to reconcile the idea of three beings possessing divine powers with the fundamental doctrine of one God.

As far as we know, the term "Trinity" did not appear in any patristic literature until around 180, when it was used by a theologian in Antioch. Tertullian of Alexandria first coined the phrase "three persons, one essence," almost a century later.

The theologian Sabellius (fl. ca. 215) took a crack at this problem when he claimed that the Father, Son, and Holy Spirit were not separate entities; instead, they were manifestations of the same God, much like water, steam, and ice are all manifestations of H_2O. A bishop of Antioch named Paul claimed that Jesus was simply a human being to whom God's Word or Spirit joined itself. The Trinity, according to Paul, consisted of the father, the holy wisdom, and the Logos, or "Word," described in the Gospel of John. In Bishop Paul's scheme, Jesus was not a member of the Trinity. Instead, the Trinity—father, holy wisdom, and Logos—descended upon Jesus, the human being, to a degree it had descended on no other prophet. *Yet Jesus remained human.*

Arius (ca. 250s–366), a priest in Alexandria, promulgated perhaps the most famous and influential heresy. (By "heresy" we mean nothing more than an opinion later judged by ruling bodies to be unorthodox, that is, an opinion that lost.) Arius claimed a secondary role for Jesus Christ in relation to God the Father. Christ, Arius argued, was subordinate to the Father. He did not share God's full divinity. Christ was not eternal. Instead, God created him from nothing to be an instrument of the world's salvation. Since the Son did not fully share God's nature, he thus could not be considered either a creator or a redeemer. For support, Arius cited the Gospel of John: "And this is eternal life, that they may know you, the only true God, and Jesus Christ whom you have sent" (John 17:3, NRSV). This verse, argued Arius, made it absolutely clear: there is only one true God. Christ, the one *sent* by God, can be nothing more than a mediator who reveals God to humans. Christ is not fully God.

A church council excommunicated and exiled Arius, but his followers multiplied and his teachings about Christ's nature and that of the Trinity spread rapidly. In-depth examinations of Arius's arguments appear below, but for now, it is important to emphasize how divisive they were. Bitter disputes about Christ's nature threatened the unity of Christianity and persuaded Constantine that he must do something.

So he did. In 325 Constantine called a meeting of church leaders to resolve the dispute in the beautiful city of Nicaea, now known as Iznik in modern Turkey. Constantine permitted bishops from throughout the empire to travel to Nicaea, but he planted spies as their traveling

Figure 6. Nicaea

companions to learn about their views. He also made sure that the delegations, probably no more than 250 people, consisted largely of anti-Arians. The meeting in Nicaea became known as the First Ecumenical Council, the first meeting with broad representation from throughout Christendom claiming to speak on behalf of the entire church. More such councils would follow, all of which helped define and clarify church doctrine between 325 and 787.

The following readings provide a sense of the early church's history and the debates that consumed it—debates central to the Christian faith. Who Christ is, of course, is *the* question of Christianity. Arguments about how God and humans can be reconciled concern the person who Christians believe is responsible for their salvation. For a sect that emerged from Judaism—a faith based squarely on the belief in one true God—it was essential to find a way to believe in Jesus as Christ without sacrificing monotheism.

Eusebius, Life of Constantine (late 330s)

Eusebius, "Life of Constantine," in *A Select Library of Nicene and Post-Nicene Fathers of the Christian Church, Second Series,* ed. Philip Schaff and Henry Wace (New York: Christian Literature Company, 1890), 1:486–91, 494–97, 504–6, 508–11, 515–18, 520–23.

Flavius Valerius Constantinus, or "Constantine the Great," was born to an army officer. He followed his father into the military and distinguished himself during wars in France and Britain. Popular with his troops, they proclaimed him emperor of the army in 306 after a successful battle at York.

Several emperors governed the Roman Empire at this time, each bearing responsibility for different portions of the realm. Power-sharing fostered frequent bickering and jockeying for position. Ambitious, cunning, and a keen military strategist, Constantine placed himself in the center of the political intrigues: leading his troops in a series of civil wars, he eventually triumphed as sole emperor.

Today Constantine is remembered less for his military victories than for his conversion to Christianity. Historians have long debated his commitment to the faith, and we will never know his personal beliefs in full or exactly what prompted his conversion. What is clear, however, is that Constantine consistently portrayed himself as a tool of God, and he attributed his military success to his conversion. He commissioned a statue of himself holding a cross with the inscription,

"By this saving sign I have delivered your city from the tyrant [a rival emperor] and restored liberty to the Senate and people of Rome."

Constantine's good friend Eusebius (who wrote the biography of Constantine we excerpt below) was born in the 260s, and he became the bishop of Caesarea in Palestine sometime around 313. Early in life Eusebius occupied himself with biblical criticism, but he proved an unimaginative theologian who mostly recycled the work of predecessors and contemporaries. His *Ecclesiastical History* holds far more interest. Though hardly a literary masterpiece, the *History* is invaluable for the extensive collections of primary sources—sources whose originals have long been lost—that Eusebius scattered throughout his narrative.

Eusebius wrote with verve about the trials Christians suffered. He lived through the worst persecutions of 303 and 304, and he watched as his best friend was led from prison to be martyred in 310. Some have suggested that Eusebius himself could have survived only by compromising his principles, but we have no evidence to support such conjectures.

Eusebius's histories share more in common with the histories of the Hebrew scriptures than with what we accept as history today. Colm

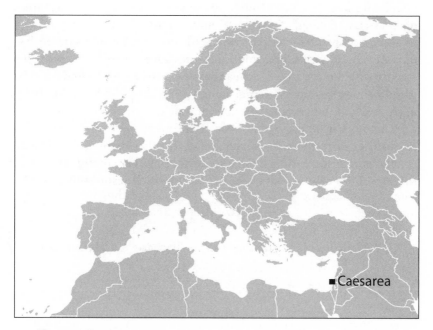

Figure 7. Caesarea

Luibhéid notes that Eusebius "thought of past and present as revealed in the perspective of a divine plan, a heavenly ordinance [that] was clarified in the texts of the Bible and exhibited in current events."[11]

Eusebius viewed the promise of God to Abraham "as an assurance that holiness would ultimately prevail throughout the world"; and "this conviction seemed to harmonize with the more recent events in history, for in Eusebius' eyes the expansion of the Roman Empire was coincident with the coming of Christ. The growth of the Roman domain since the reign of Augustus [27 BCE–14 CE] was no accident but had to be seen as part of the divine plan long ago revealed in the promise to Abraham."[12]

"Now, with the arrival of Constantine," Luibhéid continues, "this movement had gained a victory [that] was perhaps the most important since the days of Christ."[13] Constantine, both in his own mind and in Eusebius's narrative, was an instrument of God's divine will.

The following excerpts from the *Life of Constantine* recount Constantine's rise to power. One cannot divorce his faith from his military career; distinctions between politics and religion would only have puzzled him.

It is important to note that Constantine was no theologian; the particulars of the theological debates raging during his reign held little interest for him. (He described fundamental disputes about the nature of Christ as "trifling," "abstruse," and "foolish.") His main goal was to solve arguments—the particulars of any resolution mattered less than did the existence of a solution. Constantine feared that a divided church would offend God. Schism was inspired by Satan and must be cured promptly, since "internal strife within the church of God is far more evil and dangerous than any kind of war or conflict." As is evident below, Constantine paid little attention to philosophical niceties (we will explore these in greater detail in other readings). His goal, simply, was to defeat his enemies, consolidate his empire, and unite the church for whose welfare he believed himself responsible.

· Book I ·

[...]
XXV. Victories of Constantine over the barbarians and the Britons.

11. Colm Luibhéid, *The Essential Eusebius* (New York: New American Library, 1966), 13.

12. Ibid., 14.

13. Ibid., 15.

As soon then as he was established on the throne, he began to care for the interests of his paternal inheritance, and visited with much considerate kindness all those provinces that had previously been under his father's government. Some tribes of the barbarians who dwelt on the banks of the Rhine and the shores of the Western ocean, having ventured to revolt, he reduced them all to obedience, and brought them from their savage state to one of gentleness. He contented himself with checking the inroads of others, and drove from his dominions, like untamed and savage beasts, those whom he perceived to be altogether incapable of the settled order of civilized life. Having disposed of these affairs to his satisfaction, he directed his attention to other quarters of the world, and first passed over to the British nations, which lie in the very bosom of the ocean. These he reduced to submission, and then proceeded to consider the state of the remaining portions of the empire, that he might be ready to tender his aid wherever circumstances might require it. [. . .]

XXVII. That after reflecting on the downfall of those who had worshipped idols, he made the choice of Christianity.

Being convinced, however, that he needed some more powerful aid than his military forces could afford him, on account of the wicked and magical enchantments that were so diligently practiced by the tyrant,[14] he sought divine assistance, deeming the possession of arms and a numerous soldiery of secondary importance, but believing the cooperating power of the deity invincible and not to be shaken. He considered, therefore, on what god he might rely for protection and assistance. While engaged in this enquiry, the thought occurred to him, that, of the many emperors who had preceded him, those who had rested their hopes in a multitude of gods, and served them with sacrifices and offerings, had in the first place been deceived by nattering predictions, and oracles that promised them all prosperity, and at last had met with an unhappy end, while not one of their gods had stood by to warn them of the impending wrath of Heaven; while one alone who had pursued an entirely opposite course, who had condemned their error, and honored the one supreme God during his whole life, had found him to be the savior and protector of his empire, and the giver of every good thing. Reflecting on this, and well weighing the fact that they who had trusted in many gods had also fallen by manifold forms of death, without leaving behind them either family or offspring, stock, name, or memorial among men; while the God of his father had given to him, on the other hand, manifestations of his power and very many tokens; and considering further that those who had already taken arms against the tyrant and had marched to the battlefield under the protection of a multitude of gods had met with a dishonorable end (for one of them had shamefully retreated from the

14. *tyrant*—Maxentius, Constantine's rival.

contest without a blow, and the other, being slain in the midst of his own troops, became, as it were, the mere sport of death); reviewing, I say, all these considerations, he judged it to be folly indeed to join in the idle worship of those who were no gods, and, after such convincing evidence, to err from the truth; and therefore felt it incumbent on him to honor his father's God alone.

XXVIII. How, while he was praying, God sent him a vision of a cross of light in the heavens at midday, with an inscription admonishing him to conquer by that.

Accordingly he called on him with earnest prayer and supplications that he would reveal to him who he was, and stretch forth his right hand to help him in his present difficulties. And while he was thus praying with fervent entreaty, a most marvelous sign appeared to him from Heaven, the account of which it might have been hard to believe had it been related by any other person. But since the victorious emperor himself long afterwards declared it to the writer of this history, when he was honored with his acquaintance and society, and confirmed his statement by an oath, who could hesitate to accredit the relation, especially since the testimony of after-time has established its truth? He said that about noon, when the day was already beginning to decline, he saw with his own eyes the trophy of a cross of light in the heavens above the sun, and bearing the inscription, "conquer by this." At this sight he himself was struck with amazement, and his whole army also, which followed him on this expedition and witnessed the miracle.

XXIX. How the Christ of God appeared to him in his sleep and commanded him to use in his wars a standard made in the form of the cross.

He said, moreover, that he doubted within himself what the import of this apparition could be. And while he continued to ponder and reason on its meaning, night suddenly came on; then in his sleep the Christ of God appeared to him with the same sign that he had seen in the heavens, and commanded him to make a likeness of that sign that he had seen in the heavens, and to use it as a safeguard in all engagements with his enemies.

XXX. The making of the standard of the cross.

At dawn of day he arose and communicated the marvel to his friends; and then calling together the workers in gold and precious stones, he sat in the midst of them and described to them the figure of the sign he had seen, bidding them to represent it in gold and precious stones. And this representation I myself have had an opportunity of seeing. [. . .]

XXXII. How Constantine received instruction, and read the sacred scriptures.

[. . .] But at the time above specified, being struck with amazement at the extraordinary vision and resolving to worship no other god save him who had appeared to him, he sent for those who were acquainted with the mysteries of his doctrines, and enquired who that god was and what was intended by the sign of the vision he had seen.

They affirmed that he was God, the only begotten Son of the one and only God: that the sign that had appeared was the symbol of immortality and the trophy of that victory over death that he had gained in time past when sojourning on earth. They taught him also the causes of his advent and explained to him the true account of his incarnation. Thus he was instructed in these matters and was impressed with wonder at the divine manifestation that had been presented to his sight. Comparing, therefore, the heavenly vision with the interpretation given, he found his judgment confirmed; and, in the persuasion that the knowledge of these things had been imparted to him by divine teaching, he determined thenceforth to devote himself to the reading of the inspired writings. [. . .]

XLI. Rejoicings throughout the provinces and Constantine's acts of grace.

Thus the pious emperor, glorying in the confession of the victorious cross, proclaimed the Son of God to the Romans with great boldness of testimony. And the inhabitants of the city, one and all, senate and people, reviving, as it were, from the pressure of a bitter and tyrannical domination, seemed to enjoy purer rays of light and to be born again into a fresh and new life. All the nations, too, as far as the limit of the western ocean, being set free from the calamities that had heretofore beset them, and gladdened by joyous festivals, ceased not to praise him as the victorious, the pious, the common benefactor: all, indeed, with one voice and one mouth, declared that Constantine had appeared by the grace of God as a general blessing to mankind. The imperial edict also was everywhere published, whereby those who had been wrongfully deprived of their estates were permitted again to enjoy their own, while those who had unjustly suffered exile were recalled to their homes. Moreover, he freed from imprisonment, and from every kind of danger and fear, those who, by reason of the tyrant's cruelty, had been subject to these sufferings.

XLII. The honors conferred upon bishops, and the building of churches.

The emperor also personally inviting the society of God's ministers, distinguished them with the highest possible respect and honor, showing them favor in deed and word as persons consecrated to the service of his God. Accordingly, they were admitted to his table, though mean in their attire and outward appearance; yet not so in his estimation, since he thought he saw not the man as seen by the vulgar eye but the God in him. He made them also his companions in travel, believing that he whose servants they were would thus help him. Besides this, he gave from his own private resources costly benefactions to the churches of God, both enlarging and heightening the sacred edifices, and embellishing the august sanctuaries of the church with abundant offerings.

XLIII. Constantine's liberality to the poor.

He likewise distributed money largely to those who were in need, and besides these showing himself philanthropist and benefactor even to the heathen, who had no claim on him; and even for the beggars in the forum, miserable and shiftless, he provided, not with money only or necessary food, but also decent clothing. [. . .] He even gave virgins, left unprotected by their parents' death, in marriage to wealthy men with whom he was personally acquainted. But this he did after first bestowing on the brides such portions as it was fitting they should bring to the communion of marriage. In short, as the sun, when it rises upon the earth, liberally imparts his rays of light to all, so did Constantine, proceeding at early dawn from the imperial palace, and rising as it were with the heavenly luminary, impart the rays of his own beneficence to all who came into his presence. It was scarcely possible to be near him without receiving some benefit, nor did it ever happen that any who had expected to obtain his assistance were disappointed in their hope.

XLIV. How he was present at the synods of bishops.

Such, then, was his general character toward all. But he exercised a peculiar care over the church of God; and whereas, in the several provinces there were some who differed from each other in judgment, he, like some general bishop constituted by God, convened synods of his ministers. Nor did he disdain to be present and sit with them in their assembly, but bore a share in their deliberations, ministering to all that pertained to the peace of God. [. . .]

XLVI. Victories over the barbarians.

Thus the emperor in all his actions honored God, the controller of all things, and exercised an unwearied oversight over his churches. And God requited him by subduing all barbarous nations under his feet, so that he was able everywhere to raise trophies over his enemies: and he proclaimed him as conqueror to all mankind and made him a terror to his adversaries; not indeed that this was his natural character, since he was rather the meekest and gentlest, and most benevolent of men. [. . .]

· Book II ·

[. . .]

XX. Constantine's enactments in favor of the confessors.

Moreover, the emperor's edicts, permeated with his humane spirit, were published among us also, as they had been among the inhabitants of the other division of the empire; and his laws, which breathed a spirit of piety toward God, gave promise of manifold blessings since they secured many advantages to his provincial subjects in every nation and at the same time prescribed measures suited to the exigencies of the churches of God. For first of all they recalled those who, in consequence of their refusal to join in idol worship, had been driven to exile or ejected from their homes by the governors of their respective provinces. In the next place, they relieved from their burdens those who for the same reason had been adjudged to serve in the civil courts and ordained restitution to be made to any who had been deprived of property. They too, who in the time of trial had signalized themselves by fortitude of soul in the cause of God and had therefore been condemned to the painful labor of the mines or consigned to the solitude of islands or compelled to toil in the public works—all received an immediate release from these burdens—while others, whose religious constancy had cost them the forfeiture of their military rank, were vindicated by the emperor's generosity from this dishonor: for he granted them the alternative either of resuming their rank, and enjoying their former privileges, or, in the event of their preferring a more settled life, of perpetual exemption from all service. Lastly, all who had been compelled by way of disgrace and insult to serve in the employments of women, he likewise freed with the rest.

XXI. His laws concerning martyrs and concerning ecclesiastical property.

[...] With regard to those holy martyrs of God who had laid down their lives in the confession of his name, he directed that their estates should be enjoyed by their nearest kindred; and, in default of any of these, that the right of inheritance should be vested in the churches. Further, whatever property had been consigned to other parties from the treasury, whether in the way of sale or gift, together with that retained in the treasury itself, the generous mandate of the emperor directed should be restored to the original owners. Such benefits did his bounty, thus widely diffused, confer on the church of God. [...]

XXIV. Law of Constantine respecting piety toward God and the Christian religion.

"Victor Constantinus, Maximus Augustus, to the inhabitants of the province of Palestine.

"To all who entertain just and sound sentiments respecting the character of the supreme being, it has long been most clearly evident and beyond the possibility of doubt how vast a difference there has ever been between those who maintain a careful observance of the hallowed duties of the Christian religion, and those who treat this religion with hostility or contempt. But at this present time we may see by still more manifest proofs and still more decisive instances, both how unreasonable it is to question this truth, and how mighty is the power of the supreme God: since it appears that they who faithfully observe his holy laws and shrink from the transgression of his commandments are rewarded with abundant blessings and are endued with well-grounded hope as well as ample power for the accomplishment of their undertakings." [...]

XXX. A law granting release from exile, from service in the courts, and from the confiscation of property.

"Let all therefore who have exchanged their country for a foreign land because they would not abandon that reverence and faith toward God to which they had devoted themselves with their whole hearts, and have in consequence at different times been subject to the cruel sentence of the courts; together with any who have been enrolled in the registers of the public courts though in time past exempt from such office; let these, I say, now render thanks to God the liberator of all, in that they are restored to their hereditary property, and their wonted tranquility." [. . .]

XXXII. And to those ignominiously employed in the mines and public works.

"Again, with regard to those who have been condemned either to the grievous labor of the mines or to service in the public works, let them enjoy the sweets of leisure in place of these long-continued toils, and henceforth lead a far easier life, and more accordant with the wishes of their hearts, exchanging the incessant hardships of their tasks for quiet relaxation. And if any have forfeited the common privilege of liberty or have unhappily suffered dishonor, let them hasten back every one to the country of his nativity, and resume with becoming joy their former positions in society, from which they have been as it were separated by long residence abroad." [. . .]

XXXVI. The church is declared heir of those who leave no kindred and the free gifts of such persons confirmed.

"But should there be no surviving relation to succeed in due course to the property of those above-mentioned, I mean the martyrs or confessors or those who for some such cause have been banished from their native land; in such cases we ordain that the church locally nearest in each instance shall succeed to the inheritance. And surely it will be no wrong to the departed that that church should be their heir, for whose sake they have endured every extremity of suffering." [. . .]

LXI. How controversies originated at Alexandria through matters relating to Arius.

[. . .] The people of God were in a truly flourishing state and abounding in the practice of good works. No terror from without assailed them, but a bright and most profound peace through the favor of God encompassed his church on every side. Meantime, however, the spirit of envy was watching to destroy our blessings, which at first crept in unperceived, but soon reveled in the midst of the assemblies of the saints. At length it reached the bishops themselves and arrayed them in angry hostility against each other, on pretense of a jealous regard for the doctrines of divine truth. Hence it was that a mighty fire was kindled as it were from a little spark, and which, originating in the first instance in the Alexandrian church, overspread the whole of Egypt and Libya and the further Thebaid.[15] Eventually it extended its ravages to the other provinces and cities

15. *Thebaid*—a region populated by monks in the upper part of the Nile River valley in northern Egypt.

of the empire, so that not only the prelates of the churches might be seen encountering each other in the strife of words but the people themselves were completely divided, some adhering to one faction and others to another. Nay, so notorious did the scandal of these become, that the sacred matters of inspired teaching were exposed to the most shameful ridicule in the very theaters of the unbelievers. [. . .]

LXIII. How Constantine sent a messenger and a letter concerning peace.

As soon as the emperor was informed of these facts, which he heard with much sorrow of heart, considering them in the light of a calamity personally affecting himself, he forthwith selected from the Christians in his train one whom he well knew to be approved for the sobriety and genuineness of his faith and who had before this time distinguished himself by the boldness of his religious profession, and sent him to negotiate peace between the dissentient parties at Alexandria. He also made him the bearer of a most needful and appropriate letter to the original movers of the strife; and this letter, as exhibiting a specimen of his watchful care over God's people, it may be well to introduce into this our narrative of his life. Its purport was as follows.

LXIV. Constantine's letter to Alexander the bishop and Arius the presbyter.

"Victor Constantinus, Maximus Augustus, to Alexander and Arius.[16]

"I call that God to witness, as well I may, who is the helper of my endeavors and the preserver of all men, that I had a twofold reason for undertaking that duty that I have now performed.

LXV. His continual anxiety for peace.

"My design then was, first, to bring the diverse judgments formed by all nations respecting the deity to a condition, as it were, of settled uniformity; and second to restore to health the system of the world then suffering under the malignant power of a grievous distemper. Keeping these objects in view, I sought to accomplish the one by the secret eye of thought while the other I tried to rectify by the power of military authority. For I was aware that, if I should succeed in establishing, according to my hopes, a common harmony of sentiment among all the servants of God, the general course of affairs would also experience a change correspondent to the pious desires of them all.

LXVI. That he also adjusted the controversies that had arisen in Africa.

"Finding, then, that the whole of Africa was pervaded by an intolerable spirit of mad folly, through the influence of those who with heedless frivolity had presumed to rend the religion of the people into diverse sects, I was anxious to check this disorder and could discover no other remedy equal to the occasion except in sending some of yourselves to aid in restoring mutual harmony among the disputants after I had removed

16. *Alexander and Arius*—see the introduction to this document.

that common enemy of mankind who had interposed his lawless sentence for the prohibition of your holy synods. [. . .]

LXVIII. Being grieved by the dissension he counsels peace.

"But, O glorious providence of God! How deep a wound did not my ears only but my very heart receive in the report that divisions existed among yourselves more grievous still than those that continued in that country! So that you, through whose aid I had hoped to procure a remedy for the errors of others, are in a state that needs healing even more than theirs. And yet, having made a careful enquiry into the origin and foundation of these differences, I find the cause to be of a truly insignificant character and quite unworthy of such fierce contention. Feeling myself, therefore, compelled to address you in this letter, and to appeal at the same time to your unanimity and sagacity, I call on divine providence to assist me in the task, while I interrupt your dissension in the character of a minister of peace. [. . .]

LXIX. Origin of the controversy between Alexander and Arius and that these questions ought not to have been discussed.

"I understand, then, that the origin of the present controversy is this. When you, Alexander, demanded of the presbyters what opinion they severally maintained respecting a certain passage in the divine law, or rather, I should say, that you asked them something connected with an unprofitable question, then you, Arius, inconsiderately insisted on what ought never to have been conceived at all, or if conceived, should have been buried in profound silence. Hence it was that a dissension arose between you, fellowship was withdrawn, and the holy people, rent into diverse parties, no longer preserved the unity of the one body. Now, therefore, you should both exhibit an equal degree of forbearance and receive the advice that your fellow servant righteously gives. What then is this advice? It was wrong in the first instance to propose such questions as these or to reply to them when propounded. For those points of discussion that are enjoined by the authority of no law, but rather suggested by the contentious spirit that is fostered by misused leisure, even though they may be intended merely as an intellectual exercise, ought certainly to be confined to the region of our own thoughts and not hastily produced in the popular assemblies nor unadvisedly entrusted to the general ear. For how very few are there able either accurately to comprehend, or adequately to explain subjects so sublime and abstruse in their nature? Or, granting that one were fully competent for this, how many people will he convince? [. . .]

LXXI. There should be no contention in matters that are in themselves of little moment.

"For as long as you continue to contend about these small and very insignificant questions, it is not fitting that so large a portion of God's people should be under the direction of your judgment, since you are thus divided between yourselves. I believe it indeed to be not merely unbecoming, but positively evil that such should be the case. But I will refresh your minds by a little illustration, as follows. You know that philosophers, though they all adhere to one system are yet frequently at issue on certain points, and differ, perhaps, in their degree of knowledge: yet they are recalled to harmony of sentiment by the uniting power of their common doctrines. If this be true, is it not far more reasonable that you, who are the ministers of the supreme God, should be of one mind respecting the profession of the same religion? [. . .] For the dignity of your synod may be preserved, and the communion of your whole body maintained unbroken, however wide a difference may exist among you as to unimportant matters. For we are not all of us like-minded on every subject, nor is there such a thing as one disposition and judgment common to all alike." [. . .]

· Book III ·

[. . .]

IV. A further notice of the controversies raised in Egypt by Arius.

[. . .] [T]he effects of that envious spirit that so troubled the peace of the churches of God in Alexandria, together with the Theban and Egyptian schism, continued to cause [Constantine] no little disturbance of mind. In fact in every city bishops were engaged in obstinate conflict with bishops and people rising against people; and almost like the fabled Symplegades,[17] coming into violent collision with each other. Nay, some were so far transported beyond the bounds of reason as to be guilty of reckless and outrageous conduct and even to insult the statues of the emperor. This state of things had little power to excite his anger, but rather caused in him sorrow of spirit; for he deeply deplored the folly thus exhibited by deranged men. [. . .]

VI. How he ordered a council to be held at Nicaea.

Then, as if to bring a divine array against this enemy,[18] he convoked a general council and invited the speedy attendance of bishops from all quarters in letters expressive of the honorable estimation in which he held them. Nor was this merely the issuing of a bare command, but the emperor's good will contributed much to its being carried into effect, for he allowed some the use of the public means of conveyance while he afforded to others an ample supply of horses for their transport. The place, too, selected for the synod, the city Nicaea in Bithynia (named from "Victory"), was appropriate to the occasion. As soon then as the imperial injunction was generally made known, all with the utmost willingness

---

17. *Symplegades*—in Greek mythology these two rocks collided at random, crushing anything caught between them.

18. *this enemy*—Satan, on whom Eusebius lays the blame for the discord.

hastened there as though they would outstrip one another in a race; for they were impelled by the anticipation of a happy result to the conference by the hope of enjoying present peace and the desire of beholding something new and strange in the person of so admirable an emperor. [. . .]

VIII. That the assembly was composed, as in the Acts of the Apostles, of individuals from various nations.

For it is said that in the apostles' age there were gathered "devout men from every nation under Heaven" [. . .] But that assembly was less,[19] in that not all who composed it were ministers of God; but in the present company, the number of bishops exceeded two hundred and fifty, while that of the presbyters and deacons in their train, and the crowd of acolytes and other attendants was altogether beyond computation. [. . .]

X. Council in the palace. Constantine, entering, took his seat in the assembly.

[. . .] As soon, then, as the whole assembly had seated itself with becoming orderliness, a general silence prevailed in expectation of the emperor's arrival. And first of all, three of his immediate family entered in succession, then others also preceded his approach, not of the soldiers or guards who usually accompanied him, but only friends in the faith. And now, all rising at the signal that indicated the emperor's entrance, at last he himself proceeded through the midst of the assembly like some heavenly messenger of God, clothed in raiment that glittered as it were with rays of light, reflecting the glowing radiance of a purple robe and adorned with the brilliant splendor of gold and precious stones. Such was the external appearance of his person; and with regard to his mind it was evident that he was distinguished by piety and godly fear. This was indicated by his downcast eyes, the blush on his countenance, and his gait. For the rest of his personal excellences he surpassed all present in height of stature and beauty of form as well as in majestic dignity of mien, and invincible strength and vigor. [. . .]

XI. Silence of the council after some words by the Bishop Eusebius.

The bishop who occupied the chief place in the right division of the assembly then rose, and addressing the emperor, delivered a concise speech, in a strain of thanksgiving to Mother of God on his behalf. When he had resumed his seat, silence ensued, and all regarded the emperor with fixed attention, on which he looked serenely round on the assembly with a cheerful aspect, and, having collected his thoughts, in a calm and gentle tone gave utterance to the following words.

19. *that assembly was less*—Eusebius lists representatives from Syria, Sicily, Phoenicia (a region centered around Lebanon), Persia, Scythia, Galatia (the highlands of modern Turkey), Pamphylia (south-central Turkey), Cappadocia (east-central Turkey), Asia, and Phrygia (central Turkey).

XII. Constantine's address to the council concerning peace.

"[. . .] I rejoice in beholding your assembly; but I feel that my desires will be most completely fulfilled when I can see you all united in one judgment, and that common spirit of peace and concord prevailing amongst you all, which it becomes you, as consecrated to the service of God, to commend to others. Delay not, then, dear friends; delay not, you ministers of God and faithful servants of him who is our common Lord and savior; begin from this moment to discard the causes of that disunion that has existed among you and remove the perplexities of controversy by embracing the principles of peace. For by such conduct you will at the same time be acting in a manner most pleasing to the supreme God, and you will confer an exceeding favor on me who am your fellow-servant."

XIII. How he led the dissident bishops to harmony of sentiment.

As soon as the emperor had spoken these words in the Latin tongue, which another interpreted,[20] he gave permission to those who presided in the council to deliver their opinions. On this some began to accuse their neighbors, who defended themselves, and recriminated in their turn. In this manner numberless assertions were put forth by each party, and a violent controversy arose at the very commencement. Notwithstanding this, the emperor gave patient audience to all alike, and received every proposition with steadfast attention, and by occasionally assisting the argument of each party in turn, he gradually disposed even the most vehement disputants to a reconciliation. At the same time, by the affability of his address to all, and his use of the Greek language, with which he was not altogether unacquainted, he appeared in a truly attractive and amiable light, persuading some, convincing others by his reasoning, praising those who spoke well, and urging all to unity of sentiment, until at last he succeeded in bringing them to one mind and judgment respecting every disputed question.

XIV. Unanimous declaration of the council concerning faith and the celebration of Easter.

The result was that they were not only united as concerning the faith, but that the time for the celebration of the salutary feast of Easter was agreed on by all. Those points also that were sanctioned by the resolution of the whole body were committed to writing and received the signature of each several member. Then the emperor, believing that he had thus obtained a second victory over the adversary of the church, proceeded to solemnize a triumphal festival in honor of God. [. . .]

20. *interpreted*—into Greek, the language of most attendees.

Incarnational Theology and Arian Controversies

T he theological debates of Constantine's reign bothered him not because he had any ardent views about which side was correct, but because he craved stability for his empire. In fact he evidenced profound uninterest in the theological particulars at the root of this controversy.

It is time now to consider those particulars.[1]

The controversy centered around a single, overriding question: Who, exactly, was Jesus?

This question occupied theologians in the Eastern Empire to a much greater degree than it did those in the West, and Eastern theologians did most of the heavy lifting in solving them.

The four canonical Gospels tell us much about Jesus's life. Matthew and Luke recount Jesus's birth (Mark and John do not). All four recount his ministry, miracles, and death. All but the earliest and most reliable versions of Mark tell of his resurrection. We learn a good deal about Jesus's actions, thoughts, values, and power in these Gospels.

Yet in these Gospels Jesus at times appears somewhat cryptic—his identity is not always clear. He speaks about himself in parables. He and his disciples refer to him, variously, as "Messiah," "Son of man," "Son of God," "Lord," and "Lamb of God." These terms have been and continue to be understood in different ways. For example, in the

---

1. Hans Hillerbrand provides an unusually lucid account of these controversies in his article "Christology," in *The New Encyclopaedia Britannica*, 15th ed. (Chicago: Encyclopaedia Britannica, 2005). This introduction draws from Hillerbrand's framework and observations.

Hebrew scriptures (the main point of reference for the Jews who surrounded Jesus) "Son of man" refers variously to all of humanity (as in the books of Psalms, Job, and Isaiah), to the prophet Ezekiel, and to a divine being (as in the book of Daniel). "Son of God" refers at various times to men, angels, and all humankind. The term "Messiah" could mean king, prophet, high priest, liberator, or all of the above; it encompassed numerous and not always complimentary expectations. "Lord" is equally problematic. In John 20:28, for example, Thomas refers to Jesus as "My Lord and my God!" But this same phrase was often used to address Roman emperors, who were understood to embody some measure of divinity.

The Gospel of John refers to Jesus as the Logos, or "Word," in its opening and most famous passage: "In the beginning was the Word [Logos], and the Word was with God, and the Word was God." Logos is a difficult concept, implying, variously, God's will, reason, and power. It indicates something that existed before Jesus's birth—the Logos existed "in the beginning"; passages in Philippians and in Second Corinthians also imply preexistence;[2] the Apostle Paul argues that Jesus descended from Heaven as a voluntary act of submission to God his Father.

But what is this Logos that existed before the birth of Jesus? How and when did it exist "with" God? To what degree "was" it God? And how could God or some aspect of God later exist in human form without compromising God's godhood?

All sorts of explanations emerged during the 100s. Some theologians argued that Jesus was entirely human. Others argued he was entirely divine. Ignatius, the bishop of Antioch we have already encountered, tried to solve the problem through a series of paradoxes: Jesus was both flesh *and* spirit, both created *and* uncreated, both suffering *and* nonsuffering. Since he was spirit, he was equal to the Father. And since he was flesh, he was subordinate to the Father.

The Roman theologian Tertullian (ca. 155–after 220) argued in the early 200s that Jesus was a mixture of two distinct elements, divine and human. Tertullian's contemporary, Sabellius, an ardent monotheist we mentioned above, countered that, no, Jesus was not really human. He was a form of the one and only God (for there can be only one God),

---

2. *imply preexistence*—Jesus "emptied himself, / taking the form of a slave, / being born in human likeness" (Philippians 2:7, NRSV); "For you know the generous act of our Lord Jesus Christ, that though he was rich, yet for your sakes he became poor" (2 Corinthians 8:9, NRSV).

a temporary mode of God's revelation. A third contemporary, Origen (ca. 185–ca. 254), believed that Jesus and God were of the same *substance,* yet he insisted that Jesus was subordinate to God. Origen argued that the Logos, although close to God and of the same substance as God, was something different from God. The Son is "eternally begotten of the Father," but is not the Father per se.

These controversies heated up during the late 200s when two brilliant and bullheaded theologians—both convinced they represented the only reasonable and orthodox (i.e., true) position—launched the series of polemics referenced in the *Life of Constantine.* Arius (ca. 250s–326) was an energetic and passionate priest ministering in Alexandria, Egypt, the center of theology in the Christian world. Alexander (?–ca. 328) was (appropriately, given his name) the bishop of the same city.

Arius argued that God the Father willed the Son—the Logos—into being. Hence God the Father existed before the Son. And although the Son existed *before time* (God willed him into existence before time began), he was not *eternal,* since the Father preceded him. The Son had a beginning; the Father did not. Nevertheless, the Son and the Father were of the same *essence.* The Son, or Logos, following the will of the Father, became human in the person of Jesus.

One of Arius's primary goals was to preserve monotheism, the Jewish insistence that there is only one God. While acknowledging that the Father and Son were of the *same essence,* he was loath to suggest that they were the *same being.*

Arius's opponents, Alexander (the bishop of Alexandria) and Alexander's successor, Athanasius—whose argument eventually won the day—took a different approach. For Athanasius, Jesus's divine nature was *identical* to God's nature. Father and Son shared the same *substance* (*homoousios: homo* = same; *ousios* = substance), not simply, as Arius maintained, the *same essence. Homoousios* for Athanasius was the key to explaining the relationship between Son and Father, and it is the term that would eventually be adopted in the Orthodox creed.

Theodoret's (ca. 393–457) Account of the Arian Controversy

Theodoret, *Ecclesiastical History,* in *Select Library of Nicene and Post-Nicene Fathers, Second Series,* ed. Philip Schaff and Henry Wace (New York: Christian Literature Company, 1892), 3:33–43.

Theodoret, whose name means "gift of God," served as the bishop of Cyrrhus in Syria. This polemicist inserted himself into the middle of several Christological controversies during the early 400s, and he reportedly converted more than one thousand followers of Marcion and numerous Arians to his understanding of Orthodox Christianity. His history of the Christian church from the Arian controversy up to 429 is hardly nonpartisan: it portrays Arians as inspired by the "devil, full of all envy and wickedness," and thus it is wonderfully indicative of the tenor of the debates. Here Theodoret reflects on controversies of the early 300s and reprints correspondence from the two main disputants: Alexander (the bishop of Alexandria) and Arius.

· Chapter I ·

[. . . The] devil, full of all envy and wickedness, the destroyer of mankind, unable to bear the sight of the church sailing on with favorable winds, stirred up plans of evil counsel, eager to sink the vessel steered by the creator and Lord of the universe. When he began to perceive that the error of the Greeks had been made manifest, that the various tricks of the demons had been detected, and that the greater number of men worshipped the creator, instead of adoring, as heretofore, the creature, he did not dare to declare open war against our God and savior; but having found some who, though dignified with the name of Christians were yet slaves to ambition and vainglory, he made them fit instruments for the execution of his designs, and by their means drew others back into their old error, not indeed by the former method of setting up the worship of the creature, but by bringing it about that the creator and maker of all should be reduced to a level with the creature. I shall now proceed to relate where and by what means he sowed these tares.[3]

Alexandria is an immense and populous city, charged with the leadership not only of Egypt but also of the adjacent countries, the Thebaid[4] and Libya. After Peter,[5] the victorious champion of the faith, had, during the sway of the aforesaid impious tyrants, obtained the crown of martyrdom,[6] the church in Alexandria was ruled for a short time by Achillas.[7] He was succeeded by Alexander,[8] who proved himself a noble defender of the doctrines of the Gospel. At that time, Arius, who had been

---

3. *tares*—weeds.

4. *Thebaid*—a region populated by monks in the upper part of the Nile River valley in northern Egypt.

5. *Peter*—the Apostle Peter, to whom Christ promised the keys of the kingdom of Heaven and whom he called the rock upon which he would build his church (Matthew 16:18–19).

6. *obtained the crown of martyrdom*—killed for his faith.

7. *Achillas*—patriarch (bishop) of Alexandria from 312 to 313.

8. *Alexander*—patriarch (bishop) of Alexandria from 313 to 326.

■ Alexandria

Figure 8. Alexandria

enrolled in the list of the presbytery[9] and entrusted with the exposition of the holy scriptures, fell prey to the assaults of jealousy, when he saw that the helm of the high priesthood was committed to Alexander. Stung by this passion, he sought opportunities for dispute and contention; and, although he perceived that Alexander's irreproachable conduct forbade his bringing any charges against him, envy would not allow him to rest. In him the enemy of the truth found an instrument whereby to stir and agitate the angry waters of the church, and persuaded him to oppose the apostolic doctrine of Alexander. While the patriarch,[10] in obedience to the holy scriptures, taught that the Son is of equal dignity with the Father, and of the same substance with God who begat him, Arius, in direct opposition to the truth, affirmed that the Son of God is merely a creature or created being, adding the famous dictum, "There once was a time when he was not,"[11] with other opinions that may be learned from his own writings. He taught these false doctrines perseveringly, not only in the church, but also in general meetings and assemblies; and he even went

9. *enrolled in the list of the presbytery*—that is, made a minister.

10. *patriarch*—a bishop of a major city, in this case Alexander of Alexandria.

11. *"There once was a time when he was not"*—a key part of Arius's argument.

from house to house, endeavoring to make men the slaves of his error. Alexander, who was strongly attached to the doctrines of the apostles, at first tried by exhortations and counsels to convince him of his error; but when he saw him playing the madman and making public declaration of his impiety, he deposed him from the order of the presbytery, for he heard the law of God loudly declaring, "If your right eye offend you, pluck it out, and cast it from you." [. . .]

• Chapter II •

[. . .] Alexander, bishop of Alexandria, perceiving that Arius, enslaved by the lust of power, was assembling those who had been taken captive by his blasphemous doctrines, and was holding private meetings, communicated an account of his heresy by letter to the rulers of the principal churches. That the authenticity of my history may not be suspected, I shall now insert in my narrative the letter that he wrote to his namesake, containing, as it does, a clear account of all the facts I have mentioned. I shall also subjoin the letter of Arius, together with the other letters that are necessary to the completeness of this narrative, that they may at once testify to the truth of my work, and make the course of events more clear.

The following letter was written by Alexander of Alexandria to the bishop of the same name as himself.

• Chapter III •
[Epistle of Alexander, bishop of Alexandria, to Alexander, bishop of Constantinople¹²]

To his most revered and likeminded brother Alexander Alexander sends greeting in the Lord.

Impelled by avarice and ambition, evil-minded persons have ever plotted against the wellbeing of the most important dioceses. Under various pretexts, they attack the religion of the church; and, being maddened by the devil, who works in them, they start aside from all piety according to their own pleasure and trample underfoot the fear of the judgment of God. [. . .]

Arius and Achillas [. . .] revile every godly apostolic doctrine, and in Jewish fashion have organized a gang to fight against Christ, denying his divinity, and declaring him to be on a level with other men.¹³ They pick out every passage that refers to the dispensation of salvation and to his humiliation for our sake; they endeavor to collect from them their own

---

12. *Alexander, bishop of Constantinople*—patriarch (bishop) of Constantinople from around 314 to 337.

13. *on a level with other men*—not a fair summary of Arius's position.

impious assertion, while they evade all those who declare his eternal divinity, and the unceasing glory that he possesses with the Father. They maintain the ungodly doctrine entertained by the Greeks and the Jews concerning Jesus Christ; and thus, by every means in their power, hunt for their applause. Everything that outsiders ridicule in us they officiously practice. They daily excite persecutions and seditions against us. On the one hand they bring accusations against us before the courts, suborning as witnesses certain unprincipled women whom they have seduced into error. On the other they dishonor Christianity by permitting their young women to ramble about the streets. Nay, they have had the audacity to rend the seamless garment of Christ, which the soldiers dared not divide.

When these actions, in keeping with their course of life and the impious enterprise that had been long concealed, became tardily known to us, we unanimously ejected them from the church that worships the divinity of Christ. They then ran hither and thither to form cabals against us, even addressing themselves to our fellow-ministers who were of one mind with us, under the pretense of seeking peace and unity with them, but in truth endeavoring by means of fair words to sweep some among them away into their own disease. [. . .] It is on this account, beloved brethren, that without delay I have stirred myself up to inform you of the unbelief of certain persons who say that "There was a time when the Son of God was not"; and "he who previously had no existence subsequently came into existence; and when at some time he came into existence he became such as every other man is." God, they say, created all things out of that which was non-existent, and they include in the number of creatures, both rational and irrational, even the Son of God. Consistently with this doctrine they, as a necessary consequence, affirm that he is by nature liable to change, and capable both of virtue and of vice, and thus, by their hypothesis of his having been created out of that which was non-existent, they overthrow the testimony of the divine scriptures, which declare the immutability of the Word and the divinity of the wisdom of the Word, which Word and wisdom is Christ. [. . .]

[. . .] Now that the Son of God was not created out of the non-existent, and that there never was a time in which he was not, is expressly taught by John the Evangelist, who speaks of him as "the only begotten Son that is in the bosom of the Father." This divine teacher desired to show that the Father and the Son are inseparable, and therefore he said "that the Son is in the bosom of the Father." Moreover, the same John affirms that the Word of God is not classed among things created out of the non-existent, for, he says that "all things were made by him," and he also declares his individual personality in the following words: "In the beginning was the Word, and the Word was with God, and the Word was God. . . . All things were made by him, and without him was not anything made that was made." If, then, all things were made by him, how is it that he who thus bestowed existence on all, could at any period have had no existence himself? The Word, the creating power, can in no way be defined as of the same nature as the things created, if indeed he was in the beginning, and all things were made by him, and were called by him out of the non-existent into being. [. . .] How then can anyone but a madman presume to enquire into the nature of the Word of God? [. . .]

But the insane folly of imagining that the Son of God came into being out of that which had no being, and that his sending forth took place in time, is plain from the words "which had no being," although the foolish are incapable of perceiving the folly of their own utterances. For the phrase "he was not" must either have reference to time or to some interval in the ages. If then it be true that all things were made by him, it is evident that every age, time, all intervals of time, and that "when" in which "was not" has its place, were made by him. And is it not absurd to say that there was a time when he who created all time, and ages, and seasons, with which the "was not" is confused, was not? For it would be the height of ignorance and contrary indeed to all reason to affirm that the cause of any created thing can be posterior to that caused by it. [. . .]

[. . .] They will not admit that any of our fellow-ministers anywhere possess even mediocrity of intelligence. They say that they themselves alone are the wise and the poor and discoverers of doctrines and to them alone have been revealed those truths that, say they, have never entered the mind of any other individuals under the sun. O what wicked arrogance! O what excessive folly! What false boasting, joined with madness and Satanic pride, has hardened their impious hearts! [. . .]

We believe as is taught by the apostolic church in an only unbegotten Father, who of his being has no cause, immutable and invariable, and who subsists always in one state of being, admitting neither of progression nor of diminution, who gave the law, and the prophets, and the Gospel; of patriarchs and apostles, and of all saints, Lord; and in one Lord Jesus Christ, the only-begotten Son of God, begotten not out of that which is not, but of the Father, who is; [. . .] since no mortal intellect can comprehend the nature of his person, as the Father himself cannot be comprehended, because the nature of reasonable beings is unable to grasp the manner in which he was begotten of the Father. [. . .]

But those who are led by the spirit of truth have no need to learn these things of me, for the words long since spoken by the savior yet sound in our ears, "No one knows who the Father is but the Son, and no one knows who the Son is but the Father." We have learned that the Son is immutable and unchangeable, all-sufficient and perfect like the Father, lacking only his "unbegotten." He is the exact and precisely similar image of his Father. For it is clear that the image fully contains everything by which the greater likeness exists, as the Lord taught us when he said, "My

Father is greater than I." And in accordance with this we believe that the
Son always existed of the Father; for he is the brightness of his glory and
the express image of his Father's person. [. . .]

Arius and Achillas, together with their fellow foes, have been expelled
from the church, because they have become aliens from our pious doctrine according to the blessed Paul, who said, "If any of you preach any
other Gospel than that which you have received, let him be accursed,
even though he should pretend to be an angel from Heaven," and "But if
any man teach otherwise, and consent not to wholesome words, even the
words of our Lord Jesus Christ, and to the doctrine that is according to
godliness, he is proud, knowing nothing," and so forth. Since, then, they
have been condemned by the brotherhood, let none of you receive them,
nor attend to what they say or write. They are deceivers and propagate
lies, and they never adhere to the truth. [. . .]

· Chapter IV ·
[Arius defends himself—Letter of Arius
to Eusebius, Bishop of Nicomedia[14]]

[. . . The] bishop[15] greatly wastes and persecutes us and leaves no stone
unturned against us. He has driven us out of the city as atheists because
we do not concur in what he publicly preaches, namely, God always, the
Son always; as the Father so the Son; the Son co-exists unbegotten with
God; he is everlasting; neither by thought nor by any interval does God
precede the Son; always God, always Son; he is begotten of the unbegotten; the Son is of God himself. [. . .] But we say and believe and have
taught and do teach that the Son is not unbegotten; and that he does
not derive his subsistence from any matter; but that by his own will and
counsel he has subsisted before time and before ages as perfect God, only
begotten and unchangeable, and that before he was begotten or created
or purposed or established he was not. For he was not unbegotten. We
are persecuted because we say that the Son has a beginning but that God
is without beginning. This is the cause of our persecution, and likewise,
because we say that he is of the non-existent. And this we say because he
is neither part of God nor of any essential being. [. . .]

14. *Eusebius, bishop of Nicomedia*—not to be confused with the Eusebius
who wrote the *Life of Constantine*. This Eusebius served as bishop of Nicomedia
and later (from 339 to 441) as patriarch of Constantinople. One of Arius's most
fervent supporters.

15. *the bishop*—Alexander.

Arius Explains His Doctrine to
Alexander of Alexandria (320)

Athanasius, *De Synodis*, in *Select Library of Nicene and Post-Nicene Fathers, Second Series,* ed. Philip Schaff and Henry Wace (New York: Christian Literature Company, 1892), 4:458.

None of Arius's original writings survives. Constantine ordered them burned, and while it is not clear whether the order was carried out, the question is moot, since Arius's other opponents destroyed what they disliked: namely, everything. It is thus difficult to get a fix on the specifics of Arius's teachings. What remains of his thought are transcriptions (or what claim to be transcriptions) of whatever his opponents chose to copy and distribute. Scholars disagree in their assessments of these documents' reliability.

Athanasius (Alexander's like-minded successor), of all people, reprinted a good deal of Arius's works. Whether he was a faithful editor is an open question. But even if Athanasius took liberties with the following text, it is still valuable for what it tells us about how Arius's opponents viewed Arius.

Our faith from our forefathers, which also we have learned from you, blessed pope,[16] is this: we acknowledge one God, alone ingenerate, alone everlasting, alone unbegun, alone true, alone having immortality, alone wise, alone good, alone sovereign; judge, governor, and providence of all, unalterable and unchangeable, just and good, God of law and prophets and New Testament; who begat an only-begotten Son before eternal times, through whom he has made both the ages and the universe; and begat him, not in semblance but in truth; and that he made him subsist at his own will, unalterable and unchangeable; perfect creature of God, but not as one of the creatures; offspring, but not as one of things begotten; [. . .] nor that he was before, was afterwards generated or new-created into a Son, as you too yourself, blessed pope, in the midst of the church and in session have often condemned; but, as we say, at the will of God, created before times and ages, and gaining life and being from the Father, who gave subsistence to his glories together with him. For the Father did not, in giving to him the inheritance of all things, deprive himself of what he has ingenerately in himself; for he is the fountain of all things. Thus there are three subsistences. And God, being the cause of all things, is unbegun and altogether sole, but the Son being begotten apart from time by

16. *pope*—patriarch; the bishop of a large city.

the Father, and being created and founded before ages, was not before his generation, but being begotten apart from time before all things, alone was made to subsist by the Father. For he is not eternal or co-eternal or co-unoriginate with the Father, nor has he his being together with the Father, as some speak of relations, introducing two ingenerate beginnings, but God is before all things as being monad[17] and beginning of all. Therefore also he is before the Son; as we have learned also from your preaching in the midst of the church. So far then as from God he has being and glories and life, and all things are delivered to him, in such sense is God his origin. For he is above him, as being his God, and before him. But if the terms "from him," and "from the womb," and "I came forth from the Father, and I am come" [Romans 11:36; Psalms 110:3; John 16:28] be understood by some to mean as if a part of him, one in essence or as an issue, then the Father is according to them compounded and divisible and alterable and material, and, as far as their belief goes, has the circumstances of a body, who is the incorporeal God. [. . .]"

Athanasius on the Incarnation (ca. 318–335)

Athanasius, "On the Incarnation of the Word," in *Christology of the Later Fathers,* ed. Edward Hardy (Philadelphia: Westminster, 1954), 55–110. Used by permission of Westminster John Knox Press.

This excerpt is from an extended study by Athanasius on the "incarnation," the phenomenon in which God became man or Word became flesh in the person of Jesus. We do not know whether Athanasius wrote this study before or after the Council of Nicaea (see the "The Creed of Nicaea," below): estimates on the date of composition range from 318 (seven years before the council) to 335 (ten years after the council).

[. . .]

2. Of the making of the universe and the creation of all things many have taken different views, and each man has laid down the law just as he pleased. For some say that all things have come into being of themselves and in a chance fashion, as, for example, the Epicureans,[18] who tell us

17. *monad*—one essence.

18. *Epicureans*—followers of Epicurus (341 BCE–270 BCE), a Roman philosopher who argued for judging whether something was good by asking whether it caused pain or pleasure. Not all Epicureans would deny a "universal providence," as Athanasius suggests here.

in their self-contempt that universal providence does not exist, speaking right in the face of obvious fact and experience. [. . .] But others, including Plato, who is in such repute among the Greeks, argue that God has made the world out of matter previously existing and without beginning. For God could have made nothing had not the material existed already; just as the wood must exist ready at hand for the carpenter to enable him to work at all. But in so saying they know not that they are investing God with weakness. For if he is not himself the cause of the material, but makes things only of previously existing material, he proves to be weak, because unable to produce anything he makes without the material. [. . .] For he could not in any sense be called creator unless he is creator of the material of which the things created have in their turn been made. [. . .] Or if, in the words of John, who says, making no exception, "All things were made by him," and "Without him was not anything made," how could the artificer[19] be another, distinct from the Father of Christ?

[. . .] God made the universe to exist through his Word, as he says first through Moses: "In the beginning God created the Heaven and the earth"; second, in the most edifying book of the Shepherd,[20] "First of all believe that God is one, which created and framed all things and made them to exist out of nothing." To which also Paul refers when he says, "By faith we understand that the worlds have been framed by the Word of God so that what is seen has not been made out of things that do appear." [. . .]

4. You are wondering, perhaps, for what possible reason, having proposed to speak of the incarnation of the Word, we are at present treating the origin of mankind. But this too properly belongs to the aim of our treatise. For in speaking of the appearance of the savior among us, we must speak also of the origin of men, that you may know that the reason of his coming down was because of us, and that our transgression called forth the loving-kindness of the Word, that the Lord should both make haste to help us and appear among men. For of his becoming incarnate we were the object, and for our salvation he dealt so lovingly as to appear and be born even in a human body. Thus, then, God has made man and willed that he should abide in incorruption; but men, having despised and rejected the contemplation of God and devised and contrived evil for themselves [. . .] received the condemnation of death with which they had been threatened, and from thenceforth no longer remained as they were made but were being corrupted according to their devices, and death had the mastery over them as king. [. . .]

19. *artificer*—artisan or creator.

20. *book of the Shepherd*—*The Shepherd of Hermas*. Although listed as a canonical book in the "Muratorian Canon" (a list of scripture compiled in the 200s), no copy survives today. Early church fathers referred to it often and considered it inspired scripture.

5. For God has not only made us out of nothing, but he gave us freely, by the grace of the Word, a life in correspondence with God. But men, having rejected things eternal, and, by counsel of the devil, turned to the things of corruption, became the cause of their own corruption in death, being, as I said before, by nature corruptible, but destined, by the grace following from partaking of the Word, to have escaped their natural state, had they remained good. [. . .] But when this came to pass men began to die, while corruption thenceforward prevailed against them, gaining even more than its natural power over the whole race, inasmuch as it had, owing to the transgression of the commandment, the threat of the deity as a further advantage against them. For even in their misdeeds men had not stopped short at any set limits, but, gradually pressing forward, have passed on beyond all measure: having, to begin with, been inventors of wickedness and called down upon themselves death and corruption; while later on, having turned aside to wrong and exceeding all lawlessness and stopping at no one evil but devising all manner of new evils in succession, they have become insatiable in sinning. For there were adulteries everywhere and thefts, and the whole earth was full of murders and plundering. And as to corruption and wrong, no heed was paid to law, but all crimes were being practiced everywhere, both individually and jointly. Cities were at war with cities, and nations were rising up against nations; and the whole earth was rent with civil commotions and battles, each man vying with his fellows in lawless deeds. Nor were even crimes against nature far from them, but, as the apostle and witness of Christ says: "For their women changed the natural use into that which is against nature; and likewise also the men, leaving the natural use of the women, burned in their lust one toward another, men with men working unseemliness and receiving in themselves that recompense of their error that was meet."

6. For this cause, then, death having gained upon men, and corruption abiding upon them, the race of man was perishing; the rational man made in God's image was disappearing, and the handiwork of God was in process of dissolution. For death, as I said above, gained from that time forth a legal hold over us, and it was impossible to evade the law, since it had been laid down by God because of the transgression, and the result was in truth at once monstrous and unseemly. For it was monstrous, first, that God, having spoken, should prove false—that, when once he had ordained that man, if he transgressed the commandment, should die the death, after the transgression man should not die, but God's word should be broken. For God would not be true if, when he had said we should die, man died not. [. . .] It was, then, out of the question to leave men to the current of corruption, because this would be unseemly, and unworthy of God's goodness.

7. [. . .] So here, once more, what possible course was God to take? To demand repentance of men for their transgression? For this one might

pronounce worthy of God, as though, just as from transgression men have become set toward corruption, so from repentance they may once more be set in the way of incorruption. But repentance would, first of all, fail to guard the just claim of God. For he would still be none the more true if men did not remain in the grasp of death; nor, second, does repentance call men back from what is their nature—it merely stays them from acts of sin. Now, if there was merely a misdemeanor in question, and not a consequent corruption, repentance would be well enough. But if, when transgression had once gained a start, men became involved in that corruption that was their nature, and were deprived of the grace that they had, being in the image of God, what further step was needed? [. . .]

8. For this purpose, then, the incorporeal and incorruptible and immaterial Word of God comes to our realm, although he was not far from us before. For no part of creation is left void of him: he has filled all things everywhere, remaining present with his own Father. But he comes in condescension to show loving-kindness upon us and to visit us. And seeing the race of rational creatures in the way to perish, and death reigning over them by corruption; seeing, too, that the threat against transgression gave a firm hold to the corruption that was upon us and that it was monstrous that before the law was fulfilled it should fall through; seeing, once more, the unseemliness of what was come to pass: that the things whereof he himself was artificer were passing away; seeing, further, the exceeding wickedness of men, and how by little and little they had increased it to an intolerable pitch against themselves; and seeing, lastly, how all men were under penalty of death, he took pity on our race, and had mercy on our infirmity, and condescended to our corruption and, unable to bear that death should have the mastery—lest the creature should perish, and his Father's handiwork in men be spent for naught—he takes a body for himself, and that of no different sort from ours. For he did not simply will to become embodied, or will merely to appear. For if he willed merely to appear, he was able to affect his divine appearance by some other and higher means as well. But he takes a body of our kind, and not merely so, but from a spotless and stainless virgin, knowing not a man, a body clean and in very truth pure from intercourse of men. For being himself mighty and artificer of everything, he prepares the body in the virgin as a temple for himself and makes it his very own as an instrument, in it manifested and in it dwelling. And thus taking from our bodies one of like nature, because all were under penalty of the corruption of death he gave it over to death in the stead of all, and offered it to the Father—doing this, moreover, of his loving-kindness, to the end that, first, all being held to have died in him, the law involving the ruin of men might be undone (inasmuch as its power was fully spent in the Lord's body, and had no longer holding ground against men, his peers), and that, second, whereas men had turned toward corruption, he might turn them again toward

incorruption, and quicken them from death by the appropriation of his body and by the grace of the resurrection, banishing death from them like straw from the fire.

9. For the Word, perceiving that not otherwise could the corruption of men be undone save by death as a necessary condition, while it was impossible for the Word to suffer death, being immortal and Son of the Father, to this end he takes to himself a body capable of death, so that it, by partaking of the Word who is above all, might be worthy to die in the stead of all, and might, because of the Word that was come to dwell in it, remain incorruptible, and that thenceforth corruption might be stayed from all by the grace of the resurrection. Whence, by offering to death the body he himself had taken, as an offering and sacrifice free from any stain, straightway he put away death from all his peers by the offering of an equivalent. For, being over all, the Word of God naturally by offering his own temple and corporeal instrument for the life of all satisfied the debt by his death. And thus he, the incorruptible Son of God, being conjoined with all by a like nature, naturally clothed all with incorruption, by the promise of the resurrection. For the actual corruption in death has no longer holding ground against men, by reason of the Word, which by his one body has come to dwell among them. [. . .]

11. God, who has the power over all things, when he was making the race of men through his own Word, seeing the weakness of their nature, that it was not sufficient of itself to know its maker nor to get any idea at all of God; because while he was uncreated the creatures had been made of naught, and while he was incorporeal, men had been fashioned in a lower way in the body, and because in every way the things made fell far short of being able to comprehend and know their maker—taking pity, I say, on the race of men, inasmuch as he is good, he did not leave them destitute of the knowledge of himself lest they should find no profit in existing at all. For what profit to the creatures if they knew not their maker? Or how could they be rational without knowing the Word [and reason] of the Father, in whom they received their very being? For there would be nothing to distinguish them even from brute creatures if they had knowledge of nothing but earthly things. Nay, why did God make them at all if he did not wish to be known by them? Whence, lest this should be so, being good, he gives them a share in his own image, our Lord Jesus Christ, and makes them after his own image and after his likeness: so that by such grace perceiving the image, that is, the Word of the Father, they may be able through him to get an idea of the Father, and, knowing their maker, live the happy and truly blessed life. But men once more in their perversity having set at naught, in spite of all this, the grace given them, so wholly rejected God and so darkened their soul, as not merely to forget their idea of God but also to fashion for themselves one invention after another. For not only did they grave idols for themselves instead of

the truth and honor things that were not before the living God "and serve the creature rather than the creator," but, worst of all, they transferred the honor of God even to sticks and stones and to every material object[21] and to men and went even further than this, as we have said in the former treatise. So far indeed did their impiety go that they proceeded to worship devils and proclaimed them as gods, fulfilling their own lusts. For they performed, as was said above, offerings of brute animals and sacrifices of men, as was meet for them, binding themselves down all the faster under their maddening inspirations. [. . .]

12. For whereas the grace of the divine image was in itself sufficient to make known God the Word and through him the Father, still God, knowing the weakness of men, made provision even for their careless-ness, so that if they cared not to know God of themselves, they might be enabled through the works of creation to avoid ignorance of the maker. But since men's carelessness, by little and little, descends to lower things, God made provision once more even for this weakness of theirs by send-ing a law and prophets, men such as they knew, so that even if they were not ready to look up to Heaven and know their creator they might have their instruction from those near at hand. [. . .]

14. [. . .] [W]hen the likeness painted on a panel has been effaced by stains from without, he whose likeness it is must come once more to en-able the portrait to be renewed on the same wood, for, for the sake of his picture, even the mere wood on which it is painted is not thrown away, but the outline is renewed upon it; in the same way also the most holy Son of the Father, being the image of the Father, came to our region to renew man once made in his likeness, and find him as one lost, by the remission of sins; as he says himself in the Gospels, "I came to find and to save the lost." [. . .] Whence, naturally, willing to profit men, he sojourns here as man, taking to himself a body like the others, and from things of earth, that is by the works of his body [he teaches them], so that they who would not know him from his providence and rule over all things may even from the works done by his actual body know the Word of God, which is in the body, and through him the Father.

15. For like a kind teacher who cares for his disciples, if some of them cannot profit by higher subjects, comes down to their level and teaches them at any rate by simpler courses, so also did the Word of God. [. . .]

16. For men's mind having finally fallen to things of sense, the Word disguised himself by appearing in a body, that he might, as man, transfer men to himself, and center their senses on himself, and men seeing him thenceforth as man, persuade them by the works he did that he is not man only, but also God, and the Word and wisdom of the true God. [. . .] Now for this cause also he did not immediately upon his coming

21. *to every material object*—to idols.

accomplish his sacrifice on behalf of all, by offering his body to death and raising it again, for by this means he would have made himself invisible. But he made himself visible enough by what he did, abiding in it, and doing such works and showing such signs as made him known no longer as man, but as God the Word. For by his becoming man the savior was to accomplish both works of love: first, in putting away death from us and renewing us again; second, being unseen and invisible, in manifesting and making himself known by his works to be the Word of the Father and the ruler and king of the universe. For he was not, as might be imagined, circumscribed[22] in the body, nor, while present in the body, was he absent elsewhere; nor, while he moved the body, was the universe left void of his working and providence; but, thing most marvelous, Word as he was, so far from being contained by anything, he rather contained all things himself; and just as while present in the whole of creation he is at once distinct in being from the universe and present in all things by his own power—giving order to all things and overall and in all revealing his own providence and giving life to each thing and all things, including the whole without being included but being in his own Father alone wholly and in every respect—thus, even while present in a human body and himself quickening it, he was, without inconsistency, quickening the universe as well, and was in every process of nature, and was outside the whole, and while known from the body by his works he was none the less manifest from the working of the universe as well. [. . .] Now, the Word of God in his man's nature was not like that; for he was not bound to his body, but was rather himself wielding it, so that he was not only in it, but was actually in everything, and while external to the universe, abode in his Father only. And this was the wonderful thing that he was at once walking as man and as the Word was quickening all things, and as the Son was dwelling with his Father. So that not even when the virgin bore him did he suffer any change, nor by being in the body was [his glory] dulled: but, on the contrary, he sanctified the body also. For not even by being in the universe does he share in its nature, but all things, on the contrary, are quickened and sustained by him. For if the sun too, which was made by him and which we see as it revolves in the Heaven, is not defiled by touching the bodies upon earth, nor is it put out by darkness, but on the contrary itself illuminates and cleanses them also, much less was the all-holy Word of God, maker and Lord also of the sun, defiled by being made known in the body; on the contrary, being incorruptible, he quickened and cleansed the body also, which was in itself mortal: "who did," for so it says, "no sin, neither was guile found in his mouth." [. . .]

18. [. . .] [T]he actual body that ate, was born, and suffered, belonged to none other but to the Lord: and because, having become man, it was

22. *circumscribed*—limited.

proper for these things to be predicated of him as man, to show him to have a body in truth and not in seeming. But just as from these things he was known to be bodily present, so from the works he did in the body he made himself known to be Son of God. Whence also he cried to the unbelieving Jews: "If I do not the works of my Father, believe me not. But if I do them, though you believe not me, believe my works, that you may know and understand that the Father is in me, and I in the Father." [. . .] For his charging evil spirits and their being driven forth, this deed is not of man, but of God. Or who that saw him healing the diseases to which the human race is subject can still think him man and not God? For he cleansed lepers, made lame men to walk, opened the hearing of deaf men, made blind men to see again, and in a word drove away from men all diseases and infirmities, from which acts it was possible even for the most ordinary observer to see his Godhead. [. . .]

19. But all this it seemed well for the savior to do, that since men had failed to perceive his Godhead shown in creation, they might at any rate from the works of his body recover their sight and through him receive an idea of the knowledge of the Father, inferring, as I said before, from particular cases his providence over the whole. For whoever saw his power over evil spirits or whoever saw the evil spirits confess that he was their Lord will hold his mind any longer in doubt whether this be the Son and wisdom and power of God? [. . .]

21. Why, now that the common savior of all has died on our behalf, we, the faithful in Christ, no longer die the death as before, agreeably to the warning of the law; for this condemnation has ceased; but corruption ceasing and being put away by the grace of the resurrection, henceforth we are only dissolved agreeably to our bodies' mortal nature at the time God has fixed for each, that we may be able to gain a better resurrection. For like the seeds that are cast into the earth, we do not perish by dissolution, but, sown in the earth, shall rise again, death having been brought to naught by the grace of the savior. Hence it is that blessed Paul, who was made a surety of the resurrection to all, says: "This corruptible must put on incorruption, and this mortal must put on immortality; but when this corruptible shall have put on incorruption and this mortal shall have put on immortality, then shall be brought to pass the saying that is written, death is swallowed up in victory. O death, where is your sting? O grave, where is your victory?" [. . .]

30. [. . .] [W]hereas on a man's decease he can put forth no power, but his influence lasts to the grave and thenceforth ceases; and actions and power over men belong to the living only; let him who will, see and be judge, confessing the truth from what appears to sight. For now that the savior works so great things among men, and day by day is invisibly persuading so great a multitude from every side, from them that dwell both in Greece and in foreign lands, to come over to his faith and all

to obey his teaching, will anyone still hold his mind in doubt whether a resurrection has been accomplished by the savior and whether Christ is alive, or rather is himself the life? [. . .] Or how, if he be not risen but is dead, does he drive away and pursue and cast down those false gods said by the unbelievers to be alive and the demons they worship? For where Christ is named and his faith, there all idolatry is deposed and all imposture of evil spirits is exposed, and any spirit is unable to endure even the name, nay, even on barely hearing it flies and disappears. But this work is not that of one dead, but of one who lives—and especially of God. [. . .]

31. But they who disbelieve in the resurrection afford a strong proof against themselves, if instead of all the spirits and the gods worshipped by them casting out Christ, who, they say, is dead, Christ on the contrary proves them all to be dead. For if it be true that one dead can exert no power, while the savior does daily so many works, drawing men to religion, persuading to virtue, teaching of immortality, leading on to a desire for heavenly things, revealing the knowledge of the Father, inspiring strength to meet death, showing himself to each one, and displacing the godlessness of idolatry, and the gods and spirits of the unbelievers can do none of these things, but rather show themselves dead at the presence of Christ, their pomp being reduced to impotence and vanity—whereas by the sign of the cross all magic is stopped and all witchcraft brought to naught, and all the idols are being deserted and left, and every unruly pleasure is checked, and everyone is looking up from earth to Heaven— whom is one to pronounce dead? Christ who is doing so many works? But to work is not proper to one dead. [. . .]

56. Let this, Christ-loving man, then, be our offering to you, just for a rudimentary sketch and outline, in a short compass, of the faith of Christ and of his divine appearing to us. But you, taking occasion by this, if you light upon the text of the scriptures by genuinely applying your mind to them, will learn from them more completely and clearly the exact detail of what we have said. For they were spoken and written by God through men who spoke of God. But we impart of what we have learned from inspired teachers who have been conversant with them, who have also become martyrs for the deity of Christ, to your zeal for learning in turn. And you will also learn about his second glorious and truly divine appearing to us, when no longer in lowliness but in his own glory, no longer in humble guise but in his own magnificence he is to come, no more to suffer, but thenceforth to render to all the fruit of his own cross, that is the resurrection and incorruption; and no longer to be judged but to judge all by what each has done in the body, whether good or evil; where there is laid up for the good the Kingdom of Heaven but for them that have done evil everlasting fire and outer darkness. For thus the Lord himself also says, "Henceforth you shall see the Son of man sitting at the right hand of power and coming on the clouds of Heaven in the glory of the Father."

And for this very reason there is also a word of the savior to prepare us for that day in these words: "Be you ready and watch, for he comes at an hour you know not." For according to the blessed Paul, "We must all stand before the judgment seat of Christ, that each one may receive according as he has done in the body, whether it be good or bad." [. . .]

For just as if a man wished to see the light of the sun, he would at any rate wipe and brighten his eye, purifying himself in some sort like what he desires, so that the eye, thus becoming light, may see the light of the sun; or as, if a man would see a city or country, he at any rate comes to the place to see it—thus he that would comprehend the mind of those who speak of God must begin by washing and cleansing his soul by his manner of living, and approach the saints themselves by imitating their works, so that, associated with them in the conduct of a common life, he may understand also what has been revealed to them by God, and thenceforth, as closely knit to them, may escape the peril of the sinners and their fire at the day of judgment, and receive what is laid up for the saints in the Kingdom of Heaven, which "eye has not seen, nor ear heard, neither have entered into the heart of man," whatsoever things are prepared for them that live a virtuous life and love the God and the Father in Christ Jesus our Lord: through whom and with whom be to the Father himself, with the Son himself, in the Holy Spirit, honor and might and glory for ever and ever. Amen.

The Creed of Nicaea (325)

"The First Ecumenical Council: The First Council of Nicaea, 325," in *Creeds and Confessions of Faith in the Christian Tradition*, ed. Jaroslav Pelikan and Valerie Hotchkiss (New Haven, CT: Yale University Press, 2003), 1:159. Used by permission of Yale University Press.

As noted in Eusebius's *Life of Constantine*, Constantine summoned all bishops of the Christian church in 325 to Nicaea (Iznik in modern Turkey) to resolve the Athanasian-Arian debate and other matters roiling the church. Some 250 to 320 bishops plus members of their retinues arrived in the city. The overwhelming majority came from the East; only five bishops arrived from Latin-speaking provinces. Still, every region of the Roman Empire except Britain sent a representative.

The council tackled a number of secondary matters. It prohibited self-castration, a practice that some particularly ardent Christians had adopted. It warned clerics against entertaining young women in their houses. It acknowledged Rome, Constantinople, and Jerusalem as holding special places of honor among the centers of Christianity. It established relatively mild procedures for receiving back into the fold believers who had apostatized, that is, renounced their faith, during the persecutions of Licinius, the emperor Constantine deposed. It prohibited clergy from practicing usury (lending money for interest); it declared invalid those baptisms performed by certain heretics; and it dictated when parishioners could stand and kneel during services.

The main order of business, however, was crafting a resolution to the Athanasian-Arian debate. It became clear immediately that Arius and his cohorts represented a minority at the council; they never stood a chance. The council's resolutions relied heavily on the writings of Athanasius; in fact Athanasius served as the council's secretary. In the end, the council drafted the following statement (which we include below first in the original Greek and then in translation), which borrowed from Athanasius's claims that the Son was "consubstantial" (*homoousios,* literally, "same substance") with the Father. Constantine promised to exile anyone who refused to endorse the creed; he made good on his promise when Arius refused.

Many Christian churches still use a variant of this creed today.

Πιστεύομεν εἰς ἕνα Θεὸν Πατέρα παντοκράτορα πάντων ὁρατῶν τε καὶ ἀοράτων ποιητήν καὶ εἰς ἕνα Κύριον Ἰησοῦν Χριστὸν τὸν Υἱὸν τοῦ Θεοῦ, γεννηθέντα ἐκ τοῦ Πατρὸς μονογενῆ τουτέστιν ἐκ τῆς οὐσίας τοῦ Πατρος Θεὸν ἐκ Θεοῦ, Φῶς ἐκ Φωτός, Θεὸν ἀληθινὸν ἐκ Θεοῦ ἀληθινοῦ, γεννηθέντα, οὐ ποιηθέντα, ὁμοούσιον τῷ Πατρί, δι' οὗ τὰ πάντα ἐγένετο τά τε ἐν τῷ οὐρανῷ καὶ τὰ ἐν τῇ γῇ, τὸν δι' ἡμᾶς τοὺς ἀνθρώπους, καὶ διὰ τὴν ἡμετέραν σωτηρίαν, κατελθόντα, καὶ σαρκωθέντα, καὶ ἐνανθρωπήσαντα, παθόντα, καὶ ἀναστάντα τῇ τρίτῇ ἡμέρᾳ, ἀνελθόντα εἰς τοὺς οὐρανούς, ἐρχόμενον κρῖναι ζῶντας καὶ νεκρούς καὶ εἰς τὸ Ἅγιον Πνεῦμα.

Τοὺς δὲ λέγοντας Ἦν ποτε ὅτε οὐκ ἦν, καὶ Πρὶν γεννηθῆναι οὐκ ἦν, καὶ ὅτι Ἐξ οὐκ ὄντων ἐγένετο, ἢ Ἐξ ἑτέρας ὑποστάσεως ἢ οὐσίας φάσκοντας εἶναι ἢ κτιστόν ἢ τρεπτόν ἢ ἀλλοιωτὸν τὸν Υἱὸν τοῦ Θεοῦ, τούτους ἀναθεματίζει ἡ ἁγία καθολικὴ καὶ ἀποστολικὴ ἐκκλησία.

We believe in one God the Father all-powerful, maker of all things both seen and unseen. And in one Lord Jesus Christ, the Son of God, the only-begotten, begotten from the Father, that is from the substance of the Father, God from God, light from light, true God from true God, begotten not made, consubstantial with the Father, through whom all things came to be, both those in Heaven and those in earth; for us humans and for our salvation he came down and became incarnate, became human, suffered and rose up on the third day, went up into the heavens, is coming to judge the living and the dead. And in the Holy Spirit.

And those who say "there once was when he was not,"[23] and "before he was begotten he was not," and that he came to be from things that were not, or from another hypostasis[24] or substance, affirming that the Son of God is subject to change or alteration—these the catholic and apostolic church anathematizes.

23. *there once was when he was not*—this and the following quotations are meant to summarize Arius's heretical positions.

24. *from another hypostasis*—from another being. See "Trinitarian Debates" below for a discussion of this difficult term.

Reaction

The Council of Nicaea's immediate accomplishments were short-lived. Constantine's son—Constantinus II, who succeeded his father in 337, reigning jointly with others until becoming sole ruler in 361—proved to be an Arian. He persecuted the once triumphant Athanasians and established councils that overturned the theological work of Nicaea. (Today's church does not recognize the councils of Constantinus as legitimate or "ecumenical" councils). In fact during Constantinus's reign Athanasius was deposed and exiled four times: in 339, 356, 362, and 365. Arianism spread far and wide during this era, setting bishop against bishop and Christian against Christian.

Julian the Apostate (361–363) Mocks Christianity

Julian, "Against the Galileans." Reprinted by permission of the publishers and the Trustees of the Loeb Classical Library from Julian: *The Works of Emperor Julian,* Loeb Classical Library Volume 3; translated by Wilmer Cave Wright, pp. 319, 325–35, 339–43, 347–49, 357, 361–65, 377–85, 389–91, 399–401, 413–15, Cambridge, Mass.; Harvard University Press, [1962]. Loeb Classical Library ® is a registered trademark of the President and Fellows of Harvard College.[1]

1. The Loeb Library requires that we note deviations from the original translation. These deviations include "that" in place of "which" in restrictive clauses; lowercase pronouns in reference to God; uppercase nouns including "Heaven," "Son," "Sprit," "Father," "Sabbath"; lowercase "day," "night," "muse," "savior";

Constantinus's successor, Julian (known to bitter Christians as "Julian the Apostate"), spent his short career (361–363) mocking Christian theology and trying to revive Rome's pagan traditions. He passed a law excluding Christians from teaching, and he wrote a long diatribe, excerpted below, against the Christian faith. Julian referred to his religious philosophy as "Hellenism," an invention that combined disparate aspects of traditional paganism with devotion to Plato's supreme being (whom Julian imagined as the sun) standing above the still-legitimate gods of old Rome. While repudiating Christianity, Julian attempted to mimic the Christian hierarchy in his neo-pagan model, appointing regional religious leaders, or metropolitans, throughout the provinces who subscribed to his mongrel faith.

In Julian's attack on Christianity below, Plato emerges as the thinker to emulate rather than Moses (whom Julian assumed wrote the book of Genesis) or the authors of the New Testament. Julian accuses Christians of hypocrisy for claiming to worship one God while simultaneously suggesting that Jesus is also God. He also ridicules suffering Jews and Christians, whose tribes and communities could not boast the glories and triumphs of pagan Rome.

Julian's mocking tone enraged Christian theologians of the time, who in turn portrayed him as the very personification of evil.

It is, I think, expedient to set forth to all mankind the reasons by which I was convinced that the fabrication of the Galileans[2] is a fiction of men composed by wickedness. Though it has in it nothing divine, by making full use of that part of the soul which loves fable and is childish and foolish, it has induced men to believe that the monstrous tale is truth. [. . .]

Now it is true that the Hellenes[3] invented their myths about the gods, incredible and monstrous stories. For they said that Kronos swallowed his children and then vomited them forth; and they even told of lawless unions, how Zeus had intercourse with his mother, and after having a child by her, married his own daughter, or rather did not even marry

---

"you" for "thee"; "did" for "didst"; "you" for "thou"; "shall" for "shalt"; "your" for "thy" and "thine"; "make for yourselves" for "make unto thee"; American spellings for British spellings, including "color," "harmonize," "honor," "neighbor," "recognize," and "savior"; "who" for "that" in reference to a person; and "to" for "unto."

2. *Galileans*—Julian's word for Christians.

3. *Hellenes*—Greeks.

her, but simply had intercourse with her and then handed her over to another. Then too there is the legend that Dionysus was rent asunder and his limbs joined together again. This is the sort of thing described in the myths of the Hellenes. Compare with them the Jewish doctrine, how the garden was planted by God and Adam was fashioned by him, and next, for Adam, woman came to be. For God said, "It is not good that the man should be alone. Let us make him a help meet like him." Yet so far was she from helping him at all that she deceived him and was in part the cause of his and her own fall from their life of ease in the garden.

This is wholly fabulous. For is it probable that God did not know that the being he was creating as a help meet would prove to be not so much a blessing as a misfortune to him who received her? Again, what sort of language are we to say that the serpent used when he talked with Eve? Was it the language of human beings? And in what do such legends as these differ from the myths that were invented by the Hellenes? Moreover, is it not excessively strange that God should deny to the human beings whom he had fashioned the power to distinguish between good and evil? [. . .] Furthermore, their God must be called envious. For when he saw that man had attained to a share of wisdom, that he might not, God said, taste of the tree of life, he cast him out of the garden, saying in so many words, "Behold, Adam has become as one of us, because he knows good from bad; and now let him not put forth his hand and take also of the tree of life and eat and thus live forever." Accordingly, unless every one of these legends is a myth that involves some secret interpretation, as I indeed believe, they are filled with many blasphemous sayings about God. For in the first place to be ignorant that she who was created as a help meet would be the cause of the fall; secondly to refuse the knowledge of good and bad, which knowledge alone seems to give coherence to the mind of man; and lastly to be jealous lest man should take of the tree of life and from mortal become immortal—this is to be grudging and envious overmuch.

[. . .] Moses indeed has said nothing whatsoever about the gods who are superior to this creator, nay, he has not even ventured to say anything about the nature of the angels. But that they serve God he has asserted in many ways and often; but whether they were generated or ungenerated, or whether they were generated by one god and appointed to serve another, or in some other way, he has nowhere said definitely. But he describes fully in what manner the heavens and the earth and all that therein is were set in order. In part, he says, God ordered them to be, such as light and the firmament, and in part, he says, God made them, such as the heavens and the earth, the sun and moon, and that all things that already existed but were hidden away for the time being, he separated, such as water, I mean, and dry land. But apart from these he did not venture to say a word about the generation or the making of the Spirit, but only this: "And the Spirit of God moved upon the face of the waters." But whether that Spirit was ungenerated or had been generated he does not make at all clear.

Now, if you please, we will compare the utterance of Plato. Observe then what he says about the creator, and what words he makes him speak at the time of the generation of the universe, in order that we may compare Plato's account of that generation with that of Moses. For in this way it will appear who was the nobler and who was more worthy of intercourse with God, Plato who paid homage to images, or he of whom the scripture says that God spoke with him mouth to mouth.

"In the beginning God created the Heaven and the earth. And the earth was invisible and without form, and darkness was upon the face of the deep. And the Spirit of God moved upon the face of the waters. And God said, 'Let there be light'; and there was light. And God saw the light that it was good; and God divided the light from the darkness. And God called the light day, and the darkness he called night. And the evening and the morning were the first day. And God said, 'Let there be a firmament in the midst of the waters.' And God called the firmament Heaven. And God said, 'Let the waters under the heavens be gathered together to one place, and let the dry land appear'; and it was so. And God said, 'Let the earth bring forth grass for fodder, and the fruit tree yielding fruit.' And God said, 'Let there be lights in the firmament of the heavens that they may be for a light upon the earth.' And God set them in the firmament of the heavens to rule over the day and over the night."

In all this, you observe, Moses does not say that the deep was created by God, or the darkness or the waters. And yet, after saying concerning light that God ordered it to be, and it was, surely he ought to have gone on to speak of night also, and the deep and the waters. But of them he says not a word to imply that they were not already existing at all, though he often mentions them. Furthermore, he does not mention the birth or creation of the angels or in what manner they were brought into being, but deals only with the heavenly and earthly bodies. It follows that, according to Moses, God is the creator of nothing that is incorporeal, but is only the disposer of matter that already existed. For the words, "And the earth was invisible and without form" can only mean that he regards the wet and dry substance as the original matter and that he introduces God as the disposer of this matter. [. . .]

[. . .] Plato gives the name gods to those that are visible, the sun and moon, the stars and the heavens, but these are only the likenesses of the invisible gods. The sun that is visible to our eyes is the likeness of the intelligible and invisible sun, and again the moon that is visible to our eyes and every one of the stars are likenesses of the intelligible. Accordingly Plato knows of those intelligible and invisible gods who are immanent in and coexist with the creator himself and were begotten and proceeded from him. Naturally, therefore, the creator in Plato's account says "gods" when he is addressing the invisible beings, and "of gods," meaning by this, evidently, the visible gods. And the common creator of both these is he who fashioned the heavens and the earth and the sea and the stars, and begat in the intelligible world the archetypes of these. [. . .]

Moses says that the creator of the universe chose out the Hebrew nation, that to that nation alone did he pay heed and cared for it, and he gives him charge of it alone. But how and by what sort of gods the other nations are governed he has said not a word—unless indeed one should concede that he did assign to them the sun and moon. However of this I shall speak a little later. Now I will only point out that Moses himself and the prophets who came after him and Jesus the Nazarene, yes and Paul also, who surpassed all the magicians and charlatans of every place and every time, assert that he is the God of Israel alone and of Judaea, and that the Jews are his chosen people. Listen to their own words and first to the words of Moses: "And you shall say to Pharaoh, Israel is my son, my firstborn. And I have said to you, 'Let my people go that they may serve me.' But you refused to let them go." And a little later, "And they said to him, 'The God of the Hebrews has summoned us; we will go therefore three days' journey into the desert, that we may sacrifice to the Lord our God.'" And soon he speaks again in the same way, "The Lord the God of the Hebrews has sent me to you, saying, 'Let my people go that they may serve me in the wilderness.'"

But that from the beginning God cared only for the Jews, and that he chose them out as his portion has been clearly asserted not only by Moses and Jesus but by Paul as well, though in Paul's case this is strange. For according to circumstances he keeps changing his views about God, as the polypus[4] changes its colors to match the rocks, and now he insists that the Jews alone are God's portion, and then again, when he is trying to persuade the Hellenes to take sides with him, he says: "Do not think that he is the God of Jews only, but also of Gentiles: indeed of Gentiles also." Therefore it is fair to ask of Paul why God, if he was not the God of the Jews only but also of the Gentiles, sent the blessed gift of prophecy to the Jews in abundance and gave them Moses and the oil of anointing, and the prophets and the law and the incredible and monstrous elements in their myths? [. . .]

But now consider our teaching in comparison with this of yours. Our writers say that the creator is the common Father and king of all things, but that the other functions have been assigned by him to national gods of the peoples and gods that protect the cities, every one of whom administers his own department in accordance with his own nature. For since in the Father all things are complete and all things are one, while in the

4. *polypus*—polyp.

separate deities one quality or another predominates, therefore Ares rules over the warlike nations, Athena over those that are wise as well as war-like, Hermes over those that are more shrewd than adventurous; and in short the nations over which the gods preside follow each the essential character of their proper god. Now if experience does not bear witness to the truth of our teachings, let us grant that our traditions are a figment and a misplaced attempt to convince, and then we ought to approve the doctrines held by you. If, however, quite the contrary is true, and from the remotest past experience bears witness to our account and in no case does anything appear to harmonize with your teachings, why do you persist in maintaining a pretension so enormous? [. . .]

[. . .] If the immediate creator of the universe be he who is proclaimed by Moses, then we hold nobler beliefs concerning him, inasmuch as we consider him to be the master of all things in general, but that there are besides national gods who are subordinate to him and are like viceroys of a king, each administering separately his own province; and, moreover, we do not make him the sectional rival of the gods whose station is subordinate to his. [. . .]

That is a surprising law of Moses, I mean the famous Decalogue![5] "You shall not steal." "You shall not kill." "You shall not bear false witness." But let me write out word for word every one of the commandments that he says were written by God himself.

"I am the Lord your God, who has brought you out of the land of Egypt." Then follows the second: "You shall have no other gods but me." "You shall not make for yourselves any graven image." And then he adds the reason: "For I the Lord your God am a jealous God, visiting the iniquity of the fathers upon the children to the third generation." "You shall not take the name of the Lord your God in vain." "Remember the Sabbath day." "Honor your father and your mother." "You shall not commit adultery." "You shall not kill." "You shall not steal." "You shall not bear false witness." "You shall not covet anything that is your neighbor's."

Now except for the command "You shall not worship other gods," and "Remember the Sabbath day," what nation is there, I ask in the name of the gods, that does not think that it ought to keep the other commandments? So much so that penalties have been ordained against those who transgress them, sometimes more severe, and sometimes similar to those enacted by Moses, though they are sometimes more humane.

But as for the commandment "You shall not worship other gods," to this surely he adds a terrible libel upon God. "For I am a jealous God," he says, and in another place again, "Our God is a consuming fire." Then if a man is jealous and envious you think him blameworthy, whereas if God is called jealous you think it a divine quality? And yet how is it reasonable

5. *Decalogue*—Ten Commandments.

to speak falsely of God in a matter that is so evident? For if he is indeed
jealous, then against his will are all other gods worshipped, and against
his will do all the remaining nations worship their gods. Then how is it
that he did not himself restrain them, if he is so jealous and does not wish
that the others should be worshipped, but only himself? Can it be that
he was not able to do so, or did he not wish even from the beginning to
prevent the other gods also from being worshipped? However, the first
explanation is impious, to say, I mean, that he was unable; and the second is in accordance with what we do ourselves. Lay aside this nonsense
and do not draw down on yourselves such terrible blasphemy. For if it is
God's will that none other should be worshipped, why do you worship
this spurious son of his whom he has never yet recognized or considered
as his own? This I shall easily prove. You, however, I know not why, foist
on him a counterfeit son. [. . .]

But what great gift of this sort do the Hebrews boast of as bestowed on
them by God, the Hebrews who have persuaded you to desert to them?
If you had at any rate paid heed to their teachings, you would not have
fared altogether ill, and though worse than you did before, when you
were with us, still your condition would have been bearable and support-
able. For you would be worshipping one god instead of many, not a man,
or rather many wretched men. And though you would be following a law
that is harsh and stern and contains much that is savage and barbarous,
instead of our mild and humane laws, and would in other respects be
inferior to us, yet you would be more holy and purer than now in your
forms of worship. But now it has come to pass that like leeches you have
sucked the worst blood from that source and left the purer. Yet Jesus,
who won over the least worthy of you, has been known by name for
but little more than three hundred years, and during his lifetime he accomplished nothing worth hearing of, unless anyone thinks that to heal
crooked and blind men and to exorcise those who were possessed by
evil demons in the villages of Bethsaida and Bethany can be classed as a
mighty achievement. As for purity of life you do not know whether he
so much as mentioned it, but you emulate the rages and the bitterness of
the Jews, overturning temples and altars, and you slaughtered not only
those of us who remained true to the teachings of their fathers, but also
men who were as much astray as yourselves, heretics, because they did
not wail over the corpse in the same fashion as yourselves. But these are
rather your own doings; for nowhere did either Jesus or Paul hand down
to you such commands. [. . .]

[. . .] "Why were you so ungrateful to our gods as to desert them for
the Jews?" Was it because the gods granted the sovereign power to Rome,
permitting the Jews to be free for a short time only, and then forever
to be enslaved and aliens? Look at Abraham: was he not an alien in a
strange land? And Jacob: was he not a slave, first in Syria, then after that

in Palestine, and in his old age in Egypt? Does not Moses say that he led them forth from the house of bondage out of Egypt "with a stretched out arm"? And after their sojourn in Palestine did they not change their fortunes more frequently than observers say the chameleon changes its color, now subject to the judges, now enslaved to foreign races? And when they began to be governed by kings—but let me for the present postpone asking how they were governed; for as the scripture tells us, God did not willingly allow them to have kings, but only when constrained by them, and after protesting to them beforehand that they would thus be governed ill—still they did at any rate inhabit their own country and tilled it for a little over three hundred years. After that they were enslaved first to the Assyrians, then to the Medes, later to the Persians, and now at last to ourselves. Even Jesus, who was proclaimed among you, was one of Caesar's subjects. [. . .]

But when he became man what benefits did he confer on his own kinsfolk? Nay, the Galileans answer, they refused to hearken to Jesus. What? How was it then that this hardhearted and stubborn-necked people hearkened to Moses; but Jesus, who commanded the spirits and walked on the sea and drove out demons, and as you yourselves assert made the heavens and the earth—for no one of his disciples ventured to say this concerning him, save only John, and he did not say it clearly or distinctly; still let us at any rate admit that he said it—could not this Jesus change the dispositions of his own friends and kinsfolk to the end that he might save them?

[. . .] But now answer me this. Is it better to be free continuously and during two thousand whole years to rule over the greater part of the earth and the sea, or to be enslaved and to live in obedience to the will of others? No man is so lacking in self-respect as to choose the latter by preference. Again, will anyone think that victory in war is less desirable than defeat? Who is so stupid? But if this that I assert is the truth, point out to me among the Hebrews a single general like Alexander or Caesar! You have no such man. And indeed, by the gods, I am well aware that I am insulting these heroes by the question, but I mentioned them because they are well known. For the generals who are inferior to them are unknown to the multitude, and yet every one of them deserves more admiration than all the generals put together whom the Jews have had.

Further, as regards the constitution of the state and the fashion of the law-courts, the administration of cities and the excellence of the laws, progress in learning and the cultivation of the liberal arts, were not all these things in a miserable and barbarous state among the Hebrews? [. . .] What kind of healing art has ever appeared among the Hebrews, like that of Hippocrates among the Hellenes and of certain other schools that came after him? Is their "wisest" man Solomon at all comparable with Phocylides or Theognis or Isocrates among the Hellenes? Certainly not. At least, if one were to compare the exhortations of Isocrates with Solomon's proverbs, you would, I am very sure, find that the son of Theodoras is superior to their "wisest" king. [. . .]

Asclepius heals our bodies, and the muses with the aid of Asclepius and Apollo and Hermes, the god of eloquence, train our souls; Ares fights for us in war and Enyo also; Hephaistus apportions and administers the crafts, and Athene the motherless maiden with the aid of Zeus presides over them all. Consider therefore whether we are not superior to you in every single one of these things, I mean in the arts and in wisdom and intelligence; and this is true, whether you consider the useful arts or the imitative arts whose end is beauty, such as the statuary's art, painting, or household management, and the art of healing derived from Asclepius, whose oracles are found everywhere on earth, and the god grants to us a share in them perpetually. At any rate, when I have been sick, Asclepius has often cured me by prescribing remedies; and of this Zeus is witness. Therefore, if we who have not given ourselves over to the spirit of apostasy, fare better than you in soul and body and external affairs, why do you abandon these teachings of ours and go over to those others? [. . .]

[. . .] "And lay it to your heart that this the Lord your God is God in the Heaven above and upon the earth beneath, and there is none else." And again, "Hear, O Israel: the Lord our God is one Lord." And again, "See that I am and there is no God save me." These then are the words of Moses when he insists that there is only one God. But perhaps the Galileans will reply: "But we do not assert that there are two gods or three." But I will show that they do assert this also, and I call John to witness, who says: "In the beginning was the Word, and the Word was with God and the Word was God." You see that the Word is said to be with God? Now whether this is he who was born of Mary or someone else [. . .] this now makes no difference; indeed I leave the dispute to you; but it is enough to bring forward the evidence that he says "with God," and "in the beginning." How then does this agree with the teachings of Moses?

[. . .] But if, as you believe, the Word is God born of God and proceeded from the substance of the Father, why do you say that the Virgin is the Mother of God? For how could she bear a god since she is, according to you, a human being? And moreover, when God declares plainly "I am he, and there is none that can deliver beside me," do you dare to call her son savior? [. . .]

[. . .] [Y]ou point out to me where there is any statement by Moses of what was later on rashly uttered by Paul, I mean that "Christ is the end of the law." Where does God announce to the Hebrews a second law besides that which was established? Nowhere does it occur, not even a revision of the established law. For listen again to the words of Moses: "You shall not add to the word that I command you, neither shall you diminish aught from it. Keep the commandments of the Lord your God that I command you this day." And "Cursed be every man who does not abide by them all." But you have thought it a slight thing to diminish and to add to the things that were written in the law; and to transgress it completely you have thought to be in every way more manly and more high-spirited, because you do not look to the truth but to that which will persuade all men.

But you are so misguided that you have not even remained faithful to the teachings that were handed down to you by the apostles. And these also have been altered, so as to be worse and more impious, by those who came after. At any rate neither Paul nor Matthew nor Luke nor Mark ventured to call Jesus God. But the worthy John, since he perceived that a great number of people in many of the towns of Greece and Italy had already been infected by this disease, and because he heard, I suppose, that even the tombs of Peter and Paul were being worshipped—secretly, it is true, but still he did hear this—he, I say, was the first to venture to call Jesus God. And after he had spoken briefly about John the Baptist he referred again to the Word that he was proclaiming, and said, "And the Word was made flesh, and dwelt among us."

Trinitarian Debates

The Creed of Nicaea faced real opposition. Julian the Apostate (361–363), the pagan Roman emperor who disavowed Christianity seventeen years after Constantine's death, found it ludicrous. In 359, even before Julian, Emperor Constantinus II (337–361) convened a council that abandoned the Creed of Nicaea and adopted a new statement. In this version the Son was no longer of the same *substance* as the Father (*homoousios*), but rather merely *like* (*homoios*) the Father, a change in terminology that suggested similarity instead of equality. "The whole world," remarked St. Jerome (ca. 347–420) some years later, "groaned in astonishment at finding itself Arian."

At another, earlier council in Antioch (341), hardline Arians insisted on a total distinction between Father and Son. More moderate Arians conceded that perhaps the Son was "similar" to the Father but not quite the same as the Father. These moderates suggested yet another term, indicating that the Son, although not of the "same substance" (*homoousios*), was "of like substance" (*homoiousios*). In the end the council adopted four different creeds!

It would be difficult to exaggerate just how rabid and ubiquitous such debates were. Christians throughout the empire, from prominent citizens to literate commoners, argued these questions at the drop of a hat. A contemporary theologian remarked that when shopping in the marketplace, "If you ask someone to give you change, he philosophizes about the begotten and the unbegotten"; "If you say to an attendant, 'Is my bath ready?' he tells you that the Son was made out of nothing."[1]

---

1. Kallistos Ware, *The Orthodox Church* (New York: Penguin, 1993), 35.

Basil the Great (ca. 330–379), who served as bishop of Caesarea (the post formerly held by Eusebius), agonized over this infighting and that surrounding another question as well—the question of the Holy Spirit's relationship to the Father and the Son, that is, the question of the "Trinity."

A savvy theologian in his own right, Basil worked with his younger brother, Gregory of Nyssa, and their good friend Gregory of Nazianzus to find a theologically compelling resolution to the relation among three different entities. These two Gregories and one Basil argued that one could accept the Nicene concept of a single substance (*homoousios*) if one understood God as consisting of three different "hypostases." "Hypostasis" can be translated literally as "that which lies beneath"; a more meaningful translation in this context would be "manifestation" or "persona" (but not "human person"). The Trinity in this scheme consists of one God in three hypostases.

This solution by Basil and the Gregories—called the "Cappadocian fathers," since they all hailed from Cappadocia in modern Turkey— became what is now standard Trinitarian doctrine in much of the Christian church.

Gregory of Nyssa on the Trinity (ca. 390)

"Gregory of Nyssa's Concerning We Should Think of Saying That There Are Not Three Gods to Ablabius," in *The Trinitarian Controversy*, ed. William Rusch (Philadelphia: Fortress, 1980), 149–61. Used by permission of Fortress Press.

In this selection Gregory of Nyssa argues for the concept of hypostases, or three types of substantive reality in the Godhead. While each hypostasis (Father, Son, and Holy Spirit) has its own characteristics, the existence of different hypostases in the Godhead should in no way suggest the existence of three gods. It is evident in Gregory's work how much more nuanced, careful, sophisticated, and difficult Christian theology had become by the end of the 300s.

[. . .] This is not a minor subject [. . .] nor is it such a kind to cause slight damage, if it were not met with a befitting review. The force of the inquiry necessarily brings one into one of two altogether incompatible positions. One is according to common opinion: to say that there are

three gods, which is wicked. The other: not to bear witness to the deity of
the Son and the Spirit,[2] which is ungodly and absurd. [. . .] Peter, James,
and John, being in one humanity, are called three men. And it is not absurd that those united according to nature, if they are several, be counted
in the plural on the basis of the term "nature." If, therefore, usage here
permits this, and no one forbids the statement of two as two or of three
as beyond two, how, in reference to the mystical beliefs in the confession
that there are three hypostases, and the claim that there is no difference
between them in nature, do we struggle somehow with the confession by
declaring there is one deity of Father, Son, and Spirit but by forbidding
the statement that there are three gods? [. . .]

Why then in our usage, when we reckon those who are shown to be
one in nature, do we name them in the plural? We say that the men are so
many and that not all are "one," but in reference to the divine nature the
argument of doctrine rejects the multitude of gods and counting the hypostases does not admit a plural meaning.

If someone were speaking superficially to simpler minds, he would
seem to say that the argument in fleeing the likeness of Greek polytheism[3]
shuns counting the gods by number, so that no one would think there is
a commonality of doctrine between the Greeks and us, if like them, we
counted the divinity not in the singular but in the plural. This statement
to the more simple would perhaps appear to be something. But with reference to those who seek that for themselves, one of the two propositions
should stand—either not to confess the deity of the three, or to name
the three together as those who share the same deity—and such a reply
does not resolve the question. Therefore it is necessary that the answer
be made more fully and that as much as possible we trace the truth. The
topic is not about ordinary things.

First, we acknowledge that there is an abuse of usage when those who
are not determined by nature, according to the term itself, are named in
the plural, and when it is said that there are many men. It is similar to
saying that there are many human natures. That such is the case is clear
to us from what follows. When summoning someone, we do not address
him by his nature, for the common character of the name would produce
a certain error, since each hearer thinks he himself is the one summoned
because the calling is not by the peculiar name but by the common name
of the nature. But we separate him from the many by saying the word
peculiarly imposed on him (I mean the signification of the subject), for
there are many who shared the nature—for example, disciples, apostles,
martyrs—but one is the "man" in all, if as has been said "man" does not
mean the peculiarity of each but the common nature. For Luke or Ste-

2. *Spirit*—Holy Spirit.
3. *polytheism*—belief in multiple gods.

phen is a man. But if anyone is a man, is he not by any means Luke or Stephen.

But through the perceived peculiarities, the topic of the individual [hypostasis] admits distinction and is viewed in number according to combination. But the nature is one; it is united to itself, undivided, a precisely undivided unit, not increased through addition, not decreased through subtraction, but being one and remaining one, even if it would appear in a multitude, undivided, continuous, perfect, and not divided by those who individually share it. And just as a people, a common folk, an army, and an assembly is always mentioned as singular but each is discovered in the plural, so in accord with the most precise reasoning also "man" properly should be said as one (singular), even if those shown to be in the same nature would be plural. Thus it would be much better to improve our blundered usage and no longer extend the name for nature to the plural than for us enslaved to carry over the identical error even to divine doctrine. But since the improvement of usage is impractical (How would anyone be persuaded not to say many men when they are shown to be of the same nature? Usage is always unchangeable.) in reference to the lower nature, in not opposing the current usage, we would not be far wrong. There is no loss here from the wrong employment of words. But in reference to divine doctrine, the indifferent employment of words is no longer, similarly, without danger, for here "minor" points are not minor.

Therefore one God must be confessed by us according to the witness of scripture, "Hear, Israel, the Lord your God is one Lord" (Deuteronomy 6:4), even if the word "deity" extends through the Holy Trinity. But I say these things according to the reasoning given by us in reference to human nature, by which we have learned that it is necessary to extend the word for nature to the plural. But the word for deity must be scrutinized more accurately by us, so that through the significance inherent in the term there might be some assistance in regard to the truth of the subject under discussion.

Therefore the word for deity seems to many peculiarly to be fixed on God's nature. As the heaven, the sun, or some other of the elements of the world is explained by peculiar names that signify the subjects, so they say in reference to the highest and divine nature that the word for deity has been suitably adapted, as some proper name, to that which is made clear. But we, following the suggestions of scripture, have learned that the divine nature is unnamable and unutterable. We say that every name, whether it has been invented from human usage or handed down from scripture, is an interpretation of the things thought about divine nature and does not encompass the significance of the nature itself. [. . .]

[. . .] [O]bserving the various activities of the transcendent power from each of the activities known to us, we fit together the names. [. . .] [O]ne is activity-energy, viewing and seeing a vision we speak of God, and as someone might say, beholding. Accordingly he sees all things and over-sees all, as he sees the thoughts when he passes through even invisible things by his power of viewing. Thus we have assumed that "deity" has been named from "view" [*theótes* from *theá*] and our observer is named God from custom and the teaching of scripture.

But if someone agrees that to view and to see is the same thing, and that the God who oversees all both is and is called overseer of all, let him calculate God's energy activity, whether it is present in one of the persons believed to be in the Holy Trinity or whether the power pervades through the three.

If the interpretation of deity is true, and visible things are beheld, and that which beholds is called God, then not reasonably would any of the persons in the Trinity be separated from such a name because of the significance of the name. Scripture bears witness to the seeing equally of the Father, Son, and Holy Spirit. "See, God, our protector," says David [Psalms 84:9]. From this we learn that, as far as God is thought out, the activity of sight is appropriate to God. David said, "See, God." But also Jesus sees the thoughts of those who pass sentence on him, since by his supreme authority he remits men's sins. For it states, "Jesus, having seen their thoughts" [Matthew 9:4]. And concerning the Spirit, Peter says to Ananias,[4] "Why has Satan filled your heart so you are false to the Holy Spirit?" [Acts 5:3]. This reveals that the Holy Spirit was a truthful and knowledgeable witness of the things dared in secret by Ananias. It was through the Spirit that these things done in secret were disclosed to Peter. For Ananias himself, as he thought, escaping the notice of all and conceal-ing his sin, became a thief of his own goods. But the Holy Spirit was with Peter and observed the covetous intent of Ananias, and through himself the Spirit gave to Peter the ability to discern these secrets. It is clear that the Spirit could not do this if he were blind to secret things.

But someone will say that the proof of the argument does not apply to the topic under investigation. For if it would be acknowledged that the name for deity applies to nature,[5] this does not already prove that it is improper to speak of gods. Quite the opposite, we are compelled to speak of gods. For in reference to human usage, we find not only the many as the sharers of the same nature, but even certain individuals of

4. *Ananias*—Acts chapter 5 tells the story of Ananias and his wife, Sapphira, who sold a plot of land, but, unlike exemplars in the community, donated only part of the profit to the apostles. Peter condemned Ananias for his parsimony, and Ananias fell down dead. When Sapphira arrived three hours later, she told Peter that she and her husband contributed their entire profit. She, too, then promptly died at Peter's feet.

5. *nature*—that is, the nature or characteristics of the deity.

the same pursuit are mentioned not individually. Accordingly, as we say, many orators, land-measurers, husbandmen, shoemakers, etc. And if the reference point for the term "deity" were nature, it would have the occasion, in accord with the previous argument, to comprehend the three persons individually and to speak of one God, because of the indivisible and inseparable character of the nature. But since it has been proven by means of the things said that the name of deity signifies activity and not nature, the argument as a result of the things proven turns in the opposite direction. Thus it is necessary rather to speak of three gods who are viewed in the same activity, as they say that three philosophers or orators are mentioned, or if there is any other name from a pursuit when there are many who share the same thing. I have more industriously worked at these things, namely, the argument of the opposing objections, so that our doctrine would be more firmly fixed, strengthened by the persistences of the contradictions. Therefore the argument again must be resumed.

Since it has been shown by us with reason and by proof that the name of deity has not as its reference point nature but activity, perhaps someone would declare with reason why men who share with one another the same pursuits are counted and named in the plural but the deity is mentioned in the singular as one God and one deity, even if the three hypostases are not distinguished from the significance reflected in "deity." He might state that as regards men, even if many partake of one activity, each individually set apart work at the thing proposed, sharing in common nothing with the individual activity of those pursuing the same thing. For if the orators are many, among the several the pursuit has one and the same name, but those who pursue it work each individually, this one practicing oratory independently, the next one doing the same thing. Therefore, among men, because the activity of each is distinguished, although in the same pursuit, they are properly mentioned in the plural. Each of them is separated into his peculiar context from the others in accord with his peculiar manner of the activity. But in reference to divine nature, we have learned that this is not the case, because the Father does something individually, in which the Son does not join, or the Son individually works something without the Spirit; but every activity that pervades from God to creation and is named according to our manifold designs starts off from the Father, proceeds through the Son, and is completed by the Holy Spirit. On account of this, the name of activity is not divided into the multitude of those who are active. The action of each in any regard is not divided and peculiar. But whatever of the anticipated things would happen, whether for our providence or to the administration of the whole and to its constitution, it happens through the three, the things that do happen are not three distinct things.

We will think through this statement from one certain example, from him, I mean, the crown of free gifts. As many things as have a share in this gift gain life. Therefore, when we ask from where this good thing came to us, we find through the guidance of the scriptures that it is from the Father, Son, and Holy Spirit. But though we presuppose that there are three persons and names, we do not reason that three lives have been given to us—individually one from each of them. It is the same life, activated by the Holy Spirit, prepared by the Son, and produced by the Father's will.

Therefore, then, the Holy Trinity works every activity according to the manner stated, not divided according to the number of the hypostases, but one certain motion and disposition of goodwill occurs, proceeding from the Father through the Son to the Spirit. Thus we do not say that those who affect one life are three who make alive, nor do we say that they are three good beings who are viewed in the same goodness, nor as regards all other aspects do we announce them in the plural. Thus we are not able to name as three those who bring to bear on us and all creation jointly and inseparably this divine power and activity of oversight. When we learned about the God of all, as scripture says that he judges the whole earth [Genesis 8:25; Romans 8:6], thus we say that he is the judge of all. And when we heard that the Father judges no one [John 5:22], we do not think that scripture wars with itself. For he who judges all the earth does it through the Son, to whom he has given all judgment. And everything that happens by the only-begotten has reference to the Father, so he is judge of all and through the whole judges no one. As it was stated, he has given judgment to the Son, and all the judgment of the Son is not estranged from the Father's will. It cannot with reason be said either that there are two judges, or that one is estranged from authority and power of judgment. Thus also in reference to the word for deity, Christ is the power of God and the wisdom of God. The power of oversight and beholding—which we say is deity, the Father, the god doing all things in wisdom—effects through the only-begotten, the Son who perfects all power in the Holy Spirit and judges. As Isaiah says, "by the spirit of judgment and the spirit of burning heat" [Isaiah 4:4]. Therefore, according to the discourse of the Gospel, which he made to the Jews, he does well by the Spirit of God, for he says, "If I by the Spirit of God cast out demons" [Matthew 12:28]; from his sharing in doing well, he comprehends every form through the unity of activity. The term for activity is not able to be distributed into many, by whom through one another a single thing is effected.

For, as it has been stated above, the principle of the power of oversight and beholding in Father, Son, and Holy Spirit is one. It starts off from the Father as from a spring; it is effected by the Son, and by the power of the Spirit it completes its grace. No activity is divided to the hypostases, completed individually by each and set apart without being viewed together. All providence, care, and attention of all, both of things in the sensible creation and of things of the heavenly nature—and the preservation of what exists, the correction of things out of tune, the teaching of things set right—is one and not three, kept straight by the Holy Trinity. It is not severed into three, according to the number of persons beheld in faith, so that each activity, viewed by itself, is of the Father alone or of the only-begotten individually or of the Holy Spirit separately. [. . .]

If every good thing, and the name for it, is attached to a power and will without beginning, it is brought into perfection at once and apart from time by the power of the Spirit through the only-begotten God. No postponement occurs, or is thought of, in the movement of divine will from the Father through the Son to the Spirit. But deity is one of the good names and thoughts, and not reasonably is the name to be used in the plural, since the unity of activity prevents a plural counting.

And the Father, savior of all men, especially of the faithful, has been named by the apostle as one [1 Timothy 4:10]. No one on the basis of this term says that the Son does not save those who believe, or that salvation happens to those who share it apart from the Spirit. But God, who is over all, becomes the savior of all, while the Son effects salvation by the grace of the Spirit. On account of this they are not named three saviors by scripture, although salvation is confessed from the Holy Trinity. Thus, according to the significance of deity already granted, there are not three gods, even if such a name coincides with the Holy Trinity. [. . .]

When we speak of gold, even if it is changed into many stamps of a coin, still it is, and is mentioned as one. But we name many current coins and many staters,[6] although we find no increase of the nature of gold by reason of the number of the staters. Therefore much gold is mentioned when it is viewed in larger weight either in vessels or in coins. But "many golds" are not named because of the quantity of the material, unless someone would say "many golds," as darics[7] or staters, in reference to which it is not the material but the small coins that receive the significance of the number. It is properly said not that there are "many golds" but that there are "many golden ones." [. . .]

[. . .] [Scripture] uses the word "God" according to a singular pattern [. . .] so that different natures of the divine substance are not introduced secretly by the plural significance of "gods." Therefore it says, "The Lord God is one Lord" [Deuteronomy 6:4], but it also proclaims by the word for deity the only-begotten of God, and it does not break up the one into a dual significance, so to name the Father and Son as two gods, even if each is proclaimed God by the holy authors. The Father is God, the Son is God, but by the same proclamation God is one, because neither in regard to nature nor activity is any difference viewed. [. . .]

6. *stater*—a small coin.
7. *daric*—a gold coin from Persia.

While confessing the un-changeableness of the nature [of the Holy Trinity], we do not deny the difference in cause and causality,[8] by which alone we seize the distinction of the one from the other. It is by the belief that one is the cause and the other is from the cause. We also consider another difference of the one who is from the cause. There is the one that depends on the first, and there is that one which is through that which depends on the first. Thus it is that the aspect of only-begotten undoubtedly remains in the Son. It is also not doubted that the Spirit is from the Father. The mediation of the Son, although it guards for him his only-begottenness, does not prevent the Spirit from a relation by nature to the Father.

But speaking of a "cause" and "from a cause," we do not through these names signify "nature" (for no one would grant that the word for cause and nature is the same), but we disclose the difference in the manner of being. Saying that one thing is caused but another is without cause, we did not separate the nature by reason of the cause. We have only disclosed that the Son does not exist unbegotten, nor the Father through begetting. First it is necessary for us to believe that something is, and then to be inquisitive about how that which is believed is, for example, its manner of existence. Therefore the topic of what is, is one thing. It is another manner how it is (its manner of existence). Thus, to say something exists unbegotten suggests how it is, but what it is, is not disclosed by this word. If you questioned a farmer about some tree, whether it is planted or exists by chance, and he answered either that the tree is not planted or that it happened from a planting, then through the answer does he who only said how it is disclose the nature, or does he leave the principle of the nature unknown and uninterpreted?

Thus also here, having learned that he is unbegotten, we have been taught how it is fitting to think of his being, but we do not hear from the word whatever it is. Therefore in saying that there is such a difference in the Holy Trinity so to believe that one is the cause and another from the cause, we would no longer be accused with dissolving the principle of the hypostases in a commonality of nature. Then the principle of cause distinguishes the hypostases in the Holy Trinity in worshipping that which is uncaused and the other that is from the cause. But the divine nature is comprehended by every thought as unchangeable and without difference. On account of this, there is properly one deity and one God, and all other aspects of names befitting God are reported in the singular.

8. *causality*—the relationship between a cause and its effect.

Priests and Bishops

Although the New Testament uses the terms "priest" and "bishop" interchangeably, the early church quickly distinguished between the two. Priests acted as advisers and teachers. Bishops led Christian communities and "celebrated" (administered) the Eucharist—"Communion" or "the last supper"—that is, the ceremony that Jesus instructed his disciples to observe.[1] By the 300s, however, it was common for both priests and bishops to celebrate the Eucharist and baptize their parishioners.

John Chrysostom on the Role of Priests
(ca. late 370s–early 380s)

John Chrysostom, "The Glory of the Priesthood," in *Six Books on the Priesthood* (Crestwood, NY: St. Vladimir's Seminary Press, 1996), 70–74. Used by permission of SPCK Publishing.

Numerous writers in the first few centuries expounded on the significance, responsibilities, and powers of priests, while outlining the ideal

---

1. Jesus "took a cup, and after giving thanks he said, 'Take this and divide it among yourselves; for I tell you that from now on I will not drink of the fruit of the vine until the kingdom of God comes.' Then he took a loaf of bread, and when he had given thanks, he broke it and gave it to them, saying, 'This is my body, which is given for you. Do this in remembrance of me.' And he did the same with the cup after supper, saying, 'This cup that is poured out for you is the new covenant in my blood'" (Luke 22:17–20, NRSV).

81

qualities to be sought in candidates. The following document comes to us from John Chrysostom—literally "John the Goldenmouth," a moniker bestowed in recognition of his eloquent preaching—who served as the bishop of Constantinople from 398 to 404.

Chrysostom and his contemporaries understood the Christian priesthood as both a continuation and a fulfillment of the priestly duties outlined in the Hebrew scriptures, or "Old Testament." Chrysostom thus spoke of the Christian priesthood as a priesthood for a new age, an "age of grace,"[2] that is, the age following Christ's sacrifice on the cross, which made grace and salvation available to all. The splendor of the Hebrew priesthood remains, but it is now surpassed and, indeed, made "trivial" by the awesome results of Christ's shed blood, which the Christian priest celebrates through the Eucharist.

The Christian priest's power, then, derives from his administration of sacramental rites that bestow grace on and bring salvation to those who receive them. Christian priests possess, in Chrysostom's words, the "authority to remit sins," making them "responsible for our birth from God." In fact Chrysostom argued in other texts that a priest exercises more power over Christians than does a king over his subjects or a father over his children.[3]

Many priests and bishops at the time fully endorsed such language about their "authority" and power; others emphasized instead their role as a vehicle through which God bestowed the grace that only God can bestow. Debates about how, exactly, priests serve as conduits for God's grace—or, to be more precise, debates about the ways God employs priests to dispense grace—would rage for centuries. But the salient point—the point on which all those eventually deemed "orthodox" could agree—was this: priests administer the church and they administer the sacraments through which God extends grace. A church without priests is no church at all; only a heretic could propose administering sacraments without a priest.

The work of the priesthood is done on earth, but it is ranked among heavenly ordinances. And this is only right, for no man, no angel, no

2. Edward Yarnold, *The Awe Inspiring Rites of Initiation: The Origins of the RCIA* (Collegeville, MN: Liturgical Press), 151.

3. See Graham Neville's "Introduction" to *Six Books on the Priesthood* (Crestwood, NY: St. Vladimir's Seminary Press, 1996), 26, in which Neville accuses Chrysostom of "a preoccupation with power."

archangel, no other created power, but the Paraclete[4] himself ordained this succession,[5] and persuaded men, while still remaining in the flesh to represent the ministry of angels. The priest, therefore, must be as pure as if he were standing in Heaven itself, in the midst of those powers.

The symbols that existed before the ministry of grace[6] were fearful and awe-inspiring: for example, the bells, the pomegranates, the stones on the breastplate, the stones on the ephod,[7] the miter,[8] the diadem,[9] the long robe, the golden crown, the holy of holies,[10] the deep silence within. But if you consider the ministry of grace you will find that those fearful and awe-inspiring symbols are only trivial. The statement about the law is true here also: "The splendor that once was is now no splendor at all; it is outshone by a splendor greater still." When you see the Lord sacrificed and lying before you[11] and the high priest standing over the sacrifice and praying and all who partake being tinctured with that precious blood,[12] can you think that you are still among men and still standing on earth? Are you not at once transported to Heaven, and, having driven out of your soul every carnal thought, do you not with soul naked and mind pure look round upon heavenly things? O, the wonder of it! O, the loving-kindness of God to men! He who sits above with the Father[13] is at that moment held in our hands, and gives himself to those who wish to clasp and embrace him—which they do, all of them, with their eyes. Do you think this could be despised? Or that it is the kind of thing anyone can be superior about?

Would you like to be shown the excellence of this sacred office by another miracle? Imagine in your mind's eye, if you will, Elijah[14] and the

4. *Paraclete*—the Holy Spirit (literally "advocate" or "intercessor").

5. *this succession*—the "apostolic succession" or the process by which a priest is ordained by a bishop, thus transferring the commission Christ bestowed on his apostles to successive generations of priests.

6. *before the ministry of grace*—before the incarnation.

7. *ephod*—a linen apron worn by Hebrew priests.

8. *miter*—liturgical headdress.

9. *diadem*—crown.

10. *holy of holies*—the inner sanctum of the Hebrew temple, which only the high priest could enter.

11. *Lord sacrificed and lying before you*—the bread and wine of the Eucharist, that is, the sacrament commemorating Christ's death.

12. *tinctured with that precious blood*—redeemed through Christ's death on the cross.

13. *He who sits above with the Father*—Jesus Christ.

14. *Elijah*—A ninth-century BCE prophet. Elijah called down fire from Heaven to consume his sacrifice to God, a feat that prophets of Baal—a Canaanite god—were unable to replicate.

vast crowd standing around him and the sacrifice lying upon the stone altar. All the rest are still, hushed in deep silence. The prophet alone is praying. Suddenly fire falls from the skies onto the offering. It is marvelous; it is charged with bewilderment. Turn, then, from that scene to our present rites, and you will see not only marvelous things, but things that transcend all terror. The priest stands bringing down not fire but the Holy Spirit. And he offers prayer at length, not that some flame lit from above may consume the offerings, but that grace may fall on the sacrifice through that prayer, set alight the souls of all, and make them appear brighter than silver refined in the fire. Can anyone, not quite mad and deranged, despise this most awe-inspiring rite? Do you not know that no human soul could ever have stood that sacrificial fire, but all would have been utterly annihilated, except for the powerful help of God's grace?

Anyone who considers how much it means to be able, in his humanity, still entangled in flesh and blood, to approach that blessed and immaculate being, will see clearly how great is the honor that the grace of the Spirit has bestowed on priests. It is through them that this work is performed and other work no less than this in its bearing upon our dignity and our salvation.

For earth's inhabitants, having their life in this world, have been entrusted with the stewardship of heavenly things and have received an authority that God has not given to angels or archangels. Not to them was it said, "Whatever things you shall bind on earth shall be bound also in Heaven; and whatever things you shall loose, shall be loosed."[15] Those who are lords on earth have indeed the power to bind, but only men's bodies. But this binding touches the very soul and reaches through Heaven. What priests do on earth, God ratifies above. The master confirms the decisions of his slaves. Indeed he has given them nothing less than the whole authority of Heaven. For he says, "Whoever's sins you forgive, they are forgiven, and whoever's sins you retain, they are retained."[16] What authority could be greater than that? "The Father has given all judgment to the Son." But I see that the Son has placed it all in their hands. For they have been raised to this prerogative, as though they were already translated to Heaven and had transcended human nature and were freed from our passions.

Again, if a king confers on one of his subjects the right to imprison and release again at will, that man is the envy and admiration of all. But although the priest has received from God an authority as much greater than that, as Heaven is more precious than earth and souls than bod-

15. *Whatever things* . . . —Jesus's promise to the Apostle Peter in Matthew 18:18.

16. *Whoever's sins you forgive* . . . —Jesus's words to his disciples after rising from the dead (John 20:23).

ies, some people think he has received so slight an honor that they can imagine someone entrusted with it actually despising the gift. God save us from such madness! For it is patently mad to despise this great office without which we cannot attain to salvation or God's good promises.

For if a man "cannot enter into the Kingdom of Heaven except he be born again of water and the Spirit,"[17] and if he who eats not the Lord's flesh and drinks not his blood[18] is cast out of everlasting life, and all these things can happen through no other agency except their sacred hands (the priests', I mean), how can anyone, without their help, escape the fire of Gehenna[19] or win his appointed crown? They are the ones—they and no others—who are in charge of spiritual travail and responsible for the birth that comes through baptism. Through them we put on Christ and are united with the Son of God and become limbs obedient to that blessed head. So they should properly be not only more feared than rulers and kings, but more honored even than fathers. For our fathers begot us "of blood and the will of the flesh"; but they are responsible for our birth from God, that blessed second birth, our true emancipation, the adoption according to grace.

The priests of the Jews had authority to cure leprosy of the body, or rather, not to cure it, but only to certify the cure.[20] And you know what rivalry there used to be for the priesthood then. But our priests have received authority not over leprosy of the body but over uncleanness of the soul, and not just to certify its cure, but actually to cure it. [. . .]

But, to return to the topic from which I digressed, God has given greater power to priests than to natural parents, not only for punishment, but also for help. The difference between the two is as great as between the present and the future life. Parents bring us into this life; priests into the life to come. Parents cannot avert bodily death nor drive away the onset of disease; priests have often saved the soul that is sick and at the point of death, by making the punishment milder for some, and preventing others from ever incurring it, not only through instruction and warning, but also through helping them by prayer. They have authority to remit sins, not only when they make us regenerate,[21] but afterwards too. "Is any among you sick? Let him call for the elders of the church, and let them pray over him, anointing him with oil in the name of the Lord. And the prayer of faith shall save him that is sick, and the Lord shall raise him up, and if he has committed sins, they shall be forgiven him." Again, natural parents

17. *born again of water and the Spirit*—to participate in the sacrament of baptism.

18. *Lord's flesh and . . . blood*—the bread and wine of the Eucharist.

19. *Gehenna*—Hell.

20. *certify the cure*—confirm that the person has been cured.

21. *make us regenerate*—make us spiritually pure and right with God.

cannot help their sons if they fall foul of the prominent and powerful, but priests have often appeased the anger of God himself, to say nothing of rulers and kings.

Will anyone still dare to accuse me of arrogance after this? I think that after what I have said, such reverence must fill the minds of my hearers that they can no longer accuse of conceit and presumption those who avoid this honor, but only those who seek it of their own accord and are determined to get it for themselves.

Early Monasticism

Georgy Florovsky, one of the great Eastern Orthodox theologians of the twentieth century (whose work we will encounter later), once observed that "Christianity entered history as a new social order, or rather a new social dimension. From the very beginning Christianity was not primarily a 'doctrine,' but exactly a community."[1] Indeed Christian churches before Constantine's conversion constituted incredibly tight-knit communities. Persecuted believers needed and supported each other within an adversarial state. They fed each other, cared for each other's poor and sick, and sheltered those in trouble. They understood themselves to be not of this world; they were "voluntary outcasts and outlaws," as Florovsky puts it, whose true home waited in the life to come following Christ's imminent return.

What, then, did it mean when the Roman state—a pagan state—abruptly became Christian? Constantine offered the church legitimacy as well as legal and financial support. Theodosius II (408–450) outlawed paganism and "heresy." Suddenly Christians alone, and only those Christians who held Orthodox beliefs, were eligible for citizenship.

But how should Christians, who previously thought of the state as something alien, work within or with a Christian empire? How could they—or *should* they—become part of what Florovsky termed

---

1. Georges [Georgy] Florovsky, "Empire and Desert," *Greek Orthodox Theological Review* 3 No. 2 (1950): 133. This introduction borrows heavily from Florovsky's essay.

a "politico-ecclesiastical institution"? Some welcomed this new institution, whose laws and rituals we explore in a later section, and embraced the notion of a Christian state. Others held deep reservations.
Should Christians embrace a state very much of this world, even if it
was Christian? What of Christ's call to forsake the world? This question, the "imperial problem," has bedeviled Christians to this day.

Some believers turned to monasticism as a way to evade the imperial problem. The 300s witnessed an exodus of devout believers, a
stream of holy men and women who fled to the deserts around the
Mediterranean to cultivate godly lives apart from the state. Florovsky
notes that this exodus did not represent an attempt to escape the burdens of social life; no person seeking an easy life would choose the
harsh environs of the desert. It was, rather, a rejection of the ideals of
a Christian empire.

> The prospect of success [for a Christian empire] was rather bright [in
> the 300s]. [But] [t]hose who fled into the wilderness did not share
> these expectations. They had no trust in the "christened Empire." They
> rather distrusted the whole scheme altogether. They were leaving the
> earthly kingdom, as much as it might have been actually "christened,"
> in order to build the true kingdom of Christ in the new land of prom-
> ise, "outside the gates," in the desert. They fled not so much from the
> world's disasters, as from the "worldly cares," from the involvement
> with the world, even under the banner of Christ, from the prosperity
> and wrong security of the world.

"Monasticism meant first of all a 'renunciation,'" continues Florovsky, "a total renunciation of 'this world,' with all its lust and pomp."[2]
Such renunciation could be framed easily as a straightforward and
obedient response to Luke 18:18–22:

> A certain ruler asked him [Jesus], "Good Teacher, what must I do to
> inherit eternal life?" Jesus said to him, "Why do you call me good? No
> one is good but God alone. You know the commandments: 'You shall
> not commit adultery; You shall not murder; You shall not steal; You
> shall not bear false witness; Honor your father and mother.'" He re-
> plied, "I have kept all these since my youth." When Jesus heard this, he
> said to him, "There is still one thing lacking. Sell all that you own and
> distribute the money to the poor, and you will have treasure in heaven;
> then come, follow me." (NRSV)

Lest there be any doubt as to Christ's intent, monks could point as
well to another passage in Luke, in which Jesus declared that "none

---

2. Florovsky, 146, 147.

Oxyrhynchus

Figure 9. Oxyrhynchus

of you can become my disciple if you do not give up all your possessions" (Luke 14:33, NRSV).

Most Christians at this time, upon being initiated into the faith, took
an oath promising to renounce "the world." The "desert fathers and
mothers" thus undertook a life different only in degree, not in principle, to the life to which other Christians, at least in theory, committed
themselves. The desert offered a perfect escape from the world, a place
where they could seek pure and perfect communion with God. Their
work was to struggle against the devil—the prince of the world—and
to transform themselves in the image of Christ, that is, to seek "theosis," or "divinization," concepts we explore later and at length.

A visitor to Oxyrhynchus, a city about 160 kilometers south of
Cairo, reported around the year 300 that "the city is so full of monasteries that the very walls resound with the voices of monks . . . The
temples and capitols of the city were bursting with monks; every quar-
ter of the city was inhabited by them . . . as far as we could ascertain
from the holy bishop of that place, we would say that he had under his
jurisdiction ten thousand monks and twenty thousand nuns."[3]

3. *Lives of the Desert Fathers*, ed. Norman Russell (Piscataway, NJ: Gorgias
Press, 2009), 67.

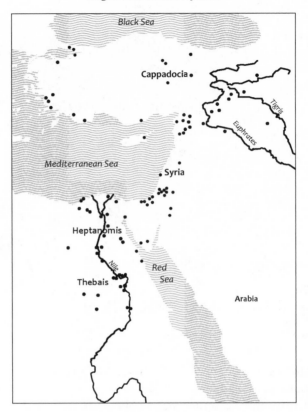

Figure 10. Christian monasteries, 300–700

In towns, on the outskirts of towns, and kilometers from any sign of civilization, monks and nuns vowed to fast, pray "without ceasing" (1 Thessalonians 5:17), and refrain from sex while living in solitude and abject poverty, awaiting Christ's return. A visitor to the Nile River valley in Egypt reported: "One can see them scattered in the desert waiting for Christ like loyal sons watching for their father, or like an army expecting its emperor, or like a sober household looking forward to the arrival of its master and liberator. For with them there is no solicitude, no anxiety for food and clothing. There is only the expectation of the coming of Christ in the singing of hymns."[4]

Some lived exposed to the elements. Some inhabited caves. Some built rickety shelters. Some lived in strict isolation; some lived in small groups of three or four; and some attracted disciples—a complication, given their commitment to solitude. They emerged from all

4. Ibid., 50.

strata of society: the aristocracy, the merchant class, the clergy, and the peasantry.

Reports of exceptional and even masochistic feats spread quickly, as did calls for reason and moderation. Questions about what constituted appropriate zeal would consume monks and nuns for centuries to come.

Sayings of the Desert Fathers (mid-500s)

The Book of Paradise, Being the Histories and Sayings of the Monks and Ascetics of the Egyptian Desert by Palladius, Hieronymus and Others: The Syriac Texts, According to the Recension of Anan-Isho of Beth Abhe, ed. and trans. E. A. Wallis Budge (London: W. Drugulin, 1904), 1:589–918.

Perhaps the most famous desert father was St. Antony: stories about his miracles and feats of asceticism made him a legendary figure, and he served as a model for countless monks.[5]

Numerous other desert fathers and mothers offered inspiring examples as well. Their acolytes eagerly memorized and repeated bits of their mentors' wisdom. The illiterate passed stories and aphorisms by word of mouth, and the literate committed them to writing. Benedicta Ward notes that countless versions and collections emerged over the centuries, "remembered and repeated, elaborated and expanded, attributed to different people and places, and written down in Syriac, Coptic [the common dialect, or vernacular, in Egypt], Greek and Latin." Sayings that survived "are very often fragments of remembered wisdom offered on request to an individual, and can therefore at times seem contradictory if they are seen as general principles."[6]

Those who compiled these sayings sometimes organized them by speaker and sometimes by topic. The collection below, roughly organized by topic and written in Syriac, was compiled and edited by Anan Isho, a Syrian monk who lived in the latter half of the 600s. Although this collection includes sayings from numerous sources, many of them unknown, some were first gathered by Palladius of Galatia (ca. 360s–420s), a Syrian bishop who spent three decades traveling

---

5. See document 4.1, "The Life of St. Antony by Athanasius," in the online supplement.

6. Benedicta Ward, "Introduction," in *The Desert Fathers: Sayings of the Early Christian Monks* (New York: Penguin, 2003), xxx.

in modern Libya, Egypt, Syria, Palestine, Iraq, and Italy to visit and interview monks.

1. When Abba Arsenius was in the palace,[7] he prayed to God and said, "O Lord, direct me how to live"; and a voice came to him, saying, "Arsenius, flee from men, and you will live."

2. And when Arsenius was living the ascetic life in the monastery, he prayed to God the same prayer, and again he heard a voice saying to him, "Arsenius, flee, keep silent, and lead a life of silent contemplation, for these are the roots that prevent a man from committing sin."

6. Abba Arsenius on one occasion went to the brethren in a certain place where there were some reeds growing, and the wind blew upon them, and they were shaken. And the old man said, "What is this rustling sound?" And they said to him, "It is the reeds, which are being shaken by the wind." And he said to them, "If a man dwells in silence and hears the twittering of a sparrow only, he will not be able to acquire that repose in his heart that he seeks; how much less then can you do so with all this rustling of the reeds about you?"

12. They used to say concerning Abba Theodore and Abba Luk that they passed fifty years with disturbed minds, and were troubled the whole time about changing their place [of abode]; and they said, "We will change in the winter"; and when the winter arrived, they said, "We will change in the summer"; and thus they did to the end of their lives.

14. Abba Battimion said, "When I went down to Scete[8] they gave me some apples to take to the brethren, and when I had knocked at the door of Abba Abhila, he said to me when he saw me, 'If these apples had been of gold I would not have wished you to knock at my door; and moreover, do not knock at the door of [any] other brother'; so I returned and placed the apples in the church and departed."

20. Abba Antony said, "As a fish when it is lifted up out of the water dies, so does the monk who tarries outside his cell."

41. Abba Poemen said, "The rule of the monk is this—to bear at all times his own blame."

46. Abba Antony said, "He who lives in the desert is free from three kinds of wars, that is to say, those of hearing, speaking, and seeing; he has only one kind to fight, namely, that of the heart."

47. Abba Alonis said, "Unless a man says in his heart, 'Only God and myself exist in this world,' he will not find rest."

7. *was in the palace*—the desert father Arsenius served as a tutor for the sons of Byzantine emperor Theodosius I (379–395).

8. *Scete*—in northern Egypt.

61. They used to say about Abba Agathon that for a period of three years he placed a stone in his mouth [and kept it there] until he had learned thoroughly how to hold his peace.

62. A certain brother went to Abba Moses in Scete, and asked him [to give him] a sentence, and the old man said to him, "Go away, and sit in your cell, and your cell will teach you everything."

65. On one occasion a brother came to Abba Isaiah, who threw a handful of lentils into a saucepan to boil them, but when they had just begun to boil he took them off the fire; and the brother said to him, "Are they not yet cooked, father?" And the old man said to him, "Is it not sufficient for you to have seen the fire? For this [alone] is greatly refreshing."

67. They used to say about Abba Macarius the Egyptian, that if he ate with the brethren, he would promise himself that if there was wine [on the table] and he drank one cup of it, he would drink no water for a whole day; now the brethren, wishing him to be refreshed, used to give him wine, and the old man took it joyfully so that he might torment his body. And when his disciple saw this, he said to the brethren, "I entreat you, for our Lord's sake, not to give him wine to drink, for if he drinks it he will go to his cell and afflict himself because of it"; and when the brethren knew this they did not give him any more wine to drink.

68. There was a certain old man who made a vow not to drink any water during the fast of forty days;[9] and when he became hot he would wash a potter's vessel, and fill it with water, and hang it up in front of him. Then the brethren asked him why he did this, and he said, "That I may labor the more, and receive a reward from God"; he said this that he might incite them to great labors.

90. Abba Theodotus used to say, "Abstinence from bread quiets the body of the monk."

97. Abba Poemen said, "Every bodily pleasure is contemptible before the Lord."

99. Abba Daniel used to say, "In proportion as the body grows, the soul becomes enfeebled; and the more the body becomes emaciated, the more the soul grows."

110. They used to say about Abba Joseph that when he was about to die, and the old men were sitting about him, he looked at the window and saw Satan sitting there; and he cried out to his disciple and said, "Bring me a stick, for this devil thinks that I have become old, and that I am no longer able to stand up against him," and as soon as he grasped the stick

---

9. *fast of forty days*—Lent, the period before Easter when Orthodox Christians abstain from all animal products, including fish, eggs, milk, and cheese. The old man's refusal to drink water is extreme, and, of course, miraculous.

in his hand, Satan, in the form of a dog, cast himself from the window, and the old men saw him taking to flight.

116. They say concerning Abba Sisoes of Babylon[10] that—wishing to vanquish sleep—he stood upright on a mountain crag, and that the angel of the Lord came and rescued him from that place, and commanded him never to do such a thing again, and not even to hand on this tradition to another.

132. They said concerning Abba John the Less that—on one occasion—he steeped the palm leaves for two baskets in water, and sewed one basket to the other without perceiving it until he came to the side of it, for his mind was held captive by the sight of God.

134. Abba Arsenius used to say, "One hour's sleep is sufficient for a monk, provided that he is strenuous."

138. A certain father said that on one occasion when the brethren were eating the food of grace, one of them laughed at table; and Abba Sisoes saw him, and burst into tears, and said, "What can there be in the heart of this brother who has laughed? It is proper that he should weep because he is eating the food of grace."

140. Certain brethren went to an old man and, making apologies to him, they said, "Father, what will we do, for Satan is hunting us?" And he said to them, "It is right for you to be watchful and to weep continually. My own thoughts are always fixed upon the place where our Lord was crucified, and I sigh and lament and weep about it always." And thus having received a good example of repentance the brethren departed and became chosen vessels.

159. They say that Abba Serapion the bishop went on one occasion to one of the brethren, and found [in his cell] a hollow in the wall, which was filled with books; and the brother said to him, "Speak to me one word by which I may live." And the bishop said to him, "What have I to say to you? For you have taken what belongs to the orphans and widows and laid it up in a hole in the wall."

162. A certain monk used to live in a cave in the desert, and a message was sent to him from his kinsfolk, saying, "Your father is grievously sick and is close to death, therefore come, and inherit his possessions. And he answered, saying, "I died to the world long before he will die, and a dead man cannot be the heir of a living one."

167. Abba Isaac, the priest of the cells, used to say that Abba Pambo said, "The type of apparel that a monk ought to wear should be such that if it were cast outside the cell for three days nobody would carry it away."

174. Abba Poemen used to say, "He who labors and keeps [the result of] his work for himself has twice the grief."

186. On one occasion thieves came to the cell of an old man and said to him, "We have come to take away everything you have in your cell";

10. *Babylon*—in the center of modern-day Iraq.

and he said to them, "My sons, take whatever you please," and they took everything they saw in his cell, and departed. Now they forgot [to take] a purse that was hanging there, and the old man took it, and ran after them, and entreated them, saying, "My sons, take this purse you left behind in your cell." [. . .]

202. They used to say that Mother Sara, who dwelt above the river and was sixty years old, had never looked out [from her abode] and seen the river.

209. A certain old man used to say, "It is a disgrace for a monk to judge the man who has injured him."

220. A lover of ascetic labors saw a man carrying a dead person on a bier, and he said to him, "Do you carry a dead man? Go and carry the living."

243. A man who wanted to be a monk came to Abba Sisoes the Theban, and the old man asked him whether he had any possessions in the world, and he said, "I have one son"; and the old man, wishing to find out whether he possessed the faculty of obedience, said to him, "Go, and throw him in the river, and then come, and you will be a monk." And because the man was obedient he went straightway to do it. Now when he had departed, the old man sent another brother to prevent him from doing this, and when the man had taken his son to throw him into the river, the brother said to him, "You will not cast him in." Then the man said to him, "My father told me that I was to cast him in," and the brother replied, "He told me that you were not to cast him in," so the man left him and came [to the old man], and through his obedience he became a chosen monk.

244. Abba Poemen used to say, "Satan has three kinds of power that precede all sin: the first is error, the second is neglect, and the third is lust. When error comes it produces neglect, and from neglect springs lust, and by lust man fell; if we watch against error, neglect will not come; and if we are not negligent, lust will not appear; and if a man does not lust, he will, through the help of Christ, never fall."

254. They say concerning Abba Paphnutius, the disciple of Abba Macarius, that when he was a youth he used to look after the oxen with his companions; and they went to take some cucumbers to the animals, and as they were going along one of the cucumbers fell, and Abba Paphnutius took it and ate it, and whenever he remembered this, he used to sit down and weep over it with great feeling.

266. Mother Sara used to say, "Whenever I put my foot on a ladder to go up, before I ascend it I set my death before my eyes."

289. Abba Poemen used to say, "If a man dwells with a youth, however much he may guard his thoughts he makes a means for sin."[11]

---

11. *he makes a means for sin*—a warning against pedophilia.

321. They used to say that the face of Abba Pambo never smiled or laughed. Now one day when devils wanted to make him laugh, they hung a feather on a piece of wood, and they carried it along and danced about in great haste, and they cried out, "Hailaw, Hailaw." Now when Abba Pambo saw them, he laughed, and the devils began to run and jump about, saying, "Wawa, Abba Pambo has laughed." Then Abba Pambo said to them, "I did not laugh [for myself], but I laughed at your weakness, and because it needs so many of you to carry a feather."

330. An old man used to say, "I await death evening, and morning, and every day."

339. Abba Daniel used to say about Arsenius that he never wished to speak about any investigation into the scriptures, although he was well able to speak [on the subject] had he been so disposed, but he could not write even a letter quickly.

354. One of the holy men used to say [. . .], "He who looks on a woman to desire her has already committed adultery with her in his heart." [. . .]

374. Another old man used to say, "When I am sewing a basket, with every stitch I put into it I set my death before my eyes before I take another stitch."

386. A certain brother was travelling on a road, and his aged mother was with him, and they came to a river, which the old woman was not able to cross; and her son took his shoulder cloth and wound it round his hands so that he might not touch his mother's body, and in this manner he carried her across the river. Then his mother said to him, "My son, why did you first wrap round your hands with the cloth, and then take me across?" And he said, "The body of a woman is fire, and through your body there would have come to me the memory of [the body of] another woman, and it was for this reason that I acted as I did."

393. On one occasion Abba Ammon came to a certain place to eat with the brethren, and there was a brother there who had with him some bad news, for it had happened that a woman had come and entered his cell; and when all the people who were living in that place heard [of this], they were troubled, and they gathered together to expel that brother from his cell. Now when they learned that the blessed Bishop Ammon was there, they came and entreated him to go with them. But when the brother learned [this], he took the woman and hid her under an earthenware vessel; and when many people had assembled, and Abba Ammon understood what that brother had done, for the sake of God he hid the matter. And he went in and sat on the earthenware vessel, and commanded that the cell of the brother should be searched, but although they examined the place they found no one there. Then Abba Ammon answered and said, "What is this that you have done? May God forgive you." And he prayed and said, "Let all the people go forth," and finally he took the brother by the hand, and said to him, "Take heed to your soul, O my

brother," and having said this he departed, and he refused to make public the matter of the brother.

419. Abba Agathon used to say, "If I could find an Arian[12] to whom I could give my body and take his in its place, I would do so, because this would be perfect love."

433. A brother went to visit a certain monk, and when he left him, he said, "Forgive me, father, for having made you to desist from your rule"; and the monk said to him, "My rule is to refresh you, and to send you away in peace."

438. A certain brother came to Abba Macarius the Egyptian, and said to him, "Father, speak to me a word by which I may live." Abba Macarius said to him, "Go to the cemetery and blaspheme the dead." So he went and blasphemed them, and stoned them with stones, and he came and informed the old man [that he had done so]. And the old man asked him, "Did they say anything to you?" And the brother said "No." And again the old man said, "Go tomorrow and praise them, and say, 'Apostles, saints, and righteous men.'" And he came back to the old man, and said, "I have praised them." And the old man asked him, "And did they answer you?" And he said "No." And the old man said to him, "You see how you praised them and they said nothing to you; and although you reviled them, they did not answer you. So let it be with yourself. If you wish to live, become dead, so that you may not care for the abuse of men or for [their] praise. For the dead care for nothing. In this way you will be able to live."

553. There was a certain old man who lived in a cell, and his thoughts said to him, "Go get yourself a woman"; then he rose up straightway and kneaded together some mud, and made the figure of a woman, and he said to himself, "Behold your wife! It is necessary for you to labor with all your might that you may be able to feed her." And he labored with his hands and twisted many ropes. Then after a few days, he rose up and made a figure of a woman, and said to his thoughts, "Behold, your wife has come forth, so it is necessary for you to work harder to keep your wife and to clothe your daughter." And doing this he vexed his body sorely. And he said to himself, "I cannot bear [all] this work, and since I am unable to bear the work, a wife is unnecessary for me." And God saw his labor, and did away his thoughts [of fornication], and he had peace.

555. They used to say that Mother Sara contended against the devil of fornication for seven years on the roof [of her house] before she vanquished him.

561. They used to say that Abba Isaac went out and found the footprint of a woman on the road, and he thought about it in his mind and destroyed it, saying, "If a brother sees it he may fall."

12. *an Arian*—a follower of Arius, who argued that Jesus was in some degree subordinate to God the father; that is, a heretic.

575. There was in Scete a certain monk who strove hard [against sin], and the enemy[13] sowed in him the remembrance of a certain woman with a beautiful face, and he troubled him greatly through her. And by the providence of God, a certain brother who came down from Egypt went to visit him, and while they were conversing together, the brother who had gone to visit him said, "Such and such a woman is dead." Now she was the very woman whose memory was being stirred up in the monk. And when the other brother heard this, he rose up, and took his head-cloth, and went by night to Egypt, and opened her grave, and he smeared himself with the filthy and putrefying matter of the dead body of the woman, and then he went back to his cell, and he set that thing of filth before him at all times, and he did battle with his thought, saying, "Behold your lust, and that which you required! Behold, I have brought it to you; take your fill of it." And he used to torture himself with [the remembrance of] that filthy thing until the war that was in him quieted.

610. On one occasion Abba Moses came to the well to draw water, and he saw Abba Zechariah praying to the stream, and the Spirit of God was resting on him like a dove.

The Life of Pachomius (n.d.)

The Life of Pachomius, trans. Apostolos N. Athanassakis
(Missoula, MT: Scholars Press, 1975), 5–167.

The Life of Pachomius is an anonymously authored biography of the man widely considered the founder of "cenobitic," or communal, monasticism, a form of monasticism much different from the hermetic life described in the *Life of St. Antony* and the *Sayings of the Desert Fathers.*

When Pachomius (ca. 292–348) first decided to become a monk, he followed the example of St. Antony and his immediate successors by adopting a solitary life. But then, according to this biography, God instructed Pachomius to build a monastery to house the first community of cenobitic monks. The site was Tabenna (Tabennesis in the text below), an island in the Nile River in upper Egypt.

Although *The Life of Pachomius* celebrates the ascetic example of Antony, and although it takes pains to demonstrate that Pachomius managed ascetic feats, it ultimately promotes an anti-individualistic (and hence somewhat anti-Antonian) ideal of monasticism as *com-*

---

13. *the enemy*—Satan.

munity. For Pachomius, monasticism—as ordered by God through an angel—centers around a godly community of "brothers" and "sisters," not isolated people devoted to individual feats.

This biography, a case study of sorts on the possibility of shared struggle and support, served as an important example for new cenobitic monasteries. Pachomius himself helped establish hundreds of such communities, and his work inspired many more. In 357–358 St. Basil (the Cappadocian father who worked on Trinitarian matters with the two Gregories) visited Pachomius's monastery, an experience that inspired Basil to form his own community patterned on Pachomius's model.

[. . .] There was a man named Pachomius, born of pagan parents in the Thebaid,[14] who, having received great mercy, became a Christian. He made progress and achieved perfection as a monk. It is necessary to recount his life from childhood on for the glory of God, who calls everyone from everywhere to his wondrous light.

It happened that the child went with his parents to an idol's temple to sacrifice to the phantoms of evil spirits in the river. And when the priest in charge of the sacrifice saw him, he had him chased away, and furiously cried, "Chase away from here the enemy of the gods!" When his parents heard this, they were greatly grieved about him because he was an enemy of the so-called gods, who are no gods at all, especially since once at another time they had given him to drink of the wine-libations in that same place, and the child forthwith vomited what he had drunk. [. . .]

Constantine the Great, the first of the Roman Christian kings, became king after the persecution. Because he was making war against some rebellious lord, he ordered the capture of many recruits. Pachomius himself was captured approximately at age twenty. And as they were sailing downstream, the soldiers who kept them under arrest brought the ship to the harbor of the city of Thebes, and there they incarcerated them. Then some merciful Christians heard about it late in the day, and they brought them food and drink and other things they needed because they were despondent. When the young man inquired about it, he heard that Christians were merciful to everyone, including strangers. Then he asked what a Christian was, and they told him, "They are men who bear the name of Christ, the only Son of God, and they do all manner of good things for everyone, placing their hope on him who made the Heaven and the earth and us men."

14. *Thebaid*—a region populated by monks in the upper part of the Nile River Valley in northern Egypt.

Upon hearing of so much grace, his heart was fired with joy and the fear of God. So he retired into privacy in the prison and, stretching his arms toward Heaven, he prayed and said, "God, maker of Heaven and earth, if you look upon my low estate, because I do not know you, the only true God, and if you free me from this affliction, I shall minister to your will all the days of my life and, loving all men, I shall serve them according to your commandment." [. . .] Pachomius came directly to the Upper Thebaid and visited the church of a little town called Chenoboskeia. There he became a catechumen[15] and was baptized. And on the night on which he was found worthy of the mystery he had a dream: he saw the dew of Heaven fall upon him; and when the dew gathered in his right hand and turned into solid honey that fell upon the earth, he heard someone say, "Heed what is taking place, for it shall come to pass in the future."

And so, moved by his love for God, he asked to become a monk. After it was explained to him that there was an anchorite[16] named Palamon, he went to him to become his fellow-anchorite. When he reached the place, he knocked on the door. The old man stooped down from above and said to him, "What do you want?" for he was abrupt in speech. He answered him and said, "I am asking you, father, to make me a monk." And he told him, "You cannot; this work of God is not simple, because many came but were unable to endure it." Then Pachomius replied, "Try me in this and see." Then the old man told him, "First try yourself for some time and then come here. My regimen is hard: in the summer I fast all day, and in the winter I eat once every two days. And by the grace of God I only eat bread and salt. I am not used to oil and wine. I stay awake always half the night, as I was taught, for prayer and the study of God's words, and many times all night." When the youth heard this from the old man, his spirit was strengthened even more so that he might endure every hardship along with him. And he told Palamon, "Through God's help and your prayers I believe that I can endure all you have told me." Then he opened the door and let him in, and clothed him with the monk's habit. Both of them pursued the toilsome regimen and also took time out for prayer. Their work consisted of spinning and weaving woolen bags. And in their work they labored not for themselves but remembering the poor as the apostle commands. And, if the old man saw during their vigils that sleep was pressing heavy on them, they both went out to the sand of the mountain. So they carried sand in baskets from place to place, forcing the body to labor so that it might stay awake for prayer. The old man used to say, "Keep awake, Pachomius, lest Satan tempt you and harm you." And, seeing his obedience in everything and the progress of his endurance, the old man rejoiced. [. . .]

15. *catechumen*—one studying the doctrines of Christianity in order to be baptized.

16. *anchorite*—one living a solitary monastic life.

Once, journeying [in the desert] for a good distance, he came to a deserted village called Tabennesis. There he prayed with God's love in his mind. And after a long prayer a voice came to him—he had not had a vision yet until that time—and told him, "Stay here and build a monastery, and many will come to you to become monks." After he heard this and realized through purity of heart, according to the scriptures, that the voice was holy, he returned to his spiritual father and told him. He was very sad because he treated Pachomius as his own child, but Pachomius used many means of persuasion, and they both journeyed to that place. They built a small dwelling, as a small monastery, that is, and the holy old man told him, "Because I believe that this comes to you from God, we shall make a solemn pledge between us, that we shall never part from each other now on in order to take turns visiting each other." And this they did for as long as Christ's true athlete, Palamon, lived. [. . .]

When his own brother according to the flesh, named John, heard about him, he came to him. Pachomius was very glad to see him, for he had never yet visited his family since he went up to the mountain after his discharge from the army. He, too, chose the same kind of life and stayed with Pachomius. Both possessed nothing, save God's law. And if they acquired something from their work, they gave most of it to the needy, and kept for themselves what was necessary for their survival. [. . .]

He spent much time battling the demons, like a champion of truth, in the fashion of the most holy Antony. For this reason he asked the Lord to keep sleep away from him so that, being awake day and night, he might defeat the enemy in accordance with the scriptural saying, "And I shall not turn away until they have vanished." For before the Lord's faith they are powerless. The Lord granted him his request for a sufficient length of time. And it was as if, through the purity of his heart, he were seeing the invisible God as in a mirror.

Sometime later, while he and some of the brothers were on an island, cutting rushes for baskets, and while he was awake and alone, praying to be taught God's perfect will, an angel sent by the Lord appeared to him, just as one had appeared to Manoah and his wife before the birth of Samson.[17] The angel said, "The Lord's will is to minister to the race of men and to reconcile them to him." He said this thrice and went away.

After he thought about the voice that he had heard and realized its meaning, he started receiving those who came to him. And after he tested their worthiness and that of their parents, he clothed them in the monk's habit, and he introduced them to monastic life gradually. The first step was to renounce the world with respect to their family and themselves and to follow the savior who taught thus. For this is what it means to bear the cross. They, on the other hand, being taught well by him and according to

17. . . . *before the birth of Samson*—see Judges 19.

the scriptures, bore fruit in a manner worthy of their call. They marveled at him exceedingly, because they saw him toiling not only through bodily hardships but also through his assumption of nearly all the care of the monastery. For he prepared the table for them at meal time. Similarly, he sowed and watered the vegetables. Then he would answer the door every time someone would knock on it, and, if any one of them was sick, Pachomius himself eagerly took care of him and ministered to him during the night. Those brothers who were neophytes[18] had not yet reached such a degree of eagerness in serving each other. But he freed them of all care by saying, "Brethren, struggle that you may attain to the object of your call; study the psalms and the lessons from the other books and especially from the Gospel. As for me, I take my rest by serving you and God, according to God's command."

[. . .] And they asked him, "Father, why are you the only one who toils in all of the works of the monastery?" And he said, "Who yokes a beast to the plow and overlooks its labor until it falls? The merciful Lord himself looking upon my indigence will support you, or will bring others who will be able to assist me in the care of the monastery." For theirs was indeed a communal monastery. And so he drew up for them a simple rule and traditions profitable to the soul, and according to scripture he prescribed for them the proper measurement of dress, equality in food portions, and decent sleeping arrangements.

God called and multiplied, and so others came to lead the ascetic life with him [. . .]

And when there was need for the Eucharist,[19] he would invite a priest from the nearest churches and he would celebrate the feast for them in that fashion. For there was no one among them invested with the clerical office.[20] He himself deliberated on the subject and frequently told them that it was not good to ask for office and glory especially in a communal monastery, lest for that very reason strife and envy and jealousy and schisms arise among many monks: "Just as when a spark from a fire, a very small one in the beginning, is cast into the threshing-floor and is not extinguished soon, it destroys a year's labors, so too a clerical office is the beginning of contemplation of the lust for power. It is good to submit to the church of God reasonably. And whenever we find someone ordained by our fathers, the bishops, let us have him perform the duties of a priest." [. . .] And whenever a clergyman came to him to become a monk, he would submit to the prescribed order according to God's law, and, like all the others, he would willingly behave according to the rules recommended by the brothers. [. . .]

18. *neophytes*—new monastic brothers.

19. *Eucharist*—Communion or the "Lord's supper."

20. *no one . . . invested with the clerical office*—no one ordained as a priest, and thus no one permitted to administer the sacraments.

When the sister of our great Father Pachomius heard reports about him she came to see him. He sent the brother who was gate-keeper of the monastery to tell her, "You have indeed heard about me that I am alive. Do not grieve because you have not seen me. But if you, too, wish to partake of this holy way of life, that we may find God's mercy, consider the matter. The brothers will make a monastery for you to retire there. Perhaps the Lord will call upon other women to be with you. For man has no hope in this world, unless he does what is good before he departs from his body to the place where he will be judged and rewarded according to his deeds." When she heard these things tears came to her eyes. She became contrite and turned her heart to her salvation. Thus a monastery was established in the village, at some distance from that of the brothers. She followed the regimen eagerly, together with other women. And as their number grew she became their mother.[21] [. . .]

If any one of the brothers who had not attained perfection yet wished to visit a woman related to him, Pachomius through his house manager would send him to the aged Peter. Thus a report was made to the mother of the monastery. It was in the presence of another reverend sister that the visit to the relative would take place in strict propriety and oblivion to kinship of flesh. [. . .]

If any one of the sisters passed away, the mothers would make a shroud for the body to be wrapped in. Then the appointed brothers would stand in solemn gathering there under a portico, while the sisters stood far from them on the other side, chanting, until the burial took place. They would go to the mountain even more solemnly, while the sisters themselves chanted behind the hearse, and their father did not cease praying until they entered the monastery with God's fear in them. They might also bury her in the monastery's cemetery. The women increased in number up to about four hundred, and, except for the rough cloak, they had the same rules as the great monastery. [. . .]

Before the communal monastery was given over to the group, there were under our Father Pachomius some monks with carnal inclinations, since not all choose the fear of God. He counseled them in many ways, but they did not obey and they did not follow the straight path. Instead, they caused him grief, and he went far away from them and, falling on his face, he prayed and said, "God, you commanded us to love our neighbors as ourselves. Look upon these souls, take pity on them and fill them with awe, so as to fear you and to know what monastic life is, in order that they, like the other brothers, might place their hope in you." After this prayer, he saw that they did not want to be in line with him, but they kept on dissenting. He took the necessary measures, and he gave them the foundation rules and the other regulations. When they realized that he would not allow them to live according to their wishes, they departed in

21. *their mother*—their abbess.

fear. And so, after their departure, the others waxed as wheat does when the darnel[22] is weeded out. [. . .]

When Pachomius saw that, as the number of the brothers increased, the monastery became too small for them, he transported some of them to Pabau,[23] another deserted village. And with them he built and enlarged a monastery, seeing that many were called by the Lord. And he appointed a steward and assistants to him to care for the brothers, and also house managers and assistants to them, according to the rules of the first monastery at Tabennesis. To make sure they would remember, he committed the rules to writing in order to have everyone proceed according to the terms, without harming his fellow man. For order is good, and only the perfect man finds no obstacles even in disorder, as it is written, "And in the days of famine they will be filled." He visited the two monasteries night and day as a servant of the good shepherd. [. . .]

No one did anything in the house without those who were to care for it. They did not even enter a cell to visit a brother. In each house the house manager or his assistant kept all the surplus clothes locked in a cell, until they needed to wash and to wear them. The books also were within a little enclosure under the care of these two officials. They had no money in their possession, and especially no gold.

Some of them died without having known money. The faithful who were in the service of the monastery were an exception. But even they entered the monastery and kept nothing in their hands for more than a day, but they gave it to the steward to keep until they might go out again. All these rules of governing are written in the book in the part that covers the stewards' duties. [. . .]

Pachomius received into his care other monasteries. [. . .] At Easter time the appointed brothers would come to where Pachomius was, and they celebrated Easter together, feasting together on the words and love of God. It was also their custom to gather again in the month of Mesore[24] in order to give a detailed written account of their work to the great steward. And if the father of each monastery wanted direction in some matter, he gave it to him, and he appointed house managers and other officers. [. . .]

While Father Pachomius was still alive, through his own dictation he committed to writing not only the account and regulations concerning the building of the communal monastery, but also many letters to fathers of monasteries. In these letters he employed names of letters, e.g., from alpha to omega, and gave them the meaning of a secret spiritual language that they understood because of their governance of souls. This he did when he had no time to visit them. These spiritual men copied these

22. *darnel*—a Eurasian ryegrass; considered a weed.

23. *Pabau*—a village in upper Egypt, the site of Pachomius's primary monastery after Tabenna.

24. *Mesore*—August.

documents in order that, by guiding them with meaningful letter and language, he might properly lead them to the perfection of being worthy of becoming books of spiritual letters. [. . .]

After Easter a disease from the Lord came upon the brothers. In all the monasteries about one hundred brothers went to their final rest—actually more than that. Pachomius himself was ill. The disease was a plague. When one was seized with fever, his color changed and his eyes became bloody. He also had the feeling of choking until he died. [. . .] Theodore ministered to abbot Pachomius, whose body became emaciated from the disease that had become chronic. His heart and his eyes were like burning fire. Two days before Pachomius died he summoned the other fathers of the monasteries and the other leaders and told them, "Behold and see that the Lord is visiting me. Choose for yourselves a man who can govern you in the Lord." And he summoned a certain Orsisius from the monastery of Chenoboskeia. [. . .]

After they prayed and departed, abbot Pachomius said to a certain brother, "Do me a favor and bring me a good cover, because this one is heavy and my body cannot bear it. I have now been ill for forty days, but I do thank God." The man went off to the steward's quarters and took a good and light cover that he placed over him. When Pachomius saw how different the mattress was he said, "Take it away, for I ought not to be treated differently from the brothers, especially now that I am freeing myself and am about to relinquish the body." [. . .]

So Pachomius gave up his holy soul on the fourteenth of the month Pachon.[25] They stayed awake all night and read from the scriptures and prayed. After the funeral rites the body was carried away to the mountain with chants and was buried. When the others descended from the mountain Theodore and three other brothers transported it to another place where it still lies until now. [. . .]

St. Basil (ca. 330–379) to Gregory of Nazianzus on Monastic Ideals (n.d.)

St. Basil, "Letter 22," in *The Fathers Speak,* ed. George Barrios (Crestwood, NY: St. Vladimir's Seminary Press, 1986). Used by permission of St. Vladimir's Seminary Press.

In a letter to Gregory of Nazianzus, Basil laid down forty-eight short principles to govern daily life in a monastery, a life detached from the world in pursuit of perfect communion with God. Many Eastern Orthodox monasteries still follow these rules today.[26]

25. *Pachon*—May.
26. See document 4.3, "Long Rules of St. Basil," in the online supplement.

1. The Christian ought to have thoughts worthy of his heavenly calling and order his life to be worthy of the Gospel of Christ.

2. The Christian must not let anything blow or drag him away from the remembrance of God, his will, and his judgments.

3. The Christian must not swear or lie, under pretense that in all things he is above the justice of the law.

4. He must not blaspheme, curse, fight, avenge himself, render evil for evil, or act in anger.

5. One should be patient, whatever one has to suffer. Even though we have the right to rebuke the one who has wronged us, we must do this not in passion for having been wronged, but in the hope of correcting a brother, according to the precept of the Lord.

6. One must not say anything against an absent brother and slander him, even if what is said is true.

7. One should turn away from one who decries a brother.

8. One should not indulge in jesting.

9. One should not play the buffoon or suffer buffoons.

10. One should not speak idle talk, for it is neither useful to those who listen, nor necessary or permissible with regard to God. Those who work should apply themselves quietly to their task and leave speeches of exhortation to those entrusted with the judicious dispensation of the word for the edification of the faith, lest the Holy Spirit of God come to grief.

11. One is not permitted to accost brethren entering [the monastery] or to speak to them before those in charge of taking care of the general order would have examined whether this is agreeable to God for the common advantage.

12. One must not be a slave to wine or crave for meat, or generally delight in any food or drink, for the athlete[27] ought to observe temperance in all things.

13. One must not hold as personal property something that is distributed to the brethren for their usage, nor store up anything; furthermore, if something is abandoned or thrown away, one must pick it up and regard it as the master's property.

14. No one may be his own master, but mind and do all things as if one had been delivered by God in bondage to the brethren, who are one's kin by the soul, each person at his own rank.

15. One must not grumble if necessary things are scarce, nor if toil is excessive, for it belongs to those in authority to decide these matters in each case.

16. One must not shout, or assume postures or a gait manifesting passion or wandering of the spirit away from the fullness of God's presence.

27. *athlete*—following the example of the Apostle Paul, Basil here compares Christian discipline to athletic training. See 1 Corinthians 9:24–27.

17. One ought to moderate one's voice as needed.

18. One must not reply to another, or treat him rashly or scornfully, but in all circumstances one ought to show fairness and respect to all.

19. One must not wink cunningly with the eye and assume attitudes or gestures that may grieve a brother or manifest some contempt.

20. One must not take pride in garments or footwear; that is vanity.

21. One ought to use inexpensive things for the needs of the body.

22. One must not spend anything beyond what is necessary and to excess; that is abuse.

23. One must not aspire to honors, or claim the first places.

24. Everyone should esteem others more than himself.

25. One must not be rebellious.

26. He who does nothing while being able to work should not eat either. But he who is busy with a task to be performed exactly ought to apply himself with all the zeal of which he is able, to the glory of Christ.

27. Everyone ought to do all things reasonably and with conviction, as approved by the leaders, even eating and drinking, to the glory of God.

28. One must not shift from one task to another without the agreement of those in charge of these sorts of things, unless being called suddenly, by evident necessity, to the help of one who lacks strength.

29. Everyone should stay at his own post and not overstep the limits of his assignment for reaching for what had not been commanded to him, unless those in charge judge that another needs help.

30. Nobody must be found wandering from workshop to workshop.

31. One should not do anything out of contentiousness.

32. One should not envy the reputation of another, or rejoice in his shortcomings.

33. One ought to deplore the faults of his brother for the love of Christ and feel sorry, but rejoice for what he did well.

34. One must not be indifferent toward sinners, nor unconcerned [about their sin].

35. If one has to reprove sinners, let it be with mercifulness, in the fear of God and in order to correct the sinner.

36. He who is reproved or blamed ought to take it with good will, realizing that it is for his own good.

37. One must not, if someone else is accused, contradict the accuser to his face or before others. If the accusation seems unreasonable, one should say a word in private to the accuser, and persuade him, or be persuaded by him.

38. Everyone as he is able should try to heal [with kindness] anyone who has something against him.

39. One must not bear a grudge against a man who has sinned and repents, but forgive him heartily.

40. He who says that he repents from sin should not only be contrite for the sin he has committed, but also make worthy fruits of repentance.

41. He who has been rebuked for first sins and was deemed worthy of pardon prepares for himself a judgment of anger worse than the previous [rebuke], if he sins again.

42. He who after a first and second warning persists in his fault ought to be reported to the hegumen,[28] if this seems better than having him rebuked in public. If he does not amend himself, let him be removed from among the others like an object of scandal and "regarded as a heathen and a publican" for the safety of those who cultivate obedience with zeal, according to the saying: "When the impious falls, the just are struck with fear"; but one should also mourn for him as for a limb severed from the body.

43. One should not let the sun set on an angry fit of a brother, lest night separate both from each other and leave an inexorable verdict in the day of judgment.

44. One should not wait for an occasion to amend oneself, because he cannot be certain of the morrow; many who have made many projects have not reached the morrow.

45. One should not let himself be fooled by a full belly, because it is a cause of nightmares.

46. One ought not be dragged into working immoderately beyond the limits of the sufficient; according to the words of the apostle, "if we have food and covering, we should be satisfied," for an abundance that exceeds the necessary displays greediness, and "greediness denotes idolatry."

47. One must not be avaricious or hoard unnecessary things.

48. He who comes to God should embrace poverty in all things and be transfixed by the fear of God, according to him who said: "Nail your flesh to the fear of me, for I have feared your judgments."

May the Lord give you to receive our instructions with full assurance and bring forth worthy fruits of the Spirit to the glory of God, through God's grace and with the cooperation of our Lord Jesus Christ, Amen!

Communal vs. Solitary Life in the "Lausiac History" (ca. 419)

Palladius, *The Lausiac History,* trans. Robert T. Meyer, Ancient Christian Writers, No. 34 (Westminster, MD: Newman Press, 1965), 46–47, 49–51.

A chamberlain named Lausus, who served in the court of the Byzantine emperor Theodosius II (408–450), ordered the compilation of short biographies and vignettes about the early desert fathers into a work now known as the "Lausiac History." The putative author of

---

28. *hegumen*—head of the monastery; "abbot" in Western parlance.

the texts, Palladius (the same Palladius mentioned in the section on the desert fathers), claimed that while researching the book he "traveled on foot and looked into every cave and cabin of the monks of the desert with all accuracy and pious motive."[29] Although scholars disagree about the source and authorship of these texts, recent research indicates that, despite obvious exaggerations, the collection can, for the most part, be considered a serious work of history that provides important insights into the lives of early Christian monks in Palestine, Syria, and Asia Minor.

This story of Paesius and Isaias illustrates the vigorous debates about the comparative virtues of the ascetic, solitary life versus the cenobitic life.

Also there were Paesius and Isaias, sons of a Spanish merchant. When their father died, they divided the estate they held, namely five thousand coins, clothes, and slaves. They deliberated and planned together: "Brother, what kind of life shall we lead? If we become merchants, such as our father was, we will still be entrusting our work to others.

"Then we would risk harm at the hands of pirates on the high seas. Come, let us take up the monastic life so that we may profit by our father's goods and still not lose our souls." The prospect of monastic life pleased them, but they found themselves in disagreement. For when they had divided the property, they each had in mind to please God, but by taking different ways of life.

Now the one shared everything among the monasteries, churches, and prisons; he learned a trade so that he might provide bread for himself and he spent his time at ascetic practices and prayer. The other, however, made no distribution of his share, but built a monastery for himself and took in a few brethren. Then he took in every stranger, every invalid, every old man, and every poor one as well, setting up three or four tables every Saturday and Sunday. In this way he spent his money.

After they both were dead, various pronouncements were made about them as though they had both been perfect. Some preferred one, some the other. Then rivalry developed among the brethren in regard to the eulogies. They went to the blessed Pambo[30] and entrusted the judgment to him, thinking to learn from him which was the better way of life. He told them: "Both were perfect. One showed the work of Abraham; the other, that of Elias."[31]

29. *Lausiac History,* 18.
30. *Pambo*—a revered desert father (d. ca. 375).
31. *Elias*—the Hebrew prophet Elijah.

One faction said: "By your feet, we implore you, how can they be equal?" And this group considered the ascetic the greater, and insisted that he did what the Gospel commended, selling all and giving to the poor, and every hour both day and night carried the cross and followed the savior even in his prayers. But the others argued heatedly, saying that Isaias had shared everything with the needy and even used to sit on the highways and gather together the oppressed. Not only did he relieve his own soul, but many others as well by tending the sick and helping them.

Pambo told them: "Again I say to you, they are both equal. I firmly insist to each of you that the one, if he had not lived so ascetically, would not be worthy to be compared with the goodness of the other. As for the other, he refreshed strangers, and thereby himself as well, and even if he appeared to carry the load of toil, he had also its relief thereafter. Wait until I have a revelation from God, and then come back and learn it."

They returned some days later and he told them: "I saw both of them standing in Paradise in the presence of God."

Christianity and the Byzantine State

Whom Christianity became the religion of the Roman Empire, church and state became forever entangled. Never again in the eastern portion of the Roman Empire, centered around Constantinople (or later in Russia—even during the Soviet era), would the two institutions function altogether separately. Emperors summoned and meddled in church councils; bishops condemned and supported emperors; emperors favored and exiled bishops; priests received payments from the state; emperors passed laws aiding and regulating the church; and Christianity became subject to and the beneficiary of the state's legal codes.

In this section we refer often to the "Byzantine Empire," by which we mean the Greek-speaking, Eastern portion of the Roman Empire (i.e., *not* the Latin-speaking, Western portion of the empire). How the Eastern, Byzantine Empire ("Byzantium") developed its own identity, and how it became separated from the Western Empire, will be explored below in the chapter titled "Great Schism."

Justinian on Imperial Authority
over the Church (ca. 535)

Deno John Geanakoplos, *Byzantium: Church, Society, and Civilization Seen through Contemporary Eyes* (Chicago: University of Chicago Press, 1984), 136–37. Used by permission of The University of Chicago Press.

Constantine imagined a single, universal, Christian society encompassing the *oikoumene*—the entire, inhabited world. Yet the precise

111

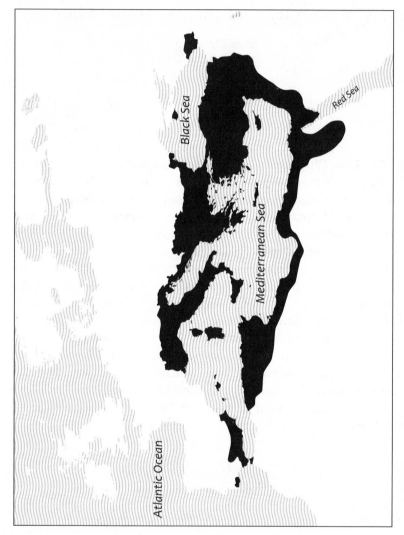

Figure 11. Byzantine Empire, 565

roles of emperor and patriarch (the head of the church in a major city such as Constantinople) were, almost from the beginning, the subject of great contention.

Constantine made clear that, unlike his pagan predecessors, he had no delusions about being divine. Yet he believed that he and his successors bore a special responsibility for the spiritual welfare of their subjects. Constantine's friend and biographer Eusebius described the emperor as an absolute ruler and God's representative on earth.

The historian Deno Geanakoplos notes that by the reign of Emperor Justinian (527–565) this ideal had evolved into the notion of a "diarchy." In Justinian's mind, emperor and patriarch shared responsibility for the spiritual and temporal well-being of the populace. Justinian articulated this ideal in the preface to a "novella" (edict) addressed to the patriarch of Constantinople. Here Justinian explained his understanding of *symphonia,* a grand vision of church and state working together in harmonious accord. Since both institutions were established by God, both must toil together to further the kingdom of God here on earth.

While beautifully conceived, this ideal worked better in theory than in practice. Justinian blatantly set himself above the church and inserted himself into all manner of church affairs. He appointed the patriarch of Constantinople. He summoned ecumenical councils. He established qualifications for bishops. He ousted patriarchs who displeased him. He granted himself privileges normally reserved for the clergy, including preaching and administering the Eucharist.

Some have termed such meddling "caesaropapism," in which the "caesar" (emperor) functions as "papa" (patriarch). Scholars can and do debate endlessly whether "caesaropapism" is an accurate means of describing church-state relations in Byzantium. What is beyond dispute, however, is that emperors exercised significant control over the church in the Byzantine Empire—control much greater than that exercised by Western emperors at the height of the Roman Catholic papacy in medieval Europe.

The greatest blessings of mankind are the gifts of God that have been granted us by the mercy on high: the priesthood and the imperial authority. The priesthood ministers to things divine; the imperial authority is set over, and shows diligence in, things human; but both proceed from one and the same source and both adorn the life of man. Nothing, therefore, will be a greater matter of concern to the emperor than the dignity and honor of the clergy; the more as they offer prayers to God without ceasing on his behalf. For if the priesthood be in all respects without blame, and full of faith before God, and if the imperial authority rightly and duly adorn the commonwealth committed to its charge, there will ensue a happy concord that will bring forth all good things for mankind. We therefore have the greatest concern for true doctrines of the Godhead and the dignity and honor of the clergy; and we believe that if they maintain that dignity and honor we shall gain thereby the greatest of gifts, holding fast what we already have and laying hold of what is yet to come. "All things," it is said, "are done well and truly if they start from a beginning that is worthy and pleasing in the sight of God." We believe that this will come to pass if observance be paid to the holy rules that have been handed down by the apostles—those righteous guardians and ministers of the word of God, who are ever to be praised and adored—and have since been preserved and interpreted by the holy fathers.

Maximus Confessor (ca. 580–662) on Imperial Power and the Church

Deno John Geanakoplos, *Byzantium: Church, Society, and Civilization Seen through Contemporary Eyes* (Chicago: University of Chicago Press, 1984), 138. Used by permission of The University of Chicago Press.

Not everyone in the empire favored imperial meddling in church affairs.[1] From the beginnings of the Byzantine Empire (see the chapter "Great Schism"), Christian prelates, particularly bishops, opposed intrusions from nonecclesiastical bodies; they took special umbrage when emperors interfered in attempts to establish and define church doctrine.

Such opposition became particularly intense when emperors during the 500s and 600s tried to placate sects that the church considered heretical, namely the Monophysites and Monotheletes. Monophysites—who were particularly strong in Syria, Egypt, and Anatolia—insisted that Christ had only one nature (as opposed to two) and that this nature was fully divine. Such certainty flew in the face of the Council of Chalcedon.[2] The Monotheletes adopted a somewhat milder version of Monophysitism, conceding that Christ had two natures yet arguing that he had only a single *will*. Christians who won the day insisted

1. See document 6.3, "Procopius on the Immorality of Justinian," in the online supplement.

2. See section 2, "Chalcedon and Non-Chalcedonian Churches," in the online supplement.

that both formulations were heretical, and they opposed any attempts emperors made to offer concessions to either group.

Such concerns prompted the theologian Maximus Confessor (who will receive more attention later) to deny that emperors did or should enjoy the same ecclesiastical responsibilities and powers as clerics.

None of the emperors was able, through compromising measures, to induce the fathers, who were theologians, to conform to the heretical teachings of their time. But in strong and compelling voices appropriate to the dogma in question, they declared quite clearly that it is the function of the clergy to discuss and define the "saving" dogmas of the universal church. And you said: "What then? Is not every emperor a Christian and a priest?" To which I responded: "He is not [a priest], for he does not participate in the sanctuary or, after the consecration of the bread, does he elevate it and say, 'The holy things [belong] to the holy.' He does not baptize nor perform the ceremony of chrismation;[3] nor does he lay on hands and ordain bishops, priests, and deacons; nor does he consecrate churches; nor does he bear the symbols of the priesthood, the *omoforion*[4] and the Gospel, as he does bear the symbols of his rule, the crown and the purple robe."

Patriarch Photios on the Powers of the Patriarch (ca. 880)

Deno John Geanakoplos, *Byzantium: Church, Society, and Civilization Seen through Contemporary Eyes* (Chicago: University of Chicago Press, 1984), 137. Used by permission of The University of Chicago Press.

Objections from those such as Maximus did not dissuade Emperor Justinian (527–565) or his predecessors from inserting themselves into doctrinal matters. But while emperors imposed themselves on the church, patriarchs also inserted themselves on occasion into affairs of state. Patriarchs regularly, for example, assumed responsibility for the administration of the government upon the death of an emperor. And patriarchs sometimes served as regents when young emperors took the throne.

3. *chrismation*—the sacrament in which a baptized Christian receives the gift of the Holy Spirit through anointing with oil.

4. *omoforion*—a liturgical vestment, essentially a brocaded scarf, worn only by bishops.

Patriarchs usually (although not always successfully) asserted their right to oversee Christian doctrine and affairs of the church. Following is one such assertion by Patriarch Photios (who appears again later) on the rights and responsibilities of the patriarchate of Constantinople.

The attributes of the patriarch are to be a teacher, to behave with equality and indifference toward all men, high as well as low; to be merciful in [administering] justice but reproving of the unbelievers, while speaking forcefully on behalf of truth and the vindication of [orthodox] doctrines before kings, and not to be ashamed.

The patriarch alone should interpret the canons adopted by those men of old and the decrees instituted by the holy synods.

The patriarch should take care of and decide whatever problems arise from what was done and arranged, in particular and in general, by the ancient fathers in ecumenical synods and in provincial synods. [. . .]

Since the constitution, analogous to man, consists of parts and members, the highest and most necessary parts are the emperor and the patriarch. For this reason the peace and happiness of the subjects in soul and body lie in the agreement and harmony of kingship and priesthood in all respects.

The [episcopal] throne of Constantinople, honored with dominion [over others], was declared by synodical votes to rank as the first [by the First Council of Constantinople in 381]. Thus, those divine laws that followed decreed that matters brought before the other thrones should be referred to that [of Constantinople] for adjudication and decision.

Basil I's Epanagoge on the Rights of Emperor and Patriarch (ca. 880)

"Passages from the *Epanagoge*," in *Social and Political Thought in Byzantium*, ed. Ernest Barker (New York: Oxford University Press, 1957), 89–97.

The following attempt to define the respective powers of emperors, patriarchs, bishops, and clergy comes from a law code—a "revision of the ancient laws"—compiled during the reign of the Byzantine emperor Basil I (867–886) and his son and successor Leo IV (886–912). This excerpt is from the introduction, or *epanagoge*.

· Title II. On the emperor and what he is ·

§1. The emperor is a legal authority, a blessing common to all his subjects, who neither punishes in antipathy nor rewards in partiality, but behaves like an umpire making awards in a game.

§2. The aim of the emperor is to guard and secure by his ability the powers that he already possesses; to recover by sleepless care those that are lost; and to acquire by wisdom and by just ways and habits those that are not [as yet] in his hands.

§3. The end set before the emperor is to confer benefits: this is why he is called a benefactor; and when he is weary of conferring benefits, he appears, in the words of the ancients, to falsify the royal stamp and character.

§4. The emperor is presumed to enforce and maintain, first and foremost, all that is set out in the divine scriptures; then the doctrines laid down by the seven holy councils; and further, and in addition, the received Romaic laws.

§5. The emperor ought to be most notable in orthodoxy and piety, and to be famous for holy zeal, both in the matter of the doctrines laid down about the Trinity, and in the matter of the views most clearly and surely defined about the nature of its being in virtue of the nature of the being of our Lord Jesus Christ according to the flesh. [. . .] This [he will do] by observing the [doctrine of the] identity of being in the three substances of the Godhead, indivisible and illimitable, and the union of the two natures substantially in the one Christ. [. . .]

§7. In his interpretation of the laws he must pay attention to the custom of the state. What is proposed contrary to the canons [of the church] is not admitted as a pattern [to be followed].

· Title III. On the patriarch and what he is ·

§1. The patriarch is a living and animate image of Christ by deeds and words typifying the truth.

§2. The aim of the patriarch is, first, to guard those whom he has received from God, in piety and soberness of life; to turn to orthodoxy and the unity of the church, so far as he can, all heretics (the name of heretics against the laws and canons is applied to those who are not in communion with the church catholic); and, finally, through the awe he inspires by his shining and most manifest and admirable action, to make those who are unbelievers imitators of the faith.

§3. The end set before the patriarch is the salvation of the souls entrusted to him, and that they should live for Christ and be crucified to the world.

§4. The attributes of the patriarch are that he should be a teacher; that he should behave equally and indifferently to all men, both high and low; that he should be merciful in justice but a reprover of unbelievers; and that he should lift up his voice on behalf of the truth and the vindication of the doctrines [of the church] before kings, and not be ashamed.

§5. The patriarch alone must interpret the canons passed by the men of old and the decrees enacted by the holy councils.

§6. The patriarch must handle and decide what has been done and arranged, in particular and in general, by the early fathers in councils and in provinces. [. . .]

§8. As the constitution consists, like man, of parts and members, the greatest and the most necessary parts are the emperor and the patriarch. Therefore the peace and felicity of subjects, in body and soul, is the agreement and concord of the kingship and the priesthood in all things.

§9. The [ecclesiastical] throne of Constantinople, honored with kingship [over other ecclesiastical thrones], was by the votes of councils designated the first and foremost;[5] therefore the divine laws following thereon ordain that the issues coming before the other thrones should be referred to the judgment and decision of that throne.

§10. The supervision and care of all metropolitanates[6] and bishoprics, and of all monasteries and churches, and further the right of judgment and of condemnation and acquittal, is reserved for their own patriarch. [. . .]

5. *designated the first and foremost*—here Basil appears, rather audaciously, to move the bishop of Constantinople from second in rank after Rome to first. The Second Ecumenical Council (the First Council of Constantinople, 381) insisted that the bishop of Constantinople ranked second to the bishop of Rome; the Council of Chalcedon (451) stipulated that Constantinople "should be magnified as Rome is in ecclesiastical matters and rank next after her."

6. *metropolitanates*—ecclesiastical provinces headed by a bishop (a "metropolitan") who oversees other bishops in the province. A metropolitan ranks directly below a patriarch.

Holy Fools

—For the message about the cross is foolishness to those who are perishing, but to us who are being saved it is the power of God. (1 Corinthians 1:18, NRSV)
—For since, in the wisdom of God, the world did not know God through wisdom, God decided, through the foolishness of our proclamation, to save those who believe. (1 Corinthians 1:21, NRSV)
—For the wisdom of this world is foolishness with God. (1 Corinthians 3:19, NRSV)
—We are fools for the sake of Christ, but you are wise in Christ. (1 Corinthians 4:10, NRSV)

The earliest account of an earnest Christian simulating madness appeared in the "Lausiac History," written around 420. A monk visiting a monastery in Egypt observed a nun who appeared to be possessed by demons. Her sisters insisted she was insane: they never saw her eat, and she never grew angry, even when abused. The visitor, however, soon discovered that her insanity and demonic possession were feigned. She was, in fact, a "fool for Christ," attempting to model the holy foolishness suggested by the passages above from 1 Corinthians. Upon learning the truth, the other nuns, mightily impressed, heaped praise upon her. She then promptly disappeared, unable to accept their accolades. A number of early accounts about holy fools followed this pattern: a person thought to be insane turned out to be a fool for Christ.

We do not know how many of these early tales derived from the lives of actual people, or, if they did, how many of the protagonists were, in fact, mentally ill. We do know, however, that such tales—transmitted both orally and in writing—established a model of behavior that came to be revered in Byzantium as well as (and especially) in Russia. Some of these holy fools certainly did suffer from mental illness or dementia. Others probably feigned foolishness to elicit alms. But other perfectly sane people adopted the ruse of foolishness as a way to follow what they understood as the Apostle Paul's behavioral ideal.

Holy fools often engaged in shocking and sometimes immoral behavior, challenging fundamental societal norms. Unconstrained by convention, holy fools could, in modern jargon, "speak truth to power": we have tales of fools condemning emperors, delivering unwanted prophecies, and conveying warnings that others dared not utter.

Life of the Holy Fool Father Simeon (ca. 642–649)

Leontius of Neapolis, "The Life of Symeon the Fool," in Derek Krueger, *Symeon the Holy Fool: Leontius' Life and the Late Antique City* (Berkeley: University of California Press, 1996), 131–71. Used by permission of the University of California Press.

The following account of Father Simeon, a monk living in the 600s, is one of the earliest written lives of a holy fool. Derek Krueger, who translated the text, argues that Simeon is largely a literary creation. Yet his biography is important, for it served as a model for other holy fools.

"The Life of Symeon the Fool" recounts a host of bizarre and repugnant antics, the significance of which is not always clear. Modern readers and scholars sometimes find it difficult to understand the purpose of Simeon's outlandish behavior. But there can be no question that his biographer, Leontius, wants us to view Simeon as a moral exemplar, however bewildering.

"The Life" includes a detailed account of Simeon's early years as a dedicated monk and desert ascetic—an account meant to demonstrate his holiness beyond a shadow of a doubt. In this tale Simeon's foolishness stems from a desire to hide his holiness and to disguise his miracles so as not to receive praise. A genuinely holy person, in this formulation, acts from altruism, shunning any recognition or reward for godly acts.

We join the tale after Simeon and his dear friend John have spent twenty-nine years in the desert, practicing asceticism and mortification in an effort to draw closer to God.

· III ·

[. . .]

Simeon said to John, "What more benefit do we derive, brother, from passing time in this desert? But if you hear me, get up, let us depart; let us save others. For as we are, we do not benefit anyone except ourselves, and have not brought anyone else to salvation." And he began to quote to him from the holy scripture such things as "Let no one seek his own good, but rather the good of his neighbor,"[1] and again, "All things to all men, that I might save all,"[2] and from the Gospel, "Let your light so shine before men, that they may see your good works and give glory to your Father who is in Heaven,"[3] and other such things. [. . .]

Simeon and John part, despite John's protestations.

Then straightaway Simeon ran ahead to the holy city of Christ our God.[4] For during that time, he thirsted greatly and burned, as he said, yearning to savor Christ's holy places. And arriving at Christ's holy and life-giving tomb, and the holy, saving, and victorious Golgotha,[5] he fulfilled his desire. He remained in the holy city for three days, visiting the Lord's all-holy places, worshipping and praying. And his every prayer was that his works might be hidden until his departure from life, so that he might escape human glory, through which human arrogance and conceit arise, and which also made the angels fall from Heaven. [. . .] For when he performed such miracles and accomplished such unexpected things, as can be learned from what follows, the pious one's works were not manifest to people. For his request was that, until his death, it might be just as if there was a veil over the hearts of those who saw the things he did. For, I say, indeed, if God did not conceal the blessed one's virtue from people so that they might not glorify him, how was it that he was not manifest to all when he cured those possessed by demons, and again when he held live coals in his hand, [or] when often he predicted the future for some, while to others he announced what had been said about him far away, when in the desert he gathered up nourishment of all sorts miraculously from nowhere, [or] when also he converted Jews or heretics to the right belief or cured the sick, or rescued others from danger? Also he often brought some disreputable women and prostitutes to lawful marriage

---

1. . . . *good of his neighbor*—1 Corinthians 10:24.
2. . . . *that I might save all*—1 Corinthians 9:22.
3. . . . *give glory to your Father who is in Heaven*—Matthew 5:16.
4. *holy city of Christ our God*—Jerusalem.
5. *Golgotha*—the hill on which Jesus was crucified.

through his jesting; others he made chaste after captivating them with money; then he spurred them on to pursue the monastic life by means of the purity he had acquired. And I am not surprised, friends of Christ, that he remained unknown while he accomplished these things in God's [name]. For he, who often makes the virtues that have been hidden from his servants manifest to all, by his plan also made manifest to all the virtues of this saint that were unknown.

As was said above, after spending three days in the holy places, he arrived in the city of Emesa.[6] The manner of his entry into the city was as follows: when the famous Simeon found a dead dog on a dunghill outside the city, he loosened the rope belt he was wearing and tied it to the dog's foot. He dragged the dog as he ran and entered the gate, where there was a children's school nearby. When the children saw him, they began to cry, "Hey, a crazy abba!"[7] And they set about to run after him and box him on the ears.

On the next day, which was Sunday, he took nuts, and entering the church at the beginning of the liturgy, he threw the nuts and put out the candles. When they hurried to run after him, he went up to the pulpit, and from there he pelted the women with nuts. With great trouble, they chased after him, and while he was going out, he overturned the tables of the pastry chefs, who [nearly] beat him to death. Seeing himself crushed by the blows, he said to himself, "Poor Simeon, if things like this keep happening, you won't live for a week in these people's hands."

According to God's plan, a phouska[8]-seller saw him, who did not know that he was playing the fool. And he said to him (for he seemed to be sane), "Would you like, my lord abba, instead of wandering about, to be set up to sell lupines?"[9] And he said, "Yes." When he set him up one day, Simeon began to give everything away to people and to eat, himself, insatiably, for he had not eaten the whole week. The phouska-seller's wife said to her husband, "Where did you find us this abba? If he eats like this, it's no use trying to sell anything! For while I observed him, he ate about a pot full of lupines." But they did not know that he had given away all the rest of the pots to fellow monks and others—the beans, the lentil soup, the desert fruits, all of it. They thought that he had sold it. When they opened the cash box and did not find a single cent, they beat him and fired him, and pulled his beard. When evening fell he wanted to burn incense. Now he had not departed from them that evening, but slept there outside their door. And not finding a shard of pottery, he put his hand

6. *Emesa*—a city in western Syria known today as Homs.
7. *abba*—father, a common word for "monk."
8. *phouska*—a soup made with vinegar.
9. *lupines*—flowers with long petals and colorful spikes, sometimes used as herbs.

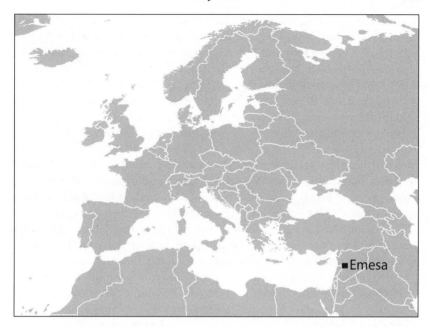

Figure 12. Emesa

in the oven and filled it with live coals and burned incense. Because God wished to save the phouska-seller, for he was a heretic of the Acephalic Severian sect,[10] his wife saw Simeon burning incense in his hand and was very frightened and said, "Good God! Abba Simeon, are you burning incense in your hand?" And when the monk heard this, he pretended to be burned and was shaking the coals in his hand and threw them into the old cloak that he wore, and said to her, "And if you do not want it in my hand, see I will burn incense in my cloak." And as in the presence of the Lord who preserved the bush[11] and the un-burnt boys,[12] neither the saint nor his cloak was burned by the coals. [. . .]

It was also the saint's practice, whenever he did something miraculous, to leave that neighborhood immediately, until the deed that he had done was forgotten. He hurried on immediately elsewhere to do something inappropriate, so that he might thereby hide his perfection.

Once he earned his food carrying hot water in a tavern. The tavern keeper was heartless, and he often gave Simeon no food at all, although he had great business, thanks to the fool. For when the townspeople were

10. *Acephalic Severian sect*—disciples of Severus of Antioch, an influential Syrian Monophysite at this time.

11. *the Lord who preserved the bush*—see Exodus 3:2.

12. *un-burnt boys*—see Daniel 3:19.

ready for a diversion, they said to each other, "Let's go have a drink where the fool is." One day a snake came in, drank from one of the jars of wine, vomited his venom in it and left. Abba Simeon was not inside; instead he was dancing outside with the members of a circus faction. When the saint came into the tavern, he saw the wine jar, upon which "Death" had been written invisibly. Immediately he understood what had happened to it, and lifting up a piece of wood, he broke the jar in pieces, since it was full. His master took the wood out of his hand, beat him with it until he was exhausted, and chased him away. The next morning, Abba Simeon came and hid himself behind the tavern door. And behold! The snake came to drink again. And the tavern keeper saw it and took the same piece of wood in order to kill it. But his blow missed, and he broke all the wine jars and cups. Then the fool burst in and said to the tavern keeper, "What is it, stupid? See, I am not the only one who is clumsy." Then the tavern keeper understood that Abba Simeon had broken the wine jar for the same reason. And he was edified and considered Simeon to be holy.

Thereupon the saint wanted to destroy his edification, so that the tavern keeper would not expose him. One day when the tavern keeper's wife was asleep alone and the tavern keeper was selling wine, Abba Simeon approached her and pretended to undress. The woman screamed, and when her husband came in, she said to him, "Throw this thrice cursed man out! He wanted to rape me." And punching him with his fists, he carried him out of the shop and into the icy cold. Now there was a mighty storm and it was raining. And from that moment, not only did the tavern keeper think that he was beside himself, but if he heard someone else saying, "Perhaps Abba Simeon pretends to be like this," immediately he answered, "He is completely possessed. I know, and no one can persuade me otherwise. He tried to rape my wife. And he eats meat as if he's godless."[13] For without tasting bread all week, the righteous one often ate meat. No one knew about his fasting, since he ate meat in front of everybody in order to deceive them.

It was entirely as if Simeon had no body, and he paid no attention to what might be judged disgraceful conduct either by human convention or by nature. Often, indeed, when his belly sought to do its private function, immediately, and without blushing, he squatted in the market place, wherever he found himself, in front of everyone, wishing to persuade [others] by this that he did this because he had lost his natural sense. For guarded, as I have often said, by the power of the Holy Spirit that dwelt within him, he was above the burning that is from the devil[14] and was not harmed by it at all. One day, when the aforementioned virtuous John,

13. *eats meat as if he's godless*—ate meat on fast days when Orthodox Christians should abstain from meat.
14. *burning that is from the devil*—lust.

the friend of God who narrated this life for us, saw him mortified from his asceticism (for it was the time after Easter and he had passed all of Lent without food), he felt both pity and amazement at the indescribable austerity of Simeon's regimen, although he lived in the city and associated with women and men. And wanting him to refresh his body, John said to him playfully, "Come take a bath, fool!" And Simeon said to him, laughing, "Yes, let's go, let's go!" And with these words, he stripped off his garment and placed it on his head, wrapping it around like a turban. And Deacon John said to him, "Put it back on, brother, for truly if you are going to walk around naked, I won't go with you." Abba Simeon said to him, "Go away, idiot, I'm all ready. If you won't come, see, I'll go a little ahead of you." And leaving him, he kept a little ahead. However, there were two baths next to each other, one for men and one for women. The fool ignored the men's and rushed willingly into the women's. Deacon John cried out to him, "Where are you going, fool? Wait, that's the women's!" The wonderful one turned and said to him, "Go away, you idiot, there's hot and cold water here, and there's hot and cold water there, and it doesn't matter at all whether [I use] this one or that." And he ran and entered into the midst of the women, as in the presence of the Lord of glory. The women rushed against him, beat him, and threw him out. The God-loving deacon [John] asked him, when he told him his whole life, "For God's sake, father, how did you feel when you entered into the women's bath?" He said, "Believe me, child, just as a piece of wood goes with other pieces of wood, thus was I there. For I felt neither that I had a body nor that I had entered among bodies, but the whole of my mind was on God's work, and I did not part from him." Some of his deeds the righteous one did out of compassion for the salvation of humans, and others he did to hide his way of life.

Then one time [some youths] were outside the city playing lysoporta,[15] of whom one was the son of Simeon's friend, John the deacon, who a few days earlier had fornicated with a married woman. As he was leaving her house, he was possessed by a demon, although no one saw it happen. Therefore the saint wanted both to chasten him and to heal him at the same time. And he said to the runners, "Truly, unless you let me play with you, I won't let you run." And they began to throw stones at him. They wanted to take him to the side where the one he wished to cure was running. Seeing this, Abba Simeon went off the opposite way instead. For he knew what he was going to do. And when they began to run, the saint rushed headlong toward the possessed boy and overtook him. When no one was looking, he punched him in the jaw, and said, "Commit adultery no more, wretch, and the devil won't draw near you." And immediately the demon threw the boy down, and everyone jumped on top of him. As

15. *lysoporta*—a game similar to red rover.

he lay on the ground foaming, the afflicted one saw the fool chasing a black dog away from him, beating it with a wooden cross. Many hours later, when the youth came to, they asked what happened to him. And he could not say anything except, "Someone said to me, 'Commit adultery no more.'" Only after Abba Simeon had died in peace, as if coming to his senses, the youth narrated the event carefully. [. . .]

Once when a large earthquake was about to seize the city, when Antioch fell, during the time of the faithfully departed Emperor Maurice[16]— for it was then that the saint came down from the desert into the inhabited world—he grabbed a whip from a school and began to strike the pillars and say to each one, "Your master says, 'Remain standing!'" And when the earthquake came, none of the pillars that he struck fell down. However he also went up to one pillar and said to it, "You neither fall nor stand!" And it was split from top to bottom and bent over a bit and stayed that way. No one figured out what the blessed one had done, but everyone said that he struck the pillars because he was out of his mind.

There was this for the glorification and admiration of God: the gestures that caused some to believe that Simeon led an irredeemable life were often those through which he displayed his miracles. For once when a plague was about to come upon the city, he went around to all the schools and began to kiss the children, saying to each of them, as in jest, "Farewell, my dear." He did not kiss all of them, but only those whom the grace of God made known to him. And he said to the teacher at each school, "In God's name, idiot, do not thrash the children whom I kiss, for they have a long way to go." The teachers mocked him, sometimes giving him a whipping; sometimes also the teacher nodded to the children and they ridiculed him publicly. When the plague came, not one of the children whom Abba Simeon had kissed remained alive, but they all died.

It was the saint's habit to enter into the houses of the wealthy and clown around, often even pretending to fondle their female slaves. For example, one day a certain circus faction member had got a slave girl of one of the notables pregnant. The slave girl did not want to expose the one who had fornicated with her, and when her mistress asked her who had seduced her, the slave girl said, "Simeon the fool raped me." Therefore, when he came into the house, according to his custom, the girl's mistress said to him, "Well, Abba Simeon, so you seduced my slave and got her pregnant." And immediately he laughed and hid his head in his right hand and said to her, while at the same time squeezing his five fingers, "Leave me alone, leave me alone, wretch, soon she will give birth for you, and you will have a little Simeon!" Until her day arrived, Abba Simeon kept bringing her wheat bread, meat, and pickled fish, and said, "Eat, my wife." When the time and the hour for her to give birth

16. *Emperor Maurice*—emperor from 582 to 602.

came, she struggled in child-birth for three days and almost died. Then her mistress said to the fool, "Pray, Abba Simeon, for your wife cannot give birth." He said to her, dancing and clapping his hands, "By Jesus, by Jesus, wretch, the child won't come out from there until she says who its father is." When the girl in danger heard this she said, "I slandered him. The child belongs to so-and-so of the circus faction." Immediately then she gave birth. And while all were amazed, some in the house believed he was a saint, while others said once again, "He prophesied this because of the devil, since he is a complete imbecile." [. . .]

One of the city's artisans wanted to unmask Simeon when he had perceived his virtue. For one time he saw Simeon at the baths conversing with two angels. Now the artisan was a Jew, and he blasphemed Christ all the time. The saint appeared to him in his sleep and told him to say nothing about what he saw. That morning he wanted to expose him, and immediately the saint stood before him, touched his lips, and sealed up his mouth. He was silenced and unable to speak to anyone. He came up to the fool and gestured to him with his hand to make it so he could speak. But Abba Simeon played the fool and gestured back to him like an idiot. He gestured to him to make the sign of the cross. To see the two of them gesturing to each other was an impressive sight. Simeon appeared to him again in a dream and the monk said, "Either you get baptized, or you will go begging." At that time he refused to obey him, but after Abba Simeon died and the Jew saw the straits he was in, and especially after the [vision he had] at the transporting of the saint's remains, then he was baptized together with his household. And as soon as he came up from the holy font, immediately he spoke. And every year he commemorated the fool and he invited beggars (to join him). [. . .]

He played all sorts of roles foolish and indecent, but language is not sufficient to paint a portrait of his doings. For sometimes he pretended to have a limp, sometimes he jumped around, sometimes he dragged himself along on his buttocks, sometimes he stuck out his foot for someone running and tripped him. Other times when there was a new moon, he looked at the sky and fell down and thrashed about. Sometimes also he pretended to babble, for he said that of all semblances, this one is most fitting and most useful to those who simulate folly for the sake of Christ. For this reason, often he reproved and restrained sins, and he sent divine wrath to someone to correct him, and he made predictions and did everything he wanted, only he changed his voice and [the position of] his limbs completely. And in all that he did, they believed that he was just like the many who babbled and prophesied because of demons. If one day one of the women whom he called his girlfriends betrayed him, he knew immediately by her spirit whether she had fornicated, and he spoke to her, opening his mouth wide and screaming, "You have lapsed, you have lapsed! Holy Virgin, Holy Virgin, strike her!" And either he prayed that a deadly disease would come to her, or often, if she continued in her un-chastity, he would send her a demon. Because of this, henceforward, he got all those who promised him to remain chaste and not betray him. [. . .]

[S]ometimes when Sunday came, [Simeon] took a string of sausages and wore them as a [deacon's] stole. In his left hand he held a pot of mustard, and he dipped [the sausages in the mustard] and ate them from morning on. And he smeared mustard on the mouths of some of those who came to joke with him. Also a certain rustic, who had leucoma[17] in his two eyes, came to make fun of him. Simeon anointed his eyes with mustard. The man was nearly burned to death, and Simeon said to him, "Go wash, idiot, with vinegar and garlic, and you will be healed immediately." As it seemed a better thing to do, he ran immediately to a doctor instead and was completely blinded. Finally, in a mad rage he swore in Syriac, "By the God of Heaven, even if my two eyes should suddenly leap [from their sockets], I will do whatever the fool told me." And he washed himself as Simeon told him. Immediately his eyes were healed, clear as when he was born, so that he honored God. Then the fool came upon him and said to him, "Behold, you are healed, idiot! Never again steal your neighbor's goats." [. . .]

Another time he was sitting with his brothers (in poverty) and warming himself near a glassblower's furnace. The glassblower was Jewish. And Simeon said to the beggars, joking, "Do you want me to make you laugh? Behold, I will make the sign of the cross over the drinking glass that the craftsman is making, and it will break." When he had broken about seven, one after the other, the beggars began to laugh, and they told the glassblower about the matter, and he chased Simeon away, branding him. As he left, Simeon screamed at the glassblower, saying, "Truly, bastard, until you make the sign of the cross on your forehead, all your glasses will be shattered." And again after the [glassblower] broke thirteen others, one after the other, he was shattered and made the sign of the cross on his forehead. And nothing ever broke again. And because of this, he went out and became a Christian. [. . .]

Now the time calls, O friends, to narrate to you [Simeon's] marvelous death, or rather sleep. For his death does not present ordinary edification, but it was more remarkable than everything I said before. It became both seal and guarantee of his triumph and confirmation that his behavior did not defile him. For when the great one perceived the profane hour, not wanting to obtain human honor after his death, what did he do? He went inside, lay down to sleep underneath the bundle of twigs in his sacred hut, and committed his spirit to the Lord in peace. When they had not seen him for two days, those who knew him said, "Let's go, let us visit the fool in case he's ill." And they went and found him lying dead under

17. *leucoma*—an eye disease.

his bundle of twigs. Then they said, "Now all will believe that he was beside himself. Behold his death is another idiocy." And two of them lifted him up without washing him, and they went out without psalm singing, candles, or incense, and buried him in the place where strangers are buried. Then when those who were bearing him and going out to bury him passed the house of the formerly Jewish glassblower, whom Simeon had made a Christian, as I said before, the aforementioned former Jew heard psalm singing, music such as human lips could not sing, and a crowd such as all humanity could not gather. This man was astounded by the verse and the crowd. He glanced out and saw the saint carried out by the two men and them alone bearing his precious body. Then the one who heard the invisible music said, "Blessed are you, fool, that while you do not have humans singing psalms for you, you have the heavenly powers honoring you with hymns." And immediately he went down and buried him with his own hands. And then he told everyone what he had heard in the angels' songs. John the deacon heard this and went running, with many others, to the place where he was buried, wishing to take up his precious remains in order to bury him honorably. But when they opened the grave, they did not find him. For the Lord had glorified him and translated him.[18] Then all came to their senses,[19] as if from sleep, and told each other what miracles he had performed for each of them and that he had played the fool for God's sake. [. . .]

18. *translated him*—transported Simeon to Heaven.

19. *all came to their senses*—realized that *they* were the fools for not having recognized Simeon's true nature.

Eastern Trends in Christian Theology

The creeds we've encountered so far, as well as works by Eusebius, Athanasius, and Gregory of Nyssa, include little that Western Christians—Roman Catholics and Protestants—cannot embrace. They contain statements that still inspire well beyond the Eastern realms in which they originated.

We now turn to aspects of early Eastern theology that, while not necessarily contrary to the Western tradition, certainly represent major differences, whether in substance or emphasis.

It is common to distinguish the Eastern theological tradition from that of the West by noting the East's emphasis upon (1) mysticism, (2) apophaticism (theology that stresses the limits of reason and what we *cannot* know about God), and (3) theosis (the process of becoming like God).[1]

To be clear: *none* of these elements is unique to the East: the Roman Catholic Church recognizes and celebrates dozens of mystics; even the most rationalistic Western theologians insist that humans are limited in what they can know about God; and Christians of all confessions seek to imitate Christ. Yet Eastern Christians tend to emphasize these elements—mysticism, apophaticism, and theosis—to a greater degree and in different ways than Christians in the West.

What we sometimes term the Western scholastic tradition reached its apogee of the high Middle Ages in the person of Thomas Aquinas

---

1. Donald Fairbairn organizes his comparative study of Eastern Orthodoxy and Western Christianity (*Eastern Orthodoxy through Western Eyes* [Louisville, KY: Westminster John Knox, 2002]), from which this introduction borrows, around these three principles.

(1225–1274).[2] Aquinas represented the extremes of scholasticism in the Roman Church. This *Doctor Angelicus* (angelic doctor) used Aristotelian logic to produce detailed, philosophical studies elucidating fine points about the nature of God. Such work, however, was largely foreign to Aquinas's contemporaries in the East, whose writings focused to a much greater extent on the unknowability of God.

Before turning to these writings, however, we should explore in some detail what, exactly, Easterners mean by the terms "mysticism," "apophaticism," and "theosis."

Andrew Louth, one of the foremost authorities on Eastern mysticism, characterizes mysticism as "a search for and experience of immediacy with God." "The mystic is not content to know *about* God," writes Louth; rather, the mystic "longs for union with God." The easy distinctions in traditional Western thought between subject (God) and object (us) begin to blur. The mystic seeks not to *understand* a divine subject (God), but rather to achieve union with God—a union that lessens or partially obliterates distinctions between the subject and object. "God no longer presents himself as object," explains Louth. "The search for God becomes a search for God's own sake, and an unwillingness to be satisfied with anything less than him."[3] Simply put, the mystic seeks experience of and union with God over knowledge of God.

As such, Eastern Orthodox mystics deemphasize cognition—intellectual comprehension—in favor of familiarity. We cannot really know God; we can only know God to the extent that God relates to us. Here early Eastern mystics drew on the work of the Greek philosopher Philo (a Jewish contemporary of Christ), who explained God in terms of God's essence (*ousia*), which is *un*knowable, versus God's energy (*energia*), which *is* knowable. Mystics participate in God's energy without trying to understand God's essence.

Hence the mystics' intellectual approach to theology is "apophatic" —mystics know there is much they do not know; they seek not to comprehend God's *ousia*. Vladimir Lossky, a twentieth-century Russian theologian, explained apophaticism as follows: "the apophatic way, or mystical theology . . . has for its object God, in so far as he

2. See document 17.2, "Thomas Aquinas on God's Essence," in the online supplement.

3. Andrew Louth, *The Origins of the Christian Mystical Tradition: From Plato to Denys* (Oxford: Oxford University Press, 1981), xv.

is absolutely incomprehensible . . . God no longer presents himself as object, for it is no more a question of knowledge but of union. Negative theology is thus a way toward mystical union with God, whose nature remains incomprehensible to us."[4]

None of this should imply that the Eastern church eschews cognition or rational deliberations about God. The works we've seen from Athanasius and Gregory of Nyssa and the edicts of ecumenical councils demonstrate just the opposite. Gregory of Nyssa's friends—Basil and Gregory of Nazianzus—also spilled a good deal of ink reasoning out the Trinity. Yet apophaticism is apparent even in their reasoned treatises: like Philo, they emphasized that we can know God's energies (*energia*)—God's actions and works, God's love for us—but never God's essence (*ousia*).

The third aspect of Eastern theology, "theosis"—sometimes termed "divinization" or "deification"—is the process of moving toward God, becoming like God, and participating in God's nature. Eastern theologians often point to three passages in scripture as the basis for pursuing theosis:

> 1. I say, "You are gods, / children of the Most High, all of you." (Psalm 82:6, NRSV)
> 2. Jesus answered, "Is it not written in your law, 'I said, you are gods'?" (John 10:34, NRSV)
> 3. "Thus he has given us, through these things, his precious and very great promises, so that through them you may escape from the corruption that is in the world because of lust, and may become participants of the divine nature." (2 Peter 1:4, NRSV)

Eastern Orthodox Christians take these passages at face value. As children of the most high and as recipients of Christ's grace, we may become "participants of the divine nature" and, in a very real sense, gods.

Proponents of theosis suggest that the Lord's prayer[5] encourages the pursuit of deification. Maximos Confessor (see below), for example, argued that the Lord's prayer petitions God for everything the Logos (Christ) accomplished through the incarnation. Baptism bestows grace

4. Vladimir Lossky, *The Mystical Theology of the Eastern Church* (Cambridge: James Clarke, 1968), 28.

5. The Lord's prayer (Matthew 6:9–13, NRSV): "Our Father in Heaven, hallowed be your name. Your kingdom come. Your will be done, on earth as it is in heaven. Give us this day our daily bread. And forgive us our debts, as we also have forgiven our debtors. And do not bring us to the time of trial, but rescue us from the evil one."

that promotes theosis. When the Apostle Paul spoke of the "riches of his [God's] glorious inheritance among the saints" (Ephesians 1:18), he meant theosis.

Teachings about theosis are often expressed in the simple formula, "God became man so man can become god." The Logos became incarnate so flesh can become divine. Our fall into sin trapped us in a life of matter, but the Logos—which became incarnate in Jesus—set humanity free to achieve its original purpose: to become like God.

Because of work by theologians such as Maximus Confessor (see below), salvation in the Eastern church began to be understood as a *process* of theosis, that is, a quest to become like God.[6] This concept of salvation as process is crucial. Unlike the later Protestant tradition, particularly the evangelical tradition, which tends to view salvation as a discreet, easily identifiable event (i.e., the "decision for Christ"), theosis (salvation) in Eastern Christianity is *process*. And as process, Eastern salvific theology looks forward toward a goal rather than backward at an accomplished fact. As process it does not see a final end in this life; we cannot achieve perfect union with God here. Roman Catholics and Protestants tend to focus on the current status of the believer in God's eyes: Protestants ask whether we are "justified" (that is, righteous in God's estimation); Roman Catholics ask whether we abide in a "state of grace." Such terminology rarely appears in the Eastern tradition, and the question of status rarely occurs. The focus instead is on a process that will lead to union with God in part in this life and in full in the life to come.[7]

In his comparison of the Eastern and Western Christian traditions, Donald Fairbairn notes that Eastern Orthodoxy adheres more closely to the "classical" or "incarnational" view of salvation than to the "juridical" or "Latin" view.[8] The juridical view common in the West was developed most eloquently by Anselm of Canterbury (1033–1109), an Italian theologian who worked in England. Prominent in the Roman Catholic Church (and hence known as the "Latin" view), the juridical understanding of salvation views Christ's death on the cross as a payment for human sin. It is "juridical" in that it perceives God's acceptance of his Son's sacrifice as satisfaction for a legal debt.

---

6. See Jaroslav Pelikan, *The Spirit of Eastern Christendom (600–1700)* (Chicago: University of Chicago Press, 1974), 8–16. This introduction borrows a number of observations from Pelikan.

7. Fairbairn, 111.

8. Ibid., 79–84.

The "classical" or "incarnational" view—far more prominent in the East—instead focuses on Christ's incarnation and the celebratory aspect of the death of God incarnate, which led to victory over sin and death. God's death in Christ is less a payment of a debt, less a legal obligation, than it is a glorious triumph over the grave. The cross is more a symbol of divine love than of satisfied legal contracts. It is the incarnation—God in man—that makes such wonders possible and opens to us the possibility that we, too, may become like God. Theosis is our path toward divinity—the very divinity embodied in Christ. It is a recognition that we may experience the power of the incarnation. Christ's death laid this path before us.

Theosis, in other words, is enabled by grace. The Holy Spirit works in us and in the church where grace abides. Eastern Orthodoxy agrees with the Protestant tradition that we are saved by grace, but it places more emphasis on our participation in this grace—that is, our participation in God's energies. These energies are sometimes described as a divine light, imagery that is prominent in the reading below from Dionysius.

Grace requires striving, and grace enables striving. Good works do not lead to salvation, and good works do not merit salvation; yet humans must participate in the grace that leads to theosis. Humanity's works do not deify humans, yet humans must participate in God's energies.

How? The following readings offer some thoughts.[9]

Dionysius the Areopagite (400s–500s) on Knowledge of the Godhead

Pseudo-Dionysius Areopagite, "The Divine Names," in *The Divine Names and Mystical Theology*. John D. Jones, translator. Pp. 120–21, 124–26, 129–30, 175–80. Copyright © 1999. Milwaukee, WI: Marquette University Press. Reprinted by permission of the publisher. All rights reserved. www.marquette.edu/mupress.

Nobody knows the true identity of "Dionysius the Areopagite," an anonymous writer confused, intentionally or not, with the man the Apostle Paul converted to Christianity in Athens (Acts 17:34). Many

---

9. See also section 7, "Eastern Trends in Christian Theology," in the online supplement.

scholars suspect that this "pseudo-Dionysius," who lived during the late 400s or early 500s, was a Syrian monk.

In Dionysius's work we find lyrical expressions of apophatic theology. God is "divinity beyond god," "unknowing, completely unintelligible," and "beyond beingness." We must "mystically accept" the incarnation, for we cannot grasp it. Instead of trying to understand God, says Dionysius, we should seek union with God. We should invoke "the source of good" through prayer so we may be "guided to it and united with it." We are not "to comprehend God according to us, but we are to stand the whole of ourselves outside of the whole of ourselves, so that we come to be wholly of God."

· Chapter II ·
Concerning Unified and Differentiated Theology and What the Divine Unity and Divine Difference Are

[. . .] [I]t is necessary that we begin again to explain the completeness of the divine unity and difference so that the meaning of all of our statements will be clear. Thus we must reject all of the various unwise things that are said, and we must wisely and systematically take up what is proper in this matter, as far as we are able. For as I have said elsewhere, the sacred mystics of our theological traditions call the divine unities the hidden and non-wandering supreme foundations of the more than ineffable and more than unknown steadfastness. But they call the divine differences the good-formed processions and manifestations of the Godhead. Further, in accordance with the sacred writings, they declare that there are specific unions and differences that are peculiar to either the unions or differences that have been spoken about.

Thus with respect to the divine unity or beyond-beingness, this is one with and common to the authoritative Trinity:

> Ground beyond being,
> Divinity beyond god,
> Goodness beyond good,
> Sameness beyond all of the whole
>   individualness that is beyond all,
> Unity beyond source of unity,
> Ineffable, many named,
> Unknowing, completely unintelligible,
> Position of all, denial of all,
>   Beyond all position and denial.
> (If one must say:)
> The abiding and foundation

of the ruling persons in one another,
wholly beyond every way of unity, and
confused in none of its parts.

Let us exemplify [this unconfused founding of the ruling persons in one another] by a sensible and familiar example. The lights of lamps that are in one room are whole and completely together in penetrating one another, yet they have an unmixed and precise distinction that lets them subsist apart from one another; they are unified in their difference and differenced in their unity. Thus, in a room that is full of many single lights we will see a light unifying all the lights into one light that is one, clear, undifferentiated illumination. And, I imagine, no one will be able to distinguish the light of this lamp from the light of the others from out of the air that encompasses all these lights. Further, he will not be able to see one light without the others among the totality of lights that are purely mixed with one another.

But if some lamp is taken out of the room all its light will be carried out with it; it will draw nothing of the other lights into itself, nor will it abandon its light to the others. For, as was said, there was a wholly un-mixed union of the totality of these lights in a complete whole such that there was no confusion of their own aspects. This, in truth, occurred in a body in which the light itself was dependent upon the material fire.

Thus, we say that the unity beyond being is founded not only beyond bodily unities but even beyond the unity of the soul and intellect. For, as a whole, the divinely formed and super-celestial lights have their unity in a pure, whole, and super-cosmic way according to their analogous par-ticipations in the unity that is apart from all.

Further, the god formation of Jesus, which is revealed in every theol-ogy, is ineffable to every Logos and unknowable to every intellect, even to those of the most honored among the highest angels. We have mystically accepted his having taken on being in a human way. We are ignorant of how he came to be formed of a maiden's blood by any other law than that of nature, and of how he walked over unstable water with dry feet while he himself had bodily mass and material weight. We are ignorant of all those other deeds indicative of the natural Logos of Jesus that is beyond nature.

Yet we have discussed these matters sufficiently in other places, and they have been celebrated beyond every natural manner by our illustrious teacher in his work titled *Theological Elements*.[10] [. . .]

From the *Theological Elements* of the most holy Hierotheus:

10. *Theological Elements*—the ostensible author of this work, Hierotheus, is most likely fictional.

The cause and fullness of all is
  the divinity of Jesus:
An ordering of consonant parts to wholeness;
  it is neither whole nor part.
Whole and part as anticipating, beyond having, and
  before-having every whole and part in itself.
A completion to the non-complete as
  source of completion,
    Non-complete to the complete as
      beyond completion and before completion.
Form producing form in those without form as
    source of form,
    Non-form in those that are formed as
      beyond form.
Being undefiedly taking a stand upon the
    totality of being;
  Beyond-being: apart from every being.
A determining of the totality of principles and orders;
  Yet, founded beyond every principle and order.
The measure of what is.
Eternity, before eternity, and beyond eternity,
Fullness in those that lack;
  Beyond fullness in those that are full.
Ineffable and unspeakable,
Beyond intellect, beyond life, and beyond being.
That beyond nature: beyond-naturally,
That beyond being: beyond beingly. [. . .]

· Chapter III ·
The Power of Prayer. Concerning the Blessed Hierotheus and the Piety and Covenant of Theology

First, if it seems right, let us investigate the most complete name of "good" that reveals the whole processions of God. Let us call upon the Trinity that is the source of good and beyond good and that manifests the whole of the supremely good providences of itself. It is necessary that we first be lifted up toward it, the source of good, by our prayers, and then, by drawing near to it, that we be initiated into the all-good gifts of what is founded around it. (For while it is present to all, not all are present to it.) Then, when we invoke it by our most holy prayers with an unpolluted intellect that is suited for the divine union, we shall be present to it. For it is not in a place, so that it would be absent from some beings or have to go from one being to another. Moreover, even the statement that it is "in" all beings falls far too short of its infinity, which is beyond all and encompasses all.

Thus, we would raise ourselves by our prayers to the more sublime ascent of the divine and good rays, just as if a brilliantly lit cord, suspended from the highest Heaven and brought down to us, is always grasped so that we ascend upwards to it by putting one hand over the other. It would seem as if we were bringing it down whereas, in fact, we do not bring it down (since it is present both above and below), but we ourselves are raised up toward the most sublime splendors of its brilliantly lit rays.

In the same way, when we are standing on a ship and are holding on to the chains, stretched out to us from a rock and, as it were, given to us to take hold of, then the rock does not come toward us; rather, we and the ship are in truth drawn toward it. Or, to consider the matter in an opposite way, if someone standing on a ship is separated from the rock on the shore, he does nothing to the standing and unmoved rock, but he is separated from it. In the same measure that he is separated from it, he is also hurled away from it. Therefore, before everything and especially before a discourse about God, it is necessary to begin with a prayer—not so that the power present both everywhere and nowhere shall come to us but so that by our divine remembrance and invocations we ourselves shall be guided to it and be united with it. [. . .]

· Chapter VII ·
Concerning Wisdom, Intellect, Logos, Truth, and Faith

Come then if you will and we will celebrate the good and eternal life as wisdom, wisdom itself and, even greater, as giver of subsistence to every wisdom and as beyond being, beyond every wisdom and understanding. For God is not only over full of wisdom such that there is no number of his understanding, but he is even founded beyond every logos, intellect, and wisdom. That divine man who is common to us and our teacher has brilliantly conceived this when he says that "the foolishness of God is wiser than men." This means not only that every human thinking is in some sort of wandering when it is judged in respect of the steadfastness and stability of the divine and most complete intellects, but that it is usual for the theologians to deny any kind of privation with respect to God.

Thus the writings call the completely lit light "invisible"; they call that which is greatly celebrated and many named "ineffable and nameless." They call that which is present in all and discoverable from all "incomprehensible and inscrutable." For this reason it is even now said that the divine apostle celebrates the foolishness of God by calling it that which appears contrary to reason and absurd in itself but that leads us to the ineffable truth before all Logos.

As I have said in other places, we are deceived into following an apparently divine and ineffable logos when we receive what is beyond us in a way that is familiar to us, when we become entangled in what is native to our sensations, and when we reject what is divine for what is ours. Now it is necessary to know that our intellect has a power toward thinking, through which it sees the intelligibles and sees that the unity through which the intellect is joined to what is beyond it is beyond the nature of the intellect. In this, therefore, we are not to comprehend God according to us, but we are to stand the whole of ourselves outside of the whole of ourselves, so that we come to be wholly of God. For it is great to be of God and not of ourselves. For thus shall what is divine be given to those who come to be with God.

Preeminently celebrating this foolish wisdom [that is] without Logos and without intellect, we shall say that it is cause of every intellect, reason, wisdom, and understanding, that every intention is of it, that every knowledge and understanding is from it, and that the total richness of wisdom and knowledge is hidden in it. Therefore, in consequence of what has already been said, the all wise and more than wise cause is the subsistence of wisdom itself both in totality and in particularity.

After this it is necessary for us to investigate how we know God, which is neither intelligible, sensible, nor in general some being among beings. It is never true to say that we know God in terms of its nature, for this is unknown, and exceeds all logos and intellect. We know God in terms of the order of all beings that are projected out of it and that have some similarity and likeness to its divine paradigms.

> According to our power,
>   we attain to that beyond all
>   by a path and order
>   in the denial and preeminence of all, and
>   in the cause of all.
> God is known
>   in all, and
>   apart from all.
> God is known
>   through knowledge, and
>   through unknowing.
> Of God there is
>   intellect, reason, knowledge,
>   contact, sensation, opinion, imagination, name, and
>   everything else.
> God is
>   not known, not spoken, not named,

not something among beings, and
not known in something among beings.
God is
all in all,
nothing in none,
known to all in reference to all,
known to no one in reference to nothing.
For we say all of this correctly about God
who is celebrated according
to the analogy of all,
of which it is the cause.
The most divine knowledge of God is
one that knows through unknowing
in the unity beyond intellect
when the intellect stands away from beings
and then stands away from itself,
it is united to the more than resplendent rays,
and is then and there illumined
by the inscrutable depths of wisdom.
Nevertheless, as we have said,
it is known from all;
(for according to the writings)
it is
productive of all,
always harmonizing the all,
cause of the indissoluble
concordance and harmony of all,
always joining together
the end of those that are prior to
the beginnings of secondaries, and
beautifying the agreement and harmony of all. [. . .]

Maximus Confessor on the Incarnation and Unity with God (early 640s)

Maximus Confessor, "Difficulty 41," in *Maximus the Confessor*,
ed. Andrew Louth (New York: Routledge, 1996), 155–62. © 1996.
Used by permission of Taylor & Francis Books UK.

Maximus Confessor (ca. 580–662) was without question the most distinguished Byzantine theologian of the 600s and arguably the most original mind in all of Byzantine theology. A man of diverse talents, Maximus served as "protosecretary" to the Byzantine emperor Hera-

clius (610–641) before leaving Constantinople to settle at a monastery in modern Scoutari, where he soon became abbot. Well-read in both pagan philosophy (Aristotle and the neoplatonists) and the writings of early church fathers, he used the tools of secular philosophy to defend the significant body of Christian doctrine developed by the 600s. Maximus developed a distinctive theology that melded academic precision with mystical contemplation of the divine.

Despite the mystical tone of his work, Maximus was a fierce and stubborn defender of Orthodox theology. He saw no contradiction between mystic reveries and rigorous argumentation. In 653 Emperor Constans II (641–668), trying to promote unity in a church beset by Monophysitism and Monothelitism, ordered Maximus arrested for Maximus's refusal to tolerate those who suggested that Christ had a single will. After a series of fruitless cross-examinations, Maximus's tormentors cut out his tongue (since it professed Christ's two wills) and cut off his hand (for refusing to sign a statement endorsing Monothelitist doctrine). He acquired the appellation "confessor" for his consistent confession of what he and his followers deemed the Orthodox faith.

Maximus wrote at length about theosis, a preoccupation that leads many historians to identify him as the prototypical Eastern theologian. The church historian John Meyendorff identifies Maximus as the "real father of Byzantine theology."[11]

Maximus makes clear that theosis cannot be achieved by humans alone—it is the work of God in humans and not a matter for the intellect; it is achieved through God's grace. Yet humans do participate in the process through right living and an energetic contemplation of the divine. To become like God humans must commune with God and align their wills with God's will. Maximus draws no firm distinctions between the life of the mind and the life of the soul: doctrine and relationship are of a piece.

Never in Maximus's work does he suggest that humans have an innate capacity to become like God. Deification is a gift from God, achievable only through God's power and grace. We must exercise our free will and participate in the process, but the Holy Spirit assists us, transforming our will so our desires become like God's desires. The debates over free will that later raged within Protestant theology were thus alien to Maximus and most of Eastern Christianity.

11. John Meyendorff, *Byzantine Theology: Historical Trends and Doctrinal Themes* (New York: Fordham University Press), 37.

Maximus's mysticism does not abandon the careful theological work of his predecessors; he sought always to remain faithful to the teachings of the early church fathers, and he emphasized the importance of philosophical, Trinitarian theology: perfect salvation requires the confession of perfect truths. Doctrine itself is a "deifying light"; grace and revelation work together to deify humanity.[12]

In the following excerpts Maximus reengages the perennial question of how Christ's two natures, human and divine, can coexist without division, that is, the formulation that led Maximus to oppose the Monophysites.[13] This lack of division in Christ, Maximus argues, can be achieved within humans through deification, and in the world and cosmos at large. The incarnation—the fusion of two natures, God and human—in the person of Christ presents us with the opportunity to overcome our own evil and destructive tendencies on the way to being defied.

Maximus introduces the following passage with a discussion of "divisions" in human beings: divisions in our nature; divisions between what our minds perceive and what our senses perceive; and divisions in what our senses perceive, including how we perceive the natural world (the "inhabited world") and Paradise.

[. . .] In order to bring about the union of everything with God as its cause, the human person begins first of all with its own division, and then, ascending through the intermediate steps by order and rank, it reaches the end of its high ascent, which passes through all things in search of unity, to God, in whom there is no division. It accomplishes this by shaking off every natural property of sexual differentiation into male and female by the most dispassionate relationship to divine virtue. This sexual differentiation clearly depends in no way on the primordial reason behind the divine purpose concerning human generation. Thus it is shown to be and becomes simply a human person in accordance with the divine purpose, no longer divided by being called male or female. It is no longer separated as it now is into parts, and it achieves this through the perfect knowledge, as I said, of its own *Logos*, in accordance with which it is. Then, by a way of life proper and fitting to saints, the human person unites Paradise and the inhabited world to make one earth, no longer is it

12. See Andrew Louth's introduction to *Maximus Confessor* (New York: Routledge, 1996)—a primary source for the observations above—for more on the themes covered here.

13. See also section 7, "Eastern Trends in Christian Theology," in the online supplement.

experienced as divided according to the difference of its parts, but rather as gathered together, since no introduction at all of partition is allowed. Then, through a life identical in every way through virtue with that of the angels, so far as is possible to human beings, the human person unites Heaven and earth, making the whole of creation perceived through the senses one with itself and undivided, not dividing it spatially by intervals in any way, since the human person has become as subtle as spirit and is no longer tied to earth by any bodily weight. Nor is it obstructed in its ascent to the heavens thanks to the perfect invisibility to these things of the mind that is genuinely hastening toward God, and wisely stretches out toward him step by step, as on an ordinary path, naturally overcoming any obstacles that stand in its way. And then the human person unites what is perceived by the mind and what is perceived by the senses with each other by achieving equality with the angels in its manner of knowing, and thus makes the whole creation one single creation, no longer divided by what it can know and what it cannot know, through its equality to the angels lacking nothing in their knowledge and understanding of the *logoi*[14] in the things that exist, according to which the infinite pouring out of the gift of true wisdom inviolably and without intermediary furnishes, so far as is permitted, to those who are worthy a concept of God beyond understanding or explanation. And finally, beyond all these, the human person unites the created nature with the uncreated through love (O the wonder of God's love for us human beings!), showing them to be one and the same through the possession of grace, the whole [creation] wholly interpenetrated by God, and become completely whatever God is, save at the level of being, and receiving to itself the whole of God himself, and acquiring as a kind of prize for its ascent to God the most unique God himself, as the end of the movement of everything that moves toward it, and the firm and unmoved rest of everything that is carried toward it, being the undetermined and infinite limit and definition of every definition and law and ordinance, of reason and mind and nature.

Since then the human person is not moved naturally, as it was fashioned to do, around the unmoved, that is its own beginning (I mean God), but contrary to nature is voluntarily moved in ignorance around those things that are beneath it, to which it has been divinely subjected, and since it has abused the natural power of uniting what is divided, that was given to it at its generation, so as to separate what is united, therefore "natures have been instituted afresh," and in a paradoxical way beyond nature that which is completely unmoved by nature is moved immovably around that which by nature is moved, and God becomes a human being, in order to save lost humanity. Through himself he has, in accordance with nature, united the fragments of the universal nature of the all, manifesting the universal *logoi* that have come forth for the particulars, by

14. *logoi*—plural of *logos*.

which the union of the divided naturally comes about, and thus he fulfills
the great purpose of God the Father, "to recapitulate everything both in
Heaven and in earth in himself," "in whom everything has been created."
Indeed being in himself the universal union of all, he has started with our
division and become the perfect human being, having from us, on our
account, and in accordance with our nature, everything that we are and
lacking nothing, apart from sin, and having no need of the natural intercourse of marriage. In this way he showed, I think, that there was perhaps
another way, foreknown by God, for human beings to increase, if the first
human being had kept the commandment and not cast himself down to
an animal state by abusing his own proper powers. Thus God-made-man
has done away with the difference and division of nature into male and
female, which human nature in no way needed for generation, as some
hold, and without which it would perhaps have been possible. There was
no necessity for these things to have lasted forever. "For in Christ Jesus,"
says the divine apostle,[15] "there is neither male nor female." Then having
sanctified the world we inhabit by his own humanly-fitting way of life
he opened a clear way into Paradise after his death, as, without a lie, he
promised the thief, "Today, you will be with me in Paradise" (Luke 23:43).
Then, since there was for him no longer any difference between Paradise
and the world we inhabit, he again made this clear to his disciples when
he was with them after his resurrection from the dead, showing that the
world is one and is not divided in itself, preserving the *Logos*[16] in accordance with which it exists free from any division caused by difference.
Then by his ascension into Heaven, he clearly united Heaven and earth,
and with his earthly body that is of the same nature and consubstantial
with ours he entered into Heaven and showed that the whole nature that
can be perceived through the senses is, by the most universal *Logos* of its
being, one, thus obscuring the peculiar nature of the division that cuts it
into two. Then, in addition to this, by passing with his soul and body, that
is, with the whole of our nature, through all the divine and intelligible
ranks of Heaven, he united the sensible and the intelligible and showed
the convergence of the whole of creation with the one according to its
most original and universal *Logos*, which is completely undivided and
at rest in itself. And finally, considered in his humanity, he goes to God
himself, having clearly "appeared," as it is written, "in the presence of
God" the Father "on our behalf," as a human being. As Word, he cannot
be separated in any way at all from the Father; as man, he has fulfilled, in
word and truth, with unchangeable obedience, everything that, as God,
he has predetermined is to take place, and has accomplished the whole
will of God the Father on our behalf. For we had ruined by misuse the

15. *the divine apostle*—the Apostle Paul.
16. *Logos*—Jesus Christ.

power that had been naturally given us from the beginning for this purpose. First he united us in himself by removing the difference between male and female, and instead of men and women, in whom above all this manner of division is beheld, he showed us as properly and truly to be simply human beings, thoroughly transfigured in accordance with him, and bearing his intact and completely unadulterated image, touched by no trace at all of corruption. With us and through us he encompasses the whole creation through its intermediaries and the extremities through their own parts. He binds about himself each with the other, tightly and indissolubly, Paradise and the inhabited world, Heaven and earth, things sensible and things intelligible, since he possesses like us sense and soul and mind, by which, as parts, he assimilates himself by each of the extremities to what is universally akin to each in the previously mentioned manner. Thus he divinely recapitulates the universe in himself, showing that the whole creation exists as one, like another human being, completed by the gathering together of its parts one with another in itself, and inclined toward itself by the whole of its existence, in accordance with the one, simple, undifferentiated and indifferent idea of production from nothing, in accordance with which the whole of creation admits of one and the same un-discriminated *Logos,* as having not been before it is. [. . .]

Maximus Confessor on the Purpose of God's Church (ca. 628–630)

Maximus Confessor, "The Church's Mystagogy," in *Selected Writings,* trans. George Berthold (New York: Paulist Press, 1985), 186–88. Copyright © 1985 by George Berthold. Paulist Press, Inc., New York/Mahwah, NJ. Reprinted by permission of Paulist Press, Inc. www.paulistpress.com.

This excerpt from Maximus discusses the essential role of the church in God's plan for us. Maximus introduces this passage by noting ways in which God "contains," "gathers," "limits," and "binds both intelligible and sensible beings to himself and to one another," thus "making them converge in each other by the singular force of their relationship to him as origin."

· Chapter 1 ·
How and in what manner the holy church of God is an image and figure of God

[. . .] It is in this way that the holy church of God will be shown to be working for us the same effects as God, in the same way as the image reflects its archetype. For numerous and of almost infinite number are the men, women, and children who are distinct from one another and vastly different by birth and appearance, by nationality and language, by customs and age, by opinions and skills, by manners and habits, by pursuits and studies, and still again by reputation, fortune, characteristics, and connections: all are born into the church and through it are reborn and re-created in the Spirit. To all in equal measure it gives and bestows one divine form and designation, to be Christ's and to carry his name. In accordance with faith it gives to all a single, simple, whole, and indivisible condition that does not allow us to bring to mind the existence of the myriads of differences among them, even if they do exist, through the universal relationship and union of all things with it. It is through it that absolutely no one at all is in himself separated from the community since everyone converges with all the rest and joins together with them by the one, simple, and indivisible grace and power of faith. "For all," it is said, "had but one heart and one mind." Thus to be and to appear as one body formed of different members is really worthy of Christ himself, our true head, in whom says the divine apostle, "there is neither male nor female, neither Jew nor Greek, neither circumcision nor un-circumcision, neither foreigner nor Scythian, neither slave nor freeman, but Christ is everything in all of you." It is he who encloses in himself all beings by the unique, simple, and infinitely wise power of his goodness. As the center of straight lines that radiate from him he does not allow by his unique, simple, and single cause and power that the principles of beings become disjoined at the periphery but rather he circumscribes their extension in a circle and brings back to himself the distinctive elements of beings which he himself brought into existence. The purpose of this is so that the creations and products of the one God be in no way strangers and enemies to one another by having no reason or center for which they might show each other any friendly or peaceful sentiment or identity, and not run the risk of having their being separated from God to dissolve into nonbeing.

Thus, as has been said, the holy church of God is an image of God because it realizes the same union of the faithful with God. As different as they are by language, places, and customs, they are made one by it through faith. God realizes this union among the natures of things without confusing them but in lessening and bringing together their distinction, as was shown, in a relationship and union with himself as cause, principle, and end. [. . .]

Marriage and Women in the Early Church

We know too little about the roles women played in the early church. Archaeologists have discovered tombstones referring to women as "presbyters," or ministers, but it remains unclear whether these women led Christian or Jewish congregations. Arguments by early church fathers *against* women serving as presbyters suggest that some women probably *did* serve as presbyters. (Why make an argument against something that isn't already occurring?)

Barbara MacHaffie suggests a number of reasons why women soon found themselves excluded from the church's ministry.[1] The Apostle Paul demanded that "women should be silent in the churches. For they are not permitted to speak, but should be subordinate, as the law also says. If there is anything they desire to know, let them ask their husbands at home. For it is shameful for a woman to speak in church" (1 Corinthians 14:34–35, NRSV). The author of 1 Timothy, at the time widely believed to be the Apostle Paul, wrote: "Let a woman learn in silence with full submission. I permit no woman to teach or to have authority over a man; she is to keep silent. For Adam was formed first, then Eve; and Adam was not deceived, but the woman was deceived and became a transgressor" (1 Timothy 2:11–14). Orthodox leaders noted that the Gospels provide no indication of Jesus choosing women as his apostles or of his commissioning any women to teach or baptize.

---

1. See Barbara MacHaffie, *Her Story: Women in Christian Tradition* (Philadelphia: Fortress, 1986), from which this introduction borrows heavily.

Fears that menstruating women might defile church buildings may have played some role in their exclusion from becoming priests or bishops. Dionysius the Great, a bishop of Alexandria (248–265), wrote in 241 that menstruating women ought not to come "to the holy table [to receive the Eucharist] or touch the holy of holies, nor to churches, but to pray elsewhere." Later church counsels prohibited "impure persons" from approaching the altar. In some regions local officials prohibited menstruating women even from entering a church.

Traditional understandings of men's and women's roles also worked against any notion of women instructing men or serving in a position of authority over men, for example, as priests or bishops.

Women did, however, serve as deacons, that is, as officials caring for the sick, poor, and imprisoned; instructing catechumens in theology; and assisting in the baptism of women. In Romans 16:1–3 Paul mentions a certain Phoebe who served as a deacon. Pliny the Younger, as we noted earlier, discovered and tortured two Christian women serving as *ministrae,* or deaconesses. By the end of the 200s we have ample evidence of women serving as deacons and visiting the sick. But as the church became more institutionalized, it found fewer roles for women. The office of deacon began to decline during the 400s and 500s, and women found themselves excluded almost entirely from official ministerial positions in both the East and the West.[2]

From its beginnings Christianity encompassed divergent and sometimes conflicting views about the relative merits of the married life and the celibate life. The Apostle Paul understood marriage as a divinely sanctioned institution beneficial to both spouses, but he also insisted that celibacy was preferable to married life. In some of Paul's work marriage emerges chiefly as a fallback position for those without the fortitude to remain chaste, that is, as a sanctioned albeit disappointing choice for those who need sex.

> "It is well for a man not to touch a woman." But because of cases of sexual immorality, each man should have his own wife and each woman her own husband. The husband should give to his wife her conjugal rights, and likewise the wife to her husband. For the wife does not have authority over her own body, but the husband does; likewise the husband does not have authority over his own body, but the wife does. Do not deprive one another except perhaps by agreement for a set time, to devote yourselves to prayer, and then come together again,

2. MacHaffie, 18–20.

so that Satan may not tempt you because of your lack of self-control. This I say by way of concession, not of command. I wish that all were as I myself am.[3] But each has a particular gift from God, one having one kind and another a different kind.

To the unmarried and the widows I say that it is well for them to remain unmarried as I am. But if they are not practicing self-control, they should marry. For it is better to marry than to be aflame with passion. (1 Corinthians 7:1–9 NRSV)

Tertullian to His Wife (ca. 200–206)

Tertullian, "To His Wife," in *Marriage in the Early Church*, ed. and trans. David Hunter (Minneapolis: Augsburg Fortress, 1992), 33–40. Used by permission of Augsburg Fortress Press.

The following letter comes from Tertullian (ca. 155–after 220), an influential theologian who lived in Carthage, a city that is now a suburb of Tunis in North Africa but was then a major outpost in Rome's African territory. Tertullian wrote in both Latin and Greek, and his knowledge of Greek philosophy allows those who so desire to place him within the Eastern tradition, although at this point in the church's history it was still too early to speak of a distinctly "Eastern" or "Western" tradition.

Tertullian wrote this letter to his wife in an attempt to persuade her not to remarry should he die first. Tertullian concedes here that remarriage is not a sin, but he also argues that it is not the favored option for a truly godly person. As in Paul's writings, which Tertullian cites copiously, we find a complex attitude toward marriage: Tertullian portrays the institution both as a gift from God and as innately inferior to the celibate life.

Tertullian's reflections on the virtues of celibacy help explain the values that drove men and women to the monastic life, as well as the reverence with which Christians viewed ascetics who chose to remain chaste and without spousal support.

We also find here a remarkably equitable view of marriage and gender relations, a view that contrasts markedly with the next excerpt from John Chrysostom. Tertullian's letter portrays spouses as equals, offering mutual support—each pulling his and her own weight in the pursuit of godliness.

3. *were as I myself am*—that is, chaste and celibate.

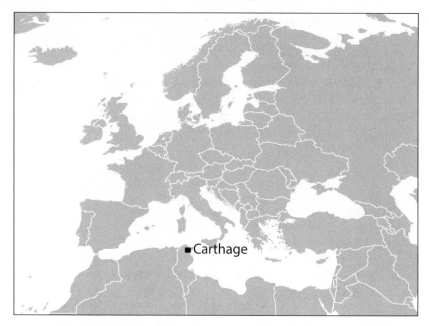

Figure 13. Carthage

[. . .] Of course, we do not reject the union of man and woman. It has been blessed by God to be the seedbed of the human race; it was devised to fill up the earth and to set the world in order. Thus it was permitted, but only once. For Adam was the one husband of Eve, and Eve his one wife; one woman, one rib. It is true that our ancient forebears, the patriarchs, were allowed not only to marry, but also to practice polygamy; they even had concubines. Now although the church existed in a figurative way in the synagogue, we can give the simple interpretation that it was necessary in the past to establish practices that later would be either abrogated or modified. The law had to come first, for it was necessary that it should first become clear that the law needed to be fulfilled; in a similar manner, the Word of God had to succeed to the law, introducing spiritual circumcision. Thus the general license of former times provided grounds for the subsequent emendations by which the Lord through his Gospel, and the apostle[4] in these last days, either eliminated excesses or regulated disorders.

But I have not set forth these remarks about the liberty granted to the old and the rigor imposed on posterity in order to argue that Christ came to dissolve marriage or to abolish sexual relations, as though from now on marriage is to be outlawed. Let them beware who, among their other perversities, teach the separation of the "two in one flesh," rejecting him

4. *the apostle*—the Apostle Paul.

who first derived the woman from the man[5] and then reunited in the marriage compact the two bodies that were taken from the harmonious union of the same material substance.

Furthermore, nowhere do we read that marriage is forbidden, since it is something good. But we have learned from the apostle what is better than this good, when he allowed marriage but preferred abstinence; the former because of the danger of temptation, the latter because of the end of time. If we examine the reasons given for each position, it is easy to see that the power to marry was granted to us out of necessity. But what necessity allows, it also depreciates. Scripture says: "It is better to marry than to burn."[6] What sort of good is it, I ask, that is commended only by comparison with an evil, so that the reason why marriage is better is because burning is worse? How much better it is neither to marry nor to burn!

For example, in times of persecution it is better to flee from town to town, as we are permitted, than to be arrested and to commit apostasy under torture. But far more blessed are those who have the courage to render the blessed testimony of martyrdom. I can say this: what is merely permitted is not good. [. . .]

Nothing should be sought merely because it is not forbidden; in fact, in a certain way such things are forbidden, since others are preferable to them. To prefer higher things is, in effect, to reject the lower. A thing is not really good simply because it is not bad; nor is something not bad simply because it does no harm. Something that is good in the true sense of the word achieves its excellence not only because it does no harm, but also because it does some good. Therefore, you ought to prefer that which does some good over that which merely does no harm. [. . .]

Now whenever [the Apostle Paul] permits marriage, he does so in such a manner as to show that he prefers us to follow his own example. Happy the person who proves to be like Paul! [. . .]

What words can describe the happiness of that marriage which the church unites, the offering strengthens, the blessing seals, the angels proclaim, and the Father declares valid? For even on earth children do not rightly and lawfully wed without their fathers' consent. What a bond is this: two believers who share one hope, one desire, one discipline, the same service! The two are brother and sister, fellow servants. There is no distinction of spirit or flesh, but truly they are "two in one flesh."[7] Where there is one flesh, there is also one spirit. Together they pray, together they prostrate themselves, together they fast, teaching each other, exhorting each other, supporting each other.

5. *derived the woman from the man*—see Genesis 2:21–23, which describes how God made woman from the rib of man.

6. *It is better to marry than to burn*—that is, it is better to marry than to be consumed with sexual desire (1 Corinthians 7:9).

7. *two in one flesh*—Genesis 2:24; Mark 10:8.

Side by side in the church of God and at the banquet of God, side by side in difficulties, in times of persecution and in times of consolation. Neither hides anything from the other, neither shuns the other, neither is a burden to the other. They freely visit the sick and sustain the needy. They give alms without anxiety, attend the sacrifice without scruple, perform their daily duties unobstructed. They do not have to hide the sign of the cross, or be afraid of greeting their fellow Christians, or give blessings in silence. They sing psalms and hymns to one another and strive to outdo each other in chanting to their Lord. Seeing and hearing this, Christ rejoices. He gives them his peace. "Where there are two," he also is present;[8] and where he is, there is no evil. [. . .]

John Chrysostom on Women

John Chrysostom, "Homily XX, Ephesians v.22–24," in *A Select Library of the Nicene and Post-Nicene Fathers of the Christian Church*, ed. Philip Schaff and Henry Wace (New York: Christian Literature Company, 1889), 13:143–52.

In this text by John Chrysostom, we find a rather patronizing view of wives. Here women are childish, foolish (although not evil or duplicitous), and in need of much love and condescending care.

"Wives, be subject to your own husbands, as unto the Lord. For the husband is the head of the wife, as Christ also is the head of the church being himself the savior of the body. But as the church is subject to Christ, so let wives also be subject to their husbands in everything."

A certain wise man,[9] setting down a number of things in the rank of blessings, set this also down in the rank of a blessing: "a wife agreeing with her husband." And elsewhere again he sets it down among blessings that a woman should dwell in harmony with her husband. And indeed from the beginning, God appears to have made special provision for this union; discussing the two as one, he said, "Male and female he created"; and again, "There is neither male nor female." For there is no relationship between man and man as close as that between man and wife if they be joined together as they should be. [. . .] For there is a certain love deeply seated in our nature, which imperceptibly to ourselves knits together these bodies of ours. Thus even from the very beginning woman sprang from man, and afterward from man and woman sprang both man and woman. Do you perceive the close bond and connection? [. . .]

8. *he is also present*—Matthew 18:20.
9. *wise man*—the author of Ecclesiastes.

[. . .] For there is nothing that so welds our life together as the love of man and wife. For this many will lay aside even their arms; for this they will give up life itself. And Paul would never without a reason and without an object have spent so many pains on this subject as when he says, "Wives, be subject to your husbands as to the Lord." Why so? Because when they are in harmony their children are well brought up, the domestics are in good order, and neighbors, friends, and relations enjoy the fragrance. But if it be otherwise, all is turned upside down and thrown into confusion. And just as when generals of an army are at peace with one another all things are in due subordination. If, on the other hand, they are at variance, everything is turned upside down. So, I say, is it also here. Therefore [Paul] says, "Wives, be subject to your own husbands, as to the Lord." [. . .]

Let us take as our fundamental position that the husband occupies the place of the "head," and the wife the place of the "body." [Paul says] that "the husband is the head of the wife as Christ also is the head of the church, being himself the savior of the body. But as the church is subject to Christ, let wives be subject to their husbands in everything."

[. . .] [Paul] had already laid down beforehand for man and wife the ground and provision of their love, assigning to each their proper place, to the one that of authority and forethought, to the other that of submission. As then "the church," that is, both husbands and wives, "is subject to Christ, so also wives submit yourselves to your husbands, as to God." "Husbands, love your wives, even as Christ also loved the church."

You have heard how great is the submission; you have extolled and marveled at Paul, how, like an admirable and spiritual man, he welds together our whole life. You did well. But now hear what he also requires at your hands; for again he employs the same example.

"Husbands," he says, "love your wives, even as Christ also loved the church."

You have seen the measure of obedience, hear also the measure of love. Would you have your wife obedient to you, as the church is to Christ? Then take the same provident care of her that Christ takes for the church. Indeed even if you must give up your life for her and to be cut into pieces ten thousand times; even to endure and undergo any suffering whatever—do not refuse. Even if you undergo all this, still will you not, even then, have done anything like Christ. For you indeed are doing it for one to whom you are already knit—but he for one who turned her back on him and hated him.[10] In the same way, then, as he laid at his feet the one who turned her back on him—who hated, spurned, and disdained him, not by menaces, nor by violence, nor by terror, nor by anything else

---

10. *one who turned her back on him and hated him*—a reference to the church's unfaithfulness to Christ.

of the kind, but by his unwearied affection—so also do you behave toward your wife. Even if you see her looking down on you and disdaining and scorning you, still by your great thoughtfulness for her, by affection, by kindness, you will be able to lay her at your feet. [. . .] Even if you suffer anything on her account, do not upbraid her, for neither did Christ do this. [. . .]

[. . .] Let us seek in a wife affectionateness, modest-mindedness, and gentleness—these are the characteristics of beauty. But let us not seek loveliness of person nor upbraid her upon these points over which she has no power. Rather, let us not upbraid at all (it is rude) nor let us be impatient nor sullen. Do you not see how many, after living with beautiful wives, have ended their lives pitiably, and how many who have lived with those of no great beauty have run on to extreme old age with great enjoyment? Let us wipe off the "spot" that is within, let us smooth the "wrinkles" that are within, let us do away with the "blemishes" that are on the soul. Such is the beauty God requires. Let us make her fair in God's sight, not in our own. Let us not look for wealth nor for that high-birth that is outward, but for that true nobility that is in the soul. Let no one entertain the possibility of getting rich by a wife, for such riches are base and disgraceful. No, by no means let anyone seek to get rich from this source. "For they who desire to be rich fall into a temptation and a snare and many foolish and hurtful lusts and into destruction and perdition." [. . .]

Not for the husband's sake alone is it said, but for the wife's sake also, that "he cherish her as his own flesh, as Christ also cherishes the church" [. . .] The wife is a second authority; let her not then demand equality, for she is under the head. Nor let him despise her as being subject, for she is the body, and if the head despise the body it will itself also perish. But let him offer love on his part as a counterweight to obedience on her part. For example, let the hands and the feet and all the rest of the members be given up for service to the head, but let the head provide for the body since it contains every sense in itself. Nothing can be better than this union. [. . .]

Do not let a wife say to her husband, "Unmanly coward that you are, full of sluggishness and dullness, and fast asleep! Here is such a one, a low man and of low parentage, who runs his risks, and makes his voyages, and has made a good fortune. And his wife wears her jewels and goes out with her pair of milk-white mules; she rides about everywhere, she has troops of slaves and a swarm of eunuchs,[11] but you have cowered down and live to no purpose." Let a wife not say these things nor anything like them. For she is the body—not to dictate to the head but to

---

11. *eunuchs*— castrated male servants, sometimes filling important positions in royal households and courts.

submit herself and obey. "But how," someone will say, "is she to endure poverty? Where is she to look for consolation?" Let her select and put beside her those who are poorer still. Let her again consider how many noble and high-born maidens have not only received nothing from their husbands, but have even given dowries to them and have spent their all upon them. Let her reflect on the perils that arise from such riches, and she will cling to this quiet life. In short, if she is affectionately disposed toward her husband she will utter nothing of the sort. No, she will rather choose to have him near her, though gaining nothing, than gaining ten thousand talents of gold, accompanied with that care and anxiety that always comes to wives from those distant voyages.

Neither, however, let the husband, when he hears these things, on the score of his having supreme authority, abuse and beat her. Instead, let him exhort. Let him admonish her as being less perfect. Let him persuade her with arguments. Let him never once lift his hand—far be this from a noble spirit—nor express insults or taunts or abuse. But let him regulate and direct her as lacking in wisdom. [. . .]

Show her that you set a high value on her company and that you are more desirous to be at home for her sake than in the market-place. And esteem her before all your friends and above the children who are born of her, and love these very children for her sake. If she does any good act, praise and admire it; if any foolish one (such as girls may chance to do) advise her and remind her. Condemn out and out all riches and extravagance and gently point out the ornament that there is in neatness and in modesty. Continually teach her the things that are profitable. [. . .]

Teach her these lessons [. . .] with much graciousness. For since the recommendation of virtue has in itself much that is stern (especially to a young and tender woman), whenever discourses on true wisdom are to be made contrive that your manner be full of grace and kindness. And above all banish the notion from her soul of "mine and yours." If she says the word "mine," say to her, "What things do you call yours? For in truth I know not; I for my part have nothing of my own. How then do you speak of 'my' when all things are yours?" Freely grant her the word. Do you not perceive that such is our practice with children? When we are holding something and a child snatches it and then wishes again to get hold of some other thing, we allow it and say, "Yes, and this is yours and that is yours." Let us do the same with a wife, for her temper is more or less like a child's. And if she says "mine," say, "why, everything is yours, and I am yours." Nor is the expression one of flattery, but of exceeding wisdom. Thus will you be able to abate her wrath, and put an end to her disappointment. [. . .]

Holy Women

Byzantine society recognized more male than female saints. A collection of saints' lives published in the late 900s or early 1000s, for example, includes the lives of some sixty-four male saints who lived during the 700s and 800s, but only eight female saints from the same period. The same collection includes only fourteen women from the 300s and 400s, four from the 500s, and zero from the 600s.[1] Alice-Mary Talbot, a leading scholar of Byzantine Christianity, suggests that such numbers reflect, at least to some degree, both "misogynistic attitudes" toward women and more "ambivalent" attitudes. The Byzantines, writes Talbot, found themselves torn between the Old Testament statement that God made humankind, both male and female in his image (Genesis 1:27), and the portrayal of Eve as causing original sin by succumbing to the temptation of the serpent (Genesis 3). The teachings of the New Testament sent mixed messages as well: Paul wrote that in Christ "there is no male and female" (Galatians 3:28) but at the same time taught that women should be subordinate to their husbands (Ephesians 5:22–24, Colossians 3:18), cover their heads while praying (1 Corinthians 11:5), and remain silent in church (1 Corinthians 14:34). Christ's chosen disciples were all male, but Mary was the instrument of humanity's salvation by giving birth to Christ.[2]

---

1. A. P. Kazhdan and A. M. Talbot, "Women and Iconoclasm," *Byzantinische Zeitschrift* 84–85 (1991–92), 392. Kazhdan and Talbot here reference the *Synaxarion of Constantinople*.

2. Alice-Mary Talbot, ed., *Holy Women of Byzantium: Ten Saints' Lives in English Translation* (Washington, DC: Dumbarton Oaks, 1996), x.

Although one can certainly identify misogynistic elements in the two saints' lives below, both are too complex to be characterized in their entirety with such a reductionist term. In each we encounter a woman who merits and receives reverence from holy men—men who then call on other men to emulate her example.

As we consider women's diminishing role in church leadership, it is important to read these tales as popular accounts, told with no official sanction from the church. The church in the East made no attempt during its first millennium to rule on who did or did not qualify for sainthood. Indeed, the official canonization of saints did not really begin until the late 1200s,[3] long after these tales spread and found their way to paper. Tales of a saint's miracles, visits to saints' shrines, the production of icons honoring saints, commoners and nobility entreating saints for help—these considerations rather than official proclamations determined who in the popular imagination was, indeed, a saint.

Life of St. Maria/Marinos (500s or 600s)

"The Life and Conduct of the Blessed Mary Who Changed Her Name to Marinos," trans. Nicholas Constas. © 1996, Dumbarton Oaks Research Library and Collection, Trustees for Harvard University. Originally published in *Holy Women of Byzantium: Ten Saints' Lives in Translation*, edited by Alice-Mary Talbot, pp. 7–12.

Stories of transvestite nuns—women posing as monks—were popular in Byzantium between the 400s and 800s. Nicholas Constas, the translator of the following text, notes that more than a dozen such stories have been found in Latin, Syriac, Coptic, Ethiopic, Armenian, and Arabic. (Writers in medieval Germany and France later produced their own variants.) Much like Alice-Mary Talbot, Constas suggests that these stories indicate "the ambiguities, tensions, and hostility that often comprised Early Christian attitudes toward women."

Although these attitudes are difficult to characterize without caricaturizing, women were generally perceived as having to transcend their inferior feminine nature to attain spiritual virility and manliness. In

---

3. Ruth Macrides, "Saints and Sainthood in the Early Palaiologan Period," in *The Byzantine Saint*, ed. Sergei Hackel (London: Fellowship of St. Alban and St. Sergius, 1981), 82–83.

this vertiginous conquest of manhood by woman, Maria/Marinos [the protagonist in the story below who poses as a man] is a hero of virile temperament, and at the same time a hero who suffers, voluntarily accepting marginalization, victimization, and helplessness. Ironically, her exploits suggest that the feminine element is part of the ambivalence of virile strength, and that it may serve to balance and amplify that strength, as well as subvert its authoritative claims to dominance and hegemony.[4]

Such ambivalence is evident throughout this story, in which a woman—that is, a member of the sex through whom "the devil wages war on the servants of God"—proves herself "perfect" and superior to the monks and the abbot with whom she lives.

There was a certain man named Eugenios who lived in purity, piety, and in the fear of God. He had an honorable and devout wife, who bore him a daughter whom he named Maria. When his wife died, the father raised the child with much teaching and in [the ways of] a pious life.

When the young girl grew up, her father said to her, "My child, behold, all that I own I place in your hands, for I am departing in order to save my soul." Hearing these things [said] by her father, the young girl said to him, "Father, do you wish to save your own soul and see mine destroyed? Do you not know what the Lord says? That the good shepherd gives his life for his sheep." And again she said [to him], "The one who saves the soul is like the one who created it."

Hearing these things, her father was moved to compunction at her words, for she was weeping and lamenting. He therefore began to speak to her and said, "Child, what am I to do with you? You are a female, and I desire to enter a monastery. How then can you remain with me? For it is through the members of your sex that the devil wages war on the servants of God." To which his daughter responded, "Not so, my lord, for I shall not enter the monastery as you say, but I shall first cut off the hair of my head, and clothe myself like a man, and then enter the monastery with you."

The [father], after distributing all his possessions among the poor, followed the advice of his daughter and cut off the hair of her head, dressed her in the clothing of a man, and changed her name to Marinos. And he charged her saying, "Child, take heed how you conduct yourself, for you are about to enter into the midst of fire, for a woman in no way enters a [male] monastery. Preserve yourself therefore blameless before God, so that we may fulfill our vows." And taking his daughter, he entered the cenobitic monastery.

4. Constas, in Talbot, 3.

Day by day, the child advanced in all the virtues, in obedience, in humility, and in much asceticism. After she lived thus for a few years in the monastery, [some of the monks] considered her to be a eunuch, for she was beardless and of delicate voice. Others considered that [this condition] was instead the result of her great asceticism, for she partook of food only every second day.

Eventually it came to pass that her father died, but [Maria, remaining in the monastery], [continued] to progress in asceticism and in obedience, so that she received from God the gift of healing those who were troubled by demons. For if she placed her hand upon any of the sick, they were immediately healed. [. . .]

One day [. . .] when Marinos had gone forth to service along with three other brethren, and while they were all lodging at the inn, it came to pass that a certain soldier deflowered the innkeeper's daughter, who then became pregnant. The soldier said to her, "If your father should learn of this, say that 'It was the young monk who slept with me.'" Her father, upon realizing that she was pregnant, questioned her closely, saying, "How did this happen to you?" And she placed the blame on Marinos, saying, "The young monk from the monastery, the attractive one called Marinos, he made me pregnant."

Thoroughly outraged, the innkeeper made his way to the monastery, shouting accusations and saying, "Where is that charlatan, that pseudo-Christian, whom you call a Christian?" [. . .] "I had but a single daughter, who I hoped would support me in my old age, but look at what Marinos has done to her, he whom you call a Christian—he has deflowered her and she is pregnant." The superior said to him, "What can I do for you, brother, since [Marinos] is not here at the moment? When he returns from his duties, however, I will have no recourse but to expel him from the monastery."

When Marinos returned with the three other monks, the superior said to him, "Is this your conduct, and is this your asceticism, that while lodging at the inn you deflowered the innkeeper's daughter? And now her father, coming here, has made us all a spectacle to the laity." Hearing these things, Marinos fell upon his face, saying, "Forgive me, father, for I have sinned as a man." But the superior, filled with wrath, cast him out saying, "Never again shall you enter this monastery."

Leaving the monastery, [Marinos] immediately sat down outside the monastery gate, and there endured the freezing cold and the burning heat. Thereafter, those entering the monastery used to ask him, "Why are you sitting outdoors?" To which he would reply, "Because I fornicated and have been expelled from the monastery."

When the day arrived for the innkeeper's daughter to give birth, she bore a male child, and the girl's father took the [infant] and brought it to the monastery. Finding Marinos sitting outside the gate, he threw the child down before him and said, "Here is the child that you have wickedly engendered. Take it." And immediately the innkeeper departed.

Marinos, picking up the child, was filled with distress and said, "Yes, I have received the just reward for my sins, but why should this wretched babe perish here with me?" Accordingly he undertook to procure milk from some shepherds, and so nursed the child as its father. But the distress that overwhelmed him was not all, for the child, whimpering and wailing, continually soiled [Marinos's] garments.

After the passage of three years, the monks entreated the superior saying, "Father, forgive this brother; his punishment is sufficient, for he has confessed his fault to all." But when they saw that the superior remained unmoved, the brethren said, "If you do not receive him back, then we too will leave the monastery. For how can we ask God to forgive our sins, when today marks the third year that he has been sitting in the open air beyond the gate, and we do not forgive him?"

The superior, considering these things, said to them, "For the sake of your love, I accept him." And summoning Marinos he said to him, "On account of the sin that you have committed, you are not worthy to resume your former position here. Nevertheless, on account of the brethren's love, I accept you back into our ranks, but only as the last and least of all." At this Marinos began to weep and said, "Even this is a great thing for me, my lord, for you have deemed me worthy to come inside the gate, so that I might thus be given the honor of serving the holy fathers."

Consequently the superior assigned him the lowliest chores of the monastery, and he performed them [all] scrupulously and with great devotion. But the child was forever following him about, crying and saying, "Dada, Dada," and such things as children say when they wish to eat. Thus, in addition to the [usual] trials and temptations that beset a monk, Marinos was continually anxious about procuring and providing sustenance for the child. When the boy grew up, he remained in the monastery, and having been raised in the practice of virtues he was deemed worthy of the monastic habit.

One day, after a considerable passage of time, the superior inquired of the brethren, "Where is Marinos? Today is the third day that I have not seen him singing in the choir. He was always the first to be found standing there before the start of the service. Go to his cell, and see whether he is lying ill." Going to his cell, they found him dead, and informed the superior, saying, "Brother Marinos has died." But the [superior] said, "In what state did his wretched soul depart? What defense can he make for the sin that he committed?" [Having thus spoken, the superior then] directed that [Marinos] be buried. But as they were preparing to wash him, they discovered that he was a woman, and shrieking, they all began to cry out in a single voice, "Lord, have mercy."

The superior, hearing their cries, asked them, "What troubles you so?" And they said, "Brother Marinos is a woman." Drawing near and seeing [for himself], the [superior] cast himself down at her feet, and with many tears cried out, "Forgive me, for I have sinned against you. I shall lie dead here at your holy feet until such time as I hear forgiveness for all the wrongs that I have done you." And while he was uttering many such lamentations, as well as things yet more remarkable, a voice spoke to him saying, "Had you acted knowingly, this sin would not be forgiven you. But since you acted unknowingly, your sin is forgiven."

The superior then sent [word] to the innkeeper to come and see him. When he arrived, the superior said to him, "Marinos is dead." The innkeeper replied, "May God forgive him, for he has made of my house a desolation." But the superior said to him, "You must repent, brother, for you have sinned before God. You also incited me by your words, and for your sake I also sinned, for Marinos is a woman." Hearing this, the innkeeper was astonished and wondered greatly at his words. And the superior took the innkeeper and showed him that [Marinos] was a woman. At this [the innkeeper] began to lament and to marvel at what had happened.

They buried her holy remains and placed them in blessed caskets,[5] all the while glorifying God with psalms and hymns. When these things were completed, the innkeeper's daughter appeared, possessed by a demon, and confessing the truth that she had been seduced by the soldier. And she was immediately healed at the tomb of the blessed Maria, and everyone glorified God because of this sign, and because of [Maria's] patient endurance, for she vigorously endured [her trials] until death, refusing to make herself known. Let us then, beloved, zealously emulate the blessed Maria and her patient endurance, so that on the day of judgment we may find mercy from our Lord Jesus Christ, to whom belongs glory and dominion to the ages of ages. Amen.

Life of St. Maria of Egypt (ca. 600s)

"The Life of St. Mary of Egypt, the Former Harlot, who in Blessed Manner Became an Ascetic in the Desert of the [River] Jordan," trans. Maria Kouli. © 1996, Dumbarton Oaks Research Library and Collection, Trustees for Harvard University. Originally published in *Holy Women of Byzantium: Ten Saints' Lives in Translation*, edited by Alice-Mary Talbot, pp. 70–93.

Numerous tales of "repentant harlots"—sexually depraved women who denounced their lascivious ways to become model ascetics—originated in Syria, Palestine, and Egypt between the 300s and the 600s.

5. *caskets*—the editors note that the plural may be nothing more than a poetic device, or it may refer to a "double casket," with an inner casket make of wood and an outer one of lead.

This tale may or may not be the work of Sophronios, patriarch of Jerusalem from 634 to 638. (An earlier version of this story can be found in a manuscript dating from the early to mid-500s.) We do not know whether Maria, the protagonist, ever existed. But the tale made its way throughout the Eastern Mediterranean into Europe, where it can be found in medieval manuscripts from Spain, France, and Italy. Maria Kouli, the translator of our version, attributes the tale's broad appeal to its subject matter (a woman with a voracious sexual appetite), its exotic locale (a desert populated by lions), and its simple, accessible style.[6]

The story opens with a monk, Zosimas, wandering in the desert during the forty days of Lent, that is, the time of reflection and penance leading up to Easter. While praying and chanting psalms, he spots a "shadowy illusion of a human body," which he pursues and overtakes, discovering a "naked figure whose body was black, as if tanned by the scorching of the sun." Zosimas learns the figure's name, Maria, and asks her to tell her life story, repeatedly pressing her for details of what turns out to be a sordid past.

These voyeuristic elements offer a certain amount of titillation, but they also serve a more serious function, namely demonstrating God's boundless grace in the face of "great shame and humiliation." Maria's transformation manifests itself in her miraculous powers—an ability to walk on water and a gift for reading minds—yet she is not perfect; she still struggles with lust. Grace rescues her from her past, but she continues to battle and work toward salvation, leaning heavily on her "guarantor and protector," the Virgin Mary. She is, in this respect, a very human saint.

We join the story as Maria narrates her life to Zosimas.

[...] "My homeland, [dear] brother, was Egypt. When my parents were still alive and I was twelve years old, I rejected my love for them and went to Alexandria. I am ashamed to think about how I first destroyed my own virginity, and how I then threw myself entirely and insatiably into the lust of sexual intercourse. But now [I feel] it is more decent for me to speak openly about what I shall briefly describe, so that you may become aware of my lust and love of pleasure. For more than seventeen years—please forgive me—I was a public temptation to licentiousness, not for payment, I swear, since I did not accept anything, although men often wished to

6. Kouli, in Talbot, 65–68.

pay me. I simply contrived this so that I could seduce many more men, thus turning my lust into a free gift. You should not think that I did not accept payment because I was rich, for I lived by begging and often by spinning coarse flax fibers. The truth is that I had an insatiable passion and uncontrollable lust to wallow in filth. This was and was considered to be my life, to insult nature [with my lust]." [. . .]

"I saw some young men standing at the seashore, about ten or more, vigorous in their bodies as well as in their movements, who seemed to me fit for what I sought (they were apparently awaiting their fellow passengers, while others had already embarked on the ships). I rushed shamelessly into their midst, as was my habit. 'Take me where you are going,' I said, 'surely you will not find me useless.' Then, uttering other even more obscene words, I made everyone laugh, while they, seeing my penchant for shamelessness, took me and brought me to the boat they had prepared for the voyage. [. . .]

"How can I possibly describe to you what followed, my dear man? What tongue can declare, or what ears can bear to hear what happened on the boat and during the journey [that followed] and the acts into which I forced those wretched men against their will? There is no kind of licentiousness, speakable or unspeakable, that I did not teach those miserable men. I am truly surprised, my father, how the sea endured my profligacy, and how the earth did not open its mouth to draw me alive down to Hades, as one who had ensnared so many souls! But, as it seemed, God sought my repentance, for he desires not the death of the sinner, but remains patient waiting for his conversion." [. . .]

They reach Jerusalem.

"At early dawn I saw everybody hurrying to the church[7] and off I went, running along with those who were running. So, I came with them to the courtyard of the church. When the time came for the divine Exaltation [of the Cross],[8] I tried to join the crowd and force my way to the entrance, pushing [my way] forward but being pushed back. Eventually, with great trouble and grief—wretched woman [that I am]—I approached the door through which one entered the church where the life-giving cross was displayed. But as soon as I stepped on the threshold of the door, all the other people entered unhindered, while some kind of divine

---

7. *the church*—likely the Church of Constantine on Golgotha, where wood from the "true cross" was housed.

8. *Exaltation [of the Cross]*—the Exaltation of the Holy Cross is a feast commemorating the Empress Helena's discovery in Jerusalem of the "true cross" on which Christ was crucified. Celebrated on 14 September.

power held me back, not allowing me to pass through the entrance [of the church]. [. . .]

"After this happened three or four times, I became fatigued and no longer had the strength to push and be pushed back, for my body was exhausted as a result of my violent effort. So I gave up and went back and stood at the corner of the courtyard of the church. Only then did I realize the cause that prevented me from laying eyes on the life-giving cross, for a salvific word touched the eyes of my heart, showing me that it was the filth of my actions that was barring the entrance to me. Then I began to cry, lamenting and beating my breast, raising sighs from the depths of my heart. As I was crying, I saw the icon of the all-holy Mother of God standing above the place where I stood. I looked straight at her and said, 'Virgin Lady, you who gave flesh to God the Word by birth, I know, I know well that it is neither decent, nor reasonable for me who is so filthy and utterly prodigal, to look upon your icon, you the ever-virginal, the chaste, you who are pure and un-dented in body and soul. For it is right that I, the prodigal woman, should be hated and abhorred by you who are pure. But since, as I heard, God to whom you gave birth became man for this reason, in order to summon sinners to repentance, help me, a lone woman who has no one to help her. Command that I, too, may be allowed to enter the church.' [. . .]

"As soon as I spoke these words I received the fire of faith just like some kind of assurance, and being encouraged by the compassion of the Mother of God, I moved from that place where I stood praying and returned and joined those people who were entering [the church]. No longer did anyone push me this way and that, nor did anyone prevent me from approaching the door through which they entered the church. Indeed, I was filled with a shivering fear and astonishment, shaking and trembling all over. [. . .] I threw myself to the ground—wretched woman [that I was]—and after I kissed that holy ground, I rushed out eagerly to [the Virgin], who had stood as guarantor for me. So I came to that place where the bond of guarantee was signed and, kneeling in front of the ever-virgin Mother of God, I said the following words: 'O, my lady, you who love goodness has shown me your love for mankind, for you did not abhor the prayers of an unworthy woman. I saw the glory that we prodigal people rightly cannot see. Glory be to God, who accepts through you the repentance of sinners.' [. . .] While I was saying these words, I heard someone crying aloud from afar, 'If you cross the [river] Jordan, you will find a fine place of repose.'"

Maria leaves the church and speaks to a bread-seller.

"'Which is the way and direction, my good man, that leads to the river Jordan?' When I learned which gate of the city leads out to that place, I passed through it at a run and began my journey filled with tears. Then I asked [the way] again and again, and went on walking for the rest of the day—I think it had been the third hour of the day when I saw the [holy] cross—and around sunset I arrived at the Church of John the Baptist, which was very near the [river] Jordan. After I prayed in the church, I immediately walked down to the Jordan and washed my face and hands with its holy water. Then I partook of the undefiled and life-giving sacraments in the Church of the Precursor,[9] ate half a loaf of bread, drank water from the Jordan, and spent the night lying on the ground. The next day I found a small boat there and crossed [the river] to the opposite bank. Once more, I asked my guide[10] to lead me wherever she pleased. So I came to this desert, and since then to this day I have fled afar off and lodged in this [wilderness], waiting for my God, who delivers those who return to Him from distress of spirit and tempest. [. . .]

"I crossed the Jordan carrying two and a half loaves of bread, which little by little dried up and became hard as rock. In this way I survived for years eating those [loaves] in small portions. [. . .]

"[F]or seventeen years I wandered in this desert struggling with those irrational desires, as if with wild beasts. Whenever I tried to take some food, I yearned for meat and fish that abound in Egypt. I longed to drink wine, which was [constantly] in my thoughts, for I used to drink a lot of wine when I was living in the world. But since I did not have even water to drink here, I was burning with terrible thirst and could not endure its deprivation. Also an irrational desire for lascivious songs entered my mind, always disturbing me profoundly and trying to seduce me into singing the demonic songs that I have learned. But immediately I would shed tears and beat my breast with my hand, and remind myself of the agreement I made when I came out to the desert. In my mind I would stand in front of the icon of the Mother of God, my guarantor, and I would weep before her, asking her to chase away those thoughts that assailed my miserable soul in this way. When I had shed enough tears and had beaten my breast as hard as I could, I used to see light shining everywhere around me. From that moment on, after that storm, I would feel constant tranquility deep inside me. [. . .]

"After I consumed those loaves of bread, as I said before, during those seventeen years, I [then] fed myself with wild plants and whatever else can be found in the desert. [. . .] I have endured cold and again the flames of summer, scorching in the burning heat and freezing and shivering in the frost, so that many times I collapsed to the ground and remained there scarcely breathing or moving. The fact is that I have struggled against many and various calamities and unbearable temptations. But from that

9. *Church of the Precursor*—the Church of John the Baptist.
10. *my guide*—the Virgin.

day until now the power of God has preserved my sinful soul and humble body in many ways." [. . .]

Maria asks Zosimas to return to his monastery, to say nothing about their encounter, and then to meet her again in a year, bearing bread and wine so she can receive the Eucharist. He does as she instructs and returns a year later to the bank of the Jordan River, where he spots her approaching from the other side.

Then he saw her making the sign of the holy cross over the Jordan—for, as he told us, there was a full moon that night—and at the same time she set foot on the water and walked on it, approaching him. When he wished to make obeisance,[11] she prevented him, crying aloud as she walked on the water, "What are you doing, revered father, you who are a priest and holding the divine gifts?" As he complied with her words, she stepped out of the water and said to the monk, "Bless me, father, bless me." He answered her trembling with fear, for he was astonished at that extraordinary sight, "Indeed, God spoke the truth when he promised that those who purify themselves liken themselves to God as much as is possible." [. . .]

Then she said to the monk, "Forgive me, father, but I beg you, fulfill one more wish of mine. Under the protection of God's grace return now to the monastery, and come again next year to that dry streambed where I met you before." [. . .] "Pray in the name of the Lord. Pray for me and remember my wretchedness." [. . .] She once more made the sign of the cross over the Jordan, stepped upon the water and walked across exactly as before. [. . .]

When [another] year passed, he went again to the desert [. . .] and ran to meet that extraordinary marvel. [. . .] [H]e reached the place that had the form of a dry streambed, and saw the blessed woman lying dead on its eastern slope, her hands folded in the proper manner and her body lying in such a way that she was facing toward the east. He ran up to her and bathed the feet of the blessed woman with his tears, for he did not dare to touch any other part [of her body].

After he wept for some time and recited psalms appropriate to the occasion, he offered a funerary prayer and said to himself, "Is it proper to bury the remains of the blessed woman? Would the blessed woman approve of this?" While he was saying these words, he saw some writing impressed on the ground beside her head, where the following words had been written: "Father Zosimas, bury the body of the humble Maria in

---

11. *make obeisance*—to bow in respect.

this place. Return dust to dust, and pray always to the Lord for me." [. . .] When the monk read these words he was overjoyed, for he had learned the name of the blessed woman. He realized that as soon as she had received the divine sacrament at the [river] Jordan, she came immediately to this place, where she died. In fact, the distance Zosimas had covered in twenty days[12] of laborious walking Maria had traversed in one hour, and had then departed straightway to God. [. . .]

A lion approaches, and Zosimas is terrified.

He made the sign of the cross, trusting that the power of the [holy woman], who was lying dead, would keep him safe. The lion in turn began to fawn upon the monk, thus not only greeting him with the movements of its body, but also showing its intentions. Then Zosimas said to the lion, "Since, wild beast, that great woman entrusted me with the burial of her dead body, and as I am an old man and do not have the strength to dig a pit (for I do not have the proper digging tool I need), and since I cannot walk back such a long distance to get a suitable tool, do what is necessary with your claws, so that we may return to the earth the body of the blessed woman." As soon as he said these words, the lion dug with its front paws a pit deep enough for the burial of her body. [. . .]

Zosimas returns to his monastery.

He narrated in detail everything from the beginning, so that all who heard the marvels of God were astonished and celebrated the blessed woman's memorial service with awe and affection. Moreover, John the father superior found certain people [in the monastery] who were in need of correction, so that even in this respect the blessed woman's words did not prove futile or fruitless. As for Zosimas, he died in that monastery when he was almost a hundred years old.

The monks continued to pass on these events by word of mouth from one generation to the other, presenting them as a model [of ascetic life], to benefit those who wish to listen. [. . .]

12. *twenty days*—Kouli notes that the preservation of Maria's body for such a long period provides another sign of her holiness.

PART II

Growth and Schisms

Holy Objects

S ome Orthodox theologians cite Mark 5:25–29 for proof that divine power can reside in items associated with holy people.

Now there was a woman who had been suffering from hemorrhages for twelve years. She had endured much under many physicians, and had spent all that she had; and she was no better, but rather grew worse. She had heard about Jesus, and came up behind him in the crowd and touched his cloak, for she said, "If I but touch his clothes, I will be made well." Immediately her hemorrhage stopped; and she felt in her body that she was healed of her disease." (NRSV)

A relic, such as Jesus's cloak in this story, is any physical object deemed to possess divine power, and which thus merits veneration. Relics may be personal items such as clothing; parts of a saint such as bones, bone fragments, hair, or entire bodies; pieces of the cross on which Christ was crucified; drinking vessels; etc. An "incorrupt" relic is a human body that has not decayed, that is, a body miraculously exempt from natural decomposition because of the dead person's holiness.

Roman Catholic and Eastern Orthodox theologians carefully distinguish between *latria* (Greek *latreia*)—a type of worship that should be offered only to God—and *dulia* (Greek *douleia*)—reverence for or veneration of icons and relics. Icons and relics may be venerated, but they should never be worshipped. To worship an icon or relic is to fall prey to idolatry.

Yet pilgrims traveling to visit relics often showed less interest in such distinctions than did theologians, and concern about improper worship prompted sporadic and largely ineffective efforts to discourage

171

veneration. Such efforts proved no match for the intensity of popular devotion and endorsements from church fathers—Basil of Caesarea, John Chrysostom, Gregory of Nazianzus, and Gregory of Nyssa. Today Eastern Orthodox churches sanction the veneration of relics, while regulating how and when bodies may be exhumed and how relics should be transported and displayed.

As we've noted in discussions about incarnational theology (the belief that God united himself with the fleshly person of Jesus), Eastern Christians never found it difficult to believe that God and God's grace can imbue matter. Incarnational theology is thus key to understanding the veneration of relics. The bodies of saints and items associated with saints—permeated with God's presence, thanks to the saints' participation in God's grace—can acquire a measure of the supernatural power that Christ himself possessed. The Russian Orthodox theologian Sergei Bulgakov (1871–1944) put it as follows:

> From the dogmatic point of view, the veneration of relics (as well as that of the icons of saints) is founded on a faith in a special connection between the spirit of the saint and his human remains, a connection that death does not destroy. In the case of the saints the power of death is limited; their souls do not altogether leave their bodies, but remain present in spirit and in grace in their relics, even in the smallest portion. The relics are bodies already glorified in earnest of the general resurrection, although still awaiting that event. They have the same nature as that of the body of Christ in the tomb, which, although it was dead and awaiting the resurrection, deserted by the soul, still was not altogether abandoned by his divine spirit.[1]

Tale of the Holy Places, of the City of Constantine (ca. 1389–1391)

"Tale of the Holy Places, of the City of Constantine, and of the Holy Relics Preserved in Jerusalem and Collected by the Emperor Constantine in the Aforementioned Imperial City." © 1984, Dumbarton Oaks Research Library and Collection, Trustees for Harvard University. Originally published in *Russian Travelers to Constantinople in the Fourteenth and Fifteenth Centuries*, edited by George Majeska, pp. 128–37.

As the center of the Byzantine Empire, Constantinople naturally became a center for relics, and churches throughout the city amassed

---

1. Sergius Bulgakov, *The Orthodox Church*, trans. Lydia Kesich (Crestwood, NY: St. Vladimir's Seminary Press, 1988), 124–25.

large collections. Relics of the Virgin Mary became especially popular; various churches claimed to own her spindle, her girdle, her robe— even her breast milk.

The following text comes to us from an ancient guidebook, a travel planner for pilgrims. Although it purports to be authored by a Russian pilgrim familiar with Constantinople, it is in all likelihood an amalgam of multiple sources. Note, for example, the abrupt switch after the first paragraph from the first to the third person; other textual evidence suggests that the Russian text may be a translation from an unknown Greek original.

Because I was in Constantinople, named by God the "Imperial City," sinful and unworthy servant of God that I am, and saw awesome wonders—how an icon of the most holy Mother of God works miracles, granting healing to the sick, and how those saints whose bodies repose there perform miracles, healing the sick, delivering from misfortune, and cleansing from sin—because I have seen this, sinful servant of God, I have written it down for the attention of true-believing Christians. [. . .]

You enter [the church of] St. Sophia [in Constantinople] from the narthex by the central west doors on the right. The doors of Noah's ark[2] and the iron chain that the Apostle Paul bore[3] are near the doors on the left; here there is much healing for Christians. Christians worship at these doors, for healing comes from them. There is a miraculous icon of the Savior high above the doors; this Savior heals many sick. A candelabrum with an iron chain hung before this Savior; attached to the chain was a little glass with oil. Beneath the little glass stands a stone pedestal with a cup and wood from Noah's ark bound with iron from the ark on the pedestal. Oil dripped into this cup from the candelabrum; the little glass with the oil came loose and [fell], breaking the cup in two and splitting the stone pedestal. The little glass did not break, however, and the oil did not spill.[4] This pedestal is bound with iron bands, with the cup attached to it so that Christians may see it and the sick be cured. From there you go straight to the sanctuary and the life-giving cross, since the life-giving cross on which they crucified the Lord is there in the sanctuary. The stone pedestal on which Christ sat as he conversed with the Samaritan woman[5]

2. *Noah's ark*—tradition holds that these doors were manufactured out of wood from Noah's ark.

3. *iron chain . . .* —worn by Paul during one of the times he was in prison for proselytizing.

4. *glass did not break . . .* —a miraculous occurrence.

5. *Samaritan woman*—see John 4:5–15.

at the well is in an oratory[6] on the right there. [. . .] If you go farther into the corner of the church on the right-hand side of the altar, leaning against the rear wall is the iron pallet on which St. George and St. Nicetas were roasted.[7] There at the end of the pallet is a stone chest on a pedestal. The relics of the forty martyrs[8] and of the fourteen thousand infants[9] are in this chest. Christians worship at this pallet and chest, for healing comes from them. [. . .]

Miracle of the True Cross (ca. 545)

Procopius, *History of the Wars, Books I and II*, trans.
H. B. Dewing (New York: Macmillan, 1914), 1:355–57.

The Byzantine historian Procopius (ca. 500–ca. 565) described a piece of "the true cross," which could be found in the city of Apamea in northwestern Syria.

[. . .] Now there is a piece of wood one cubit[10] in length in Apamea, a portion of the cross on which the Christ in Jerusalem once endured punishment not unwillingly, as is generally agreed, and which in ancient times had been conveyed there secretly by a man of Syria. And the men of olden times, believing that it would be a great protection both for themselves and for the city, made for it a wooden chest and deposited it there;

6. *oratory*—a small chapel or place for prayer.

7. *St. George and St. Nicetas were roasted*—Majeska notes that the author perhaps confuses his saints. He probably has in mind St. Lawrence of Rome (ca. 225–258), a deacon to whom, according to legend, the holy grail (the cup from which Christ drank at the last supper) was entrusted. When a Roman prefect demanded that Lawrence turn over the grail and other treasures, he refused and was grilled to death on a gridiron.

8. *forty martyrs*—soldiers purportedly killed by Licinius, Constantine's rival for the Roman throne.

9. *fourteen thousand infants*—Matthew 2:16–18 reports that King Herod (ca. 73–74 BCE), a Jewish king in Judea governing on behalf of the Romans, grew distressed over reports about a new "king of the Jews," that is, Jesus, being born in Bethlehem. According to Matthew, he thus ordered that all boys in Bethlehem under the age of two be murdered. Tradition holds that more than ten thousand children were killed (fourteen thousand in this account). Some scholars believe that no more than twenty children under the age of two may have lived in Bethlehem at that time.

10. *one cubit*—approximately 46 centimeters.

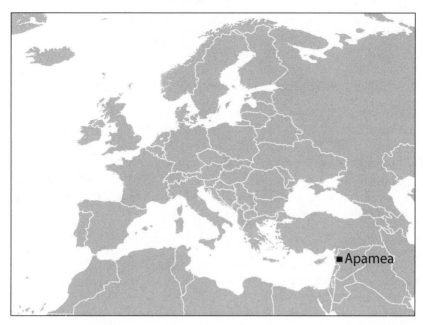

Figure 14. Apamea

and they adorned this chest with much gold and with precious stones and they entrusted it to three priests who guard it in all security; and they bring it forth every year and the whole population worships it during one day. Now at that time the people of Apamea, upon learning that the army of the Medes[11] was coming against them, began to be in great fear. And when they heard that Chosroes[12] was absolutely untruthful, they came to Thomas, the chief priest of the city, and begged him to show them the wood of the cross, in order that after worshiping it for the last time they might die. And he did as they requested. Then indeed it befell that a sight surpassing both description and belief was there seen. For while the priest was carrying the wood and showing it, above him followed a flame of fire, and the portion of the roof over him was illuminated with a great and unaccustomed light. And while the priest was moving through every part of the temple, the flame continued to advance with him, keeping constantly the place above him in the roof. So the people of Apamea, under the spell of joy at the miracle, were wondering and rejoicing and weeping, and already all felt confidence concerning their safety. And

11. *Medes*—Persians.

12. *Chosroes*—King Khosrau I of Persia (531–579), who waged war against the Byzantines in Syria.

Thomas, after going about the whole temple, laid the wood of the cross in the chest and covered it, and suddenly the light had ceased.

Relics in Constantinople (ca. 1105 or 1106)

Einar Joranson, "The Problem of the Spurious Letter of Emperor Alexius to the Court of Flanders," *American Historical Review* 55 No. 4. (July 1950): 815.

Seeking military aid for Constantinople against pagan invaders, the Byzantine emperor Alexius (1081–1118) in the early 1100s cited his city's relics as one reason the count of Flanders owed Constantinople his assistance.

Therefore, before Constantinople is captured by [the invaders], you most certainly ought to fight with all your strength so that you may joyfully receive in Heaven a glorious and ineffable reward. For it is better that you should have Constantinople than the pagans, because in that [city] are the most precious relics of the Lord, to wit: the pillar to which he was bound; the lash with which he was scourged; the scarlet robe in which he was arrayed; the crown of thorns with which he was crowned; the reed he held in his hands, in place of a scepter; the garments of which he was despoiled before the cross; the larger part of the wood of the cross on which he was crucified; the nails with which he was affixed; the linen cloths found in the sepulcher after his resurrection; the twelve baskets of remnants from the five loaves and the two fishes; the entire head of St. John the Baptist with the hair and the beard; the relics or bodies of many of the innocents,[13] of certain prophets and apostles, of martyrs and, especially, of the protomartyr[14] St. Stephen,[15] and of confessors and virgins, these latter being of such great number that we have omitted writing about each of them individually. Yet all the aforesaid the Christians rather than the pagans ought to possess; and it will be a great muniment[16] for all Christians if they retain possession of all these, but it will be to their detriment and doom if they should lose them. [. . .]

13. *the innocents*—children killed by Herod, king of Judea, who, according to Matthew 2:13–18, ordered the death of boys two years old and younger in his attempt to kill the Christ child.

14. *protomartyr*—first martyr for the faith.

15. *St. Stephen*—the evangelist mentioned in the book of Acts who was stoned to death for preaching the Gospel.

16. *muniment*—means of defense.

St. Sophia as a Miraculous Church (early 1200s)

Robert of Clari, *The Conquest of Constantinople,* trans.
Edgar Holmes McNeal (New York: Columbia University Press, 1936), 106–7.

This text does not describe relics, but rather the miraculous powers associated with a holy place, in this case the church of Hagia Sophia in Constantinople.[17] The text is by Robert of Clari, a knight from northern France who fought in the infamous siege of Constantinople in 1204. (See the section "Fourth Crusade" below.)

The church of Saint Sophia was entirely round, and within the church there were domes, round all about, which were borne by great and very rich columns, and there was no column that was not of jasper[18] or porphyry[19] or some other precious stone, nor was there one of these columns that did not work cures. There was one that cured sickness of the reins when it was rubbed against, and another that cured sickness of the side,[20] and others that cured other ills. [. . .]

On the ring of the great door of the church, which was all of silver, there hung a tube,[21] of what material no one knew; it was the size of a pipe such as shepherds play on. This tube had such virtue as I shall tell you. When an infirm man who had some sickness in his body like bloat, so that he was bloated in his belly, put it in his mouth, however little he put it in, when this tube took hold it sucked out all the sickness and it made the poison run out of his mouth and held him so fast that it made his eyes roll and turn in his head, and he could not get away until the tube had sucked all the sickness out of him. And the sicker a man was the longer it held him, and if a man who was not sick put it in his mouth, it would not hold him at all, much or little. [. . .]

17. See section 9, "Architecture—Hagia Sophia," in the online supplement.

18. *jasper*—a reddish-brown quartz.

19. *porphyry*—a reddish igneous rock with crystals.

20. *sickness of the reins . . . sickness of the side*—a kidney illness . . . appendicitis.

21. *a tube*—Edgar Holmes McNeal notes that scholars can only speculate about this tube. The term may refer to the spout on some kind of vessel. One scholar has suggested that the tube connected to an air pump, which priests used to feign the miracle described here.

Missions to the North: Balkans and Rus'

Although missionary efforts by the Eastern churches between the 1100s and the early 1700s pale when compared with those of the Roman Catholic Church and subsequent Protestant denominations,[1] it is important to remember that Eastern missionaries are responsible for the very existence of Eastern Christianity in much of the world. Byzantine missionaries engaged in vigorous proselytization during the 700s, 800s, and 900s.

Authorized missionary activity among the Slavs can be traced back to a dispute between a Moravian prince (ruling what is now the Czech Republic, Slovakia, Hungary, southern Poland, western Romania, and northern bits of Croatia and Serbia) and a Germanic emperor.

Some history is in order. Prince Rastislav of Moravia (846–870) owed his position to the support of the Germanic emperor, Louis the German (843–876), who personally selected and brought Rastislav to power in 846, expecting him to behave as a compliant and faithful subject.

He did not.

When Rastislav refused to comply with a number of German demands, Louis responded to the upstart's ingratitude by attacking Moravia in 855. The attack failed, but it did ignite in Rastislav an abiding fear of and resentment toward German influence in his country.

Rastislav particularly resented Germanic, or "Frankish," missionaries, whom he viewed as vehicles for Louis's meddling in Moravia.

---

1. See section 30, "Orthodoxy in the Diaspora: Missions to Alaska," in the online supplement.

Figure 15. European territory inhabited by East Slavic tribes, 700–850

Seeking a counterweight, he invited Constantinople in 863 to send its own missionaries to Moravia, hoping that close ties with the Byzantine Empire would protect his realm from the bullying Germanic Franks. (Frankish missionaries, like most missionaries from the West, insisted that their converts adopt the Latin liturgy celebrated throughout Frankish lands.) Loath to permit the Latinization of his country, Rastislav embraced Byzantine missionaries willing to bring the Gospel to his Slavic subjects in their own language.

Byzantium, in turn, had something to gain by supplying Rastislav with missionaries: it viewed Moravia as a potential ally against Bulgaria. The Bulgarians—Asiatic nomads who settled in the Balkans during the mid-600s—had adopted the Slavic language and local customs as they built their community into a significant military force. The Byzantines worried that the Bulgarians might form a

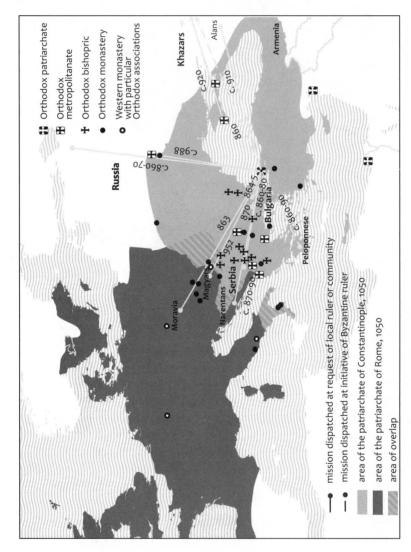

Figure 16. Byzantine missions, 800s and 900s

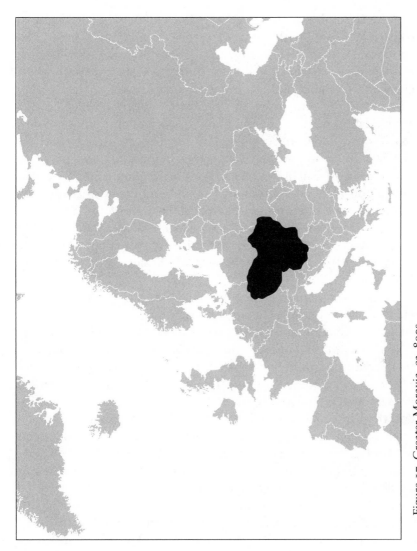

Figure 17. Greater Moravia, ca. 890s

union with the Franks, posing an even more formidable threat to the Byzantine Empire than did the Franks alone. A Byzantine-Moravian alliance might offset this threat. Byzantium thus hoped to Christianize Moravia rather than wait for missionaries from the Franks to do the same.

So the Byzantine emperor, Michael III (842–867), dispatched two brothers, Kirill and Methodius, as missionaries to Moravia in 863, the same year Rastislav filed his request. Before departing, Kirill translated the New Testament and some liturgical texts into Slavonic—a remarkable feat since the Slavs had no written language and no alphabet: Kirill first had to create an alphabet (see below), which he may have modeled on a cursive form of the Greek alphabet.

Kirill's translation of scripture facilitated Christianity's relatively quick spread among the Slavs. Such translations, however, triggered abundant skepticism in Rome: most of Christendom at the time read scripture only in Latin, Greek, or Hebrew, and Frankish clergy condemned the new translations as heretical. Pope Adrian II (867–872), however, appreciated the success of Kirill and Methodius's work: he approved the translations, endorsed education for the Slavic clergy, and in 869 formally appointed Methodius as an archbishop of the Slavs.

Around this time, another important ethnic group entered the scene unbidden. Scandinavian Vikings, or "Varangians," who in the 750s had conquered areas in what is now northwestern Russia, began moving south toward Byzantium. How, exactly, the Scandinavians came to rule the Slavic tribes in northwestern Russia—the Rus'[2]—is a matter of fierce debate. (Some Russian chronicles wishfully imagine that the Varangians were "invited.") We do know, however, that by the mid-800s, the Varangians controlled a loose alliance of tribes, including a settlement in Kiev. In 860, three years before Kirill and Methodius left for Moravia, two Varangian chieftains—Askold and Dir—laid siege to Constantinople, plundering the villages and monasteries that surrounded the city. (The attack upon the city itself failed.)

Such "contact" introduced the Rus' to Byzantine Christianity. Within a few years, converts in Kievan Rus' (the region around Kiev that expanded mostly west, north, and east) had grown so numerous that Photios, the patriarch of Constantinople (858–867, 878–886), dispatched a bishop to the Rus'. (Photios was determined to expand

---

2. In discussions below we use *the Rus'* to reference Slavic tribes and people and *Rus'* (more formally *Kievan Rus'*) to reference the region they inhabited.

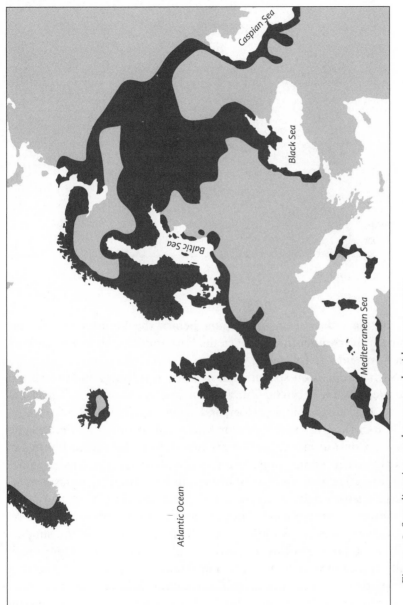

Figure 18. Scandinavian settlements and raids, 700s–1000s

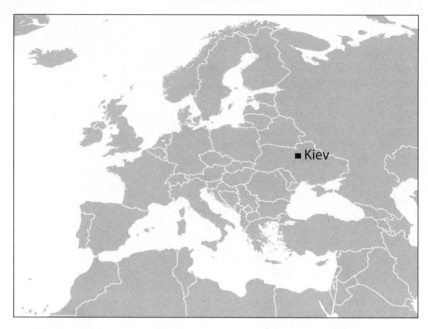

Figure 19. Kiev

Byzantine influence in this region before the Latins could do the same.) The competition between the East and West to win Slavic converts was now in full swing.

Such competition spawned all manner of disputes and ill will. An excellent example can be found in Bulgaria's conversion to Christianity in 864. It is a complex story, and some background is helpful.

In 857 the Byzantine emperor Michael III deposed Patriarch Ignatius of Constantinople (846–857, 867–878) and installed Photios in his place. The Roman pope Nicholas I (858–867) refused to recognize Photios, a layman, as a lawful bishop. In his refusal Nicholas also asserted his own right to oversee all affairs of the church.

However, Pope Nicholas hinted that if Constantinople would return some territory Rome had lost, he might recognize the supposedly unsuitable Photios as patriarch after all. Nicholas optimistically took the first step, approving Photios's appointment with the expectation of a territorial quid pro quo. (Nicholas had his eye on the province of Illyricum in the Balkans, a region that spanned unchristianized territory in Bulgaria and seemed a prime field for missionary work.) Photios, however, did not reciprocate, and Nicholas grew enraged.

Meanwhile, the Bulgarian tsar Boris I (852–889) was toying with the idea of adopting Christianity in his realm. Sensing an opportunity in the dispute between Nicholas and Photios, he corresponded with both Rome and Constantinople, playing the two sides against one another and provoking what would become known as the Photian Schism.[3]

In 866 Pope Nicholas dispatched an epistle to Boris, criticizing a number of practices in the Greek church and warning about the dangers of associating with Greek missionaries. The epistle infuriated the Greeks since they considered Bulgaria a rightful part of their (not Rome's) ecclesiastical territory. Photios responded by calling a council in 867 that condemned the pope's action.

But Photios's ambitions extended well beyond Bulgaria.[4] He was determined to exert Byzantine influence throughout the Slavic world, and in the 860s he dispatched a bishop to Kiev. We do not know how successful this bishop was; in fact, we find little solid evidence of Christianity in Rus' until the reign of Prince Igor (913–945), who, if not baptized himself, was at least sympathetic toward Christianity. After Igor's death, his wife Olga consented to be baptized, sometime between the years 946 and 960.

Several motives probably prompted Olga's conversion. Certainly she viewed her new faith as an opportunity to strengthen ties and foster trade between Rus' and Byzantium. It is likely that Olga expected the Greeks to appoint a bishop in Kiev, since the Bulgarian church had received its own patriarch in 927. When Constantinople did not, Olga sent ambassadors to the Franks requesting clergy. The dispatched clergy, however, did not fare well: resistance from local pagans as well as from a Christian community now accustomed to a liturgy in Slavonic prompted a backlash, and the missions failed.

Christianity became the official religion of Rus' in 988 with the baptism of Olga's grandson, Prince Vladimir. According to the *Primary Chronicle*,[5] a tale probably more fiction than fact, Vladimir sought a religion capable of uniting the turbulent and fractious tribes of Rus'. He dispatched envoys to the Muslim Turks, the Germans, and the Greeks in the hope of finding such a religion. He finally settled on

3. See section 18.4, "Photian Schism," in the online supplement.

4. See document 18.4.1, "Pope Nicholas I on Papal Jurisdiction," in the online supplement.

5. See document 10.3, "Tales from *The Russian Primary Chronicle*," in the online supplement.

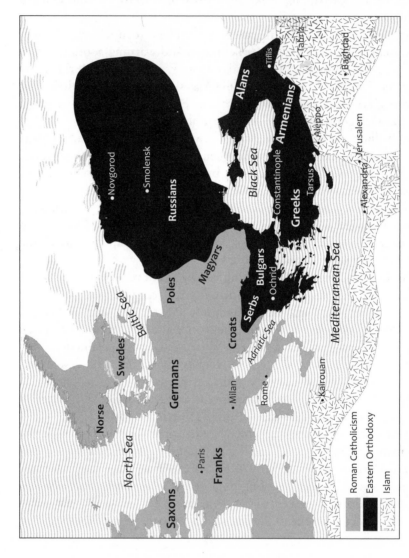

Figure 20. Christianity and the Slavs, ca. 1000

Christianity as practiced by the Byzantine church, an unsurprising choice given the history of trade between Kiev and Constantinople. Vladimir must also have noted that the Rus' were historically more receptive to the Greek faith than to its Latin counterpart, largely because of the familiar sound of Church Slavonic.

In sum, the conversions of Moravia, Bulgaria, and Rus' were part and parcel of the political machinations rulers adopted to unite their subjects under a common religion and to link their realms to the powerful Byzantine Empire. Moravians, Bulgarians, and the Rus' valued their autonomy; but they saw in Byzantium an accommodating ally and a protector, which would allow them to worship in their native tongue while staving off unwanted attention from the Franks.

But as Rus' grew into Russia and established itself as a powerful Christian nation in its own right, this desire for autonomy would evolve into aggressive claims for influence over other nations, including a bold assertion that Moscow was now the center of Orthodox Christianity.

Kliment Okhridski (ca. 840–916) on Kirill, Missionary to the Slavs

Kliment Okhridski, "Life and Acts of Our Blessed Teacher Konstanin the Philosopher, the First Enlightener of the Slavic Tribe," trans. Spass Nikolov, in *Kiril and Methodius: Founders of Slavonic Writing, A Collection of Sources and Critical Studies,* ed. Ivan Duichev (Boulder, CO: East European Monographs, 1985), 72–75, 78.

The next two texts provide some of the best extant information about the lives of Kirill (here "Konstantin") and Methodius, Byzantine missionaries to the Slavs. The author, Kliment Okhridski, served as a disciple to both Kirill/Konstantin and Methodius, and he joined their missions to Moravia. After the deaths of his mentors, Okhridski played a leading role in educating local clergy in the Slavic language and in fighting Germanic influence in the region.

Okhridski here recounts Kirill/Konstantin's creation of a new alphabet and the controversy that ensued over the translation of scripture into the vernacular. As noted earlier, Kirill/Konstantin and Methodius eventually won the support of Pope Adrian II, despite strong opposition from other clergy in the West.

**It is important to remember that these tales were composed to pro-
mote a religious message; Okhridski did not consider himself bound
by modern standards of historical research.**

[. . .] The Moravian prince, Rastislav, at the inspiration of God, held
counsel with his barons and the Moravians sent envoys to Emperor Michael[6] with these words: "Our people have discarded the heathen ways
and hold the Christian law, but we have no teacher to instruct us in our
own tongue in the true Christian faith, so that other countries, seeing this,
might do as we did. Therefore, master, send us such a bishop and teacher,
because from you there always comes a good law for all countries."

The emperor held counsel, sent for Konstantin [Kirill] the philosopher,
let him hear this plea, and told him: "I know, philosopher, how fatigued
you are; but it is necessary that you go there for none else could do this
task like you." The philosopher replied, "Though I am fatigued and ailing
in my body, I will gladly go there, only provided they have an alphabet in
their language." [. . .]

The philosopher retired to his hermitage and, as was his wont, devoted
himself to prayer along with his disciples. And God, who listens to the
prayers of his servants, soon revealed this to him and he immediately
composed the alphabet and began to write the evangelical text, "In the
beginning was the word, and the word dwelt with God, and the word
was God."[7] [. . .]

[The emperor] sent the philosopher on this mission with many gifts,
writing such a missive to Rastislav: "God whose will it is that all men
should come to know the truth and raise themselves into a higher dignity, on seeing your faith and your diligence, has made for the fulfillment
of your desire by inventing now in our days letters in your language—
something that has been until now, but only in the very first days so that
you too may affiliate yourselves to the great nations that praise the Lord
in their own language. And now we are sending you this man to whom
God revealed these letters, a man righteous, pious and a philosopher of
great learning. Receive him as you would a gift greater and dearer than
gold and silver, than jewels and fleeting earthly riches." [. . .]

And when [Konstantin] arrived in Moravia, Rastislav received him
with great honors and after gathering disciples for him, gave them to
him to be tutored. And over a brief spell of time he translated the whole
ecclesiastical canon and taught them the matins,[8] the hourly prayers, the

6. *Emperor Michael*—Michael III, emperor of Byzantium from 842 to 867.
7. *In the beginning . . .* —John 1:1.
8. *matins*—a liturgy conducted at night; usually set to end at daybreak.

vespers,[9] the post-vespers and the liturgy. And then according to the prophetic words, "The ears of the deaf were unstopped," and they heard the words of the scriptures, "and the man who stammers spoke plain." And God was pleased with this, and the devil was disgraced.

And when the divine teaching began to spread, the wicked and [. . .] envious, trebly-accursed devil could not suffer this good deed to be successful; but, entering into his own vessels,[10] began to stir many, saying, "God is not to be praised in this way. If that were pleasing to God, could he not have made it so as from the very beginning that they might write speech with letters of their own, and thus praise the Lord? But he only chose three languages—Hebrew, Greek, and Latin—in which it is seemly to give praise to the Lord." This was spoken by the Latin clerics, prelates, priests, and their disciples. The philosopher fought them as David fought the gentiles. Having overcome them with the word of the scripture, he called them trilinguals, or trebly-heathen, or Pilates, since Pilate[11] had written the inscription on the cross of the Lord in three languages. [. . .]

And spending forty months in Moravia, [Konstantin] went to ordain his disciples. And on his way he was received by Kotsel, the prince of Panonia,[12] who, strongly desirous to master the Slavonic lore, gave him some fifty disciples to be taught in the new learning. And paying him great homage, he sent him along his way. And the philosopher, preaching the Gospel without charge, took from Rastislav and Kotsel neither gold, nor silver, nor anything else, but only begged from them nine hundred captives and set them free.

And when he was in Venice, there fell upon him bishops, priests, and monks, like crows upon a falcon, who raised the trilingual-trebly-heathen heresy, saying, "Tell us, man, how is it that you now invent books for the Slavs, and teach them? None has so far invented such books [. . .] We only know of three languages in which it is becoming to praise God with books: Hebrew, Greek, and Latin." And the philosopher answered: "Does not God send rain on the just and the unjust alike? And does not the sun rise on the evil and on the good?" Do not we all breathe the air equally? How come you are not ashamed to single out only three tongues, leaving all other tribes and peoples deaf and blind? Tell me, do you think God powerless to give them this, or do you think him envious and loathe to give it? We on our part know of many peoples who have books and give praise to God each in its own tongue. [. . .]

9. *vespers*—evening prayer of thanksgiving.

10. *entering into his own vessels*—entering into his own people.

11. *Pilate*—Pontius Pilate, who conducted Jesus's trial.

12. *Panonia*—territory that includes portions of present-day Austria, Croatia, Hungary, Serbia, Slovenia, Slovakia, and Bosnia and Herzegovina.

And when the pope in Rome heard of him, he sent for him to come to Rome. [. . .] And the pope, having received the Slavic books, consecrated them and placed them in the church of the Virgin Mary, which is called "the manger." Then the pope commanded the two bishops Formosa and Gauderik to ordain the Slav disciples. And after they were ordained, mass was forthwith celebrated in the Slavonic language at the Church of the Holy Apostle Peter. [. . .]

The Glagolitic Alphabet

We do not know with certainty whether the Cyrillic alphabet, variants of which are used today in Slavic countries, or the Glagolitic alphabet came first. (The text above does not tell us which alphabet Kirill concocted; it is possible he invented both.) Although the letters of the Cyrillic and Glagolitic alphabets look quite different, they contain approximately the same number of letters and identical sound values for letters, strongly suggesting a common origin. Even the casual observer will immediately recognize that the Cyrillic alphabet is based on the Greek alphabet. Cyrillic also incorporated letters from Hebrew, for which Greek has no equivalent.

Figure 21. Croatia and Montenegro

Figure 22. Passage from the Gospel of Mark in the Zograf Codex, ca. late 900s to early 1000s

We know that the Glagolitic alphabet appeared in Moravia with the Slavic liturgy in the second half of the 800s. The Cyrillic alphabet eventually displaced the Glagolitic in eastern Slavic lands, but the Glagolitic remained important for some time in the West, where the pope made special allowances for its use. It can still be found today in the liturgies of some communities in Dalmatia (western Croatia) and Montenegro.

Part of the Zograf Codex (shown here), dated to the 900s or early 1000s, is written with the Glagolitic alphabet. It was found in 1843 at the Zograf Monastery on Mount Athos in northeastern Greece.

Iconoclastic Controversy

I t is difficult to overstate the importance in Eastern Orthodoxy of icons—artistic representations of Christ, the saints, prophets, evangelists, martyrs, angels, and the Mother of God.[1] Iconographers craft these pictures to remind observers of the pictures' holy prototypes and the prototypes' qualities that merit emulation. As such, icons aid in prayer, spiritual reflection, and the pursuit of holiness.

We know little about the origins of icons. Tradition holds that the author of the Gospel of Luke painted the first icon. A popular legend speaks about the icon of the Mandilion, a piece of cloth imprinted with the image of Christ. According to one variant of this tale, popular in Byzantium, Christ pressed his face onto a piece of linen, imprinting his image on the cloth, which he sent to King Abgar of Edessa (in what is now southeastern Turkey) to heal the king of an illness. This *acheiropoietoi* icon (an icon "not made by hands," that is, created not from the handiwork of any artist) is said to be the basis for subsequent *acheiropoietoi* icons, or icons in which artists modeled Christ's face on the image first imprinted on the linen.

Although the earliest surviving icons date only from the 500s, written documents from the 300s mention them. Eusebius (ca. 263–339), for example, reports seeing icons of Christ and his apostles. By the 600s icons were ubiquitous in the Byzantine Empire. They appeared

---

1. Fiona Nicks and Jean Maurice Gouillard ("Iconoclasm," 7:280–83) and Lynn Jones ("Icon," 7:278–80) provide concise histories of icons and iconoclasm, from which this introduction borrows, in *New Catholic Encyclopedia* (Detroit: Thomson/Gale, 2003).

in churches, hanging individually on walls and collectively on screens, or iconostases, that separated church sanctuaries from the naves. Icons occupied prominent places in private homes. Soldiers carried them into battle and priests carried them aloft in religious processions. Commoners believed they cured illness, warded off evil, and facilitated miracles.[2]

Icons also spawned tremendous controversy. Critics characterized claims about their miraculous powers as naive and even blasphemous. How, some theologians asked, could one possibly reconcile iconography with the first commandment? "You shall not make for yourself an idol, whether in the form of anything that is in Heaven above, or that is on the earth beneath, or that is in the water under the earth. You shall not bow down to them or worship them; for I the Lord your God am a jealous God" (Exodus 20:4–5, NRSV). Eusebius and the theologian Origen (ca. 185–ca. 254) both warned against attempts to depict Christ. Such warnings, however, had little effect during the early centuries of the church: iconography flourished.

This all changed dramatically when the state inserted itself into such debates in the early 700s. Around 724 two bishops in Asia Minor won the support of the Byzantine emperor Leo III (717–741) in condemning the veneration of images. The condemnation appalled Patriarch Germanus I (715–730). How, Germanus asked, could the state denounce such a long-standing practice?

Emperor Leo, for his part, was not at all pleased to find the patriarch questioning his authority. He demanded that Germanus sign a document condemning images of the saints, a demand tantamount to demanding Germanus's resignation, which Germanus tendered in 730. Leo ordered that the icon of Christ hanging over the main palace gate in Constantinople be removed. Byzantine officials destroyed countless icons, crosses, and relics. Despairing monks denounced what they considered an unforgivable sacrilege, but most of the church's leaders acquiesced.

We can only speculate about Leo's motives. Some scholars believe he acted out of fear, inspired by the military successes of Islamic tribes—a now-constant threat to the Byzantine Empire—whose prohibition against human figures in art may have suggested to Leo a divine preference for those who opposed images. Why risk violating God's order to Moses about images (see Exodus 20:4–5, quoted

2. See section 12, "Icons: Aesthetics and Forms," in the online supplement.

above) when God's protection is so badly needed against invaders who themselves scrupulously obey this order? Others note that Leo's family came from a region populated by Monophysites, whose insistence on a single, divine nature in Christ called into question any depiction of his human form. Fiona Nicks and Jean Maurice Gouillard argue that a series of disasters—a volcanic eruption in 726 and territorial losses to the Slavs, Avars, and Arabs—may have persuaded Leo that iconography had prompted God's wrath.[3]

John of Damascus (ca. 676–749) Defends Icons

John of Damascus, *On the Divine Images*, trans. David Anderson
(Crestwood, NY: St. Vladimir's Seminary Press, 1980), 15–33, 52–53, 58–62.
Used by permission of St. Vladimir's Seminary Press.

During Leo's attacks on icons, John of Damascus—a representative of the Jerusalem patriarch, who supported icons—issued a carefully reasoned and theologically astute defense. (The iconoclasts [those who opposed icons] spent little time during this era crafting theological arguments of their own.)

The crux of John's argument derives from his unquestionably Orthodox theology of the incarnation. If God became man—that is, if God assumed flesh and blood and became visible in the person of Christ—then why can we not paint an image of God in the flesh? The invisible God became visible in Christ; Christ himself thus validated physicality and the depiction of that physicality. The incarnation is a recognition that humans need tangible representation of the intangible.

John directly refutes charges that iconography equals idolatry by distinguishing between "veneration" (*latreia*), that is, the honor one pays to icons; and "adoration" (*douleia*), that is, the worship that God alone merits. In venerating icons, John argues, "I do not worship matter." Instead, I *venerate* the icon and in so doing "worship the creator of matter who became matter for my sake, who willed to take his abode in matter; who worked out my salvation in matter."

· First Apology ·

[. . .]

4. I heed the words of him who cannot deceive: "The Lord our God, the Lord, is one," and, "You shall adore the Lord your God, and worship

3. Nicks and Gouillard, "Iconoclasm," 7:281.

him alone," and, "You shall not have strange gods." "You shall not make for yourself a graven image or any likeness of anything that is in Heaven above, or that is in the earth beneath," and, "All worshippers of images are put to shame, who make their boast in worthless idols." And again, "The gods who did not make the heavens and the earth shall perish from the earth and from under the heavens." In this way and in a similar manner God spoke in times past to the fathers by the prophets, but last of all in these days he has spoken to us by his only-begotten Son, by whom he made the ages. He says: "This is eternal life, that they know you, the only true God, and Jesus Christ, whom you have sent." I believe in one God, the source of all things, without beginning, uncreated, immortal and unassailable, eternal, everlasting, incomprehensible, bodiless, invisible, uncircumscribed,[4] without form. I believe in one superessential being, one Godhead greater than our conception of divinity, in three persons: Father, Son, and Holy Spirit, and I adore him alone. I worship one God, one Godhead, but I adore three persons: God the Father, God the Son made flesh, and God the Holy Spirit, one God. I do not adore the creation rather than the creator, but I adore the one who became a creature, who was formed as I was, who clothed himself in creation without weakening or departing from his divinity, that he might raise our nature in glory and make us partakers of his divine nature. Together with my king, my God and Father, I worship him who clothed himself in the royal purple of my flesh, not as a garment that passes away, or as if the Lord incarnate constituted a fourth person of the Trinity—God forbid! The flesh assumed by him is made divine and endures after its assumption. Fleshly nature was not lost when it became part of the Godhead, but just as the word[5] made flesh remained the word, so also flesh became the word, yet remained flesh, being united to the person of the word. Therefore I boldly draw an image of the invisible God, not as invisible, but as having become visible for our sakes by partaking of flesh and blood. I do not draw an image of the immortal Godhead, but I paint the image of God who became visible in the flesh, for if it is impossible to make a representation of a spirit, how much more impossible is it to depict the God who gives life to the spirit?

5. Now some say that God commanded Moses the lawgiver: "You shall worship the Lord your God, and adore him alone," and, "You shall not make yourself a graven image, or any likeness of anything that is in Heaven above, or that is in the earth beneath."

They truly are in error, brothers, for they do not know the scriptures, that the letter kills, but the spirit gives life. They do not find in the written word its hidden, spiritual meaning. I can justly say to those people:

---

4. *uncircumscribed*—without limits.

5. *word*—John 1:1 refers to Jesus before his incarnation as "the Word."

he who teaches you this will also teach you the following. Listen to the lawgiver's interpretation, which you read in Deuteronomy: "The Lord spoke to you out of the midst of the fire; you heard the sound of words but saw no form; there was only a voice." And shortly thereafter: "Take good heed to yourselves. Since you saw no form on the day that the Lord spoke to you at Horeb out of the midst of the fire, beware lest you act corruptly by making a graven image for yourself, in the form of any figure, the likeness of male or female, the likeness of any beast that is on the earth, or the likeness of any bird that flies in the air." And again, "Beware lest you lift up your eyes to Heaven, and when you see the sun and the moon and the stars, all the host of Heaven, you be drawn away and worship them and serve them."

6. You see that the one thing aimed for is that no created thing can be adored in place of the creator, nor can adoration be given to any save him alone. Therefore to worship him always means to offer him adoration. For again he says: "You shall have no other gods before me. You shall not make for yourself a graven image, or any likeness of anything that is in Heaven above, or that is on the earth beneath. You shall not worship them or adore them, for I am the Lord your God." And again, "You shall tear down their altars, and dash in pieces their pillars, and burn their Asherim[6] with fire; you shall hew down the graven images of their gods, for you shall not worship other gods." And again, "You shall make for yourself no molten gods."

7. You see that he forbids the making of images because of idolatry, and that it is impossible to make an image of the immeasurable, uncircumscribed, invisible God. For "You heard the sound of words, but saw no form; there was only a voice." This was Paul's testimony as he stood in the midst of the Areopagus:[7] "Being then God's offspring, we ought not to think that the deity is like gold, or silver, or stone, a representation by the art and imagination of man."

8. These commandments were given to the Jews because of their proneness to idolatry. But to us it is given, on the other hand, as Gregory the Theologian[8] says, to avoid superstitious error and to come to God in the knowledge of the truth; to adore God alone, to enjoy the fullness of divine knowledge, to attain to mature manhood, that we may no longer be children, tossed to and fro and carried about with every wind of doctrine. We are no longer under custodians, but we have received from God the ability to discern what may be represented and what is uncircumscript.[9]

---

6. *Asherim*—plural of Asherah, a fertility goddess and mother of the Canaanite god Baal.

7. *Areopagus*—the "hill of Ares" in Athens where the court of justice met.

8. *Gregory the Theologian*—Gregory of Nazianzus (329–389).

9. *uncircumscript*—unlimited.

"You cannot see my form," the scripture says. What wisdom the lawgiver has! How can the invisible be depicted? How does one picture the inconceivable? How can one draw what is limitless, immeasurable, infinite? How can a form be given to the formless? How does one paint the bodiless? How can you describe what is a mystery? It is obvious that when you contemplate God becoming man, then you may depict him clothed in human form. When the invisible one becomes visible to flesh, you may then draw his likeness. When he who is bodiless and without form, immeasurable in the boundlessness of his own nature, existing in the form of God, empties himself and takes the form of a servant in substance and in stature and is found in a body of flesh, then you may draw his image and show it to anyone willing to gaze upon it. Depict his wonderful condescension, his birth from the virgin, his baptism in the Jordan, his transfiguration on Tabor, his sufferings that have freed us from passion, his death, his miracles that are signs of his divine nature, since through divine power he worked them in the flesh. Show his saving cross, the tomb, the resurrection, the ascension into the heavens. Use every kind of drawing, word, or color. Fear not; have no anxiety; discern between the different kinds of worship. Abraham bowed down to the sons of Hamor, men who had neither faith nor knowledge of God, when he bought the double cave intended to become a tomb.[10] Jacob bowed to the ground before Esau, his brother, and also before the tip of his son Joseph's staff. He bowed down, but he did not adore. Joshua, the son of Nun, and Daniel bowed in veneration before an angel of God, but they did not adore him. For adoration is one thing, and that which is offered in order to honor something of great excellence is another. [. . .]

11. Again, visible things are corporeal models that provide a vague understanding of intangible things. Holy scripture describes God and the angels as having descriptive form, and the same blessed Dionysius[11] teaches us why. Anyone would say that our inability immediately to direct our thoughts to contemplation of higher things makes it necessary that familiar everyday media be utilized to give suitable form to what is formless, and make visible what cannot be depicted, so that we are able to construct understandable analogies. If, therefore, the word of God, in providing for our every need, always presents to us what is intangible by clothing it with form, does it not accomplish this by making an image using what is common to nature and so brings within our reach that for which we long but are unable to see? A certain perception takes place in the brain, prompted by the bodily senses, which is then transmitted to the

10. *sons of Hamor* . . . —Abraham bestowed honor upon the owners of the cave by bowing to them.

11. *Dionysius*—Dionysius the Areopagite, or "pseudo-Dionysius," an anonymous, fifth-century theologian.

faculties of discernment, and adds to the treasury of knowledge something that was not there before. The eloquent Gregory says that the mind
that is determined to ignore corporeal things will find itself weakened
and frustrated. Since the creation of the world the invisible things of God
are clearly seen by means of images. We see images in the creation that,
although they are only dim lights, still remind us of God. For instance,
when we speak of the holy and eternal Trinity, we use the images of the
sun, light, and burning rays; or a running fountain; or an overflowing
river; or the mind, speech, and spirit within us; or a rose tree, a flower,
and a sweet fragrance. [. . .]

   14. Worship is the means by which we show reverence and honor. Let
us understand that there are different degrees of worship. First of all there
is adoration, which we offer to God, who alone by nature is worthy to be
worshipped. Then, for the sake of him who is by nature to be worshipped,
we honor his friends and companions, as Joshua, the son of Nun, and
Daniel bowed in worship before an angel, or as David[12] venerated God's
holy places, when he says, "Let us go to his dwelling place; let us worship
at his footstool," or as when the people of Israel once offered sacrifices
and worshipped in his tent,[13] or encircled the temple in Jerusalem, fixing
their gaze upon it from all sides and worshipping as their kings had commanded, or as Jacob bowed to the ground before Esau, his elder brother,
and before pharaoh, the ruler whose authority was established by God.
Joseph's brothers prostrated themselves in homage on the ground before
him. Other worship is given to show respect, as was the case with Abraham [. . .].[14] Either do away with worship completely, or else accept it in
the manner and with the esteem it deserves. [. . .]

   16. In former times God, who is without form or body, could never be
depicted. But now when God is seen in the flesh conversing with men, I
make an image of the God whom I see. I do not worship matter; I worship the creator of matter who became matter for my sake, who willed
to take his abode in matter; who worked out my salvation through matter. Never will I cease honoring the matter that wrought my salvation! I
honor it, but not as God. How could God be born out of things that have
no existence in themselves? God's body is God because it is joined to his
person by a union that shall never pass away. The divine nature remains
the same; the flesh created in time is quickened by a reason-endowed soul.

---

   12. *Joshua . . . Daniel . . . David*—major righteous figures from Hebrew
scripture.

   13. *tent*—perhaps a reference to the Hebrew tabernacle, the holy place of worship the Israelites carried as a tent during their journey from Egypt through the
wilderness to the promised land.

   14. *Jacob . . . Joseph . . . Abraham*—more righteous figures from Hebrew
scripture.

Because of this I salute all remaining matter with reverence, because God has filled it with his grace and power. Through it my salvation has come to me. Was not the thrice-happy and thrice-blessed wood of the cross matter? Was not the holy and exalted mountain of Calvary[15] matter? What of the life-bearing rock, the holy and life-giving tomb, the fountain of our resurrection,[16] was it not matter? Is not the ink in the most holy Gospel-book matter? Is not the life-giving altar made of matter? From it we receive the bread of life![17] Are not gold and silver matter? From them we make crosses, patens,[18] chalices! And over and above all these things, is not the body and blood[19] of our Lord matter? Either do away with the honor and veneration these things deserve, or accept the tradition of the church and the veneration of images. [. . .]

17. We use all our senses to produce worthy images of him, and we sanctify the noblest of the senses, which is that of sight. For just as words edify the ear, so also the image stimulates the eye. What the book is to the literate, the image is to the illiterate. Just as words speak to the ear, so the image speaks to the sight; it brings us understanding. For this reason God ordered the ark[20] to be constructed of wood that would not decay, and to be gilded outside and in, and for the tablets to be placed inside, with Aaron's staff and the golden urn containing the manna,[21] in order to provide a remembrance of the past, and an image of the future. Who can say that these were not images, heralds sounding from far off? They were not placed aside in the meeting-tent, but were brought forth in the sight of all the people, who gazed upon them and used them to offer praise

15. *Cavalry*—where Christ was crucified.

16. *life-bearing rock . . . life-giving tomb . . . fountain of our resurrection* — referring to the tomb in which Jesus was buried and from which he was resurrected.

17. *bread of life*—in John 6:35 Jesus declares, "I am the bread of life. Whoever comes to me will never be hungry, and whoever believes in me will never be thirsty" (NRSV).

18. *paten*—small plate for holding bread during the Eucharist.

19. *body and blood*—a reference to the Eucharist, Christians' commemoration of Christ's death on the cross by eating bread (representing Christ's body) and drinking wine (representing Christ's blood). See the description in Matthew 26:27–28 of Jesus's "last supper" with his disciples.

20. *ark*—ark of the covenant, a chest described in the book of Exodus that contained the stone tablets on which were inscribed the Ten Commandments and other holy items.

21. *manna*—according to both the Hebrew books of Exodus and Numbers (and the Qur'an), God miraculously provided the Israelites with "manna," a flaky food that appeared on the ground like frost, during their sojourn in the wilderness.

and worship to God. Obviously they were not adored for their own sake, but through them the people were led to remember the wonders of old and to worship God, the worker of wonders. They were images serving as memorials; they were not divine, but led to the remembrance of divine power. [. . .]

19. Some would say: Make an image of Christ and of his mother, the Theotokos,[22] and let that be enough. What foolishness! Your own impious words prove that you utterly despise the saints. If you make an image of Christ, and not of the saints, it is evident that you do not forbid images, but refuse to honor the saints. You make images of Christ as one who is glorified, yet you deprive the saints of their rightful glory, and call truth falsehood. The Lord says, "I will glorify those who glorify me." The divinely inspired apostle[23] writes, "So through God you are no longer a slave but a son, and if a son, then an heir." And "if children, then heirs, heirs of God and fellow heirs with Christ, provided we suffer with him in order that we may also be glorified with him." You are not waging war against images, but against the saints themselves. St. John the Theologian,[24] who leaned on the breast of Christ, says "We shall become like him." Just as something in contact with fire becomes fire not by its own nature, but by being united, burned, and mingled with fire, so it is also, I say, with the assumed flesh of the Son of God. By union with his person, that flesh participates in the divine nature and by this communion becomes unchangeably God; not only by the operation of divine grace, as was the case with the prophets, but by the coming of grace himself. The scripture calls the saints gods, when it says, "God has taken his place in the divine council; in the midst of the gods he holds judgment." St. Gregory interprets these words to mean that God takes his place in the assembly of the saints, determining the glory due each. The saints during their earthly lives were filled with the Holy Spirit, and when they fulfill their course, the grace of the Holy Spirit does not depart from their souls or their bodies in the tombs, or from their likenesses and holy images, not by the nature of these things, but by grace and power.

20. God told David[25] that through his son a temple would be built, and that his resting-place would be prepared. As the books of Kings tell us, Solomon,[26] while he was building the temple, also made the cherubim. "And he overlaid the cherubim with gold and carved all the walls of the house roundabout with carved figures of cherubim and palm trees

22. *Theotokos*—God-bearer: the Virgin Mary.

23. *divinely inspired apostle*—Paul.

24. *St. John the Theologian*—the author of the Gospel of John.

25. *David*—one of Israel's great kings, "a man after [God's] own heart" (1 Samuel 13:14, NRSV), whom the Gospels identify as an ancestor of Jesus.

26. *Solomon*—the son of King David, known for his exceptional wisdom. Another of Israel's great kings.

and open flowers, in the inner and outer rooms." Is it not even better to adorn the Lord's house with holy forms and images, instead of beasts and plants? What has become of this law that declares "You shall make for yourself no graven image?" Solomon was given the gift of wisdom, and built the temple, the image of Heaven. He made the likenesses of bulls and lions, which the law forbade. Now if we make images of Christ, and images of the saints, which are filled with the Holy Spirit, will they not increase our reverence? [. . .]

21. We depict Christ as our king and lord, then, and do not strip him of his army. For the saints are the Lord's army. If the earthly emperor wishes to deprive the Lord of his army, let him also dismiss his own troops. If he wishes in his tyranny to refuse due honor to these valiant conquerors of evil, let him also cast aside his own purple.[27] For if the saints are heirs of God and co-heirs with Christ they will also share in the divine glory and dominion. If they have partaken of Christ's sufferings, and are his friends, shall they not receive a share of glory from the church on earth? "No longer do I call you servants," God says, "but I have called you friends." Shall we strip them of the glory given them by the church? What audacity! What effrontery of mind, to fight with God, refusing to follow his commands! You who refuse to bow before images also refuse to bow before the Son of God who is the living image of the invisible God, and his unchanging likeness. I bow before the images of Christ, the incarnate God; of our lady, the Theotokos and mother of the Son of God; and of the saints, who are God's friends. In struggling against evil they have shed their blood; they have imitated Christ who shed his blood for them by shedding their blood for him. [. . .]

24. If you speak of pagan abuses, these abuses do not make our veneration of images loathsome. Blame the pagans, who made images into gods! Just because the pagans used them in a foul way, that is no reason to object to our pious practice. Sorcerers and magicians use incantations and the church prays over catechumens;[28] the former conjure up demons while the church calls upon God to exorcise the demons. Pagans make images of demons that they address as gods, but we make images of God incarnate, and of his servants and friends, and with them we drive away the demonic hosts. [. . .]

· Second Apology ·

[. . .]

5. If we attempted to make an image of the invisible God, this would be sinful indeed. It is impossible to portray one who is without body:

27. *purple*—the color of royalty, hence John suggests it is better for an emperor to forfeit his throne than to refuse "due honor" to icons.

28. *catechumens*—new Christians, not yet baptized and still receiving instruction in the faith.

invisible, uncircumscribed, and without form. Again, if we made images of men and believed them to be gods, and adored them as if they were so, we would be truly impious. We do neither of these things. But we are not mistaken if we make the image of God incarnate, who was seen on earth in the flesh, associated with men, and in his unspeakable goodness assumed the nature, feeling, form, and color of our flesh. For we yearn to see how he looked, as the apostle says, "Now we see through a glass darkly." Now the icon is also a dark glass, fashioned according to the limitations of our physical nature. Though the mind wear itself out with effort, it can never cast away its bodily nature. [. . .]

11. If anyone should dare to make an image of the immaterial, bodiless, invisible, formless, and colorless Godhead, we reject it as a falsehood. If anyone should make images to give glory, honor, and worship to the devil and his demons, we abhor them and deliver them to the flames. Or if anyone makes idols of men, birds, reptiles, or any creature, we anathematize[29] him. Just as the holy fathers pulled down the temples and altars of the demons, and raised churches on the same spot that they named for the saints whom we honor, so also they threw down the images of demons, and instead raised up the images of Christ, the Theotokos, and the saints. Even under the old dispensation, Israel never built temples named for men or celebrated the memory of men. The human race was under the curse, and death was the condemnation, and the source of grief. A corpse was reasoned to be unclean; likewise anyone who touched it. But since divine nature has assumed our nature, we have been given a life-bearing and saving remedy, which has glorified our nature and led it to incorruption. Therefore we celebrate the death of the saints; churches are built in their honor, and their icons are painted. [. . .]

12. What right have emperors to style themselves lawgivers in the church? What does the holy apostle say? "And God has appointed in the church first apostles, second prophets, third teachers and shepherds, for building up the body of Christ." He does not mention emperors. And again, "Obey your leaders and submit to them; for they are keeping watch over your souls, as men who will have to give account." And again, "Remember your leaders, those who spoke to you the word of God; consider the outcome of their life, and imitate their faith." Emperors have not preached the word to you, but apostles and prophets, shepherds and teachers. When God gave commands to David concerning the house David intended to build for him, he said to him, "You may not build a house for my name, for you are a warrior and have shed blood." "Pay all of them their dues," the Apostle Paul says, "taxes to whom taxes are due, revenue to whom revenue is due, respect to whom respect is due, honor to whom honor is due." Political prosperity is the business of emperors;

29. *anathematize*—to curse or to relinquish to Satan.

the condition of the church is the concern of shepherds and teachers. Any other method is piracy, brothers. Saul rent Samuel's cloak,[30] and what was the consequence? God tore the kingdom away from him, and gave it to David the meek. Jezebel pursued Elijah,[31] who escaped her clutches, but the day came when pigs and dogs would lick up her blood, and her body would be trampled by horses. Herod killed John,[32] but worms ate Herod. And in our own day blessed Germanus,[33] a shining example by his words and deeds, is punished with exile, and with him how many more bishops and fathers whose names are unknown? Is this not piracy? When the scribes and Pharisees surrounded our lord, supposedly to listen to his teaching, and questioned him, "Is it lawful to pay taxes to Caesar, or not?" He answered them, "Bring me a coin." And when they had brought it he said, "Whose likeness and inscription is this?" They said, "Caesar's." Then he said to them, "Render therefore to Caesar the things that are Caesar's, and to God the things that are God's." We will obey you, O emperor, in those matters that pertain to our daily lives: payments, taxes, tributes; these are your due and we will give them to you. But as far as the government of the church is concerned, we have our pastors, and they have preached the word to us; we have those who interpret the ordinances of the church. We will not remove the age-old landmarks that our fathers have set, but we keep the tradition we have received. For if we begin to erode the foundations of the church even a little, in no time at all the whole edifice will fall to the ground.

The arguments of John of Damascus did not immediately win the day. Emperor Leo III's successor, Constantine V (743–775), sanctioned new persecutions against iconophiles (defenders of, or literally "lovers of," icons). He summoned a council of Byzantine bishops to his palace, where the bishops equated pictures with idols and argued that representing Christ in a human body suggested a false separation of his human nature from his divine nature. The council, held in Constantinople, declared itself to be an "ecumenical" council, but Eastern churches today do not recognize the council as valid.[34]

30. *Saul rent Samuel's cloak*—an example from scripture of a king tearing a prophet's coat.

31. *Jezebel pursued Elijah*—an example from scripture of an evil queen pursuing a prophet.

32. *Herod killed John*—an example from scripture of a king killing a prophet.

33. *Germanus*—patriarch of Constantinople (715–730), who defended the veneration of images in defiance of Emperor Leo III.

34. See document 11.1, "Council of Constantinople on Images," in the online supplement.

The persecution of iconophiles increased after the Council of Constantinople. Andrew of Crete, an iconophilic monk, was executed around 762. Emperor Constantine V, who summoned the council condemning icons, seized monasteries that housed iconophiles, paraded disobedient monks in the Hippodrome, and replaced generals in the army whose loyalty he questioned.

Such persecution moderated significantly after the death of Constantine V in 775 and ceased entirely when Empress Irene assumed the throne in 797. Irene had always supported iconography in private; now she found herself in a position to support it officially. When she was regent, she appointed a loyalist as patriarch in 784 and summoned an ecumenical council in 786 to overturn the work of the previous Council of Constantinople (754). Opposition from the army, however, frustrated her plans.

A second council met successfully in Nicaea in 787.[35] Irene's favorite, Patriarch Tarasius, ran roughshod over the opposition, admitting iconoclastic bishops to the council's deliberations only after they renounced their views. The council insisted that the veneration of icons was not akin to idol worship.[36]

Irene's reforms did not last. The Byzantine army, a breeding ground for iconoclastic fervor, supported the rise to the imperial throne in 813 of the iconoclastic Leo V (813–820).

Leo's ethnicity, Armenian rather than Greek, troubled many in the empire, particularly in the monasteries. Leo almost completely alienated the monasteries when he dismissed the iconophilic patriarch and forced the church's synod to annul the Second Council of Nicaea.

The Iconoclastic Views of Leo V (813–820)

Deno John Geanakoplos, *Byzantium: Church, Society, and Civilization Seen through Contemporary Eyes* (Chicago: University of Chicago Press, 1984), 157. Used by permission of The University of Chicago Press.

As noted above we do not know with certainty why Leo opposed the veneration of icons so fiercely. Yet the following text, written by Leo, suggests that his concerns stemmed from worry about the health of his empire and his own well-being.

35. See document 11.2, "The Second Council of Nicaea on Icons," in the online supplement.

36. See ibid. for the council's statement.

Why are the Christians suffering defeat at the hands of the pagans?[37] It seems to me it is because the icons are worshipped and nothing else. And [for this reason] I intend to destroy them. For you see that those emperors who accepted and worshipped them died either as a result of exile or in battle. But those alone who have not worshipped them died each one in his own bed and after death were buried with honor in the imperial tombs at the church of the holy apostles. Thus I too wish to imitate these latter emperors and destroy the icons in order that I and my son may live for a long time and our line may reign until the fourth and fifth generation.

Such views prompted vituperative attacks from iconophiles. The most fiery, perhaps, was Theodore "the Studite," abbot of the venerable Studios monastery in Constantinople. In response to Leo's actions Theodore commanded the monks in his charge to march through the monastery's vineyard holding icons above their heads so those passing by on the other side of the monastery's walls could see them. Leo V rebuked Theodore, which only emboldened him to write to friends throughout the empire, airing his grievances with Leo. To nobody's surprise, Leo exiled Theodore to a remote fortress in Bithynia (in what is now northwestern Turkey), from where he composed polemics refuting his iconoclastic foes.[38]

The views of John of Damascus and Theodore the Studite eventually triumphed. When Empress Theodora (815–867) became regent on behalf of her son in 842, she restored images, a decision that would never again be revoked by a Byzantine emperor. She hastily summoned a synod (843) to reaffirm the Council of Nicaea and its stance in favor of icons. Today the Eastern Orthodox churches recognize Theodora as a saint.

In the final analysis, persecutions against the iconophiles served only to make icons more popular than ever. From there on out, icons would hold a central place in Orthodox worship. They would accompany troops into battle, adorn churches, and travel with missionaries into Slavic lands, where the Slavs embraced the art form and developed it in new ways.[39]

37. *pagans*—Muslims.

38. See document 11.3, "Theodore the Studite Refutes Iconoclasts," in the online supplement.

39. See section 12, "Icons: Aesthetics and Forms," in the online supplement for more on thematic and artistic issues.

Hesychasm

T he drifting apart of the Eastern and Western branches of Christendom," wrote Sir Steven Runciman, the eminent historian of
Byzantium, was "clearly marked in their respective attitudes
towards mysticism."[1] We've already explored the importance in the
East of apophatic theology—the fundamental assertion that God's
true nature can never be known, at least purely through the intellect.
Gregory of Nazianzus said that anyone who claimed to know God
was "depraved." Apophatic theology continued to dominate Eastern
thought into the Middle Ages, prolonging a tradition increasingly at
odds with the scholastic and philosophical approach to theology in
the Western church, which reached its zenith in the work of Thomas
Aquinas (1225–1274). Aquinas and his followers sought to ascertain
through reason, logic, and Aristotelian philosophy important aspects
of God's nature—an endeavor many of his Eastern counterparts considered foolish, arrogant, and possibly even heretical.[2]

As already noted, this is not to say that Eastern theologians de-
spaired of communing with God or of becoming like God. Quite the
opposite. Gregory of Nyssa spoke of God's "luminous darkness,"
namely God's ability to make himself known while remaining un-

---

1. Steven Runciman, *The Great Church in Captivity: A Study of the Patriarch-
ate of Constantinople from the Eve of the Turkish Conquest to the Greek War of
Independence* (Cambridge: Cambridge University Press, 1968), 128. Chapter 6,
"The Theology of Mysticism," informs much of this introduction.

2. See document 17.2, "Thomas Aquinas on God's Essence," in the online
supplement.

knowable. In earlier readings we saw Eastern theologians assert that the Christian's goal is not to know God in an intellectual fashion (a delusional venture) but to be with God and become like God. Deification can be achieved through prayer, that is, quiet supplication and the abandonment of all other obligations. Diligent, unrelenting prayer leads its practitioners to the light of God—the mystical experience of God's energies. Apophatic theology and the practice of prayer, wrote Runciman, "resolved the paradox between the knowable and the unknowable." Although one can never know God's *essence,* one can know, experience, and absorb God's *energies.*

Evagrius Ponticus (345–399) was one of the first theologians to outline the practice that would become known in the Middle Ages as "hesychasm."[3] The term "hesychast," which originally referred simply to a desert ascetic such as Evagrius, came eventually to indicate a person who sought inner peace, quietude, and mystical union with God through prayer. Hesychasts hearkened back to Evagrius's insistence that such communion follow contrite repentance—utter remorse—evidenced by the abundant weeping he called "the gift of tears." Tears and contrition enable a state of prayer characterized by "a habitual state of imperturbable calm," which "matches to the heights of intelligible reality the mind that loves wisdom and which is truly spiritualized by the most intense love."[4]

The truly penitent can escape the passions, temptations, and other claims on human attention that prevent communion with God. For those in a state of prayer, prayer becomes the true, God-infused activity of the intellect: the "prayer of the mind." Although some of Evagrius's other teachings (such as the preexistence of human souls) led to his condemnation as a heretic at the Fifth Ecumenical Council (the Second Council of Constantinople in 553), his teachings on prayer remained widely influential.

Hesychast writings circulated throughout Eastern Christendom under the names of various authors, including the pseudonymous "Macarius," whose work found an especially receptive audience on Mount Athos, a peninsula in northeastern Greece, which served as a home for numerous monasteries. Macarius and his devotees developed the

3. See document 4.4, "Evagrius Ponticus's Guide to Monastic Life," in the online supplement.

4. "Introduction," in Gregory Palamas, *The Triads,* trans. John Meyendorff (New York: Paulist Press, 1983), 2.

Figure 23. Mount Athos

"Jesus Prayer," or the "prayer of the heart," as a means of achieving union with God. The prayer consisted simply of repeating the word "God," "Lord," or "Jesus" over and over, with the goal of keeping "one's mind in one's heart," that is, keeping these names constantly in one's thoughts—as constant as a heartbeat. Conducted properly, the Jesus Prayer could be prayed with every breath and with every beat of the heart: physiology intertwined with psychology and spirituality. Macarius pointed to the incarnation—God's complete identification with a corporeal being—as evidence of the interdependence between the body and spirit. Grace resides not only in the soul and mind, but also in the body. The soul can thus work in concert with the body through prayer; hence Christological doctrine became for the hesychasts much more than a theoretical construct: it became a model for the combined efforts of mind and body to become like God.

Gregory Palamas (1296–1359) on Hesychasm, Prayer, and Deification

Excerpts from *Gregory Palamas: The Triads*, edited by John Meyendorff, translation by Nicholas Gendle, pp. 41–64, 66–68. Copyright © 1983 by Paulist Press, Inc., New York/Mahwah, NJ. Reprinted by permission of Paulist Press, Inc. www.paulistpress.com.

From the late 1200s we find written instructions from Nikephoros, a hesychast monk on Mount Athos, on breathing techniques to help supplicants turn prayer into a physiological act. Like Macarius, Nikephoros believed that body, soul, and spirit form a unity: physical acts yield spiritual benefits. He instructed supplicants to sit alone in a corner of their cells, bend forward, focus their eyes on their navels, and search for their hearts where intellect and soul reside.[5]

Some Byzantine Christians found such instructions troubling. Should we focus so intently on ourselves in order to reach God? Is it healthy to distance ourselves so completely from temporal concerns and responsibilities? Breathing exercises and the search for "the light" smacked of mystical currents within Islam and Hinduism, currents that may indeed have influenced some early hesychasts. Western scholasticism, which had by this time reached the East through translations of Thomas Aquinas's work into Greek, was, of course, completely antithetical to such practices.

Barlaam of Calabria (ca. 1290–1348), an Italian theologian living in Constantinople, distrusted the hesychasts' mystical bent and their relegation of reason and philosophy to the realm of secondary (and, for some, even irrelevant) concerns. Only through the cultivation of the intellect, argued Barlaam, could humans hope to achieve full perfection. While not a pure scholastic—Barlaam dismissed those who discounted everything that could not be perceived by the intellect—intellectual inquiry remained for him an indispensable tool in the search for God and personal perfection. Barlaam rejected the hesychasts as *omphaloscopoi*, or "naval gazers," considering them,

5. See Meyendorff's introduction, ibid.

in John Meyendorff's terms, "intellectually unqualified fanatics." The breathing tutorials in particular struck Barlaam as nonsense, as did the suggestion that the body (not only the mind) could be transfigured by the divine light.

Gregory Palamas (1296–1359) devoted himself to refuting Barlaam's criticism. At age twenty Gregory joined one of the great monasteries on Mount Athos, but Ottoman raids on the peninsula around 1325 forced many monks, including Palamas, to flee. He took refuge in Thessaloniki, where he formed a prayer group with other monks; there, he practiced the Jesus Prayer alone, for five days every week. He returned to Mount Athos in 1331 and began writing refutations of Barlaam.

Palamas considered himself orthodox to the core, and he took Barlaam's criticisms personally. As an ordained priest who served for a short period as an abbot, Palamas believed himself completely faithful to church doctrine. One of his prime goals in the following excerpt is to demonstrate that hesychasm is compatible with Orthodox Christianity; the reader will notice that in his arguments Palamas relies on Gregory of Nyssa's distinction between God's essence and God's energies.

Palamas ultimately emerged triumphant in these squabbles. Two councils in Constantinople in 1341 rebuked Barlaam, who left Byzantium in disgrace to live in Italy with his more scholastically inclined colleagues. Later councils in 1347 and 1351 endorsed Palamas's theology. (This triumph did not lead to an easy life: when Palamas was traveling to Constantinople in 1354, his ship was captured by Ottoman pirates, who beat him and held him prisoner; eventually ransomed by Serbs, Palamas returned to Thessaloniki, where he served as bishop for the last three years of his life.)

The following excerpt, intended as a response to Barlaam as well as an introduction to hesychasm for the uninitiated, was originally titled *For the Defense of Those Who Practice Sacred Quietude.* Published in three segments of three books, it is commonly known as *The Triads.*

· Part I ·
Section ii

1. My brother, do you not hear the words of the apostle, "Our bodies are the temple of the Holy Spirit, which is in us," and again, "We are the house of God"? For God himself says, "I will dwell in them and will walk in them and I shall be their God." So why should anyone who possesses mind grow indignant at the thought that our mind dwells in that whose

nature it is to become the dwelling place of God? How can it be that God at the beginning caused the mind to inhabit the body? Did even he do ill? Rather, brother, such views befit the heretics, who claim that the body is an evil thing, a fabrication of the wicked one.

As for us, we think the mind becomes evil through dwelling on fleshly thoughts, but that there is nothing bad in the body, since the body is not evil in itself. [. . .] Likewise, there is nothing evil in the fact that the mind dwells in the body; what is evil is "the law that is in our members, which fights against the law of the mind."

2. [. . .] We improve the rational part by rejecting all that impedes the mind from elevating itself toward God (this part of the law we call "watchfulness"). He who has purified his body by temperance, who by divine love has made an occasion of virtue from his wishes and desires, who has presented to God a mind purified by prayer, acquires and sees in himself the grace promised to those whose hearts have been purified. He can then say with Paul: "God, who has ordered light to shine from darkness, has made his light to shine in our hearts, in order that we may be enlightened by the knowledge of the glory of God, in the face of Jesus Christ"; but he adds, "We carry this treasure in earthen vessels." So we carry the Father's light in the face of Jesus Christ in earthen vessels, that is, in our bodies, in order to know the glory of the Holy Spirit. [. . .]

3. [. . .] We ourselves know exactly that our rational part is not confined within us as in a container, for it is incorporeal, nor is it outside of us, for it is conjoined to us; but it is in the heart, as in an instrument. [. . .] And the great Macarius[6] says also, "The heart directs the entire organism, and when grace gains possession of the heart, it reigns over all the thoughts and all the members; for it is there, in the heart, that the mind and all the thoughts of the soul have their seat."

Thus our heart is the place of the rational faculty, the first rational organ of the body. Consequently, when we seek to keep watch over and correct our reason by a rigorous sobriety, with what are we to keep watch, if we do not gather together our mind, which has been dissipated abroad by the senses, and lead it back again into the interior, to the selfsame heart which is the seat of the thoughts? [. . .]

4. [. . .] And if, according to the apostle, "God has given his Spirit to cry in our hearts, Abba, Father," how is it we too do not pray with the Spirit in our hearts? If, as the Lord of the prophets and apostles teaches, "the kingdom of God is within us," does it not follow that a man will be excluded from the kingdom if he devotes his energies to making his mind go out from within himself? [. . .]

6. *Macarius*—the "pseudo" Macarius, the unknown author of homilies that influenced the hesychasts.

5. There are, however, those who assert that the mind is not separate from the soul but is interior to it, and who therefore question how it can be recalled within. It would seem such people are unaware that the essence of the mind is one thing, its energy another. Or rather, they are well aware of this, and prefer to range themselves with the deceitful, and prevaricate over an ambiguity. "For such men, sharpened to controversy by dialectic, do not accept the simplicity of the spiritual doctrine," as the great Basil[7] says. [. . .]

6. The father of lies[8] is always desiring to lead man toward those errors that he himself promotes; but up to now (as far as we know) he has found no collaborator who has tried to lead others to this goal by good words. But today, if what you tell me is true, it seems he has found accomplices[9] who have even composed treatises toward this end, and who seek to persuade men (even those who have embraced the higher life of hesychasm) that it would be better for them to keep the mind *outside* of the body during prayer. They do not even respect the clear and authoritative words of John, who writes in his *Ladder of Divine Ascent*,[10] "The hesychast is one who seeks to circumscribe[11] the incorporeal in his body."

This is exactly the tradition, and our spiritual fathers have also handed it down to us, and rightly so. For if the hesychast does not circumscribe the mind in his body, how can he make to enter himself the one who has clothed himself in the body,[12] and who thus penetrates all organized matter, insofar as he is its natural form? For the external aspect and divisibility of matter is not compatible with the essence of the mind, unless matter itself truly begins to live, having acquired a form of life conformable to the union with Christ. [. . .]

7. [. . .] On the other hand, it is not out of place to teach people, especially beginners, that they should look at themselves, and introduce their own mind within themselves through control of breathing. A prudent man will not forbid someone who does not as yet contemplate himself to use certain methods to recall his mind within himself, for those newly approaching this struggle find that their mind, when recollected, continually

---

7. *the great Basil*—Basil of Caesarea (ca. 329–379). See "St. Basil (ca. 330–379) to Gregory of Nazianzus on Monastic Ideals."

8. *father of lies*—Satan.

9. *accomplices*—Barlaam.

10. *The Ladder of Divine Ascent*—an ascetic treatise for monks—written by St. John Climacus (ca. 579–649), a hermit living in the Sinai Peninsula—on attaining salvation through the practice of virtue and the avoidance of vice. John likened the pursuit of salvation to ascending a ladder toward Heaven.

11. *circumscribe*—encompass.

12. *one who has clothed himself in the body*—Christ.

becomes dispersed again. It is thus necessary for such people constantly to bring it back once more; but in their inexperience, they fail to grasp that nothing in the world is in fact more difficult to contemplate and more mobile and shifting than the mind.

This is why certain masters recommend them to control the movement inwards and outwards of the breath, and to hold it back a little; in this way, they will also be able to control the mind together with the breath—this, at any rate, until such time as they have made progress, with the aid of God, have restrained the intellect from becoming distracted by what surrounds it, have purified it and truly become capable of leading it to a "unified recollection." One can state that this recollection is a spontaneous effect of the attention of the mind, for the to-and-fro movement of the breath becomes quieted during intensive reflection, especially with those who maintain inner quiet in body and soul. [. . .]

8. In the case of those who have made progress in hesychasm, all this comes to pass without painful effort and without their worrying about it, for the perfect entry of the soul within itself spontaneously produces such inner detachment. But with beginners none of these things comes about without toil; for patience is a fruit of love, "for love bears all," and teaches us to practice patience with all our strength in order to attain love; and this is a case in point.

But why delay over these matters? Everyone who has the experience can only laugh at the contradictions of the inexperienced; for they have learned not through words but effort, and the experience that indicates the pains they take. It is effort that brings the useful fruits, and challenges the sterile views of the lovers of disputation and ostentation. [. . .]

9. [. . .] Maintain this watch, this attention, this self-control, or rather mount guard, be vigilant, keep watch! For it is thus that you will make the disobedient flesh subject to the spirit, and "there will no longer be a hidden word in your heart." "If the spirit of him who dominates"—that is to say, of the evil spirits and passions—"lifts himself up over you," says scripture, "on no account shift your ground"; in other words, never leave any part of your soul or any member of your body without surveillance.

In this way, you will become unapproachable to the spirits that attack you from below, and you will be able to present yourself with boldness to "him who searches the reins and the heart"; and that indeed without his scrutinizing you, for you will have scrutinized yourself. Paul tells us, "If we judge ourselves, we will not be judged." You will then have the blessed experience of David[13] and you will address yourself to God, saying, "The shadows are no longer darkness thanks to you, and the night

13. *David*—King David, on whom God bestowed repeated blessings.

will be for me as clear as the day, for it is you who have taken possession of my reins." [. . .]

· Part II ·
Section ii

[. . .]

5. When we return to interior reflection, it is necessary to calm the sensations aroused by external activities. But why should one calm those provoked by the dispositions of the soul, the good dispositions? Is there a method of ridding oneself of them, once one has returned into oneself? And indeed, for what reason should one seek to dispose of them, since they in no way impede one, but rather contribute to the greatest possible extent to our integration?

For this body that is united to us has been attached to us as a fellow-worker by God, or rather placed under our control. Thus we will repress it, if it is in revolt, and accept it, if it conducts itself as it should. The hearing and sight are more pure and more easily conformed to reason than the touch, but nonetheless one will pay them no attention, nor be disturbed by them in any way, except when what we see or hear affects us disagreeably. [. . .]

6. In every case, those who practice true mental prayer must liberate themselves from the passions, and reject any contact with objects that obstruct it, for in this way they are able to acquire undisrupted and pure prayer. As for those not yet arrived at this degree, but who seek to attain it, they must gain the mastery over every sensual pleasure, completely rejecting the passions, for the body's capacity to sin must be mortified; that is, one must be released from domination by the passionate emotions. Similarly the judgment must vanquish the evil passions that move in the world of mind, that is, it must rise above the sensual delights.

For it is the case that if we cannot taste mental prayer, not even as it were with the slightest touch of our lips, and if we are dominated by passionate emotions, then we certainly stand in need of the physical suffering that comes from fasting, vigils and similar things, if we are to apply ourselves to prayer. This suffering alone mortifies the body's inclination to sin, and moderates and weakens the thoughts that provoke violent passions. Moreover, it is this that brings about within us the start of holy compunction, through which both the stain of past faults is done away and the divine favor especially attracted, and which disposes one toward prayer. For "God will not despise a bruised heart," as David says; and according to Gregory the Theologian,[14] "God heals in no more certain way than through suffering." This is why the Lord taught us in the Gospels that prayer can do great things when combined with fasting. [. . .]

14. *Gregory the Theologian*—Gregory of Nazianzus.

8. [. . .] But it is not only bodily activities that ought to be abandoned by one who strives toward the divine union, but also intellectual ones: "All the divine lights, and every elevation toward all the holy summits must be left behind," as the great Denys[15] says. [. . .] "And how can these things come from grace," asks Barlaam, "when one does not perceive them during the mental prayer that unites man to God? They serve no purpose, whereas all that comes from him is to some purpose." [. . .]

12. [. . .] [J]ust as the divinity of the Word of God incarnate is common to soul and body, since he has deified the flesh through the mediation of the soul to make it also accomplish the works of God; so similarly, in spiritual man, the grace of the Spirit, transmitted to the body through the soul, grants to the body also the experience of things divine, and allows it the same blessed experiences as the soul undergoes. [. . .]

When the soul pursues this blessed activity, it deifies the body also; which, being no longer driven by corporeal and material passions— although those who lack experience of this think that it is always so driven—returns to itself and rejects all contact with evil things. Indeed, it inspires its own sanctification and inalienable divinization, as the miracle-working relics of the saints clearly demonstrate.

What of Stephen,[16] the first martyr, whose face, even while he was yet living, shone like the face of an angel? Did not his body also experience divine things? Is not such an experience and the activity allied to it common to soul and body? Far from nailing the soul to terrestrial and corporeal thoughts and filling it with darkness, as the philosopher alleges, such a common experience constitutes an ineffable bond and union with God. It elevates the body itself in a marvelous way, and sets it far apart from evil and earthly passions. For as the prophet says, "Those whom God has filled with power have been lifted far above the earth." [. . .]

14. [. . .] Although God makes those who pray sincerely go out of themselves, rendering them transcendent to their natures and mysteriously ravished away to Heaven, yet even in such cases, since they are concentrated within themselves, it is through the mediation of their souls and body that God effects things supernatural, mysterious and incomprehensible to the wise of this world. [. . .]

19. [. . .] But if one uses these things properly, then through the knowledge of created things, spiritually understood, one will arrive at knowledge of God; and through the passionate part of the soul that has been orientated toward the end for which God created it, one will practice the

15. *Denys*—bishop of Paris, martyred ca. 250.

16. *Stephen*—one of Jesus's disciples. According to the book of Acts, Jewish authorities accused Stephen of blasphemy and ordered him stoned to death. See Acts 6:8–7:59

corresponding virtues: with the concupiscent appetite,[17] one will embrace charity, and with the irascible, one will practice patience. It is thus not the man who has killed the passionate part of his soul who has the preeminence, for such a one would have no momentum or activity to acquire a divine state and right dispositions and relationship with God; but rather, the prize goes to him who has put that part of his soul under subjection, so that by its obedience to the mind, which is by nature appointed to rule, it may ever tend toward God, as is right, by the uninterrupted remembrance of him. [. . .]

Section iii

[. . .]

8. [. . .] The monks know that the essence of God transcends the fact of being inaccessible to the senses, since God is not only above all created things, but is even beyond Godhead. The excellence of him who surpasses all things is not only beyond all affirmation, but also beyond all negation; it exceeds all excellence that is attainable by the mind. This hypostatic light,[18] seen spiritually by the saints, they know by experience to exist, as they tell us, and to exist not symbolically only, as do manifestations produced by fortuitous events; but it is an illumination immaterial and divine, a grace invisibly seen and ignorantly known. *What* it is, they do not pretend to know.

[. . .] This light is not the essence of God, for that is inaccessible and incommunicable; it is not an angel, for it bears the marks of the master. Sometimes it makes a man go out from the body or else, without separating him from the body, it elevates him to an ineffable height. At other times, it transforms the body, and communicates its own splendor to it when, miraculously, the light that deifies the body becomes accessible to the bodily eyes. Thus indeed did the great Arsenius[19] appear when engaged in hesychastic combat; similarly Stephen, while being stoned, and Moses, when he descended from the mountain. [. . .]

11. [. . .] But hesychasts know that the purified and illuminated mind, when clearly participating in the grace of God, also beholds other mystical and supernatural visions—for in seeing itself, it sees more than itself: it does not simply contemplate some other object, or simply its own image, but rather the glory impressed on its own image by the grace of God. This radiance reinforces the mind's power to transcend itself, and accomplish that union with those better things that is beyond understanding. By this union, the mind sees God in the Spirit in a manner transcending human powers.

17. *concupiscent appetite*—lust; sexual desire.
18. *hypostatic light*—the light of God or the mystical experience of God.
19. *Arsenius*—a Roman tutor who became a desert ascetic in Egypt.

[. . .] You claim that the mind can see God only when purified not only of the passions but of ignorance as well: yet the saints make no mention of the latter. They purify themselves of evil passions and transcend all knowledge by uninterrupted and immaterial prayer, and it is then that they begin to see God. [. . .]

16. [. . .] Let us not, then, turn aside incredulous before the superabundance of these blessings; but let us have faith in him who has participated in our nature and granted it in return the glory of his own nature, and let us seek how to acquire this glory and see it. How? By keeping the divine commandments. For the Lord has promised to manifest himself to the man who keeps them, a manifestation he calls his own indwelling and that of the Father, saying, "If anyone loves me, he will keep my word, and my Father will love him, and we will come to him and will make our abode with him," and "I will manifest myself to him." [. . .]

17. We have here a proof [. . .] that this contemplation of God is not a form of knowledge, even though Barlaam's greatest desire is that the opposite should be true. For our own part, if we refuse to call this contemplation "knowledge," it is by reason of its transcendence—just as we also say that God is not being, for we believe him to be above being. [. . .]

33. Since the reality that transcends every intellectual power is impossible to comprehend, it is beyond all beings; such union with God is thus beyond all knowledge, even if it be called "knowledge" metaphorically, nor is it intelligible, even if it be called so. For how can what is beyond all intellect be called intelligible? In respect of its transcendence, it might better be called ignorance than knowledge. It cannot be a part or aspect of knowledge, just as the super-essential is not an aspect of the essential. Knowledge as a whole could not contain it, nor could this knowledge, when subdivided, possess it as one of its parts. [. . .]

68. It is time to repeat those divine words: "We give thanks to you, Father, Lord of Heaven and earth, because," uniting yourself to us and making yourself manifest to us by yourself, "you have hidden these things from the wise and prudent," who are prudent only by their own account and learned only in their own eyes. [. . .]

We must transcend ourselves altogether, and give ourselves entirely to God, for it is better to belong to God, and not to ourselves. It is thus that divine things are bestowed on those who have attained to fellowship with God.

Great Schism

T he 400s to the 1200s witnessed a progressive, albeit gradual, estrangement between churches in the East and churches in the West, marked by crises both big and small as well as by attempts at reconciliation—some successful and some not. Thousands of books and articles have tried to explain the schism. Scholars disagree on particulars, but nearly all agree that the causes were numerous. Divergent explanations and interpretations differ mainly in the relative import granted to each.

Kallistos Ware, the author of a popular history of the Eastern Orthodox Church, rightly notes that "long before there was an open and formal schism between East and West, the two sides had become *strangers* to one another."[1] The questions are why and how did members of the same faith become strangers?

Distance, certainly, played an important role. Constantinople sits nearly fourteen hundred kilometers east of Rome as the crow flies and twenty-two hundred kilometers by boat: south toward Sicily, east across the Mediterranean Sea, northeast around the Greek peninsula, up through the Aegean Sea, and east across the Sea of Marmara. Communications moved slowly, with difficulty, and infrequently. Travel was dangerous: as noted above, pirates kidnapped Gregory Palamas during a trip to Constantinople.

Although the Roman Empire remained in theory one empire throughout its history, it had begun to function as two different em-

---

1. Kallistos Ware, *The Orthodox Church* (Baltimore: Penguin, 1963), 52. This introduction borrows from the structure of Ware's survey.

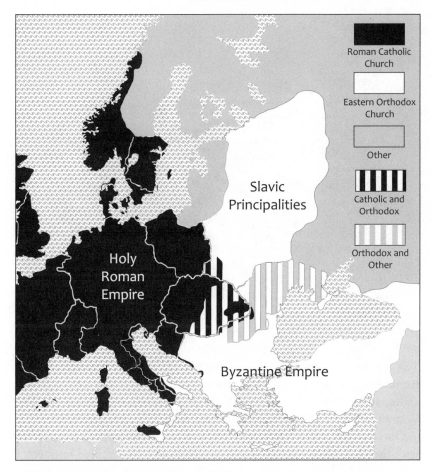

Figure 24. Eastern Orthodox and Roman Catholic lands, 1054

pires by the end of the 200s, each ruled by a co-emperor. (Recall that Constantine served as co-emperor with Licinius before claiming the throne exclusively for himself.) Constantine's relocation of the capital city to Constantinople only exacerbated divisions. After Constantine died, an alternating series of dual and single emperors followed. The last member of Constantine's family line, Theodosius I (379–395), proved to be the last emperor to rule a unified empire.

The Western Empire endured endless setbacks and repeated invasions from "barbarian" tribes while struggling to raise revenue for its defense. The rural populace fled to cities for protection, creating overcrowding and chaos and making the borders harder to defend.

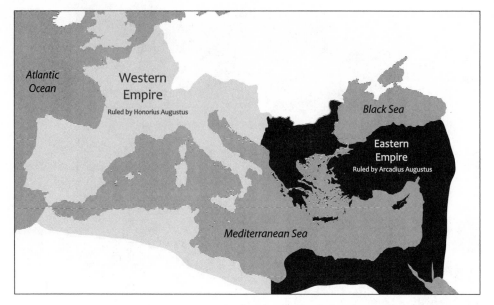

Figure 25. Roman Empire after the death of Theodosius I, 395

The Visigoths, a nomadic, Germanic tribe from the northeast, sacked Rome in 410 and mounted additional attacks over the next few decades. In 476 the illiterate Visigoth chief Odoacer deposed the last Roman emperor of the West, Romulus Augustus (475–476).

Odoacer, an Arian Christian, was hardly one to make communion with the Orthodox East a top priority. Although he retained important aspects of the Roman government—the senate, the legal system, and the tax structure—the Western Empire faded to a shadow of its former self. Various barbarian chiefs carved it up in the decades that followed.

The Eastern Empire, in contrast, enjoyed relative stability during this period. Flush with money from trade across Eurasia and North Africa, the Eastern, or Byzantine, emperors imagined themselves the rightful rulers of the *entire* empire. A few even tried (mostly without success) to recapture the Italian peninsula. Justinian, the phenomenally ambitious emperor of the East from 527 to 565, *did* make some significant gains on the peninsula and in North Africa. These gains, however, were short-lived, and the conquered territories soon slipped from Byzantine hands. After Justinian, never again would a Byzantine emperor make significant gains in the West.

Different languages made communication between East and West difficult. Many of the early church fathers were bilingual—if not

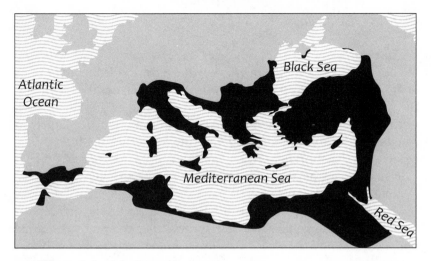

Figure 26. Justinian's empire, 555

fluent then at least reasonably comfortable in both Greek and Latin. But with the division of the empire, knowledge of Greek began to die in the West. By the mid-400s few Westerners could read, let alone speak, Greek: Latin served as *the* language of the educated classes. And by the 600s few in Byzantium could or cared to speak Latin, the language of nearly all theological discourse in the West. Scholars in the East and scholars in the West read literature and wrote works indecipherable to each other. Discourses on God, the Trinity, liturgical practices, and all manner of doctrine composed in one region remained largely unknown in the other.

Yet distance, language, and the fall of empires constitute only several pieces of a complex story. In accounting for the schism we must also consider theological controversies (particularly disputes over the *filioque*, an addition to the Creed of Nicaea), ecclesiastical politics (the claims of the Roman See), secular politics (the rise of the Holy Roman Empire, which imagined itself as the successor to the fallen Roman Empire, and its support of the papacy), personalities (the self-righteous Patriarch Photios and irascible Pope Adrian), the escalation of tensions through written condemnations (the anathemas of 1054), the enduring outrage caused by war and plunder (the Fourth Crusade in 1204), and failed attempts to repair the rifts (the councils of Lyons[2] and Ferrara-Florence).

We now examine each of these factors in turn.

2. See document 18.7, "Council of Lyons," in the online supplement.

CLAIMS OF THE ROMAN SEE

The term "pope" derives from the Greek *pappas,* or "father" (*papa* in Latin). Early in the church's history the term applied to all bishops in the West. In fact the patriarch of Alexandria still uses the title today. By 1073, however, Pope Gregory VII declared that only the bishop of Rome could use the moniker, making official a practice largely in place since the 800s. Many Eastern Orthodox dislike the title and often refer to the "bishop of Rome" rather than to the "pope."

Roman popes have long claimed to be successors to St. Peter, Jesus's unruly but devoted disciple. We have no evidence that Peter ever served as a bishop in Rome or that he died in Rome, as tradition asserts, although some archaeologists believe that Peter may be buried under what is now St. Peter's Basilica in Rome. And assertions about Peter's service and death in Rome have undergirded the bishop of Rome's claims to successorship since the early 100s.

The Roman Catholic Church, of which the pope is the head, often references Jesus's words to Peter in Matthew 16:18–19: "And I tell you, you are Peter, and on this rock I will build my church, and the gates of Hades will not prevail against it. I will give you the keys of the kingdom of heaven, and whatever you bind on earth will be bound in heaven, and whatever you loose on earth will be loosed in heaven" (NRSV). This "Petrine" theory of the papacy takes this verse to indicate Jesus's designation of Peter as his representative on earth. The theory also holds that this designation passes to each of Peter's successors, that is, to each succeeding bishop of Rome. In fact the papal coat of arms consists of two keys, topped by a crown.

Most bishops, including those in the East and in the West, were and still are willing to concede a "primacy of honor" to the bishop of Rome. Rome was, after all, the original seat of the empire and arguably the most important city in the history of the early church. But many bishops, especially those in the East, also insist that the pope, while enjoying "primacy of honor," should function as the "first among equals."

So what, exactly, do "primacy of honor" and "first among equals" really mean?

They mean different things to different people, and the phrases often did more to confuse than to clarify questions about roles.

Disputes about the bishop of Rome's prerogatives and powers arose almost from the beginning of the institutional church. The bishop of Carthage, for example, clashed with Bishop Stephen I of Rome (254–257) when Stephen made unwelcome claims about his (Stephen's)

Figure 27. Papal coat of arms

doctrinal authority within the church. Disputes intensified during the 400s. After the Visigoths conquered Rome, the bishop of Rome found himself without the oversight of a powerful emperor. Thus, unlike the bishop of Constantinople, the bishop of Rome enjoyed more latitude to make claims about his rights than did bishops in the East.

A furor erupted when in 451 the Council of Chalcedon granted the patriarch of Constantinople and the bishop of Rome equal privileges (*isa presbeia*).[3] Said Canon 28:

> we do also enact and decree the same things concerning the privileges of the most holy church of Constantinople, which is new Rome. For the fathers rightly granted privileges to the throne of old Rome, because it was the royal city. And the one hundred fifty most religious bishops gave equal privileges to the most holy throne of new Rome, justly judging that the city is honored with the sovereignty and the senate and enjoys equal privileges with the old imperial Rome.

3. See section 2, "Chalcedon and Non-Chalcedonian Churches," in the online supplement.

Leo I, the bishop of Rome during this council, angrily objected and
ordered the canon removed from the council's official documents.

A century and a half later, the forceful and ambitious Roman
bishop Gregory I ("Gregory the Great," 590–604) conceded that he
and his church were part of the Byzantine Empire, but subsequent
actions belied this concession. Concerned about the Lombards, a Germanic tribe that threatened both his realm and Byzantine territory in
Italy, Gregory turned his attention and that of his church toward the
Franks, Germanic tribes to the north and west. It was the Franks with
whom the papacy would eventually align itself whole-heartedly in the
700s and the Franks who supported the pope's claims to represent
all of Christendom. We will examine the papacy's relationship with
Charlemagne, the great emperor of the Franks, below.

For now, however, we offer some documents illustrating wide-
ranging and often incompatible conceptions of the papacy in the East
and West.[4]

St. Jerome to Pope Damasus on the Chair of St. Peter (375)

"Jerome, *Ep.* 15, to Pope Damasus," in Edward Giles,
Documents Illustrating Papal Authority, A.D. 96–454
(London: SPCK, 1952), 148–50. Used by permission of SPCK Publishing.

**St. Jerome, most famous for translating the Bible into Latin, had
this to say about the chair of St. Peter, which he viewed as the logical
court of appeal for resolving disputes in the church.**

1. Since the East, dashed against itself by the accustomed fury of its
peoples, is tearing piecemeal the undivided tunic of Christ,[5] woven from
the top throughout, and foxes are destroying the vine of Christ, so that
among the broken cisterns that have no water it is hard to locate the
sealed fountain and the enclosed garden, I have considered that *I ought to
consult the chair of Peter,* and the faith praised by the mouth of the apos-

4. See also section 18.2, "Claims of the Roman See," in the online supplement.

5. *tearing piecemeal the undivided tunic of Christ*—Jerome traveled in Syria,
and he refers here to a schism in Antioch fueled by doctrinal disputes and competing claims of rival bishops.

tle, asking now food for my soul, from the place whence I received the garment of Christ.[6] Neither the vast expanse of ocean, nor all the breadth of land that separates us could preclude me from seeking the precious pearl.[7] "Wherever the body is, there will the eagles be gathered together." Now that evil children have squandered their patrimony, you alone keep your heritage intact. There the fertile earth reproduces a hundredfold the purity of the Lord's seed. Here the corn, cast into the furrows, degenerates into darnel[8] or wild oats. It is now in the West that the sun of justice rises; while in the East Lucifer who fell has set his seat above the stars. "You are the light of the world." "You are the salt of the earth." You are vessels of gold and silver. Here the vessels of clay or wood await the iron rod and eternal fire.

2. Yet though your greatness terrifies me, your kindness attracts me. From the priest I ask the salvation of the victim; from the shepherd, the safety of the sheep. Away with envy! The canvassing of the Roman height recedes. I speak with the successor of the fisherman,[9] with the disciple of the cross. Following none in the first place but Christ, *I am in communion with your beatitude—that is with the chair of Peter. On that rock I know the church is built.* [. . .]

Council of Rome on the Bishop of Rome's Role in Legal Disputes (378)

"Document 94: The Council of Rome, A.D. 378, *To the Emperors*," in Edward Giles, *Documents Illustrating Papal Authority, A.D. 96–454* (London: SPCK, 1952), 127–28. Used by permission of SPCK Publishing.

A gathering of bishops in 378 sought to clarify procedures for resolving disputes within the church. The council produced the following resolution on the bishop of Rome's role in such disputes.

[. . .] But if a [legal] question [. . .] arises in more distant parts, let the examination be transferred by the local courts to the metropolitan;[10] or if

6. *garment of Christ*—see Galatians 3:27: "As many as you as were baptized into Christ have clothed yourselves with Christ" (NRSV).

7. *precious pearl*—see Matthew 13:45–46: "the kingdom of heaven is like a merchant in search of fine pearls; on finding one pearl of great value, he went and sold all that he had and bought it" (NRSV).

8. *darnel*—a Eurasian ryegrass; considered a weed.

9. *successor of the fisherman*—Peter worked as a fisherman.

10. *metropolitan*—an important regional bishop.

he is a metropolitan himself, he should be ordered of necessity to journey to Rome without delay, or to those judges whom the Roman bishop may appoint, so that those who shall have been deposed be kept away from the bounds of the city in which they exercised the priesthood, lest they again impudently usurp that which they have been deprived of by law. Certainly, if either the metropolitan or any other priest be suspected of favor or iniquity, it is lawful to appeal either to the Roman bishop or to a council of fifteen neighboring bishops. [. . .]

Gregory Nazianzus on the Bishop of Rome (382)

"Gregory Nazianzen, *Carmen de Vita Sua*," in Edward Giles,
Documents Illustrating Papal Authority, A.D. 96–454
(London: SPCK, 1952), 130. Used by permission of SPCK Publishing.

Gregory of Nazianzus, the great Trinitarian theologian and bishop of Constantinople whose work we have already encountered, spoke about the glory of the "two Romes": Rome and Constantinople.

Truly nature has not given us two suns; but she has given us two Romes, as lights of the whole world, an old dominion and a new; the one differs from the other as the latter outshines the East and the former the West. But the beauty of the one balances exactly in the scales with the beauty of the other. Regarding the faith that they uphold, the ancient Rome has kept a straight course from of old, and still does so, *uniting the whole West* by sound teaching, as is just, since *she presides over all* and guards the universal divine harmony.

Council of Rome on the Primacy of Rome (382)

"Council of Rome, a.d. 382, *Post has omnes*," in Edward Giles,
Documents Illustrating Papal Authority, A.D. 96–454
(London: SPCK, 1952), 131–32. Used by permission of SPCK Publishing.

The same year that Gregory spoke about the glory of "two Romes" (382), a council in Rome clearly set Rome above the other major bishoprics.

After all these writings of the prophets, evangelists, and apostles that we set out above, and on which, by God's grace, the catholic church is founded, we think this should also be noticed: that though all the catholic churches diffused throughout the world are but one bridal chamber of Christ, yet the holy Roman church has been set before the rest by no conciliar decrees, but has obtained the primacy by the voice of our Lord and savior in the Gospel: "You are Peter and upon this rock . . . shall be loosed in Heaven."[11] There is added also the society of the most blessed Apostle Paul, "a chosen vessel," who was crowned on one and the same day, suffering a glorious death with Peter in the city of Rome,[12] under Caesar Nero;[13] and they alike consecrated the above-named Roman church to Christ the Lord, and set it above all others in the whole world by their presence and venerable triumph.

The first see of the apostle Peter is therefore the Roman church, "not having spot or wrinkle or any such thing."

But the second see was consecrated at Alexandria, in the name of blessed Peter, by his disciple Mark the Evangelist; and he, being directed by Saint Peter into Egypt, preached the word of truth, and perfected a glorious martyrdom.

And the third see of the most blessed apostle Peter is at Antioch, which is held in honor because he lived there before he came to Rome, and there, first, the name of the new race of Christians arose.

One year later, in 383, the church in the East suggested that Constantinople held a privilege of honor second to that of Rome, "because it is new Rome."[14]

Pope Innocent on the Prerogatives of the Roman Church (416)

"Innocent, *Ep.* 25, to Decentius, bishop of Eugubium (*Si instituta*),"
in Edward Giles, *Documents Illustrating Papal Authority*, A.D. 96–454
(London: SPCK, 1952), 194–95. Used by permission of SPCK Publishing.

In 416 Pope Innocent I felt compelled to remind those who "neglect the head of their institution" of Rome's importance in Christianizing the empire, and by implication, its authority within the empire.

11. "*You are Peter and upon this rock . . . shall be loosed in Heaven*"—an abbreviated version of Christ's words to Peter in Matthew 16:18–19.

12. *death with Peter in the city of Rome*—as already noted, there is no evidence that Peter died in Rome.

13. *under Caesar Nero*—a number of early, unreliable sources assert that Emperor Nero (54–68) killed the apostles Peter and Paul.

14. "Council of Constantinople, Canon 3," in Edward Giles, *Documents Illustrating Papal Authority*, A.D. 96–454 (London: SPCK, 1952), 130.

[. . .] Who does not know or observe that [the church order] was delivered by Peter, the chief of the apostles, to the Roman church, and is kept until now, and ought to be retained by all, and that nothing ought to be imposed or introduced that has no authority, or seems to derive its precedents elsewhere—especially since it is clear that in all Italy, the Gauls,[15] Spain, Africa, Sicily and the adjacent islands, no one formed these churches except those whom the venerable apostle Peter or his successors made priests? Or let them discover that any other apostle be found to have been or to have taught in these provinces. If not, they ought to follow that which the Roman Church keeps, from which they undoubtedly received them first; but while they are keen on foreign statements, they seem to neglect the head of their institution.

Theodore the Studite (759–826) on the Pentarchy and Roman Authority

Francis Dvornik, *Byzantium and the Roman Primacy*
(New York: Fordham University Press, 1966), 101.

Although the major patriarchates (i.e., the most important bishoprics in the Christian world—traditionally Alexandria, Antioch, Constantinople, Jerusalem, and Rome) jockeyed for position throughout the church's early centuries, Eastern patriarchs generally agreed, sometimes happily and sometimes grudgingly, to the notion of a "pentarchy." This pentarchy of five patriarchates was to function, at least in theory, as a collegial unit, jointly administering major ecclesiastical matters through regular consultation and consensus. Rome's claims of primacy, of course, violated this notion. Here, Theodore the Studite outlines in a letter to a colleague his understanding of the pentarchy.

The right to judge [worldly affairs] rests with the emperor and the secular tribunal. But here [in our discussion] it is a question of divine and heavenly decisions and those are reserved only to him to whom the Word of God has said: "Whatever you bind on earth will be bound in Heaven, and whatever you shall loose on earth shall be loosed in Heaven" (Matthew 16:19). And who are the men to whom this order was given? The apostles and their successors. And who are their successors? He who occupies the throne of Rome and is the first; the one who sits upon the

15. *Gauls*—the area that now consists of France, Belgium, and northern Italy.

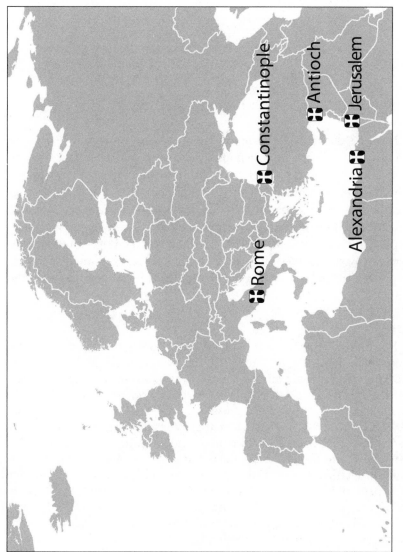

Figure 28. The "Pentarchy," or five patriarchates

throne of Constantinople and is the second; after them, those of Alexandria, Antioch and Jerusalem. That is the pentarchic authority in the church. It is to them who all decisions belong in divine dogmas. The emperor and the secular authority have the duty to aid them and to confirm what they have decided.

Archbishop Niketas on Roman Primacy (1136)

Steven Runciman, *The Eastern Schism: A Study of the Papacy and the Eastern Churches during the XIth and XIIth Centuries* (Oxford: Clarendon, 1955), 116.

In 1136 the Holy Roman emperor (a position examined in some detail below) dispatched Bishop Anselm from northern Germany to Constantinople to discuss the possibility of the East and West taking joint military action against the ruler of Sicily. While in Constantinople, the Byzantine emperor John Komnenos invited Anselm to debate Archbishop Niketas of Nicomedia (modern Izmit, near Constantinople) on theological differences that had emerged over the centuries between East and West. The tone of the debate, facilitated by an interpreter, was polite, but Niketas made clear his unhappiness with the Roman papacy.

My dearest brother, we do not deny the Roman Church the primacy among the five sister patriarchates; and we recognize her right to the most honorable seat at an ecumenical council. But she has separated herself from us by her own deeds when through pride she assumed a monarchy that does not belong to her office. [. . .] How shall we accept from her decrees that have been issued without consulting us and even without our knowledge? If the Roman pontiff, seated on the lofty throne of his glory, wishes to thunder at us and, so to speak, hurl his mandates at us from on high, and if he wishes to judge us and even to rule us and our churches, not by taking counsel with us but at his own arbitrary pleasure, what kind of brotherhood, or even what kind of parenthood can this be? We should be the slaves, not the sons, of such a church, and the Roman see would not be the pious mother of sons but a hard and imperious mistress of slaves.

Thomas Aquinas on Papal Power (1258–1264)

Thomas Aquinas, "Of the Episcopal Dignity, and That Therein
One Bishop is Supreme," in *Of God and His Creatures: An Annotated
Translation (with Some Abridgement) of the Summa Contra Gentiles of
Saint Thos. Aquinas,* ed. and trans. Joseph Rickaby S.J. (London: Burns
& Oates, 1905), 399–401. Revised with occasional reference to
Thomas Aquinas, *Summa Contra Gentiles,* trans. Charles O'Neil
(South Bend, IN: University of Notre Dame Press, 1975), 4:290–95.

**Here Thomas Aquinas, the great theologian of the medieval Roman
church, argues that a strong pope is essential for peace and a unified
faith.**

[. . .]

2. The agreement of all the faithful in faith is one requirement for the
unity of the church. When questions of faith arise, the church would be
rent by diverse judgments were it not preserved in unity by the judgment
of one. But in necessary things Christ has not failed his church, which he
loved, and for which he shed his blood. For the Lord says even about the
synagogue, "What more is there that I should have done for my vineyard,
but have not done?" (Isaiah 5:4). We cannot doubt, then, that one man
presides over the whole church by the ordinance of Christ.

3. None can doubt that the government of the church is excellently
arranged—arranged as it is by he[16] through whom "kings reign and lawgivers enact just things" (Proverbs 8:15). But the best form of government
ensures the peace and unity of its subjects; and one man is a better source
of unity than many together. [. . .]

7. If anyone says that the one head and one shepherd is Christ—who
is the one spouse of the one church—his view is inadequate to the facts.
For Christ clearly makes the sacraments of the church efficacious: it is he
who baptizes, he who forgives sins, he who is the true priest who offered
himself on the altar of the cross, and it is by his power that his body is
consecrated at our altars.[17] Nevertheless, because he was not going to be
present in bodily form with all his faithful, he chose ministers and dis-
pensed his gifts to his faithful people through the ministers' hands. And
because he would be absent in the future, it was necessary for him to issue his commission to someone to take care of the universal church in his
stead. Hence he said to Peter before his ascension, "Feed my sheep" (John

16. *he*—Christ.

17. *it is by his power that his body is consecrated on our altars*—that is, it is by
the power of Christ that the bread becomes his body during the Eucharist.

11:17); and before his passion, "You in turn confirm your brethren"[18] (Luke 22:32); and to Peter alone he promised, "To you I will give the keys to the kingdom of Heaven" (Matthew 16:19).

8. Nor can it be said that although he gave this dignity to Peter, it does not pass from Peter to others.[19] For Christ instituted his church to last until the end of the world, according to the text, "He shall sit on the throne of David and in his kingdom to confirm and strengthen it in justice and judgment from now and forever" (Isaiah 9:7). Therefore, in constituting his ministers for the time, he intended their power to pass to posterity for the benefit of his church to the end of the world, as he himself says, "Lo, I am with you to the end of the world" (Matthew 28:20).

9. By this we cast out the presumptuous error of some, who endeavor to withdraw themselves from obedience and subjection to Peter, not recognizing his successor the Roman pontiff, the pastor of the universal church.

Pope Boniface VIII on the Spiritual Authority of the Papacy (1302)

"The Bull, 'Unam Sanctam,'" in *Select Historical Documents of the Middle Ages,* ed. Ernest F. Henderson (London: George Bell and Sons, 1905), 435–37.

This final document represents the height of papal claims.[20] Although the arguments are somewhat convoluted, the claims are not. Here Pope Boniface VIII excoriates Easterners who do not recognize papal authority. And in a theme that would spawn centuries of conflict between popes and kings, Boniface insists that temporal authority is subject to the papacy's spiritual authority.

We are compelled, our faith urging us, to believe and to hold—and we do firmly believe and simply confess—that there is one holy catholic and apostolic church, outside of which there is neither salvation nor remission of sins [. . .], which represents one mystic body, of which body the head is

18. *You in turn confirm your brethren*—here Aquinas suggests Peter's (and, by inference, the pope's) power to ordain other ministers.

19. *pass from Peter to others*—a reference to "apostolic succession," the doctrine that the ordination of bishops passes unbroken from Christ to Peter, from Peter to his successors, and from these successors to other bishops up to the present.

20. See also section 18.2, "Claims of the Roman See," in the online supplement.

Christ. [. . .] In this church there is one Lord, one faith, and one baptism. There was one ark of Noah, indeed, at the time of the flood, symbolizing one church; and this being finished [. . .] had, namely, one Noah as helmsman and commander. And, with the exception of this ark, all things existing upon the earth were, as we read, destroyed. This church, moreover, we venerate as the only one. [. . .] She is that seamless garment of the Lord that was not cut but that fell by lot.[21] Therefore of this one and only church there is one body and one head—not two heads as if it were a monster: Christ, namely, and the vicar of Christ, St. Peter, and the successor of Peter. For the Lord himself said to Peter, "Feed my sheep." "My sheep," he said, using a general term, and not designating these or those particular sheep; from which it is plain that he committed to him *all* his sheep. If, then, the Greeks[22] or others say that they were not committed to the care of Peter and his successors, they necessarily confess that they are not of the sheep of Christ; for the Lord says, in John, that there is one fold, one shepherd, and one only. We are told by the word of the Gospel that in this his fold there are two swords—a spiritual, namely, and a temporal. For when the apostles said, "Behold here are two swords"—when, namely, the apostles were speaking in the church—the Lord did not reply that this was too much, but enough. Surely he who denies that the temporal sword is in the power of Peter wrongly interprets the word of the Lord when he says, "Put up your sword in its scabbard." Both swords, the spiritual and the material, therefore, are in the power of the church; the one, indeed, to be wielded for the church, the other by the church; the one by the hand of the priest, the other by the hand of kings and knights, but at the will and sufferance of the priest. One sword, moreover, ought to be under the other, and the temporal authority to be subjected to the spiritual. For when the apostle says "there is no power but of God, and the powers that are of God are ordained," they would not be ordained unless sword were under sword and the lesser one, as it were, were led by the other to great deeds. [. . .] But that the spiritual exceeds any earthly power in dignity and nobility we ought the more openly to confess the more spiritual things excel temporal ones. [. . .] For, the truth bearing witness, the spiritual power has to establish the earthly power, and to judge it if it be not good. Thus concerning the church and the ecclesiastical power is verified the prophecy of Jeremiah: "See, I have this day set

21. *seamless garment . . . that fell by lot*—see John 19:23–24: "When the soldiers had crucified Jesus, they took his clothes and divided them into four parts, one for each soldier. They also took his tunic; now the tunic was seamless, woven in one piece from the top. So they said to one another, 'Let us not tear it, but cast lots for it to see who will get it.' This was to fulfill what the scripture says, 'They divided my clothes among themselves, and for my clothing they cast lots'" (NRSV).

22. *Greeks*—Easterners.

you over the nations and over the kingdoms," and the other things that
follow. Therefore if the earthly power err it shall be judged by the spiritual power; but if the lesser spiritual power err, by the greater. But if the
greatest, it can be judged by God alone, not by man, the apostle bearing
witness. A spiritual man judges all things, but he himself is judged by no
one. This authority, moreover, even though it is given to man and exercised through man, is not human but rather divine, being given by divine
lips to Peter and founded on a rock for him and his successors through
Christ himself whom he has confessed; the Lord himself saying to Peter:
"Whatsoever you shall bind," etc. Whoever, therefore, resists this power
thus ordained by God, resists the ordination of God. [. . .] Indeed we declare, announce, and define that it is altogether necessary to salvation for
every human creature to be subject to the Roman pontiff. [. . .]

FILIOQUE

The Roman church's insertion of a single word—*filioque*—into the
Creed of Nicaea launched furious arguments and accusations that
continue to this day.

The creed, as revised at the First Council of Constantinople in 381,
asserts that the Holy Spirit "proceeds from the Father": literally, τὸ
ἐκ τοῦ Πατρὸς ἐκπορευόμενον, or "from the Father proceeding." The
Western church later inserted one word, *filioque*, into the Latin translation of the creed, resulting in *ex Patre Filioque procedit*, or "from
the Father *and the Son* proceeds."

Thus, where the original creed describes the Holy Spirit as proceeding *only* from the Father, the Western church decided that the Holy
Spirit proceeds from the Father *and from the Son*.

The origins of the *filioque* remain obscure. The phrase probably first
appeared somewhere in Spain as a tool to counter Arianism: suggesting
that the Holy Spirit proceeds from the Father *and from the Son* might,
in some eyes, increase the importance of the Son, thus suggesting, as
the Arians' opponents insisted, that the Son is fully equal to the Father.

The church in Spain formally adopted the phrase at the Council of
Toledo in 589. It then slowly made its way east into France and Germany. Charlemagne, who became the first "Holy Roman emperor,"
adopted the phrase at a church council in 794, and Frankish monks
began using it in the early 800s. It appeared regularly in Frankish
Masses later in the 800s. When Henry II was crowned Holy Roman
emperor in 1014, the officiants recited the creed with the *filioque*.

The addition of the *filioque* to the creed seems not to have garnered
much attention in the East until the 800s. But when it did, it led to
centuries of outrage.

Why?

The Creed of Nicaea was adopted first in 325 and then revised in 381, both times at councils of the church that both the East and West recognized as ecumenical and thus universally binding. The councils' delegates painstakingly examined and agonized over each and every word. How dare a single portion of the church, said the Easterners, now introduce a novelty into this oh-so-carefully constructed creed without consulting anyone in the East? Only another ecumenical council (nearly impossible by the 800s) had the authority to enact such a change. This addition of the *filioque*, fumed the Easterners, was unilateral (without question), arrogant (perhaps), and designed to insult (probably not).

Second, many in the East believed the *filioque* to be bad theology. However simplistic, there is much truth in the common observation that the East pays more attention than the West to the individual natures and unique roles of Father, Son, and Holy Spirit. The *filioque,* argued opponents in the East, merged and confused the distinct hypostases, or manifestations, of Father and Son. John of Damascus had famously argued that the distinction between the Son and the Holy Spirit stems from the means by which each originates from the Father: the Son is "begotten" from the Father while the Holy Spirit "proceeds" from the Father. To say now that the Holy Spirit proceeds from the Father *and from the Son* confuses the proper distinction between Father and Son.

Third, the Byzantine Empire faced dire threats in the 800s and 900s from Islamic enemies to the East. During a time of uncertainty and fear, that is, during a time when the protection of God was more crucial than ever, any theological novelties or errors that might compromise correct understandings of (and thus right relations with and protection from) the triune God could not be tolerated.

Patriarch Photios Condemns Rome
over the *Filioque* (867)

Deno John Geanakoplos, *Byzantium: Church, Society, and Civilization Seen through Contemporary Eyes* (Chicago: University of Chicago Press, 1984), 205. Used by permission of The University of Chicago Press.

Here Patriarch Photios of Constantinople condemns the *filioque*. (We encountered Photios earlier in "Missions to the North: Balkans and Rus'.")[23]

23. For a defense of the *filioque* by an Easterner, see document 18.1.1, "Maximus Confessor Defends the *Filioque*," in the online supplement.

Where have you learned [that the Holy Spirit proceeds from the Son]? From what Gospel is [*filioque*] taken? From which council does this blasphemy come? Our Lord and God says, "the Spirit that proceeds from the Father." But the fathers of this new impiety state, "the Spirit that proceeds from the Son."

Who will not close his ears against the enormity of this blasphemy? It goes against the Gospel, it is arrayed against the holy synods, and it contradicts the blessed and holy fathers: Athanasius the great, Gregory renowned in theology, the [royal] robe of the church [who is] the great Basil, and the golden-mouth of the *oikoumene*,[24] that sea of wisdom truly named Chrysostom. But why should I mention this father or that one? This blasphemous term, which militates against God, is at the same time armed against everyone: the holy prophets, the apostles, bishops, martyrs, and the voices of God himself.

CHARLEMAGNE AND THE POPE ASSERT THEMSELVES

The conquest of Rome by the Visigoths in the 400s left the Western Empire in shambles. Gone were all Roman territories in modern Spain, France, England, and much of northern Africa. Religious scholarship languished. Popes feuded with minor princes. A center could not be found.

The Byzantine Empire, centered in Constantinople, proved unable (and mostly unwilling) to assist churches in the West. Finding no meaningful offers of help or alliances (military or other) from Constantinople, the Roman church—bereft of patronage and protection—looked elsewhere.

It looked in particular to the Franks, that is, Germanic tribes living north and east of the lower Rhine River. First identified by the Romans in the 200s, the Franks (sometimes called "Germans") converted to Christianity by the 500s. During the next three centuries they expanded throughout Central Europe: by the 800s they had moved through modern France ("France" derives from "Frank"), east into the Bavarian and Saxon portions of modern Germany, and south into the northern parts of modern Italy. In short, they controlled all of west-central Europe.

But for all their success, the Franks in these early centuries constituted a rather motley conglomeration of forces: sometimes cooperating and often squabbling. In 751 Pepin (or "Pippin") the Short became

24. *oikoumene*—an ancient Greek word for the inhabited world. Often used by the church to denote all of Christendom.

sole ruler of all Frankish tribes and devoted himself to unifying them into an effective force. Pippin's illegitimate son Charles continued his father's efforts by embarking on a series of wars that made the Franks *the* major power in Europe. The Byzantine Empire watched, wary and impotent, as the Franks expanded into Italy and the Balkans.

Charles, or "Charlemagne" ("Charles the Great"), allied himself closely with the Western church, conflating the work and responsibilities of church and state to a degree not seen in the West for centuries. He expected bishops to enforce his royal councils' edicts. He claimed and asserted the right to discipline clerics, oversee church property, and define doctrine. Concerned about disarray in the church that had festered since the fall of the Roman Empire, Charlemagne reformed the church's hierarchy and clarified ecclesiastical responsibilities.

The papacy, weak and without a protector, mostly welcomed these moves. And because Charlemagne controlled the appointment of bishops and abbots, the Western church had little choice *but* to welcome these moves. With Charlemagne's assertion of royal prerogatives in religious matters came significant financial support for the church.

Charlemagne also recognized the papacy's control of the papal states, areas of northern and central Italy, which Charlemagne's Frankish predecessors and then Charlemagne himself guaranteed for the Western church in return for the church's cooperation with the Franks. In 781 Charlemagne explicitly identified lands—including parts of Tuscany, Corsica, and Lombardy—in which popes would serve as spiritual *and temporal* sovereigns.

In gratitude for Charlemagne's protection and largess, Pope Leo III crowned Charlemagne in 800 as *Augustus Romanorum*, "emperor of the Romans." The coronation served as an unequivocal declaration that he, Charlemagne, was the rightful heir to the political and religious legacy of Christian Rome. Such a declaration also served as a dig at the Byzantine Empire, which, of course, understood itself—with more justification than did Charlemagne's empire—as the true heir to the glories of the now-defunct Roman Empire.

Charlemagne took seriously the need to improve the rather lax moral standards of the Western clergy, to provide better education (including basic literacy) for priests, and to standardize divergent liturgical practices. He brought to these tasks the energy manifest in all areas of his life. (He hunted with a passion, wore out five wives, and doted on at least eighteen children—his coterie of concubines makes it difficult to establish firmly the number of his progeny.) Although

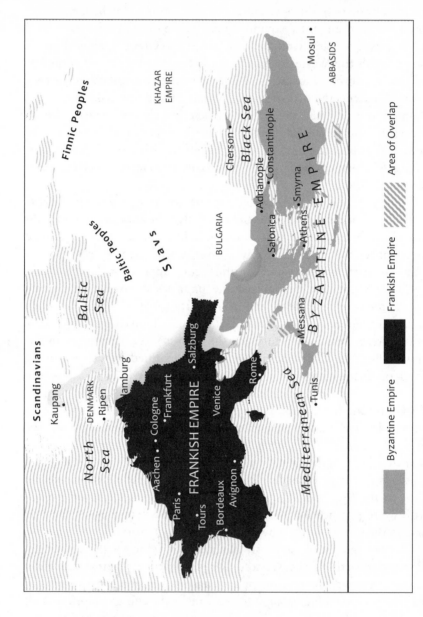

Figure 29. Charlemagne's territory, 814

Scandinavians

Finnic Peoples

North Sea

Kaupang •

DENMARK
• Ripen

Hamburg

Baltic Sea

Baltic peoples

Slavs

KHAZAR EMPIRE

• Cologne
Aachen •   • Frankfurt
       • Salzburg
FRANKISH EMPIRE

Paris •
Tours •
Bordeaux •
       • Avignon

• Venice

• Rome

BULGARIA

Black Sea

• Cherson

• Adrianople
       Constantinople •

       • Salonica   • Smyrna

       • Athens

Mediterranean Sea

Messana •

• Tunis

BYZANTINE EMPIRE

Mosul •

ABBASIDS

Byzantine Empire   Frankish Empire   Area of Overlap

illiterate, Charlemagne promoted and funded scholarship within his realm to a degree never before seen. He vastly improved the educational system. Bishops and abbots reinvigorated monastic schools and founded new ones. He created a court library to house theological works and a royal scriptorium to copy them, and he ordered that these copies circulate throughout his realm. Members of Charlemagne's court wrote religious poetry, history, biblical exegesis, theological tracts, and epistles.

Efforts in the East to educate clergy paled in comparison.

All these measures, of course, irked the Byzantines, who questioned the right of an upstart Western emperor to insert himself so willfully into the affairs of the church. Perhaps what bothered the Byzantines most, however, was Charlemagne's careful cultivation of the papacy, his treatment of the pope as the church's supreme religious authority, and his understanding of himself and the pope as partners in reestablishing *the* Christian empire. As Robert Sullivan writes, Charlemagne and his court understood this new Christian empire, although centered in Germany, as comprising

> all who adhered to the orthodox faith proclaimed by the Roman Church. This community accepted the dominion of a monarch increasingly hailed as the "new David" and the "new Constantine," the guardian of Christendom and executor of God's will. Concern for the welfare of the *imperium Christianum* was heightened by the perceived unfitness of the heretical emperors in Constantinople to claim authority over the Christian community—especially after a woman, Irene, became Eastern emperor in 797. In a larger sense, developments in the eighth century produced the perception in [Charlemagne's] world that the Latin West and the Greek East were diverging in ways that negated the universalist claims of the Eastern emperors.[25]

Charlemagne's activities directly challenged the church in the East. Who was he, the Easterners asked, to take charge of clerical education? What gave him the right to revise liturgical practice? Who was Charlemagne to grant lands from the true Roman Empire (which Byzantium still imagined itself to be) to the bishop of Rome? Here, concluded the Byzantines, was an arrogant man making dangerous claims about religious and secular authority, building a new empire in which Byzantium had no real place.

25. Robert Sullivan, "Charlemagne," in *New Encyclopaedia Britannica* (Chicago: Encyclopaedia Britannica, 2007).

Charlemagne to Pope Leo III on Relations with the Papacy (796)

"Charles to Leo III: Early 796," in *Charlemagne: Translated Sources*, ed. and trans. P. D. King (Lambrigg: P. D. King, 1987), 311–12.

After learning of Pope Adrian I's death in December 795, Charlemagne dispatched a letter to his successor, Pope Leo III. Charlemagne's eagerness to retain and strengthen ties with the papacy is evident here.

Charles, by the grace of God, king of the Franks and the Lombards and patrician of the Romans, to Leo, pope: the greeting of perpetual bliss in Christ.

[. . .] I was overwhelmed by the news of [Pope Adrian's] death [. . .]

But it was a great solace that the divine grace provided for us in causing you [. . .] to be chosen in his place, that there should be one who might make daily intercession with the blessed Peter, prince of the apostles, for the stability of the whole church and well-being of myself and my *fideles*[26]—indeed, for the prosperity of the entire realm given to us by God— and who might adopt us, with a father's loving kindness, as his son.

And to confirm that we are of one pacific heart with you in this most sweet love, we have sent Angilbert—who is close to us and serves as our intimate counselor—to your holiness [. . .] And we have charged him with all matters that seem pertinent to our wishes or your needs, so that you and he, deliberating together, may discuss whatever is perceived to be necessary for the exaltation of God's holy church, the stability of your *honor* and the security of our patriciate.[27] [. . .]

For just as I entered upon a pact with the most blessed father who was the predecessor of your holy fatherhood, so I desire your blessedness, to the end that, by the divine grace that the prayers of your apostolic holiness call upon, apostolic blessing may attend me everywhere I may be and the most holy see of the Roman Church may always, by God's gift, be defended by our devotion. It is our function—to the extent that divine goodness aids us—externally to defend Christ's holy church on every side by force of arms against the incursions of the pagans and the devastations of the infidels, internally to strengthen it in knowledge of the catholic faith. It is yours, most holy father, to aid our struggle with hands raised to

26. *fideles*—faithful ones.
27. *patriciate*—noble rank.

God, like Moses, to the end that, with you interceding and God guiding and granting, the Christian people should at all times and in all places enjoy victory over the enemies of his holy name and the name of our Lord Jesus Christ be glorified throughout the whole world. [. . .]

Account of Charlemagne Being Crowned Emperor (late 900s)

"Moissac Chronicle," in *Charlemagne: Translated Sources*, ed. and trans. P. D. King (Lambrigg: P. D. King, 1987), 144.

Pope Leo III crowned Charlemagne *Augustus Romanorum*, "emperor of the Romans," in 800. A greater rhetorical challenge to the Byzantine emperors cannot be imagined. The following account is from the *Moissac Chronicle*, a compilation of primary sources assembled in the late 900s.

[. . .] And since the name of emperor was at this time lacking among the Greeks and they had female rule[28] among them, it then seemed to the Apostolicus Leo[29] and to all the holy fathers present at that council,[30] as well as to the rest of the Christian people, that they ought to bestow the name of emperor upon Charles himself, king of the Franks, who held Rome itself, where the caesars had always been accustomed to have their seat, and the rest of the seats, which he held throughout Italy, Gaul and Germany; since Almighty God had granted all these seats into his power, it seemed to them to be right that, with the help of God and at the request of the entire Christian people, he should have that name. King Charles was himself unwilling to deny this request of theirs and, having submitted with all humility to God and the petition of the sacerdotes[31] and the entire Christian people, received the name of emperor, with the consecration of the Lord Pope Leo, on the very day of the nativity of our Lord Jesus Christ. And his very first action there was to recall the holy Roman church from its internal discord to peace and harmony. [. . .]

28. *female rule*—rule by Empress Irene (797–802).
29. *Apostolicus Leo*—Pope Leo III (795–816).
30. *that council*—an assembly of bishops, abbots, priests, and deacons summoned by Charlemagne to the city of Mainz in 800.
31. *sacerdotes*—priests.

Einhard on Charlemagne, Constantinople, and Rome (ca. 817–836)

Einhard: The Life of Charlemagne, trans. Samuel Epes Turner (Ann Arbor: University of Michigan Press, 1960), 43, 56.

This excerpt comes from a biography of Charlemagne written by a member of his court. It frankly acknowledges suspicions in the East about Charlemagne and his intentions.

[. . .] The emperors of Constantinople, Nicephorus, Michael, and Leo,[32] made advances to Charles, and sought friendship and alliance with him by several embassies; and even when the Greeks suspected him of designing to wrest the empire from them, because of his assumption of the title emperor, they made a close alliance with him, that he might have no cause of offense. In fact, the power of the Franks was always viewed by the Greeks and Romans with a jealous eye, whence the Greek proverb: "Have the Frank for your friend, but not for your neighbor." [. . .]

He cherished the church of St. Peter the apostle at Rome above all other holy and sacred places, and heaped its treasury with a vast wealth of gold, silver, and precious stones. He sent great and countless gifts to the popes; and throughout his whole reign the wish that he had nearest at heart was to re-establish the ancient authority of the city of Rome under his care and by his influence, and to defend and protect the church of St. Peter, and to beautify and enrich it out of his own store above all other churches. [. . .]

ANATHEMAS OF 1054

Perhaps the most spectacular controversy between the medieval church in the East and church in the West erupted over bread. Rome insisted on using unleavened bread (*azyma,* i.e., bread made *without* yeast) in the Eucharist. Constantinople used leavened bread (bread made *with* yeast) and accused Rome of endorsing "Judaic" practices, since Jews celebrate Passover with unleavened bread.

Roman attempts to impose Western practices, including the use of unleavened bread, on Byzantine churches in southern Italy peeved Patriarch Michael Cerularius of Constantinople (1043–1058), who or-

---

32. *Nicephorus, Michael, and Leo*—Nicephorus I (802–811), Michael I (811–813), and Leo V (813–820).

dered all Roman churches in that city either to use leavened bread or to close. Cerularius also circulated a letter to all bishops in the West, including the pope, condemning the use of unleavened bread.

One recipient of this letter was the irascible Cardinal Humbert, Pope Leo IX's secretary. Humbert translated the letter into Latin and angrily gave it to Pope Leo. Leo, now angry himself, ordered a point-by-point response—including a defense of papal supremacy.

Here we should note that the Byzantine emperor Constantine IX never authorized Cerularius's letter. In fact the letter upset Constantine, who craved the papacy's support in warding off Norman invaders. Constantine forced Cerularius to write a conciliatory letter to Pope Leo, offering to work through the dispute and forge a common alliance against the Normans. Leo responded by dispatching Cardinal Humbert and two other papal legates to Constantinople.

Pope Leo, who apparently meant well, could not have picked a worse representative than Humbert. Though intelligent, Humbert could be a cantankerous pill. So could Cerularius. When Cerularius received Humbert's delegation, he did so with what Humbert considered to be haughty contempt. Humbert and company, miffed by the reception, stomped out of the palace hosting the reception.

Subsequent negotiations, begun on such a sour note, went nowhere, and on 16 April 1054, Humbert and his angry companions marched into the great church of Hagia Sofia and placed a bull of excommunication against Patriarch Cerularius on the altar. (It is significant that Humbert did not consult Pope Leo before issuing the excommunication; in fact Leo had just died.) The church synod in Constantinople responded by excommunicating the papal legates.

It is tempting to identify 1054 as the formal date of irreparable schism between East and West. But those living in the decades that followed seemed not to view the anathemas as an especially big deal. The anathemas were, after all, aimed at particular individuals, not against the offices those individuals occupied, nor against the churches they served. Nothing in the anathemas suggested that communion between East and West had broken. Rome and Constantinople still communicated amiably at times. In 1089, for example, the Byzantine emperor Alexius appealed to Rome for assistance against the Normans. The pope and patriarch continued to exchange embassies, and there is no evidence that the populace at large viewed the anathemas as indicative of schism, or, for that matter, even knew about them.

Still, as is evident in the following documents, the vituperations leveled in 1054 were difficult to forgive or forget. And they illustrate the extreme distrust that had accumulated over the centuries and would continue to accumulate.

Cardinal Humbert's Anathema against Patriarch Michael I (1054)

Deno John Geanakoplos, *Byzantium: Church, Society, and Civilization Seen through Contemporary Eyes* (Chicago: University of Chicago Press, 1984), 208–9. Used by permission of The University of Chicago Press.

The bull of excommunication issued by Cardinal Humbert's delegation against Patriarch Cerularius appears here. The Byzantine counter-excommunication, issued by the synod Cerularius assembled, immediately follows. Jaroslav Pelikan and Valerie Hotchkiss note that the modern reader cannot avoid being struck by how "both sides have intermingled dogma (the *filioque*), polity (Roman primacy), church law (clerical celibacy), liturgical practice (leavened versus unleavened bread in the Eucharist), and custom (for example, bearded versus clean-shaven priests)."[33]

Humbert, by the grace of God cardinal-bishop of the Holy Roman Church [et al.]:

The holy Roman, first, and apostolic see, toward which, as toward the head, belongs the special solicitude of all churches, for the sake of the peace and benefit of the church, has deigned to appoint us legates to this city in order that, according to our instructions, we might come over and see whether in fact the clamor still continues that, without ceasing, comes to [Rome's] ears or, if that is not so, in order that the holy see might find out about it. Therefore, above all else, let the glorious emperors, the clergy, the senate, and the people of this city of Constantinople, and the entire catholic church, know that we have noted here a great good, on account of which we deeply rejoice in the Lord, but also we have perceived a very great evil because of which we are extremely saddened.

For, with respect to the pillars of the empire and its wise and honored citizens the city is most Christian and orthodox. However, with regard to Michael[34] falsely called patriarch, and his followers in folly, too many

33. Jaroslav Pelikan and Valerie Hotchkiss, eds., *Creeds & Confessions of Faith in the Christian Tradition* (New Haven, CT: Yale University Press, 2003), 1:309.

34. *Michael*—Patriarch Michael Cerularius.

tares and heresies are daily sown in its midst. For as the Simoniacs[35] sell God's gift; as the Valesians[36] castrate their guests and promote them not only to the priesthood but even to the episcopate; as the Arians rebaptize people already baptized (especially Latins) in the name of the Holy Trinity; as the Dynamists[37] affirm that, excepting for the Greek church, Christ's church and the true sacrifice [of the Mass] and baptism have perished from the whole world; as the Nicolaites[38] permit and defend [carnal] marriage for ministers of the holy altar;[39] as the Severians[40] maintain that the law of Moses is accursed; as the Pneumatomachians[41] or Theoumachians[42] have deleted from the creed the procession of the Holy Spirit from the Son; as the Manicheans[43] declare, among other things, that anything fermented is alive; as the Nazarenes[44] maintain the bodily cleanliness of the Jews to such a point that they deny baptism to infants who die before the eighth day after birth and [deny] Communion to menstruating women or those about to give birth or if [the women] were pagan they forbid them to be baptized; also [the Nazarenes], preserving their hair and beards, do not receive into communion those who, according to the custom of the Roman Church, cut their hair and shave their beards. Although admonished by our Lord Pope Leo regarding these errors and many other of his deeds, Michael [Cerularius] himself has with contempt disregarded these warnings. Moreover, to us [Leo's] ambassa-

---

35. *Simoniacs*—those who engage in simony, that is, buying or selling church offices.

36. *Valesians*—a sect mentioned by Epiphanius, a Cyprian bishop in the late 300s, that castrated its members.

37. *Dynamists*—those who believed that Jesus, though inspired by the spirit of God, was a mere mortal and not the son of God.

38. *Nicolaites*—a sect mentioned in the book of Revelation about which we know little. Some church fathers surmised that the Nicolaites were guilty of promiscuity.

39. *[carnal] marriage for ministers of the holy altar*—Eastern priests are allowed to marry; Roman Catholic priests are not.

40. *Severians*—followers of Severus; Monophysites.

41. *Pneumatomachians*—followers of Bishop Macedonius of Constantinople in the 300s. Also known as the "spirit fighters," they denied the divinity of the Holy Spirit.

42. *Theoumachians*—another sect that denied the divinity of the Holy Spirit.

43. *Manicheans*—followers of the Persian religious philosopher Mani (216–274), who believed in an age-old conflict between darkness and light. Mani's thought combined elements of esoteric Christianity, Buddhism, and Persian Zoroastrianism.

44. *Nazarenes*—Hebrews mentioned in the book of Numbers, set apart and specially consecrated to God. They abstained from alcohol and allowed their hair to grow uncut.

dors who are seeking faithfully to stamp out the cause of such great evils, he denied his presence and any oral communication, and he forbade [us the use of] churches to celebrate Mass in, just as earlier he had closed the Latin churches [in Constantinople], and, calling the Latins *azymites,* he hounded them everywhere in word and deed. Indeed, in the persons of its sons, he cursed the apostolic see, in opposition to that he signed himself "ecumenical patriarch." Therefore, not putting up with this unheard-of slander and insult to the first, holy apostolic see, and seeing the catholic faith assaulted in many ways, we, by the authority of the undivided and Holy Trinity and that of the apostolic see, whose embassy we constitute, and by the authority of all the orthodox fathers of the seven [ecumenical] councils and that of the entire catholic church, whatever our most reverend lord the pope has denounced in Michael and his followers, unless they repent, we declare to be anathematized:

May Michael, false neophyte patriarch, who only out of human fear assumed the monastic habit, now known notoriously to many because of his extremely wicked crimes, and with him Leo the archdeacon called bishop of Ochrida, and his treasurer Michael, and Constantine who with profane feet trampled upon the Latins' sacrifice [the Eucharist], and all their followers in the aforesaid errors and presumptions, be anathematized, Maranatha,[45] with the Simoniacs, Valesians, Arians, Donatists,[46] Nicolaites, Severians, Pneumatomachians, Manichaeans, and Nazarenes, along with all heretics, indeed with the devil and his angels, unless by some chance they repent. Amen. Amen. Amen.

Edict of Michael I and the Synod of Constantinople (1054)

"Michael Cerularius and the Synod of Constantinople, The Edict, 1054," in *Creeds and Confessions of Faith in the Christian Tradition,* ed. Jaroslav Pelikan and Valerie Hotchkiss (New Haven, CT: Yale University Press, 2003), 1:311–17. Used by permission of Yale University Press.

Patriarch Michael Cerularius and his synod responded as follows.

1. Edict concerning the writ of excommunication placed on the altar by the Roman legates against the most holy patriarch, Lord Michael, in the month of July [. . .]

45. *Maranatha*—"Our Lord, come!"
46. *Donatists*—Christians who argued that priests and bishops who renounced Christianity during the persecutions of Diocletian (303–305) were not fit to administer the sacraments, even if they sought forgiveness for their renunciations.

3. The evil one, it seems, never has his fill of wickedness. Therefore he never ceases to attack pious people and is always devising some sort of new plot against the truth. [. . .] [T]here now come some men who are wicked, abominable, and (for right believers) downright unspeakable, men who have come up out of the darkness. Having their origin in the West, they arrived in this devout and God-protected city,[47] out of which the wellsprings of orthodoxy flow as from some deep and elevated place and the pure streams of right belief gush forth into the entire civilized world and the rivers water all the souls under the sun with correct dogmas. Bursting into it like lightning or an earthquake or a hailstorm or, to put it more appropriately, like a boar out of the forest, they tried to overthrow the orthodox message with a diversity of dogmas, so that they laid a writ on the sacramental altar of the great church of God,[48] by which they pronounced an anathema on us, or rather on the orthodox church of God and all those orthodox who, simply because they have a desire to believe correctly and to preserve the orthodox faith, have not been carried away by their false doctrines. They also attack us on other grounds: that we refuse to shave our beards as they do and to alter the natural human appearance; also, that we do not decline to receive holy Communion from presbyters who are married; in addition to all this, that we are not willing to adulterate, with false reasoning and alien terminology as well as with overweening presumption, the sacred and holy creed,[49] which has been endowed with unassailable authority by all the conciliar and ecumenical decrees; that we do not say, as they do, that the Holy Spirit proceeds from the Father and the Son (O, the machinations of the evil one!), but from the Father; that we desire not to contravene the scripture when it says, "You shall not mar the edges of your beard"; that we do not want to concede that God the creator made something seemly for women that he pronounced to be unseemly for men. It is also obvious that they despise the fifth canon of the synod of Gangra[50] concerning those who have a loathing for matrimony when it says: "If anyone separates himself from a married presbyter, as though it were not proper, when he has celebrated the liturgy, to receive the oblation[51] from him, let him be anathema." [. . .] [No one should demand] at the time of ordination that [a deacon] abstain from intercourse with his own lawful wife, lest we be compelled to insult marriage, which God has instituted and blessed with his own presence: as the voice of the Gospel cries out, "What God has joined together, let not man put asunder"; and as the apostle teaches, "Marriage is honorable

47. *God-protected city*—Constantinople.
48. *great church of God*—Hagia Sofia in Constantinople.
49. *creed*—Nicene Creed.
50. *synod of Gangra*—a synod held sometime in the 300s, about which we know little.
51. *oblation*—act of offering the eucharistic elements to God.

in all things, and the marriage bed undefiled"; and "Are you bound to a wife? Do not seek to be free." [. . .]

4. In addition to all of this and totally without understanding, they say that the Spirit proceeds not only from the Father but "also from the Son." For they do not get this statement from the evangelists, nor does this blasphemous dogma derive from an ecumenical council. For the Lord our God says "the spirit of truth, who proceeds from the Father"; but the fathers of this novel piece of impiety say "the Spirit, who proceeds from the Father and the Son." But once again they do not see that because the distinctive attribute of the Spirit is discerned in his proceeding from the Father, just as the distinctive attribute of the Spirit is discerned in his proceeding from the Father, just as the distinctive attribute of the Son is discerned in his being begotten, then if the Spirit proceeds also from the Son, as their wicked teaching maintains, the Spirit will be distinguished from the Father by more distinctive attributes than the Son is. For to come from the Father is common to the Spirit and the Son, but the procession from the Father is peculiar to the Spirit, though not also to the Son. [. . .]

6. [Here Cerularius and his synod reproduce the papal legates' writ of excommunication.]

7. That is the content of this wicked and despicable writ. Our humble person, being unwilling to let such an insult and shameless presumption against true belief stand without scrutiny and be left unpunished, spoke to our mighty and holy emperor about the matter. [. . .]

8. In accordance with the dispensation of the orthodoxy-loving autocrat,[52] the wicked writing itself, as well as those who perpetrated it and those who contributed to its composition and those who gave assistance to the perpetrators, were subjected to an anathema in the grand privy council and in the presence of the representatives of the emperor. The judgment took place on the fourth day, which is the first day of the present month. But on the twenty-fourth day of the present month of July [. . .] with a large crowd in attendance, an anathema was pronounced again upon the same wicked writing itself, as well as upon those who perpetrated it and wrote it and who gave any assistance or counsel to the deed. [. . .]

FOURTH CRUSADE

If distance, language, theological disputes, and papal claims divided East from West, the Fourth Crusade of 1204 ensured a total rupture. The story of the Fourth Crusade is a sordid one, which might be darkly

---

52. *autocrat*—emperor.

comic were the results less tragic. Many in the Eastern church talk about its humiliations and injustices as if they occurred yesterday.

By the end of the 1000s Muslim forces had conquered roughly two-thirds of the Christian world, defeats that prompted endless hand-wringing and speculation about which sins or lack of zeal had prompted God to abandon "his people." One response—or rather a series of disjointed responses, each with its own particular motivations and goals—was the Crusades, campaigns supported between 1096 and 1270 by popes, bishops, kings, and emperors and staffed by standing armies, mercenaries, untrained peasants, priests, monks, and even children that were designed to halt the spread of Islam and to recapture formerly Christian regions. Although crusader campaigns spread as far west as Spain and as far east as the Baltics, much of the rhetoric and activity focused on capturing the "Holy Land"—that is, Jerusalem and its environs—which Muslim forces had overrun several centuries earlier. (Jerusalem first fell in 638 to Umar, a companion of and successor to the Prophet Muhammad.) The crusaders' motives— often a mix of righteous ideals and greed—were complex, malleable, and frequently confused.

Some of the campaigns realized significant territorial gains, as crusaders drove out Muslim troops and established Christian feudal states. Other campaigns turned into utter debacles, with thousands of deaths the only meaningful result.

Anna Komnenos on the Franks (ca. 1148)

Anna Comnena, *The Alexiad*, trans. E. R. A. Sewter
(New York: Penguin, 2003), 308–9.

Although the crusaders viewed themselves as a liberating force, our earlier discussions of East-West relations should make it easy to imagine the mistrust with which the "liberated" Eastern Christians viewed this influx of armies composed of English, French, Germanic, papal, and other soldiers from multiple points west. The following brief example of that mistrust is from a history of the First Crusade (1096–1099) written by the daughter of the Byzantine emperor Alexius I (1081–1118).

[Emperor Alexius] had no time to relax before he heard a rumor that countless Frankish armies were approaching. He dreaded their arrival, knowing as he did their uncontrollable passion, their erratic character and their irresolution, not to mention the other peculiar traits of the Kelt,[53] with their inevitable consequences: their greed for money, for example, which always led them, it seemed, to break their own agreements without scruple for any chance reason. He had consistently heard this said of them and it was abundantly justified. [. . .]

Crusader's Criticism of the Greeks (ca. 1148)

Odo of Deuil, from *De profectione Ludovici VII in orientem:*
The Journey of Louis VII to the East, by Virginia Gingerick Berry,
trans., pp. 56–59, 65–67, 99. Copyright © 1948 Columbia University Press.
Reprinted with permission of the publisher.

Crusaders also mistrusted the Easterners. The following account from the Second Crusade (1145–1149) was written by the chaplain to Prince Louis VII of France, a pious if eccentric leader who vowed to embark on a crusade to atone for his sins.

[If] our priests celebrated Mass on Greek altars, the Greeks afterward purified them with propitiatory offerings and ablutions, as if they had been defiled. [. . .] [E]very time they celebrate the marriage of one of our men, if he has been baptized in the Roman way, they rebaptize him before they make the pact. We know other heresies of theirs, both concerning the treatment of the Eucharist and concerning the procession of the Holy Spirit, but none of these matters would mar our page if not pertinent to our subject. Actually, it was for these reasons that the Greeks had incurred the hatred of our men, for their error had become known even among our lay people. Because of this they were judged not to be Christians, and the Franks considered killing them a matter of no importance and hence could with the more difficulty be restrained from pillage and plundering. [. . .]

[. . .] [T]he Greeks degenerated entirely into women; putting aside all manly vigor, both of words and of spirit, they lightly swore whatever they thought would please us, but they neither kept faith with us nor maintained respect for themselves. In general they really have the opinion that anything that is done for the holy empire cannot be considered perjury. Let no one think that I am taking vengeance on a race of men hateful to me and that because of my hatred I am inventing a Greek whom I have not seen. Whoever has known the Greeks will, if asked, say that when they are afraid they become despicable in their excessive debasement and

53. *Kelt*—Frank.

when they have the upper hand they are arrogant in their severe violence to those subjected to them. [. . .]

[Constantinople] is squalid and fetid and in many places harmed by permanent darkness, for the wealthy overshadow the streets with buildings and leave these dirty, dark places to the poor and to travelers; there murders and robberies and other crimes that love the darkness are committed. Moreover, since people live lawlessly in this city, which has as many lords as rich men and almost as many thieves as poor men, a criminal knows neither fear nor shame, because crime is not punished by law and never entirely comes to light. In every respect she exceeds moderation; for, just as she surpasses other cities in wealth, so, too, does she surpass them in vice. [. . .]

Niketas Choniates (ca. 1155–1215) on the Sack of Constantinople

Niketas Choniates, O *City of Byzantium, Annals of Niketas Choniatēs,* trans. Harry J. Magoulias (Detroit: Wayne State University Press, 1984), 312–20. © 1984 Wayne State University Press, with the permission of Wayne State University Press.

Perceptions such as those in the excerpt above preceded the Fourth Crusade, which was an utter debacle, dizzying in its rapid devolution from an idealistic quest to a catastrophe of ineptitude. But some history is in order.

In 1199 Pope Innocent III called for a crusade, usually numbered the "fourth," to recapture Jerusalem. Securing transportation proved to be the main challenge. How does one convey some 33,500 soldiers from north-central Europe to the Middle East? The ruler (doge) of Venice, which was at that time the great center of shipping in Italy, agreed to transport the troops, hoping to make a nice profit by building the ships required. By 1201 around 12,000 soldiers had arrived in Venice, expecting to sail from its port. There they found, just as the doge had promised, dozens of warships and transports. In fact they found three times as many ships as needed, since only around one-third of the expected forces actually showed up.

The Venetians, of course, insisted that the crusaders pay for the entire fleet. No money—no transportation.

The troops had no money.

The Venetians grew angry. What were they supposed to do with the remainder of a fleet they had spent a good year constructing?

The troops, too, were angry. How were they supposed to reach the Holy Land after traveling all the way to Venice?

The doge and the Venetians proposed a solution. As satisfaction for the debt the crusaders had no hope of paying, would they agree to stop on their way to Jerusalem to conquer, on behalf of the doge, the city of Zara on the Croatian coast?

This suggestion disgusted some of the troops. They were on a religious mission, they insisted. A good number refused and headed home. Pope Innocent's representative on the crusade, however, endorsed the move as the only way to prevent the entire trip from ending before it even began.

Nonetheless, Pope Innocent threatened to excommunicate anyone who participated in a campaign for Zara. The crusaders' leaders elected not to share Innocent's threat with their troops, so the ships sailed. The troops attacked Zara. Zara fell. And Innocent excommunicated the troops.

And then events took an even stranger turn.

The recently deposed Byzantine emperor, Alexius IV, offered the troops two hundred thousand silver marks, twenty ships, and ten thousand more troops to make another pit stop, this time in Constantinople.

Why? To conquer the city and reinstall him as emperor.

Some of the crusaders agreed. Others did not and abandoned this mission that now bore little resemblance to the one they had originally joined. Pope Innocent opposed the plan, but had no way to intervene.

So the remaining crusaders joined Alexius IV, and in late June of 1203 he and roughly eight thousand troops arrived at the outskirts of Constantinople—only to discover that the denizens of the city had no desire to welcome Alexius IV back as emperor. They had, after all, just deposed him. They taunted and jeered the soldiers and their former emperor. Disillusioned, humiliated, and goaded by the Venetians, who craved booty to offset their investment in the fleet, the troops laid siege to the city, and, after a long battle, breached the walls.

A Byzantine nobleman and government official wrote the following account of the sack of his city. Little introduction is necessary: the account speaks for itself and helps explain the anger that persists to this day.

[. . .]

The enemy, who had expected otherwise, found no one openly venturing into battle or taking up arms to resist; they saw that the way was

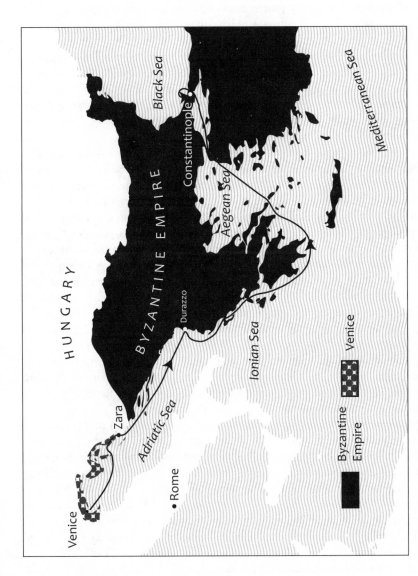

Figure 30. Route of the Fourth Crusade

open before them and everything there for the taking. The narrow streets were clear and the crossroads unobstructed, safe from attack, and advantageous to the enemy. The populace, moved by the hope of propitiating them, had turned out to greet them with crosses and venerable icons of Christ as was customary during festivals of solemn processions. But their disposition was not at all affected by what they saw, nor did their lips break into the slightest smile, nor did the unexpected spectacle transform their grim and frenzied glance and fury into a semblance of cheerfulness. Instead, they plundered with impunity and stripped their victims shamelessly, beginning with their carts. Not only did they rob them of their substance but also the articles consecrated to God; the rest fortified themselves all around with defensive weapons as their horses were roused at the sound of the war trumpet.

What then should I recount first and what last of those things dared at that time by these murderous men? O, the shameful dashing to earth of the venerable icons and the flinging of the relics of the saints [. . .] How horrible it was to see the divine body and blood of Christ poured out and thrown to the ground! These forerunners of Antichrist, chief agents and harbingers of his anticipated ungodly deeds, seized as plunder the precious chalices and patens;[54] some they smashed, taking possession of the ornaments embellishing them, and they set the remaining vessels on their tables to serve as bread dishes and wine goblets. Just as happened long ago, Christ was now disrobed and mocked, his garments were parted, and lots were cast for them by this race; and although his side was not pierced by the lance, yet once more streams of divine blood poured to the earth.

The report of the impious acts perpetrated in the great church are unwelcome to the ears. The table of sacrifice,[55] fashioned from every kind of precious material and fused by fire into one whole—blended together into a perfection of one multicolored thing of beauty, truly extraordinary and admired by all nations—was broken into pieces and divided among the despoilers, as was the lot of all the sacred church treasures, countless in number and unsurpassed in beauty. They found it fitting to bring out as so much booty the all-hallowed vessels and furnishings that had been wrought with incomparable elegance and craftsmanship from rare materials. In addition, in order to remove the pure silver which overlay the railing of the bema,[56] the wondrous pulpit and the gates, as well as that which covered a great many other adornments, all of which were plated with gold, they led to the very sanctuary of the temple itself mules and asses with packsaddles; some of these, unable to keep their feet on the

54. *patens*—plates for the eucharistic bread.
55. *table of sacrifice*—altar.
56. *bema*—the raised platform on which the altar sat.

smoothly polished marble floors, slipped and were pierced by knives so that the excrement from the bowels and the spilled blood defiled the sacred floor. Moreover, a certain silly woman[57] laden with sins, an attendant of the Erinyes,[58] the handmaid of demons, the workshop of unspeakable spells and reprehensible charms, waxing wanton against Christ, sat upon the synthronon[59] and intoned a song, and then whirled about and kicked up her heels in dance. [. . .]

There were lamentations and cries of woe and weeping in the narrow ways, wailing at the crossroads, moaning in the temples, outcries of men, screams of women, the taking of captives, and the dragging about, tearing in pieces, and raping of bodies heretofore sound and whole. They who were bashful of their sex were led about naked, they who were venerable in their old age uttered plaintive cries, and the wealthy were despoiled of their riches. [. . .]

The sons of Ishmael[60] did not behave in this way, for when the Latins overpowered Zion[61] the Latins showed no compassion or kindness to their race. Neither did the Ishmaelites[62] neigh after Latin women. [. . .] Thus the enemies of Christ dealt magnanimously with the Latin infidels, inflicting upon them neither sword, nor fire, nor hunger, nor persecution, nor nakedness, nor bruises, nor constraints. How differently, as we have briefly recounted, the Latins treated us who love Christ and are their fellow believers, guiltless of any wrong against them. [. . .]

O city, city, eye of all cities, universal boast, superabundant wonder, wet nurse of churches, leader of the faith, guide of orthodoxy, beloved topic of orations, the abode of every good thing! O city that has drunk at the hand of the Lord the cup of his fury! [. . .] The cup of your destruction is magnified, says Jeremiah, who was given to tears as he lamented over ancient Zion. What malevolent powers have desired to have you and taken you to be sifted? What jealous and relentless avenging demons have made a riotous assault upon you in wild revel? [. . .]

COUNCIL OF FERRARA-FLORENCE

By the 1430s the Byzantine Empire teetered on the brink of extinction. The Turks had reached Constantinople's eastern flank: nothing but the Bosporus and the Sea of Marmara stood between them and

---

57. *silly woman*—a prostitute.
58. *Erinyes*—"furies," mythological personifications of vengeance.
59. *synthronon*—row of seats on either side of the bishop's throne.
60. *sons of Ishmael*—Muslims.
61. *Zion*—Jerusalem.
62. *Ishmaelites*—Muslims.

the city. On the western front, the Ottoman border had moved to within eighty kilometers of the city. The Byzantine Empire remained nothing more than a small patch of land, sandwiched on two sides by a mighty, advancing army. The Byzantine emperor desperately needed help wherever help could be found.

Back in Rome the papacy faced its own troubles. A number of long-standing political—and, to a lesser degree, theological—disputes gave rise to the "conciliar movement," whose members argued that authority in the Western church ought to rest with councils rather than with the pope alone. The movement boasted some success in 1417 when church leaders extracted a promise from Pope Martin V to summon periodic councils. One of these councils convened in the Italian city of Ferrara in 1438. (When plague struck the city of Ferrara, the gathering moved to Florence, hence the council's dual name.)

The reunion of East and West found its way onto the agenda, since both the Eastern and Western churches had something to gain from resolving the schism: Western conciliarists hoped union with the East would reduce the power of the pope in the Western church; Easterners hoped reunion with Rome might save the Byzantine Empire from the approaching Turks.

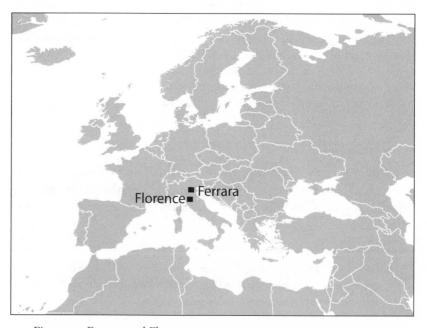

Figure 31. Ferrara and Florence

Some seven hundred delegates from the East arrived in Ferrara, including the Byzantine emperor, the patriarch of Constantinople, and representatives from Antioch, Alexandria, and Jerusalem.

Pope Eugenius IV (1431–1447) presided. At first, questions of protocol consumed the delegates. Where should the pope, patriarch, and emperor sit during the deliberations? What did seating arrangements indicate about prestige or privileges? Eventually conversation turned to a series of substantive and intense debates on the major issues separating East from West.

It soon grew clear that neither East nor West wished to make any concessions on the *filioque,* but the Byzantine emperor John VIII (1425–1448), desperate to strike an accord, leaned hard on his Eastern delegates to compromise.

In the end, the council found agreement on all major issues, largely due to concessions from the Easterners on the *filioque,* yeast in eucharistic bread, the doctrine of Purgatory,[63] and the powers of the pope. The Westerners did not persuade the Byzantine delegates that Roman positions were superior; instead, Emperor John persuaded his delegates they had no choice but to capitulate. On 6 June 1439 all but two of the Eastern bishops signed the agreement, while insisting it would be valid only if ratified by a meeting of a synod of the Eastern church.

The delegates returned home to face the scorn of a populace that accused them of selling out.

Patriarch of Constantinople Objects to Kissing the Pope's Foot (1438)

Deno John Geanakoplos, *Byzantium: Church, Society, and Civilization Seen through Contemporary Eyes* (Chicago: University of Chicago Press, 1984), 222. Used by permission of The University of Chicago Press.

Of all the foreign customs facing the Eastern delegates who arrived at the council, the custom of kissing the pope's foot rankled them most. Who was the pope, they wondered, to expect such subservience from eminent bishops who had traveled so far? This account derives

---

63. *Purgatory*—in Roman Catholic doctrine, Purgatory is a place of suffering where those who die in a state of grace—those not destined for Hell but not yet sufficiently pure for the ascent to Heaven—become ready through suffering for that eventual ascent. Most in the Eastern church did not accept this doctrine.

from the memoirs of Sylvester Syropoulos, a cleric from Constantinople who vigorously opposed reunion.

The patriarch exclaimed:

Whence has the pope this right? Which synod gave it to him? Show
me from what source he derives this privilege and where it is written. The
pope claims he is the successor of St. Peter. But if he is successor to Peter,
then we too are the successors of the rest of the apostles. Did they kiss
the foot of St. Peter? [. . .]

Resolutions of the Council of Ferrara-Florence (1439)

"Decrees of the Union of the Council of Basel-Ferrara-Florence-Rome,
1431–45," in *Creeds and Confessions of Faith in the Christian Tradition*, ed.
Jaroslav Pelikan and Valerie Hotchkiss (New Haven, CT: Yale University Press,
2003), 1:753–55. Used by permission of Yale University Press.

**A bull from Pope Eugenius IV describes the agreements signed by
the delegates. While noting that the council approved the agreements,
Eugenius fails to note that two Greek metropolitans refused to sign:
Mark Eugenicus of Ephesus and Isaias of Stauropolis. It should be
clear in the following document that the remaining Greek representatives yielded to the Latins on nearly every point of contention: *filioque*, yeast, Purgatory, and the powers of the pope.**

1. [. . .] Let the heavens be glad and let the earth rejoice. For the wall
that divided the Western and the Eastern church has been removed, peace
and harmony have returned, since the corner-stone, Christ, who made
both one, has joined both sides with a very strong bond of love and
peace, uniting and holding them together in a covenant of everlasting
unity. After a long haze of grief and a dark and unlovely gloom of long-
enduring strife, the radiance of hoped-for union has illuminated all.

2. Let mother church also rejoice. For she now beholds her sons hitherto in disagreement returned to unity and peace, and she who hitherto
wept at their separation now gives thanks to God with inexpressible
joy at their truly marvelous harmony. Let all the faithful throughout the
world, and those who go by the name of Christian, be glad with mother
catholic church. [. . .]

5. For when Latins and Greeks came together in this holy synod, they
all strove that, among other things, the article about the procession of

the Holy Spirit should be discussed with the utmost care and assiduous investigation. [. . .]

6. [. . .] The Greeks asserted that when they claim that the Holy Spirit proceeds from the Father, they do not intend to exclude the Son; but because it seemed to them that the Latins assert that the Holy Spirit proceeds from the Father and the Son as from two principles and two spirations,[64] they refrained from saying that the Holy Spirit proceeds from the Father and the Son. The Latins asserted that they say the Holy Spirit proceeds from the Father and the Son not with the intention of excluding the Father from being the source and principle of all deity, that is of the Son and of the Holy Spirit, nor to imply that the Son does not receive from the Father, because the Holy Spirit proceeds from the Son, nor that they posit two principles or two spirations; but they assert that there is only one principle and a single spiration of the Holy Spirit, as they have asserted hitherto. Since, then, one and the same meaning resulted from all this, they unanimously agreed and consented to the following holy and God-pleasing union, in the same sense and with one mind.

7. [. . .] We declare that when holy doctors and fathers say that the Holy Spirit proceeds from the Father through the Son, this bears the sense that thereby also the Son should be signified, according to the Greeks indeed as cause, and according to the Latins as principle of the subsistence of the Holy Spirit, just like the Father. [. . .]

9. We define also that the explanation of those words "and from the Son" was licitly and reasonably added to the creed for the sake of declaring the truth and from imminent need.

10. Also, the body of Christ is truly confected in[65] both unleavened and leavened wheat bread, and priests should confect the body of Christ in either, that is, each priest according to the custom of his Western or Eastern church.

11. Also, if truly penitent people die in the love of God before they have made satisfaction for acts and omissions by worthy fruits of repentance, their souls are cleansed after death by cleansing pains; and the suffrages of the living faithful avail them in giving relief from such pains, that is, sacrifices of Masses, prayers, almsgiving and other acts of devotion that have been customarily performed by some of the faithful for others of the faithful in accordance with the church's ordinances.

64. *spirations*—a recognition that the Holy Spirit proceeds from both the Father and the Son, that is, the Father and the Son both function as live-giving sources for the Spirit. "Spiration" specifically invokes the Father and Son as creative forces, literally "breathing" life.

65. *confected in*—"composed of" or "made of." The point is that either leavened or unleavened bread may serve as Christ's body in the Eucharist.

12. Also, the souls of those who have incurred no stain of sin whatsoever after baptism, as well as souls who after incurring the stain of sin have been cleansed whether in their bodies or outside their bodies, as was stated above, are straightaway received into Heaven and clearly behold the triune God as he is, yet one person more perfectly than another according to the difference of their merits.

13. But the souls of those who depart this life in actual mortal sin, or in original sin alone, go down straightaway to Hell to be punished, but with unequal pains.

14. We also define that the holy apostolic see and the Roman pontiff hold the primacy over the whole world and the Roman pontiff is the successor of blessed Peter prince of the apostles, and that he is the true vicar of Christ, the head of the whole church and the father and teacher of all Christians, and to him was committed in blessed Peter the full power of tending, ruling and governing the whole church, as is contained also in the acts of ecumenical councils and in the sacred canons.

15. Also, renewing the order of the other patriarchs that has been handed down in the canons, the patriarch of Constantinople should be second after the most holy Roman pontiff, third should be the patriarch of Alexandria, fourth the patriarch of Antioch, and fifth the patriarch of Jerusalem, without prejudice to all their privileges and rights.

Greek Participant at Florence Describes Disputes (1438 or 1439)

Deno John Geanakoplos, *Byzantium: Church, Society, and Civilization Seen through Contemporary Eyes* (Chicago: University of Chicago Press, 1984), 223–24. Used by permission of The University of Chicago Press.

The Greek delegate Sylvester Syropoulos reported in his memoirs on private conversations among the Byzantine delegates that were conducted after the agreements were written but before they were signed. "Latinizers" is Syropoulos's pejorative term for Byzantine delegates who favored union with Rome.

[Some] said: "The difference is small that separates us from the Latins, and if our side should wish it, this difference could he easily bridged. When the bishop of Ephesus [Mark] responded that the difference, on the contrary, was great, they replied to him: "It is *not* heresy and you should not call it that, for none of the scholars and holy men[66] who lived before you

---

66. *holy men*—church fathers.

have called it heresy." Then the bishop of Ephesus replied: "It *is* a heresy and those who have preceded us have considered it to be that. Only they did not want to condemn the Latins as heretics because they had hopes of converting them and were seeking their friendship. If you wish it, I shall myself show you why they [in the past] were considered heretics." At once the bishops of Mytilene[67] and of Lacedaemon[68] angrily exclaimed: "Who are you to treat the Latins as heretics?" They rose near the patriarch and, together approaching closer to the bishop of Ephesus, they chastised him shamelessly with reproaches and sarcasm. "How long," they cried, "shall we bear in silence what you say?" And they could hardly restrain themselves from rushing upon him to tear him in pieces with their teeth and hands. Finally they said: "We are going to tell the pope that you called him a heretic and either you will prove it or suffer as you deserve." And they left very troubled. Then the grand *protosynkellos*,[69] about to leave but still near the patriarch, said: "I know very well that if we achieve union [the Latins] will anathematize us before we have even reached Venice. If we do not achieve it, on the other hand, they will still anathematize us. It would be better, then, to make union and as a result have them anathematize us." Questioned by the *protekdikos*,[70] he expressed this idea still more clearly, leaving his hearers perplexed.

Muscovite Reaction to Ferrara-Florence (1437–1441)

"The Voskresensk Chronicle Concerning the Council of Florence and Its Aftermath, 1437–1441," in *A Source Book for Russian History from Early Times to 1917*, ed. George Vernadsky (New Haven, CT: Yale University Press, 1972), 1:126–27. Used by permission of Yale University Press.

Metropolitan Isidor of Kiev and Moscow (1458–1463) emerged as one of the chief Eastern defenders of reunion at the council. Reaction to his "betrayal" was ferocious in Muscovy, the principality centered around Moscow, which would grow into what we now know as Russia. Here a Muscovite chronicle speculates on Isidor's intentions and reports on his reception when he returned home from Florence.

[. . .] He concealed an evil intention in his heart, wishing to seduce God's people from the true path of the holy faith and to unite with the

67. *Mytilene*—city on the island of Lesbos.
68. *Lacedaemon*—ancient Sparta.
69. *protosynkellos*—chief deputy of the patriarch.
70. *protekdikos*—a cleric who presided over a tribunal of priests.

Latins, deeming that he alone was wiser than all the rest. [. . .] And thus Isidor came into the Roman region, into a city called Ferrara, where in the forty-seventh year[71] the Roman pope Eugenius had assembled the false-minded Eighth Council, repudiated by God. [. . .]

The tsar[72] and the patriarch expressed their intention of holding the council in the Latin city of Florence [. . .] and they did thus, taking much gold, and the tsar and the patriarch, and Isidor in agreement with them, went to their city of Florence to carry out their evil treachery. [. . .] Then they held a great council with the pope, and came to an agreement among themselves, and certified it firmly in a document. And the tsar signed it, and Metropolitan Isidor with him. [. . .] [In August 1439] they dispersed, covered with the darkness of faithlessness. Alas for this pernicious deceit! Alas for the joining of abomination to Greek Orthodoxy! For the gloom of darkness had replaced the living light, and the faith of piety was surrendered to the Latins; the Orthodox tsar and patriarch fell into the deceit of the Latin heresies; caught in nets of gold they perished through the lies of Isidor; having taken gold they turned away from God and joined with the Latins.

Isidor came to the Russian land, into the God-protected city of Moscow [in March 1441], to the pious and Orthodox grand prince Vasily Vasilevich,[73] concealing within himself the deceit of the Latin heresy. [. . .] And he ordered that the Latin cross[74] be carried before him. [. . .] Then during the commemorative prayers of the holy service he mentioned first and lauded, instead of the holy ecumenical patriarchs, the Roman pope Eugenius, to whom he had delivered the holy faith of Greek Orthodoxy for gold. Upon the conclusion of the holy service Isidor ascended the pulpit and ordered that the edict of the false-minded and apostate council be read in a loud voice. In it were written the Latin deceits, hateful and foreign to God: separating the Holy Trinity, saying that the Holy Spirit proceeds from the Son as well as from the Father, and joining to this their sophistry concerning unleavened bread, saying that it is proper for the body of Christ to be transformed both as fermented and un-fermented bread; and concerning the dead it was written thus: those who have met death with humility, in the true faith and in penitence to God, but have not succeeded in performing the penance for their sins that their confessors have pronounced, such men will be purified after death by the purification of sins. But they did all this among themselves through sophistry, in order to deceive the true Orthodox faith and, having deceived it, to sever Christianity from the law of God.

71. *forty-seventh year*—1438.

72. *The tsar*—Emperor John VIII.

73. *Vasily Vasilevich*—Grand Prince Vasily II.

74. *Latin cross*—Latin crosses tend to be simpler: a plain cross with four points. Eastern crosses sometimes have eight points.

The grand prince, after hearing these things, and when he had seen the edict with the enactments of their false-minded council, and heard from [Isidor's] lips the name of the pope mentioned first, recognized the heresy of that rapacious wolf Isidor, did not accept the blessing from his hand, and called him a heretical Latin deceiver; and, quickly accusing him, he covered him with shame and called him a wolf rather than a shepherd and teacher; and he soon ordered that he be removed from his throne as metropolitan, as a mad deceiver and apostate from the faith, and ordered him to go into a monastery. [. . .] Isidor [. . .] left stealthily at night, the doors being open, took to flight with his pupil the monk Grigory, and thus fled to Rome, whence he had come and brought the evil Latin heresies. The God-knowing worker of piety, the Orthodox grand prince Vasily Vasilevich, did not send anyone after him to bring him back, not wishing to detain him, as someone bereft of reason and hateful to God.

FALL OF CONSTANTINOPLE

Nothing—not heroic resistance, pleas to Western powers for military assistance, or compromises on doctrine—could save Constantinople from the Ottoman invaders. In the spring of 1453, the city's inhabitants endured a siege of nearly two months, repulsing a number of assaults on the city's walls. But Ottoman engineering and sheer numbers proved too much: on 29 May 1453 (Byzantine calendar), Sultan Mehmed II, with a force numbering somewhere between eighty thousand and two hundred thousand troops, captured the city, which the Turks control to this day. With Constantinople now subject to a Muslim state and more isolated from the West than ever, the great schism was complete.

Account of the Ottoman Siege of Constantinople (early 1600s)

"An Anonymous Greek Chronicle," in Marios Philippides, *Emperors, Patriarchs and Sultans of Constantinople, 1373–1513* (Brookline, MA: Hellenic College, 1990), 43–51. Used by permission of Holy Cross Orthodox Press, Brookline, Massachusetts.

[In 1453[75] Sultan Mehmed] rushed, like a wild beast, toward [Constantinople] with a countless multitude, from land and sea. The land was

75. *In 1453*—although compiled sometime in the early 1600s, this document draws from a number of much earlier documents.

filled with men and horses while the sea was full of long ships, the greatest number possible. They manned the ships with individuals from the regions of the emperor by the Black Sea. They had been recruited by force. When the ships arrived, they were prevented from entering the harbor by the chain [stretched across the mouth by Byzantine defenders]. So they resorted to a marvelous and astonishing tactic: they unfurled the sails, put the oars in their places, and dragged the ships over land. A multitude of countless soldiers pulled the ships to the very high hills to the accompaniment of drums and trumpets and then dragged them down to the sweet waters. Thus, they took command of the harbor. Then they constructed quays with empty containers and planks [. . .] and attacked the walls of the city, as there was nothing to prevent them.

Thus, he besieged the city by land and sea. [The Sultan] destroyed with the big cannon the section of the walls from the Gate called Charsia to the Gate of Saint Romanos. Many sections of the walls were brought down. Those sectors were fortified nevertheless with stockades made of brushwood and cotton. There happened to be present, in those days, a nobleman from Genoa called Giustiniani [. . . who said,] "I can guard the demolished sector with my soldiers; I will defend it for the name of Christ." [. . .] This nobleman took his position and fought for many days, preventing them from entering the fortifications. But observe our sin and God's departure: while he was at his post fighting, a shot from an arquebus[76] hit him on the right leg; he collapsed like a corpse. His own men took him, went to the ships, made sail, and escaped as far as the island of Chios,[77] where he died. It was rumored that he had been shot from within the fortifications but no one knows how it really came about.

While the nobleman was still alive, the Constantinopolitans decided to send a vessel in the night with forty young men on board to set fire to the armada in secret. [. . .] But the Franks [. . .] who were befriending the Turks, discovered this and lit a fire on top of the tall tower. So they brought their cannons from the galleys and sank the vessel. Thus those admirable young men drowned.

The Constantinopolitans were at a loss; there was nothing that they could do against such a countless multitude (almost one man against one thousand). When the demolished sector failed to be approached by the mob, the Constantinopolitans realized that a strong attack would be launched on the following day. So they came out to the outer fortifications, as they feared that they would come close to the great walls. The Turks charged, entered the demolished sector, took charge of the great walls, and raised their standard on the towers. But the army of the city was outside. When they heard the shouting and saw the standards on the

76. *arquebus*—a primitive smoothbore (non-rifled) firearm.
77. *Chios*—an island off the eastern coast of Greece.

towers, they rushed to enter through the Charsia Gate in order to expel the Turks. And they perished in the press; they could not enter because of the dead bodies blocking the entrance (the gates of Charsia and of Saint Romanos were congested, all the way up to the arches). Later, the captives, women and children, could not be brought out but had to be lowered by rope from the walls.

So the capture of the renowned city took place in the year 6961,[78] on May 29, Tuesday morning. Great is your patience, Lord of the universe! Who can say that he knew the Lord's mind or that he had knowledge of his plans? Who cannot cry or mourn over the pillage of the happiest and most prosperous city in the world? What heart is made of stone and fails to feel the anguish of that calamity? Alas, one could see sacred vessels snatched from monasteries, churches being forced open, and widespread pillage. What is one to say about the abduction of nuns who lived in God and had maintained their virginity? What about the daughters of noblemen, who were also nuns, and were now being led, with curses, to the market to be polluted by the impious and were forced to bend their heads as slaves? Priests and monks were tied with ropes and were taken away. Who can describe such a calamity and such God-sent wrath? What a terrible fate it is, to fall into the hands of the living God! What can one say about the imperial tombs that were pried open? Bones were thrown around in jest; they hoped to find within the golden thread from the vestments. They trampled over the remains of Emperor Constantine and those of other emperors and threw them into heaps of manure. Am I to sing again David's lamentation for Jerusalem?[79] They placed the mortal remains of your slaves as if to display them in a vegetable shop; they offered the flesh of your saints as prey to the birds of Heaven; they poured the blood as if it were water, to the beasts of the earth, all around Jerusalem, and there was no one to bury them: "You make us a reproach to our neighbors, a scorn and a derision to them who are about us." [. . .]

When, Lord, when will your wrath come to an end? [. . .] You are just; we deserve everything that you have sent upon us. So we were delivered into the hands of lawless foes and most hateful apostates, into the hands of an unjust and most wicked emperor, throughout the entire earth, on account of our sins. [. . .] Shudder, O sun; groan, O earth; shake and cry out: Glory to you, enduring Lord.

78. *year 6961*—1453.

79. *David's lamentation for Jerusalem*—here the Greek chronicler equates Constantinople with the holy city of Jerusalem.

Rise of Islam and Turkish Expansion

The Ottoman tribes that conquered Constantinople in 1453, established the vast Ottoman Empire, and governed the Balkans for centuries thereafter probably first emerged in southern Siberia around 3000 BCE. Chinese documents refer to Turkish tribes as early as the 500s CE, and we know that these same tribes fought each other for control of Mongolia between the 700s and 1000s before migrating west. Genghis Kahn united one of these Turkish tribes—the Mongols—in the early 1200s and then led a formidable army east into China and west into southern Russia and Eastern Europe. As the Turks conquered Arabic regions, they began to adopt the Islamic faith of their Arab subjects, abandoning their polytheistic beliefs and practices.

Christians in Europe and the Balkans watched with trepidation as the Turks relentlessly chipped away at Byzantine territory, expanding ever westward during the 1300s, 1400s, 1500s, and 1600s.

The Byzantines were right to worry: when the Turks seized Constantinople in 1453, the Ottoman sultan allowed his troops to pillage the capital for three days. He ordered that the altar, iconostasis (an enormous wall covered with icons), bells, and holy vessels be removed from the grand church of Hagia Sofia and the church converted into a mosque. The Turks plastered over interior mosaics and constructed four minarets outside.

The fall of Constantinople in 1453 brought an inglorious end to the Byzantine Empire. The traditional center of Eastern Orthodoxy now stood subject to an Islamic state.

Yet it would be simplistic to argue that the church was severely persecuted, or at least that it was persecuted to the degree that Christian

266

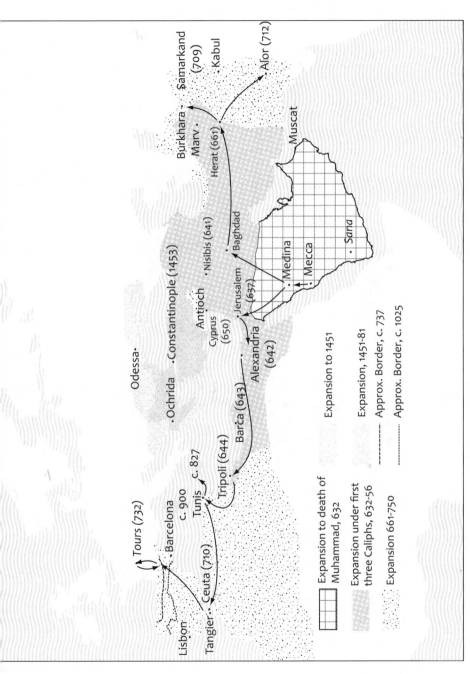

Figure 32. Expansion of Islam to 1481

Tours (732)
Lisbon
Barcelona
c. 900
Tunis · c. 827
Ceuta (710)
Tangier ·
Tripoli (644)
Barca (643)
Alexandria (642)
Odessa ·
· Ochrida · Constantinople (1453)
Antioch
Cyprus (650)
Jerusalem (637)
· Nisibis (641)
Baghdad
Medina
Mecca
Bukhara ·
Marv ·
Herat (661)
Samarkand (709)
· Kabul
Afor (712)
Muscat
· Sana

Expansion to death of
Muhammad, 632

Expansion under first
three Caliphs, 632-56

Expansion 661-750

Expansion to 1451

Expansion, 1451-81

Approx. Border, c. 737

Approx. Border, c. 1025

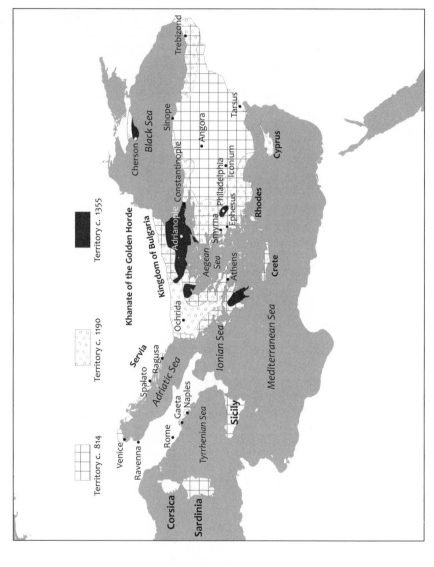

Figure 33. Decline of the Byzantine Empire

Territory c. 814

Territory c. 1190

Territory c. 1355

Khanate of the Golden Horde

Kingdom of Bulgaria

Servia

Sicily

Corsica

Sardinia

Rhodes

Crete

Cyprus

Venice
Ravenna
Rome
Gaeta
Naples

Spalato
Ragusa

Ochrida
Adrianople
Constantinople
Cherson
Sinope
Trebizond

Athens
Smyrna
Philadelphia
Ephesus
Iconium
Angora
Tarsus

Black Sea
Aegean Sea
Adriatic Sea
Ionian Sea
Tyrrhenian Sea
Mediterranean Sea

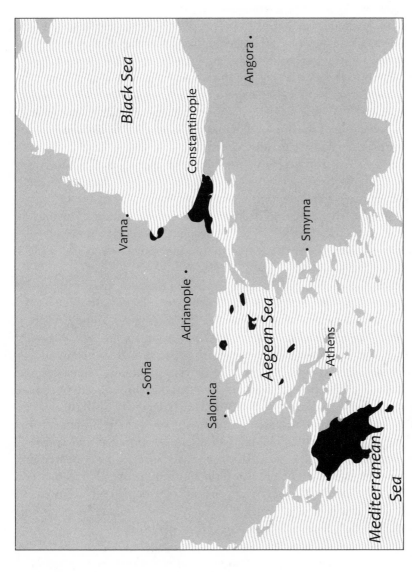

Figure 34. Byzantine Empire, 1430

rulers of the time often persecuted non-Christian institutions in areas they conquered. Muslims classified (and still classify) Christians and Jews as "people of the book," that is, people who, like Muslims, received scripture from God. According to Muslims, Christians and Jews enjoyed revelations from God *before* Allah (Arabic for "God") issued additional revelations to his prophet Muhammad between 609 and 632. These new revelations, compiled by scribes shortly after Muhammad's death, constitute Islam's most holy book, the Qur'an. Islam understands the Qur'an as a completion of Hebrew and Christian scripture rather than a challenge to or replacement of it. Christianity, according to Islamic theology, is more incomplete than wrong. And because people of the book recognize the same God of Abraham as do Muslims, they deserve tolerance.

The new Muslim overlords thus allowed their Christian subjects a good deal of freedom. The patriarchate remained in place. Christians could worship freely as long as they remained loyal to the Ottoman state, paid their taxes, and declined to proselytize among Muslims (a capital crime). The Turks viewed Ottoman Christians as the *Rum millet,* or "Roman nation," a semiautonomous body, though still subject to the sultan.

But while the patriarchate of Constantinople survived within the Ottoman state, the patriarch's role changed substantially. The Turks referred to the patriarch as the *millet-bachi,* or head of the Christian millet. They invested the patriarch with responsibility for governing, taxing, and administering justice within the millet on behalf of the Ottomans. Thus, in one sense, the patriarch actually gained power under the Turks: his jurisdiction now spread through all Ottoman lands with a Christian populace. This arrangement made it easy, as John Meyendorff notes, for the patriarch to "practically ignore his colleagues"; "his power ceased to be purely canonical and spiritual but became political as well. To the enslaved Greeks, he appeared not only as the successor of the Byzantine patriarchs but also as the heir of the emperors."[1] The patriarchs of Constantinople even adopted attire associated with the former emperors: a miter shaped like a crown, long hair, eagle insignias, and other royal symbols.

The patriarch's subjugation to the Ottoman sultan and elevation within the Ottoman Empire meant greater isolation for the patriarch-

1. John Meyendorff, "Eastern Orthodox Christianity," in *New Encyclopaedia Britannica* (Chicago: Encyclopaedia Britannica, 2010).

ate—isolation not only from Rome, but also from other precincts of the Eastern church, especially in Russia. Powerful and enmeshed in political issues, yet cut off from other Christian people, the center of Eastern Christendom found itself even more removed from the West than before.

Muslims Appear in Palestine
(ca. late 700s to early 800s)

"The Zuqnin Chronicler," in Robert Hoyland, *Seeing Islam as Others Saw It: A Survey and Evaluation of Christian, Jewish and Zoroastrian Writings on Early Islam* (Princeton, NJ: Darwin Press, 1997), 413–14. © 1997 Darwin Press.

The author of the following text lived in the Zuqnin monastery in northern Mesopotamia, from where he wrote a history of the world, beginning with creation. The fourth part of his grand work, from which this excerpt draws, attends to the Islamic conquests, which, the author contends, are "our fault."

The Arabs subdued the land of Palestine as far as the river Euphrates, while the Romans fled and crossed over to the east of the Euphrates, and the Arabs gained authority over them in [Palestine]. The first king was a man from among them by the name of Muhammad.[2] This man they also called a prophet because he had turned them away from cults of all kinds and taught them that there was one God, maker of creation. Also he laid down laws for them, because they had been firm adherents of the worship of demons and adoration of idols and particularly of trees. And since he had shown them the one God, and they had conquered the Romans in battle under his direction, and he had appointed laws for them according to their desire, they called him prophet and messenger of God. They are a very covetous and carnal people, and any law—whether prescribed by Muhammad or another God-fearing person, which is not set in accord with their desire—they neglect and abandon. But what is in accord with their will and complements their desires, though it be instituted by one contemptible among them, they hold to it, saying: "This was appointed by the prophet and messenger of God, and moreover it was charged to him thus by God." [. . .]

2. *Muhammad*—the founder of Islam.

Apocalyptic Prediction of the Rise of Islam (ca. 640)

"Ps.-Ephraem," in Robert Hoyland, *Seeing Islam as Others Saw It: A Survey and Evaluation of Christian, Jewish and Zoroastrian Writings on Early Islam* (Princeton, NJ: Darwin Press, 1997), 260–62.

The next excerpt appears in the first extant Christian apocalyptic work to appear in Syria during the Islamic occupation. (Some scholars believe that the work in its present form derives from an unknown fourth-century text.) This version probably assumed its present form around 640, that is, around the time of the Islamic conquest of Damascus. Arabs in this text are described (as per the biblical account) as the children of Abraham's slave Hagar.[3]

A people shall rise up from the desert, the offspring of Hagar, handmaid of Sarah. [. . .] They are awakened to come in the name of the Ram, the messenger of the son of perdition. And there will be a sign in the sky as says our Lord in his Gospel.[4] [. . .] The plunderers will spread over the earth, in the valleys and on mountain tops, and they will enslave women, children and men, old and young [. . .] They open roads in the mountains and paths in the valleys. They will plunder to the ends of creation and take possession of the cities. Lands will be ravaged and corpses abound upon the earth. All peoples will be laid low before the plunderers. And just when the peoples had endured long on the earth and were hoping that now would come peace, they will exact tribute and all will indeed fear them. Injustice will increase upon the earth and obscure the clouds. [. . .]

They take the wife away from her husband and slay him like a sheep. They throw the babe from her mother and drive her into slavery; the child calls out from the ground and the mother hears, yet what is she to do? And so it is trampled under the feet of the horses, camels and infantry. [. . .] They separate the children from the mother like the soul from within the body, and she watches as they divide her loved ones from off her lap, two of them to go to two masters, herself to another. [. . .] Her children cry out in lament, their eyes hot with tears. She turns to her loved ones, milk pouring forth from her breast: "Go in peace, my darlings, and may God accompany you."

3. *Hagar*—Muslims honor Hagar (a handmaid to Abraham's wife, Sarah; Hagar became Abraham's second wife) as the father of Ishmael, an ancestor of Muhammad. See Genesis 16:1–6.

4. *as says our Lord in his Gospel*—Matthew 24:30.

Fictional Disputation between a Monk and an Arab (early 700s)

"A Monk of Beth Hale and an Arab Notable," in Robert Hoyland, *Seeing Islam as Others Saw It: A Survey and Evaluation of Christian, Jewish and Zoroastrian Writings on Early Islam* (Princeton, NJ: Darwin Press, 1997), 465–69. © 1997 Darwin Press. All rights reserved. Used by permission.

We know next to nothing about the provenance of the following text, a supposed transcript of a disputation between a Christian monk and an Islamic notable. The author is a partisan Christian, and he stacks the debate from the outset: the clever monk inevitably forces his debating partner to admit the truth of Christianity and then proclaim, "were it not for fear of the authorities and of disgrace before men, many would become Christians." Robert Hoyland argues that this disputation is a literary fabrication, recalling earlier (and similar) accounts of disputations between Christians and Jews. It does, however, give some insight into serious if naive attempts by Eastern Christianity to engage Islamic theology.[5]

With God's help we shall write down the debate that took place between a man of the Arabs and a certain monk of the monastery of Beth Hale.[6] [. . .]

This Arab man [. . .] was one of the chief men before the emir [. . .] and by reason of a malady that he had, he came to us and remained with us for ten days. He spoke freely with us and debated much about our scriptures and their Qur'an. When he saw our rites performed at the appropriate seven times in accordance with what the blessed David said: "Seven times a day I praise you for your judgments, O righteous one," he called me to him. And because he had acted as steward in the government for a long time and because of his exaltedness and our lowliness, he would speak with us via an interpreter. He began by reproving us for our faith, saying: "You make prayers much, night and day you are not silent, and you outdo us in prayer and fasting and in your petitions to God. However, in my own opinion, your faith rules out that your prayers will be accepted." [. . .]

---

5. For more detailed exploration of Christians' and Muslims' views of each other, see section 18.8, "Rise of Islam and Turkish Expansion," in the online supplement.

6. *monastery of Beth Hale*—this could refer either to a monastery near Mosul (a city in northern Iraq) or to one near Hira in Saudi Arabia.

The monk said: "Speak with me respectfully so that I shall speak with you as is fitting. [. . .] I know that in every matter, whatever it is, I should respect you because of your authority and importance; but when you desire from me the truth of my faith, I know that I shall not show you favor. [. . .]

The Arab then poses the following questions, to which the monk has ready answers.

1. "Is not our faith better than any faith that is on the earth [. . .] for we observe the commandments of Muhammad and the sacrifices of Abraham? [. . .] And this is a sign that God loves us and is pleased with our faith, namely, that he gives us dominion over all religions and all peoples?"

Answer: There are and have been many other rulers in the world besides the Arabs.

2. "Why do you not profess Abraham and his laws, when he is the father of the prophets and of kings, and scripture bears witness to his righteousness?"

Answer: Christ has brought a new covenant, the old being merely a model of the new.

3. "Since God is lofty and exalted [. . .] why do you degrade him and announce 'to him is a son,' and why, when he is one, do you say 'Father, Son and Holy Spirit?'"

[The monk provides proofs from scripture and logic.]

4. "How is Muhammad our prophet considered in your eyes?"

Answer: "A wise and God-fearing man who freed you from idolatry and brought you to know the one true God."

5. "Why do you act perversely and worship images and crosses and the bones of saints?"

Answer: The image is a reminder of the original; the cross is symbolic and has miraculous power; relics are important for intercession.

6. "Why do you reject all [other] directions and prostrate in the direction of the east?"[7]

Answer: The Paradise of Eden is there, thence we came and thither we hope to return. [. . .]

One question still bothers the Arab.

---

7. *prostrate in the direction of the east*—five times each day Muslims face Mecca and ritually bow, prostrate themselves, and then sit on the ground, reciting verses from the Qur'an.

"Though I know that your faith is true and that your way of thinking is superior to ours, what is the reason that God has delivered you into our hands, and that you are led by us like sheep to the slaughter, and that your bishops and priests are killed and the rest crushed and enslaved night and day by the king's taxes, which are harsher than death. [. . .]"

The monk replies by citing words from Moses to the Israelites.

"Not because of your righteousness has God brought you into the land of promise, but because of the wickedness of its inhabitants"[8] [. . .]

Pact between Christians and Their Muslim Occupiers (800s)

"The Pact of Umar," in *The Medieval Record,* ed.
Alfred Andrea (New York: Houghton Mifflin, 1997), 94.

Muslims confronted the challenge of governing non-Muslim populations long before the Turks conquered Constantinople. The following document, which probably assumed its present form in the 800s, claims to be a pact of peace granted by the caliph (the Islamic head of state), Umar I, to Syrian Christians around 637. Most Western scholars question its veracity, finding its terms more restrictive than what we know of Islamic demands of the time. Still, it provides some sense of what Christians expected from Muslim occupiers.

In the name of God, the merciful, the compassionate!
This is a writing to Umar from the Christians of such and such a city. When you marched against us[9] we asked of you protection for ourselves, our posterity, our possessions, and our co-religionists; and we made this stipulation with you, that we will not erect in our city or the suburbs any new monastery, church, cell or hermitage; that we will not repair any of such buildings that may fall into ruins, or renew those that may be situated in the Muslim quarters of the town; that we will not refuse the Muslims entry into our churches either by night or by day; that we will open the gates wide to passengers and travelers; that we will receive any Muslim traveler into our houses and give him food and lodging for three nights; that we will not harbor any spy in our churches or houses or conceal any enemy of the Muslims.

8. *but because of the wickedness of its inhabitants*—Deuteronomy 9:5.
9. *you marched against us*—Muslims marched against Syrian Christians.

That we will not teach our children the Qur'an; that we will not make a show of the Christian religion nor invite anyone to embrace it; that we will not prevent any of our kinsmen from embracing Islam if they so desire. That we will honor the Muslims and rise up in our assemblies when they wish to take their seats; that we will not imitate them in our dress, either in the cap, turban, sandals, or parting of the hair; that we will not make use of their expressions of speech, nor adopt their surnames; that we will not ride on saddles, or gird on swords, or take to ourselves arms or wear them, or engrave Arabic in inscriptions on our rings; that we will not sell wine;[10] that we will shave the front of our head; that we will keep to our own style of dress, wherever we may be; that we will wear belts round our waists.

That we will not display the cross upon our churches or display our crosses or our sacred books in the streets of the Muslims or in the market-places; that we will strike the clappers[11] in our churches lightly; that we will not recite our services in a loud voice when a Muslim is present; that we will not carry palm-branches[12] or our images[13] in procession in the streets; that at the burial of our dead we will not chant loudly or carry lighted candles in the streets of the Muslims or their market-places; that we will not take any slaves that have already been in the possession of Muslims, nor spy into their houses, and that we will not strike any Muslims.

All this we promise to observe, on behalf of ourselves and our co-religionists, and receive protection from you in exchange; and if we violate any of the conditions of this agreement, then we forfeit your protection and you are at liberty to treat us as enemies and rebels.

10. *wine*—Muslims may not drink alcohol.

11. *clappers*—the Ottomans did not allow Christians to ring bells, so they summoned congregants to church with wooden clappers.

12. *not carry palm-branches*—not process on Palm Sunday with palm branches.

13. *images*—icons. Islam views icons as a form of idolatry.

Rise of the Moscow Patriarchate

In 1238, a confederation of Mongol tribes known as the Tartars invaded Kievan Rus' (or just Rus'). By the end of 1240, Mongol Tatars controlled most of the region, including Slavic fiefdoms centered upon the major cities of Moscow, Kiev, Novgorod, Vladimir, and Suzdal. Defeated princes in all these cities paid taxes and obeisance to their new Tartar overlords.

The overarching story of political life in Rus' from the 1200s into the 1500s is that of independent princes competing against each other for power, while also collaborating with and sometimes fighting against the Tartars. All princes desired freedom from the "Tatar yoke" and also more power at the expense of other Slavic princes.

The princes of Moscow, or Muscovy, proved especially savvy in their collaboration with the Tatars. They married the daughters of Mongol nobles; they collected taxes from other princes on behalf of the Mongols; and they negotiated alliances with important Mongol figures. By the time the Grand Duchy of Moscow freed itself from Tatar rule in 1480, Moscow was the major power in the region. And by the 1800s Muscovy, now Russia, was *the* power in the East.

By the early 1400s Muscovy had its own metropolitan plus fifteen other bishops. Three of these bishops—of Novgorod, Rostov, and Suzdal—bore the title "archbishop." In theory all fifteen bishops and the metropolitan fell under Constantinople's control. In practice, however, the metropolitan of Moscow chomped at the bit to assert his independence.

We have already witnessed the fall of Metropolitan Isidor of Moscow after his concessions at the Council of Ferrara-Florence. After

277

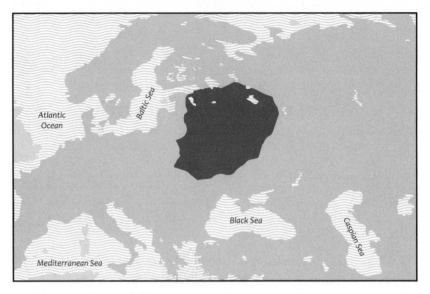

Figure 35. Kievan Rus', ca. 1000

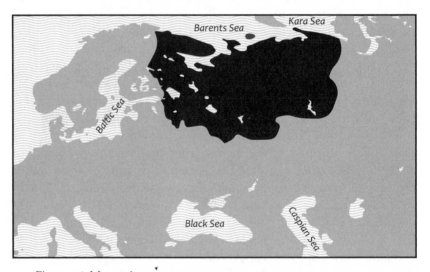

Figure 36. Muscovite state, ca. 1500

deposing Isidor, Grand Prince Vasily of Moscow took the extraordinary step of appointing Isidor's replacement, Metropolitan Iona,
without consulting Constantinople. Such a step violated canon law,
and it signaled at least two things to the Orthodox world at large.
First, Moscow's deep unhappiness with Constantinople's concessions
to Rome. The Russian church, which had never enjoyed the close ties

with Rome that Constantinople intermittently enjoyed, had no desire to establish such relations now. Second, this appointment without permission constituted a de facto statement that Russia no longer owed fealty to Constantinople. It would now function as an "autocephalous," or independent, church.

Filofei Argues That Moscow Is the Third Rome (ca. 1510)

"Filofei on Moscow as the Third Rome, ca. 1510," in
A Source Book for Russian History from Early Times to 1917,
ed. George Vernadsky (New Haven, CT: Yale University Press,
1972), 1:127. Used by permission of Yale University Press.

Some in Russia interpreted the fall of Constantinople as God's punishment for concessions to the Latins at Ferrara-Florence. Constantinople, according to this theory, had forfeited its right to lead the Eastern church, and this right now fell to Moscow. Moscow was thus the "Third Rome," succeeding Constantinople, the "Second Rome." The leader of a monastery in Pskov, Filofei, made just such an argument in a letter to Grand Prince Vasily III of Moscow (1505–1533).

It is fitting to respect and to obey the tsar, the prince, or other rulers, because it is God's will that we should obey and submit to the rulers; for they are concerned about us and take care of us. [. . . But] it is fitting to serve the rulers with body, not with soul, and to render them royal honors, but not divine ones, as the Lord says: "Render therefore to Caesar the things that are Caesar's, and to God the things that are God's" (Matthew 22:21). If you respect and obey [the secular ruler] in such a way, it will not do any harm to your soul, because in such a manner you will learn to fear God; for the tsar is God's servant when he benefits the people or punishes [the guilty]. But if the tsar dominates the people and if he himself is dominated by wicked passions and sins—avariciousness, anger, falsity, arrogance, fury, and, the worst of all, unbelief and blasphemy—such a tsar is not a servant of God but a servant of the devil—not a tsar, but a tyrant. [. . .] And you must not obey such a tsar or a prince who inclines you to unbelief and falsity, even if he torments you and threatens you with death.

To the Orthodox Christian tsar and ruler over all,[1] who holds the reins over the holy divine altars of the holy ecumenical catholic

---

1. *Orthodox Christian tsar and ruler over all*—Grand Prince Vasily III (1505–1533).

apostolic church [. . .], which shines in place of Rome and Constantinople. For the churches of ancient Rome fell because of the falsehood of the Apollinarian heresy;[2] the churches of Constantinople, the second Rome, their doors have been cleft by the axes and halberds[3] of the Muhammadans; but now the holy catholic apostolic church of your mighty realm, the third new Rome, shines to the ends of the earth in its Orthodox Christian faith.

[. . .] And may your rule, pious tsar, know that all the realms of the Orthodox Christian faith have converged into your single realm. You are the only Christian tsar in all the world; it befits you, the tsar, to rule in fear of God.

Perceive, pious tsar, how all the Christian realms have converged into yours alone. Two Romes have fallen, and the third stands, and a fourth there shall not be. Your Christian realm shall not pass under the rule of another.

Muscovite Response to the Fall
of Constantinople (ca. 1533–1541)

"The Muscovite Response to the Fall of Constantinople, as Revised by the Voskresensk Chronicle, ca. 1533–1541," in *A Source Book for Russian History from Early Times to 1917*, ed. George Vernadsky (New Haven, CT: Yale University Press, 1972), 1:159–60. Used by permission of Yale University Press.

Some Byzantine legends mentioned a "russet-haired people" who would liberate Constantinople from the Turks. Russian chroniclers copied these tales, changing *rusyi* ("russet-haired") to *ruskii* ("Russian"), thus depicting themselves as potential liberators. This version is from the *Voskresensk Chronicle*. Here again we find an assertion that Constantinople fell because of its sins.

[. . .] [Since the fall of Constantinople happened] because of our sins, the lawless Muhammad seated himself on the tsar's throne, the noblest of all on earth, [. . .] But understand, O accursed ones! If all the signs concerning this city that were foretold [. . .] have come to pass, the last shall not be avoided but shall likewise come to pass; for it is written: "The Russian race with the former founders[4] shall conquer all the Muham-

2. *Apollinarian heresy*—denying the Holy Spirit's place in the Godhead.
3. *halberds*—axe blades topped with a spike, mounted on a long shaft.
4. *former founders*—Greeks.

madans and shall receive the city of the seven hills[5] with its former lawful masters[6] and shall reign in it.

Account of Establishing the Moscow Patriarchate (1589)

"An Anonymous Account of the Establishment of the Patriarchate in Moscow, 1589," in *A Source Book for Russian History from Early Times to 1917*, ed. George Vernadsky (New Haven, CT: Yale University Press, 1972), 1:175–76. Used by permission of Yale University Press.

A manuscript from the late 1500s, copied in 1619, gives the following account of how the head of the Muscovite church became patriarch of Moscow and all Russia. The decision by Constantinople followed lengthy negotiations with officials in Moscow. In the end, Patriarch Jeremiah of Constantinople agreed to recognize Iov, metropolitan of Moscow, as a "patriarch." This is yet another indication of the Russian church's growing pretensions as it sought to join the ranks of those cities (Rome, Jerusalem, Antioch, Alexandria, and Constantinople) whose bishoprics call themselves patriarchates.

But as much as piety declined in ancient Rome and in other countries, so much and more did grace shine in the most glorious and reigning city of Moscow; and in the lands of the Russian metropolitanate many metropolitans and archbishops and bishops shone as does the sun amidst the stars, and miracles caressed the earth. [. . .]

[. . .] Thus many metropolitans and archbishops and bishops came to this pious tsar from the holy city of Jerusalem, and from Tsar'grad,[7] and from other places [. . .] [and] declared to the pious tsar that in the Greek land the holy churches and monasteries of God were suffering from much destruction and plunder through the rule of the pagans.

[. . .] Therefore, having heard these things, the true defender of piety, the pious Tsar Feodor Ivanovich[8] [. . .] being inflamed by divine zeal, convoked a council of piety in the ruling city of Moscow, with the

---

5. *city of the seven hills*—Constantinople.
6. *former lawful masters*—Greeks.
7. *Tsar'grad*—Constantinople.
8. *Tsar Feodor Ivanovich*—Tsar Feodor I (1594–1598).

primate[9] of the holy church in the Russian land, and with the archbishops and bishops, and with other churchmen, and with the magnates:
"I desire, if it be pleasing to God and if the divine scriptures do not
oppose it, that there be erected a most exalted patriarchal throne in the
ruling city of Moscow." [. . .] Hearing these words, the most eminent
metropolitan, and the other prelates, and the noble boiars[10] praised
the counsel of the pious tsar [. . .] but said, however: "Pious tsar! If it
pleases your pious sovereignty, may this be made known to the four
ecumenical patriarchs through an epistle [. . .] lest it be imagined, O pious tsar, by other peoples [. . .] that a patriarchal throne was erected in
the ruling city of Moscow solely through the power of the tsar alone."
The pious tsar, hearing these things, readily agreed, even though he
could have erected a most exalted patriarchal throne by his power as
tsar and autocrat;[11] but he thought it proper to bear obedience to the
will of God and the counsel of the prelates, all the more since he was
in every way an obedient son of the holy church: and straightway he
ordered the word to be made deed, and thus an epistle from the tsar
and the prelates was soon dispatched to the four patriarchs[12] and to
many metropolitans with such an inquiry. The envoys went eagerly
on their way, and, by the grace of God, the [reply] sought was received.
[. . .] And thus [. . .] the ruling city of Moscow and all great Russia was
chosen and elevated to the most exalted patriarchal throne in the Russian metropolitanate.

Patriarch Jeremiah on the Glory of the Moscow Patriarchate (1653)

"Patriarch Jeremiah's Address, 1589," in *A Source Book for Russian
History from Early Times to 1917*, ed. George Vernadsky (New Haven, CT:
Yale University Press, 1972), 1:176. Used by permission of Yale University Press.

**Before granting a patriarchate to Moscow in 1589, Patriarch Jere-
miah of Constantinople supposedly addressed Tsar Feodor Ivanovich
as follows. (It is difficult to imagine the patriarch of Constantinople
issuing such a fawning statement.) This account is from the 1653 edition of the *Kormchaia kniga*, a Russian collection of church laws.**

9. *primate*—chief church official.

10. *boiars*—feudal lords.

11. *his power as tsar and autocrat*—of course the tsar had no such right.

12. *four patriarchs*—note the number "four" rather than "five": the envoys
were not dispatched to Rome.

You wish to honor and to adorn the great and holy church [of Russia] [. . .] with the lofty throne of the patriarchate, and with that great deed to glorify and enhance all the more the reigning city, Moscow, and all your great Russian tsardom. [. . .] For the ancient Rome has fallen through the Apollinarian heresy.[13] The second Rome, which is Constantinople, is held by the Ishmaelites[14]—the godless Turks. And the third Rome—your great Russian tsardom, O pious Tsar—has surpassed them all in piety, and all pious people have been united in your tsardom. And you alone on earth are called a Christian tsar everywhere and among all Christians. And by God's providence and the grace of the most pure Virgin, and thanks to the prayers of the new miracle workers of the great Russian tsardom [. . .] and through your church's request to God, and in accordance with your royal purpose, this great deed will be accomplished.

13. *Apollinarian heresy*—denying the Holy Spirit's place in the Godhead.
14. *Ishmaelites*—Muslims.

PART III

Modernity and Upheavals

Byzantine Rite Catholics

Documents that we have already examined reflect the fierce competition between Eastern and Western Christianity for influence in what is now Bulgaria. After the fall of Constantinople in 1453 and Russia's emergence as the primary Orthodox power in the East, jockeying for influence shifted north to other areas on Russia's western flank, that is, to the territories of modern Ukraine and western Poland. Both the Russian Empire in the East and the commonwealth of Poland-Lithuania in the West coveted these regions.

The Polish-Lithuanian commonwealth encompassed ethnically and religiously diverse populations: Circassians (Muslim), Russians (Orthodox), Belarusians (Orthodox), and Poles (Roman Catholic). Orthodox and Roman Catholics could be found throughout Ukraine, and the papacy and the patriarch of Moscow both sought jurisdiction over each.

This competition took a wild turn at the end of the 1500s. King Sigismund III (1587–1632) of Poland-Lithuania, a loyal Roman Catholic, distrusted his Orthodox subjects, recognizing that Orthodoxy constituted a significant component of the Ukrainian nationalism that sought independence from his rule.

Orthodox Christians in Poland-Lithuania distrusted Sigismund and the Jesuit missionaries who worked with his support to convert them to Roman Catholicism. The counterreformation—the Roman church's attempt to bring back into the fold believers who fled during the Protestant reformations—was now in full swing and enjoying some significant success. (See "Engaging the West through Creeds" below for more on the Protestant reformations.) This success prompted some

287

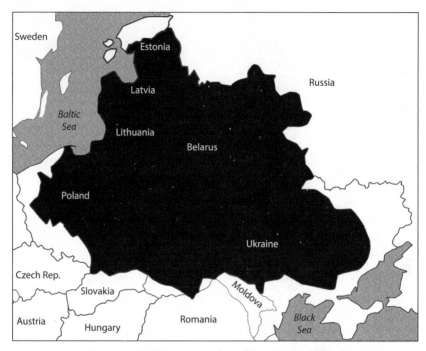

Figure 37. Polish-Lithuanian commonwealth at its maximum extent, 1619

Polish Catholics to imagine, however fantastically, that they might entice all Slavs to pledge allegiance to Rome.

Adding to this confidence was the recognition that not all Orthodox priests in Poland-Lithuania were happy with the Eastern church or with Patriarch Jeremias II of Constantinople (1572–1584), whose patriarchate oversaw Orthodox Christians in Poland-Lithuania. Jeremias fretted about the moral laxity of his Polish-Lithuanian clergy, and he tried to stiffen their collective moral spine by removing offending priests from office and by appointing "confraternities": church committees charged with monitoring the work of priests. Such appointments did not go over at all well with Orthodox priests in Poland-Lithuania. Some resented efforts to dictate personal behavior. Others distrusted in principle actions by a patriarchate under the authority of Muslim Turks. Other nationalists in the commonwealth worried less about Constantinople's meddling than about Russia's growing power in the region; they feared Eastern Orthodoxy risked becoming *Russian* Orthodoxy and a vehicle for military and political intervention by the Russian state.

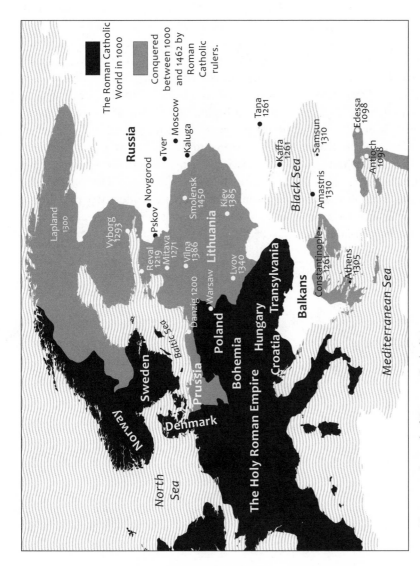

Figure 38. Spread of Roman Catholicism

These suspicions and resentments help explain an extraordinary decision by a synod of Polish-Lithuanian Orthodox bishops in 1595 to
approve a union with the Roman Catholic Church. (Six of the eight
bishops in the synod voted for the union, including three Russian
bishops and the metropolitan of Kiev, Mikhail Ragoza.) The terms of
the union were unique: those Orthodox who would unite with Rome
("Uniates," to their detractors) agreed to accept Roman Catholic doctrine and recognize the pope as the supreme head of the church. In return, they could retain the trappings of Eastern Orthodoxy: the Eastern
liturgy, religious art, and devotional traditions. Many thus referred to
themselves as "Byzantine Rite Catholics," since they observed the Byzantine liturgy, yet pledged allegiance to the Roman Catholic Church.

Churches in Russia and Constantinople reacted with fury. Rome,
they argued, had snatched Christians from Orthodoxy, turning them
from the true faith toward Latin heresies. Orthodox clerics felt out-
foxed, humiliated, and abandoned. And secular leaders worried about
their ability to assert political influence in regions now allied with
Western Christianity.

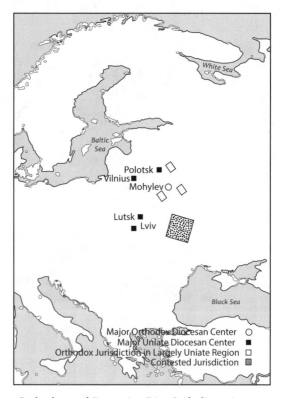

Figure 39. Orthodox and Byzantine Rite Catholic regions, 1770

Konstantin Ostrozhsky on the Union of Brest (1595)

"The Church Union of Brest: Prince Constantine Ostrozhsky's Circular,
June 25, 1595," in *A Source Book for Russian History from Early Times
to 1917,* ed. George Vernadsky (New Haven, CT: Yale University Press,
1972), 1:285–86. Used by permission of Yale University Press.

**On 25 June 1595, twenty-four days after the Orthodox bishops
signed the "Articles of Union," Prince Konstantin Ostrozhsky (1526–
1608), a layman who opposed the agreement, sent the following letter
to Orthodox clergy and laity.**

Outside the one true faith, implanted in Jerusalem and nourishing
[Christians] as the source of the ever-flowing word of God, there is no
other faith. [. . .] But [. . .] at the present time, through the devious wiles of
the all-cunning devil, the enemy and foe of the Christian race, the leading
hierarchs [leaders] of our true faith, seduced by the glories of this world
and cast into darkness by love of pleasure, our pretended pastors, the
metropolitan[1] with his bishops, have turned into wolves and abandoned
the one true faith of the holy Eastern church; they have renounced the
most holy patriarchs, our pastors and ecumenical teachers, have adhered
to the Western [church authorities], have cloaked themselves in hypocrisy
as in sheep's clothing, to conceal the wolf that lies hidden within, and do
not reveal their intent, but have secretly agreed among themselves, as did
Christ's betrayer, Judas, with the Jews, to lead astray surreptitiously all
the pious Christians of this region and to cast them into perdition along
with themselves, as is revealed by their pernicious and clandestine correspondence. [. . .]

Metropolitan Ragoza's Edict on Brest (1596)

"Brest: The Edict of the Uniate Metropolitan Mikhail Ragoza, October 8,
1596," in *A Source Book for Russian History from Early Times to 1917,* ed.
George Vernadsky (New Haven, CT: Yale University Press, 1972), 1:286–87.
Used by permission of Yale University Press.

**Ostrozhsky's protest did nothing to stop those determined to pro-
ceed. King Sigismund of Poland recognized the union on 24 September 1595, and Pope Clement VIII praised it later that year. In May
1596 King Sigismund asked the metropolitan of Kiev, Mikhail Ragoza**

1. *the metropolitan*—the metropolitan of Kiev, Mikhail Ragoza.

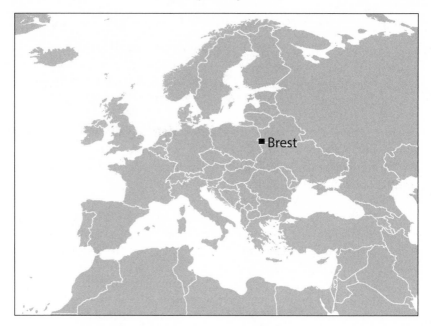

Figure 40. Brest

(1589–1599), to assemble a council in Brest (a city on the border of modern Poland and Belarus) to settle unresolved details. The council met on 6 October.

Things did not go well. Delegates quickly broke into feuding and irreconcilable groups. Those who wanted union with Rome and those who did not refused even to recognize each other. Those seeking union prepared the following encyclical, issued on 8 October 1596. Note that they cite Metropolitan Isidor (the representative at Ferrara-Florence who, according to many Orthodox Christians in Slavic lands, betrayed the faith) as an example to emulate—hardly a way to inspire trust among the Russians.

We, the undersigned metropolitan and bishops of the Greek rite,[2] by God's will assembled at a legitimate council in the cathedral church of Saint Nicholas in Brest [. . .] make known for all time to come that, taking into consideration that the autocratic nature of God's church was founded and confirmed in the Gospel through the words of our Lord

2. *Greek Rite*—Eastern Orthodox rites.

Jesus Christ, we [acknowledge] that the church of Christ, standing firmly upon Peter alone, as upon a rock, was governed and administered by him solely, so that the single head of a single body and the single master of a single house and the collector of God's tithes placed over mankind might look after the proper maintenance and general welfare of all. [. . .] In no lesser degree did the patriarchs of Tsar'grad,[3] from whom this Russian land adopted the holy faith, recognize for a long time the supremacy of the Roman see of Saint Peter and subordinate themselves to it and receive their blessings from it; even though they apostatized from it many times, they always reunited with it and returned in obedience to it; finally at the Council of Florence in the year of our Lord 1438, through the patriarch Joseph and the caesar[4] of Tsar'grad, John Paleologus, they returned in complete obedience, recognizing that the pope of Rome is the father and teacher and ruler of all Christendom and is the true vicar of Saint Peter. At the Council of Florence was likewise present our archbishop of Kiev and all Russia, the metropolitan Isidor, who brought home to Russia the union of the patriarchate of Constantinople and all the churches subordinate to it and confirmed this obedience to the church of Rome and its supremacy. [. . .] The patriarchs of Constantinople once again apostatized from this union of churches, and for this sin of apostasy and rupture of religious unity they fell into the power of the heathen Turks; this was followed by many errors and evil deeds, and a lack of proper supervision in these Russian lands, and much open simony,[5] so that heresy spread and took possession of all Russia, with churches desolated and the glory of God profaned. Not wishing to participate in such a great sin and in the pagan bondage that was the fate of the patriarchs of Constantinople, nor wishing to support them in their schism and rupture of the unity of the holy church, seeking to protect churches from desolation and human souls from perdition through the heresies that have now appeared, and heedful of our own salvation and the salvation of the spiritual flock entrusted to us by God, we took counsel and last year dispatched envoys to the most holy father, Clement VIII, the Roman pope, [. . .] requesting that he receive us in obedience to him as supreme pastor of the ecumenical catholic church and deliver and absolve us from the supremacy of the patriarchs of Constantinople, while maintaining our rites and ceremonials of the Eastern Greek and Russian churches, not making any changes in our churches but allowing us to continue in the traditions of the holy Greek fathers for all time to come. This [the pope] has done, and he has sent [us] his charters and envoys to this effect, telling us to convoke a synod and make a confession of holy faith, and render obedience to the

3. *Tsar'grad*—Constantinople.
4. *caesar*—emperor.
5. *simony*—selling religious offices for money.

Roman see of Saint Peter, to Clement VIII and his successors. All this we have done today at this synod.

Edict of the Orthodox Dignitaries at Brest (1596)

"Brest: The Edict of the Orthodox Dignitaries, October 9, 1596," in
A Source Book for Russian History from Early Times to 1917,
ed. George Vernadsky (New Haven, CT: Yale University Press, 1972), 1:287.
Used by permission of Yale University Press.

The Orthodox dissenters at Brest issued their own encyclical.

[. . .] In addition to their other misdeeds, that apostate, the metropolitan of Kiev, Galicia,[6] and all Russia, Mikhail Ragoza by name, together with the bishops who aided him in his evil intent [. . .], finally refused to heed our canonical invitation and accordingly to appear at a synod before us, to answer for their godless acts. [. . .] Outraged by these men, the divine holy Eastern church authorizes and definitively decrees through us at this council that the above-named Metropolitan Mikhail, along with the said bishops, shall be deposed and [. . .] stripped of all their episcopal vestments, and deprived of all administration and authority, and even of the name of bishop [. . .] and cast out and excluded [from the church]. [. . .]

Letter from a Participant at Brest (1596)

"Brest: A Letter from a Participant," in *A Source Book for Russian History from Early Times to 1917,* ed. George Vernadsky (New Haven, CT: Yale University Press, 1972), 1:287–88. Used by permission of Yale University Press.

An anonymous participant and opponent of the union wrote the following letter.

In October [. . .] there was a great synod in Brest for the sake of an agreement between the Greeks and the Romans,[7] at which the metropolitan Ragoza and the prelates, [. . .] having forsaken holy ecumenical

---

6. *Galicia*—the southeastern portion of modern Poland and the west-central portion of the modern Ukraine.

7. *Greeks and the Romans*—Eastern Orthodox and Roman Catholics.

Greek Orthodoxy, secretly and shamefully repaired to the communion of the Roman pope [. . .] for which they were all feted at the castle by the Romans, and were diverted like bears by buffoons' music and rattles; though in reality they were being laughed at.[8] But [the prelates who joined the Roman Catholic Church] were not able to seize and draw after them a single sheep, but were alone in surrendering themselves to the wolf; while the entire flock, praise be to God, being safely protected by God himself [and] united in heart and word, remained to praise God in its ancient orthodoxy [. . .]

Edict of Mikhail Ragoza (1596)

"Brest: The Edict of Mikhail Ragoza, October 10, 1596," in
A Source Book for Russian History from Early Times to 1917, ed.
George Vernadsky (New Haven, CT: Yale University Press, 1972),
1:288–89. Used by permission of Yale University Press.

Metropolitan Ragoza issued the council's final edict on 10 October 1596, condemning those who refused to recognize the union.

By the will and at the command of his royal grace,[9] we assembled a council [. . .] [but certain bishops and their confederates] refused to gather with me, their metropolitan and superior, in the church [designated as] the usual meeting-place for the synod; but in defiance of his royal grace's authority and mine, their elder pastor's, they held some kind of meeting in an unwonted and unseemly place, in a house where heretical meetings often took place and blasphemous sermons [were read]; and there, in that shameful house, they allowed Masses to be said, and they gathered secretly with heretics and with persons who did not belong to the council. More than once did we remind them that they should stop these clandestine meetings and sit with me, their elder archbishop, and the other bishops in the usual place, in the cathedral church where councils were formerly held, and determine, discuss, and reach decisions concerning God's church. But since they have acted both against the authority of the sovereign and against our pastoral will, and have congregated with heretics in violation of our laws and canons, and have allowed Masses to be celebrated in an alien diocese against regulations, we therefore, by virtue of the authority given to me by God and by my superior,[10] through the

8. *being laughed at*—by the Roman Catholics.
9. *his royal grace*—King Sigismund III of Poland-Lithuania.
10. *my superior*—the pope.

authority of the council, and with all my brethren, the reverend bishops who are with us here, deprive [the following men] of their ecclesiastical rank [. . .] [and] we hereby depose and remove them from their episcopal sees and dignities forever, so that they should not dare to wear a stole[11] around their neck, or to perform any holy offices of any kind, for all time to come and without any absolution by God the Father and the Son and the Holy Spirit. And if anyone should recognize those whom we have cursed as bishops or priests, may he himself and his house be accursed by the Father and the Son and the Holy Spirit. [. . .]

11. *stole*—a band of cloth that is part of a deacon's or a priest's vestments.

Peter the Great's Reorientation
of Russian Orthodoxy

W hen Peter the Great—arguably Russia's most influential
ruler of all time—assumed the throne in 1682, he encountered a powerful and ambitious Moscow patriarchate.[1] The
Russian church in the 1600s owned roughly one-fifth of all peasants
(held as serfs) in Russia. Some eighty-six thousand people served as
monks, priests, and bishops. The patriarchate possessed significant
wealth and exercised considerable influence in state affairs, and it un-
abashedly insisted that it represented and safeguarded Christianity in
Russia.

Patriarch Ioakim on Prerogatives of the Church (1690)

"The Testament of Patriarch Joachim, March 17, 1690," in *A Source
Book for Russian History from Early Times to 1917*, ed. George Vernadsky
(New Haven, CT: Yale University Press, 1972), 1:361–63. Used by
permission of Yale University Press.

Patriarch Ioakim of Moscow (1674–1690) wrote the following letter eight years after Peter took the throne. It illustrates well the Russian church's conception of itself and its rights. Ioakim insists here
that Peter exercise his power to protect the church against foreign influence, while also arguing that his (Ioakim's) own "episcopal power"
gives him the right to provide "guidance" for Peter.

1. See section 25, "Patriarch Nikon and the Old Belief," in the online supplement.

297

[. . .] [M]ay our sovereign never allow any Orthodox Christians in their realm to entertain any close friendly relations with heretics and dissenters—with the Latins,[2] Lutherans, Calvinists,[3] and godless Tatars[4] (whom our Lord abominates and the church of God damns for their God-abhorred guiles); but let them be avoided as enemies of God and defamers of the church. May they command by their tsarist decree that men of foreign creeds who come here to this pious realm shall under no circumstances preach their religion, disparage our faith in any conversations, or introduce their alien customs derived from their heresies for the temptation of Christians; they should be strictly forbidden to do all this on pain of severe punishment. [. . .]

I again implore their most serene tsarist majesties, the pious tsars, and call upon them before God, our savior, that they prohibit in the whole realm all accursed foreign heretics and dissenters from exercising any kind of command in their regiments; but let them order that these enemies of Christendom be completely removed from such positions. For these dissenters do not agree in faith with us, Christians, who are in possession of true Orthodoxy; they are completely at variance with us in interpreting the tradition of the fathers; they are alien to our mother, the Orthodox church. Of what help could such accursed heretics be to the Orthodox host? They only bring on the wrath of God. The Orthodox pray to God according to the rules and customs of the church, while they, the heretics, sleep, and perform their abominable deeds, despising Christian prayer. The Christians honor the most pure Mother of God, the Virgin Mary, and invoke in every way her aid and that of all the saints; but the heretics—the military commanders—being ungodly, revile it and blaspheme; in no way do they respect the most holy Mother of God and all the saints; they do not honor the holy icons; they scoff at all Christian piety. Christians observe the fasts; heretics—never. [. . .]

In [our] Christian regiments [we have] these God-abhorred living idols, the heretics, who malign our holy faith and piety: these Lutherans, Calvinists, and Latins, who dispense injustice; indeed, more—as superiors, they are wolves set over hapless Christian lambs, on whom they heap every insult. No good can come from allowing a heretic—a non-Orthodox man—to hold in bondage, to command, or to judge the Orthodox Christians in the pious tsarist realm. Are there no Orthodox men fit to fill these positions and to perform in them capably? Indeed, by God's grace, the Russian tsardom abounds in pious men among the subjects of the tsarist realm, who are well versed in military science and skilled in leading troops. [. . .]

2. *Latins*—Roman Catholics.

3. *Calvinists*—Protestants who follow the teachings of John Calvin.

4. *Tatars*—Muslims.

With all my soul I implore and beg of you, our great and most pious sovereigns and tsars, to follow these precepts, and, by my episcopal power, I lay down this testament of mine for the guidance of all pious autocrats. [. . .]

Postscript: Let me remind you again not to allow, under any circumstances, the heretic dissenters to build Roman temples,[5] Lutheran churches, or Tatar mosques anywhere in your realm or dominions, nor to bring in any new Latin and alien customs, nor to introduce the wearing of foreign dress: for it is not through such practices that piety will spread in a Christian realm or faith in our Lord will grow. [. . .]

Manifesto Creating the Ecclesiastical College or Holy Synod (1721)

"(l. 30). My Petr" Pervyi, tsar' i samoderzhet" vse-rossiiskii," in *Uchrezhdenie Dukhovnoi Kollegii i dukhovnyi reglament k voprosu ob otnoshenii tserkvi i gosudarstva v rosii*, ed. P. V. Verkhovskoi (Rostov na donu, 1916), 6–7. Translated by Bryn Geffert. CC BY-SA.

Ioakim's missive against "alien customs" made little impression on Peter, who initiated a herculean effort to wrest Russia into the modern era by adopting and imposing upon his realm Western art, culture, technology, governance, and economic practices. Peter jettisoned the Russian calendar, which tried to reckon dates from the creation of the world (the year 1672 in Russia was considered the year 7180). He modernized Church Slavonic orthography into the modern Russian script. He built a state-of-the-art Western navy; modeled his government's bureaucracy on Sweden's; and made education compulsory for children of the nobility. Books published in the West flooded into Russia. Peter supported the first Russian newspaper. He built a new capital, St. Petersburg, on the shores of the Baltic Sea, employing European architects, who ignored traditional Russian forms. To make his subjects appear more Western, he imposed a special tax on nobles who refused to shave their beards.

Eastern Orthodox Christianity did not suite this Western-minded tsar. Peter disliked the long Orthodox liturgy, preferring instead Lutheran services and sermons. He scoffed at miracle-working icons. He equated monasticism with laziness.

Close ties in Russia between church and state hampered Peter's quest to create a strong, secular state. Such a state needed more revenue, and

---

5. *Roman temples*—Roman Catholic churches.

Peter envied the church its wealth. So he forbade church leaders from collecting taxes. He forced monasteries to share their revenue with the state, and he forbade them from building new structures. In 1701 Peter created a government agency, the "Monastery Department," to supervise church courts and administer church land. This department effectively annexed large swaths of monastic land to the state.

Peter's vision of a secular state, governed by a strong emperor, had no place for an independent patriarch with his own base of power. So in 1721 Peter took the extraordinary step of creating the "Most Holy Governing Synod," essentially a government cabinet subject to his will, to govern the Russian church. He abolished the patriarchate, the governance model that had served Russia for 132 years, and Jerusalem, Constantinople, Antioch, Alexandria, and Rome for centuries. Every occurrence in the liturgy of the word "patriarch" disappeared, replaced by "Holy Synod." The Holy Synod oversaw a cadre of spiritual inspectors known as "inquisitors" who bore responsibility for monitoring the actions of bishops and priests. In place of the patriarch, Peter appointed a "chief procurator," that is, a departmental secretary.

In effect, Peter transformed the Russian church from (depending on one's point of view) either a rival power base or an institution meant to share power with and guide the state, into a body fully subordinate to the state. As Lindsey Hughes notes, "Long gone were the days when a patriarch could assert," as did Patriarch Nikon of Moscow (1652–1660), that "the tsar must be lower than the prelate and obedient to him." The clergy under Peter "had no more power to resist the tsar's commands than did secular officials."[6]

We Peter the First, the tsar and autocrat of all Russia, etc.:
Among the many lofty obligations borne by us by virtue of the dominion given to us by God for the reformation of all the Russian people and other subjects of our rule: having examined the ecclesiastical rank and finding within it much disorganization and great deficits in its affairs, we should be troubled by fear lest we appear ungrateful to the Most High[7] if—having received from him such great help in the reformation of both the military and civilian ranks—we should disregard the reforma-

6. Lindsey Hughes, *Peter the Great: A Biography* (New Haven, CT: Yale University Press), 148.
7. *Most High*—God.

tion of the ecclesiastical rank as well, and—when the nonpartisan judge[8] requires an answer in response to his great trust in us—we do not have an answer.

In light of the example provided by pious kings in the Old Testament and New Testament, having accepted responsibility for reforming the ecclesiastical rank, and not perceiving any better method to achieve this than conciliar government—because [governing the church] is too much for one person without inherited authority[9]—we establish an ecclesiastical college—that is, an ecclesiastical, conciliar cabinet—which will, according to the following regulation, govern all spiritual affairs in the Russian church.

And we order all our true subjects of both the ecclesiastical and secular ranks to accept [the college] as an important and strong cabinet, to bring extreme spiritual matters to it for adjudication, decisions, and resolutions; to be satisfied with its judgments and decisions, [and] to heed its decrees in all matters [. . .]

Oath of the Holy Synod (1721)

"(l. 32). Prisiaga chlenov' Dukhovnoi Kollegii," in *Uchrezhdenie Dukhovnoi Kollegii i dukhovnyi reglament k voprosu ob otnoshenii tserkvi i gosudarstva v rosii*, ed. P. V. Verkhovskoi (Rostov na donu, 1916), 10–11. Translated by Bryn Geffert. CC BY-SA.

All members of the Ecclesiastical College (Holy Synod) were required to sign the following oath.

I, the one named below, promise and swear before Omnipotent God and before his Holy Gospels:

That I have an obligation, that I want the obligation, and that I will always in every way strive to seek in the advice and judgments and in all matters of this ecclesiastical cabinet the utmost truth and utmost justice, and to act in everything according to the written stipulations of the ecclesiastical regulation and anything agreed to thereafter by the ecclesiastical cabinet and determined to be pleasing to his majesty the tsar.

In all this I shall act according to my conscience, not working toward my own ends, not contaminated by envy, covetousness, or obstinacy, and

8. *nonpartisan judge*—God.

9. *because [governing the church] is too much for one person without inherited authority*—a reference to the patriarch. Peter wrote these words into the declaration by hand.

in no way captivated by passion for anything other than the fear of God, always bearing in mind his incorruptible judgment, with sincere love for God and neighbor, holding in all my thoughts, words, and deeds the ultimate aim of the glory of God, the salvation of human souls, and the edification of the entire church, working not for myself but for the Lord Jesus. [. . .]

I swear before Omnipotent God that I want and that I have an obligation to my natural, true tsar and supreme sovereign, Peter the First, the all-Russian autocrat, etc., etc., etc., and to those who follow as his Tsarist Majesty's lofty and legal successors, who according to the pleasure of his autocratic Tsarist Majesty's power, are appointed or will be appointed as worthy to assume the throne [. . .] to be a true, good, and obedient servant. I will defend and protect to the extreme limits of my intellect and body his Tsarist Majesty's autocracy, strength, and power, and all rights and prerogatives belonging to him, ordained by him, or to be ordained by him [. . .]

In conclusion to my vow I kiss the words and cross of my Savior. Amen.

Ecclesiastical Regulation (1721)

"The Ecclesiastical Regulation, Part 1," in James Cracraft, *Major Problems in the History of Imperial Russia* (Lexington, MA: D. C. Heath, 1994), 120–23.

The following "ecclesiastical regulation" constitutes Peter's justification for establishing the Ecclesiastical College (later named the Holy Synod). Here Peter acknowledges his fear that subjects are inclined to think of the patriarch as "a kind of second sovereign, equal to or even greater than the autocrat himself, and to imagine that the ecclesiastical order is another and better state."

[. . .] What is an ecclesiastical college [Holy Synod], and what are the grave reasons for [establishing] it?

An administrative college is nothing else than an administrative body in which certain matters are subject to the control not of a single person but to that of the several qualified persons appointed by the supreme authority. [. . .] And such colleges, varying according to the business and needs of the state, the most potent all-Russian tsar, the most-wise Peter the first, has established for the good of the fatherland beginning in the year 1718.

And as a Christian sovereign, guardian of Orthodoxy and all good order in the holy church, and having observed the needs of the ecclesiastical order and desiring that it should be better administered, he has deigned to establish an ecclesiastical college. [. . .]

Lest anybody imagine, however, that this kind of administration is unsuitable [for the church] and that the spiritual affairs of an entire society might be better directed by a single person,[10] as the affairs of a particular diocese are directed by its bishop, we here put forth [nine] weighty reasons to prove that government by council is indeed the best, and better than one-man rule, especially in a monarchical state such as our Russia.

1. In the first place, truth is more surely discovered by a council than by a single person. An old Greek proverb says that second thoughts are wiser than first; thus how much more wisely will many thoughts, rather than one, resolve some issue. [. . .] In government by council proposals are examined by many minds [. . .] so that a doubtful matter is more surely elucidated and quickly explained, and what is required to resolve it is seen without difficulty.

2. And so far as there is more certain knowledge, there is great power to do things. For people are more inclined to accept and obey the decision of a council than the decree of a single person. The power of monarchs is autocratic, which God himself commands us to obey in good conscience; yet monarchs have their advisors, not only for the sake of better ascertaining the truth but in order that disobedient subjects should not slander them by saying that they rule by force and caprice rather than by justice and truth. How much more so, then, should this be the case in church government, where the authority is not monarchical and the person governing is forbidden to lord it over the clergy. When only one person rules, his adversaries may slander him alone and so detract from the force of his decisions. But this is not possible when decisions proceed from a council.

3. And this is especially true when an administrative college is founded by the monarch and is under his authority. For a college is not some faction secretly joined to promote its own interest but rather is composed of persons gathered together for the common good by order of the autocrat after consultation with his advisors.

4. This is also important: when one person rules, procrastinations and interruptions in business often occur because of the overwhelming demands made upon him or because of his sickness or infirmity, and when he dies, business stops altogether. It is otherwise with government by council: if one member is absent, say even the chief person, the others carry on, and business continues its uninterrupted course.

5. But what is particularly advantageous, in such a college there is no room for partiality, intrigue, or bribery. [. . .] Should one member be partial to or adversely prejudiced against a person on trial, the second,

---

10. *single person*—a patriarch.

third, and so on will be free of any such prejudice. How could bribery prevail when matters are decided not arbitrarily but only after regular and serious consideration? For any individual member will be wary lest he be unable to show good cause for his opinion and so be suspected of having taken a bribe. This would be particularly true if the college were composed of persons who could not possibly conspire together in secret, that is, of persons of different rank and station—bishops, abbots, and members of the secular clergy who are in positions of authority. In truth it cannot be seen how such persons could dare to reveal to one another a nefarious plot, let alone conspire in wrongdoing.

6. Similarly, a college enjoys greater freedom of mind to administer justice, for unlike a single governor it need not fear the wrath of the mighty. To put pressure on many persons, and moreover persons of different rank, is not so easy as pressuring one person.

7. And this is most important: the fatherland need not fear from a conciliar government the sedition and disorders that proceed from the personal rule of a single church leader. For the common folk do not perceive how different is the ecclesiastical power from that of the autocrat, but, dazzled by the great honor and glory of the supreme pastor,[11] they think him a kind of second sovereign, equal to or even greater than the autocrat himself, and imagine that the ecclesiastical order is another and better state. Thus the people are accustomed to reason among themselves, a situation in which the tares[12] of seditious talk by ambitious clerics multiply and act as sparks that set dry twigs ablaze. Simple hearts are perverted by these ideas, so that in some matters they look not so much to their autocrat as to the supreme pastor. And when they hear of a dispute between the two, they blindly and stupidly take sides with the ecclesiastical ruler rather than the secular one, and dare to conspire and rebel against the latter. The accursed ones deceive themselves into thinking that they are fighting for God himself, that they do not defile but hallow their hands even when they resort to bloodshed. Criminal and dishonest persons are pleased to discover such ideas among the people: when they learn of a quarrel between their sovereign and the pastor, because of their animosity toward the former they seize on the chance to make good their malice, and under pretense of religious zeal do not hesitate to take up arms against the Lord's anointed; and to this iniquity they incite the common folk as if to the work of God. And what if the pastor himself, inflated by such lofty opinions of his office, will not keep quiet? It is difficult to relate how great are the calamities that thereby ensue.

These are not mere inventions: would to God that they were. But in fact this has more than once occurred in many states. One need only in-

11. *supreme pastor*—patriarch.
12. *tares*—weeds.

vestigate the history of Constantinople since Justinian's time to discover much of this. Indeed the pope by this very means achieved so great a pre-eminence, and not only completely disrupted the Roman empire, while usurping a great part of it for himself, but more than once has profoundly shaken other states and almost completely destroyed them. Not to mention similar threats that have occurred among us.

In government by an ecclesiastical council there is no room for such mischief. For here the president himself enjoys neither the great glory that dazzles the people nor excessive luster and notoriety; there can be no lofty opinions of him; nor can flatterers exalt him with inordinate praises, because what is well done by such an administrative council cannot possibly be ascribed to the president alone. The very name president is not a proud one, for it means nothing more than "he who presides," and neither can he think highly of himself nor can others extol him. Moreover, when the people see that this administrative council[13] has been established by decree of the monarch with the concurrence of the senate, they will remain meek and put away any hope of receiving aid in their rebellions from the ecclesiastical order.

8. Church and state will further benefit from such an administrative council since not only each of its members, but the president himself, is liable to the judgment of his brothers, that is of the college itself, in case of notable transgression. This is not what happens when one supreme pastor rules, for he is unwilling to be tried by his subordinate bishops. And should he be compelled thus to stand trial, the common folk, who are ignorant of the processes of law and judge blindly, would be suspicious of such a trial and subject it to abuse. Hence it would be necessary to summon a general council to try such a pastor, which can only be managed at great trouble and expense for the entire country. And at the present time (when the Eastern patriarchs live under the Ottoman yoke, and the Turks are more than ever wary of our state), it would seem impossible.[14]

9. Finally such an administrative council will become a kind of school of ecclesiastical government. For in the exchange of the many different opinions, counsels, and sound arguments required by current business each member can be conveniently instructed in ecclesiastical administration and, by daily practice, learn how best to administer the house of God. Hence the most suitable members of the college will deservedly advance to the episcopal rank [of bishop]. And thus in Russia, with God's help, grossness will soon disappear from the ecclesiastical order, and the best results may be hoped for.

13. *administrative council*—the Ecclesiastical College/Holy Synod.

14. *it would seem impossible*—Cracraft suggests that here Peter has in mind the schism created by Patriarch Nikon's reforms: see section 25, "Patriarch Nikon and the Old Belief," in the online supplement.

Engaging the West through Creeds

The historian Jaroslav Pelikan (1923–2006) once delivered a lecture that he subtitled with a question: "Where Does Orthodoxy Confess What It Believes and Teaches?"[1] On the face of it, this seems a straightforward query, one that most Roman Catholics and Protestants could answer in regard to their own confessions with little trouble.

It is a more difficult question, however, for the Eastern Orthodox, who have never been as enamored of creeds and doctrinal statements as Roman Catholics and Protestants. A twentieth-century Bulgarian Orthodox scholar once remarked, "The West incessantly asks us for the symbolical books [doctrinal statements] of Orthodoxy. We have no need of them."[2]

How to explain this?

Pelikan notes what he terms the "inseparable connection" in Eastern Orthodoxy between *lex orandi* (the rule of prayer) and *lex credendi* (the rule of faith), or the degree to which faith expresses itself in prayer and worship rather than in creeds. Those who study Eastern Orthodoxy, Pelikan continues, "whether sympathetic or critical, agree on the proposition that the Divine Liturgy According to Saint John

---

1. Jaroslav Pelikan, "The Eastern Orthodox Quest for Confessional Identity: Where Does Orthodoxy Confess What It Believes and Teaches?" *Modern Greek Studies Yearbook* 14/15 (1998/1999): 21–36.

2. "L'Occident nous demande sans cesse nos livres symboliques de l'orthodoxie. Nous n'avons pas besoin d'en avoir"; S. Herbert Scott, *The Eastern Churches and the Papacy* (London: Sheed & Ward, 1928), 351.

Chrysostom [i.e., the primary Orthodox the church service], as the premier Eastern Orthodox confession of faith, is an especially forceful illustration of the universal principle of lex orandi lex credendi."[3] In other words, liturgy and worship rather than doctrinal statements express belief.[4]

Second, Pelikan notes Eastern Orthodoxy's devotion to the faith as expressed in documents of the seven ecumenical councils conducted between 325 and 787. The Eastern church recognizes *only* these councils as truly ecumenical, and thus *only* these expressions of faith have the support of the entire Eastern church. No body since 787 can claim to be universally representative, and thus no body since 787 can issue statements with equivalent authority. As the Russian theologian Nikolai Glubokovsky (1863–1937) wrote, "The faith of the seven ecumenical councils is sufficient for us!"[5]

Third, Eastern Orthodoxy after the ecumenical councils had no ready means of issuing statements of faith. Without a figure such as the Roman pontiff, such things as papal encyclicals, bulls, epistles, and constitutions could not be easily issued. Although the patriarchal synod of Constantinople did at times issue decrees, it never claimed that those decrees bore the same authority that Rome claimed for its decrees. And the synod of Constantinople never suggested that its decrees bore the same import as statements from ecumenical councils.

The Eastern reluctance to produce anything resembling a statement of faith wavered, however, when Protestant reformers in the West began to issue their own. The Protestant statements, Pelikan suggests, prompted a Newtonian "equal and opposite reaction," that is, a felt need by the Orthodox to issue point-by-point refutations to the strange doctrine emerging in Germany, England, and Switzerland. Orthodox creeds began to emerge in some abundance.[6]

Some history is in order here.

In our work so far, all documents illustrating relations between East and West have focused on tensions between the church in the East and the Roman church in the West. Constantinople and Rome stood as the two major centers of power in Christendom up until the 1500s.

---

3. Pelikan, 25.

4. See document 14.1, "Divine Liturgy of St. John Chrysostom," in the online supplement.

5. Pelikan, 27.

6. See section 19, "Post-Conciliar Doctrine," in the online supplement.

This is not to say that all in the West welcomed the Roman church's power. In 962—that is, 148 years after Charlemagne's death—Pope John XII (955–964) crowned the Germanic prince Otto I "Holy Roman emperor" (962–973), or ruler of the "Holy Roman Empire," that is, the vast collection of the lands consolidated by Charlemagne. This formal invention of the Holy Roman Empire, while strengthening both Pope John and Emperor Otto, also exacerbated questions as to who should wield primary power in this region: the Holy Roman emperor, the pope, or princes governing states within the empire? Germanic rulers often chafed at papal claims. Jockeying for position and influence was constant. Princes resented taxes levied by the papacy, and they questioned why government officials should be subject in some matters to an ecclesiastical leader in Rome.

Theological developments in the West also bred distrust of Rome. In the 1300s the English theologian John Wycliffe (ca. 1320–1384) began railing against the Roman church's sale of indulgences, that is, grants from the church remitting punishment for sins. The Roman Catholic Church claimed that indulgences drew upon a storehouse of merit built up by the virtues of the saints, penance performed by the saints, and Christ's own sacrifice. Rome's sale of indulgences (often to finance the construction of churches) enraged Wycliffe and, later in the early 1500s, the German monk Martin Luther (1483–1546). The Bohemian reformer Jan Hus (1369–1415) was executed as a heretic for opposing indulgences.

Western reformers protested a number of other practices in the Roman Catholic Church. Some, like Wycliffe, wanted to read the Bible in the vernacular, a practice Rome forbade, insisting that the Bible be distributed only in Latin. (This position, of course, ran contrary to earlier allowances for the Bible's translation into Slavic languages.) Some of Hus's more radical followers rejected any church doctrine not derived directly from scripture. Numerous reformers criticized what they considered the rapacity of the Roman Catholic Church and the immoral conduct of priests and bishops. Princes and emperors resented the church's demands that church land be exempt from taxation. Peasants without land resented the very existence of church estates.

In 1517 Martin Luther posted his ninety-five theses, criticizing, among many other things, the theory and practice of indulgences. The church condemned Luther, which only steeled his resistance. He mulled over the seven sacraments of the church and concluded that only two, marriage and baptism, were true sacraments. (He denied sacramental status for the Eucharist, penance, confirmation, holy orders, and the anointing of the sick.) When the pope issued a bull threatening excommunication, Luther burned it in public.

Although Charles V (1519–1556), the Holy Roman emperor at this time, had his own beefs with the papacy, he worried about the implications of Luther's revolt for the stability of his empire. In 1521 Charles summoned Luther to appear before him and the rulers of the German principalities that comprised the Holy Roman Empire. The archbishop of Trier acted as the emperor's spokesman at the assembly and told Luther he had no right to question the doctrines of the church. Luther responded, "Unless I am convicted by scripture and plain reason—I do not accept the authority of popes and councils, for they have contradicted each other—my conscience is captive to the word of God. I cannot and will not recant anything, for to go against conscience is neither right nor safe." For this Luther was declared an outlaw. He went into hiding for a year, writing tracts and treatises while translating the Bible into German.

Some rulers of German principalities, themselves chaffing under the demands of their emperor, found something inspiring in Luther's resistance. Princes who supported Luther's theology, and even some who did not, saw in Protestantism a way to distance themselves from their emperor and from rival princes. Lutheran theology also became a way for residents of particular states to oppose their own prince. In 1524 peasants angry over exploitation by religious and secular landowners revolted. The Holy Roman Empire had become a tinderbox of economic, political, and religious claims and counterclaims.

So in 1530 Emperor Charles V summoned the German princes to the city of Augsburg, hoping the assembly might restore political and religious unity in his empire (or at least enough unity to focus his empire's attention on repulsing an Ottoman invasion). The Protestant theologian Philipp Melanchthon produced for the assembly a statement of Lutheran tenets, which he hoped might prove acceptable to the emperor and other Roman Catholics. The first twenty-one articles bent over backward to demonstrate that Lutheran doctrine was compatible with the established doctrine of the Roman Catholic Church: in fact article twenty-one claimed that Lutherans "dissent in no article of faith from the catholic church."

The remaining seven articles attacked what Lutherans considered errors in Roman Catholicism. These included the practice of distributing only bread, not wine, to parishioners during the Eucharist ("Communion under one kind"); the requirement that priests remain

Figure 41. Augsburg

celibate; the understanding of the Catholic Mass as an "expiatory sacrifice," that is, as a sacrifice that expiates guilt (only Christ's sacrifice on the cross, argued the reformers, constitutes an expiatory sacrifice); mandatory confession; understandings of grace; certain monastic practices; and claims regarding the authority of bishops. Overall, the document adopted a conciliatory tone, using intentionally vague language, for example, on questions such as justification (how humans become righteous and free from sin in the eyes of God) and confession.

But papal loyalists at Augsburg could not accept the confession in its entirety: they endorsed nine of the articles without qualification, six with qualification, and dismissed thirteen outright. Lutheran princes at the assembly asked that the confession be read in public. Their request was denied. Two Saxon chancellors—one with a Latin copy and one with a German copy—read it anyway. The schism between the reformers and the loyalists had proved irreconcilable. Resultant feuds erupted into the civil arena and led to civil war that tore the empire apart and ended only with the Peace of Augsburg in 1555.

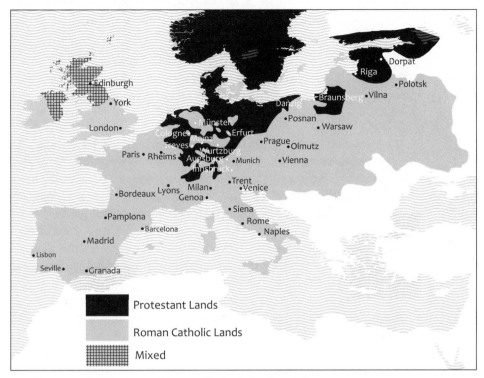

Figure 42. Protestant and Roman Catholic lands, 1648

We rehearse this history here to make one big point: the Eastern church now found itself in schism not only with Western Christendom (i.e., Roman Catholicism), but also (and not by choice) with a new offshoot of Western Christendom, which itself was now in schism with the papacy.

On many of the points where Protestant reformers diverged from the papacy, they also diverged from Eastern Orthodoxy. Eastern and Roman Catholic understandings of the Eucharist, monasticism, grace, justification, and episcopal authority have far more in common with each other than with Protestant interpretations.

Luther and a number of his allies, however, failed at first to recognize this fact. In 1520 Luther boasted, quite erroneously, that "Muscovites, White Russians, Greeks, Bohemians, and many other great lands in the world . . . believe as we do, baptize as we do, preach as we do, live as we do." His colleagues and successors would be sorely disappointed in the years ahead to learn how wrong he was.

Confession of Patriarch Dositheos and the Synod of Jerusalem (1672)

"Dositheus and the Synod of Jerusalem, 'Confession, 1672,'" trans. J. N. W. B. Robertson, in *Creeds and Confessions of Faith in the Christian Tradition,* ed. Jaroslav Pelikan and Valerie Hotchkiss (New Haven, CT: Yale University Press, 2003), 1:615–26, 628–35. Used by permission of Yale University Press.

In 1672 Patriarch Dositheos II of Jerusalem convened a council to refute a statement of faith authored by Patriarch Kyrillos Loukaris, the sometime patriarch of Constantinople, who had, to his colleagues' bafflement, fallen completely under the spell of Protestant theology.

In the estimation of one scholar, this council proved to be the most important modern council of the Eastern church and the church's "closest approximation" to Roman Catholic efforts at the Council of Trent (1545–1563) to define and defend traditional doctrine in the face of the Protestant reformations.[7]

In Dositheos's response below he refutes Protestant elements of Loukaris's confession point by point. The *filioque* is wrong. Not all Christians have the right to interpret scripture for themselves. The authority of scripture is not superior to the authority of the church. In fact the church cannot err. Salvation and justification require faith *and* works, not just faith, as many Protestants insisted. The church needs leaders and order. Protestants are wrong to talk about original sin. The writings of bishops and the church fathers are extraordinarily important. There are seven sacraments, not two. We should pay reverence to the Virgin, to icons, and to the saints. God's presence in the eucharistic elements is real. And scripture that Protestants classify as apocryphal (i.e., not reliable enough to enter the canon of scripture) is central.

Note that Dositheos's use of "catholic church" does not denote the Roman Catholic Church; it refers to what he considers the true universal church, that is, the Eastern Orthodox Church. The "Calvinists" he references are followers of John Calvin (1509–1564), a radical Protestant whom Kyrillos Loukaris admired.

[. . .]

7. See "Trent, Council of (1545–63)" in *The Oxford Dictionary of the Christian Church,* 3rd ed. (New York: Oxford University Press, 1997).

· Decree 2 ·

We believe that the divine and sacred scripture is taught by God. And therefore we ought to believe it without doubting, yet not otherwise than as the catholic church has interpreted and delivered it. For every foul heresy does indeed receive the divine scripture, but interprets it perversely, using metaphors and homonymies and sophistries[8] of human wisdom, confusing what ought to be distinguished and trifling with what ought not to be trifled with. For if we were to receive it otherwise, with each man holding every day a different sense concerning it, the catholic church would not, as she does by the grace of Christ, continue to be the church until this day, holding the same doctrine of faith and always believing it identically and steadfastly, but would be rent into innumerable parties and subject to heresies. [. . .] Therefore the witness of the catholic church is, we believe, not inferior in authority to that of the divine scripture. For one and the same Holy Spirit being the author of both, it is quite the same to be taught by the scripture and by the catholic church. Moreover, when anyone speaks from himself, he is liable to err, to deceive and be deceived. But for the catholic church, as never having spoken or speaking from herself but from the Spirit of God—who being her teacher, she is unfailingly rich forever—it is impossible to err in any way, or to deceive at all or be deceived; but like the divine scripture, she is infallible and has perpetual authority.

· Decree 3 ·

We believe that from eternity the supremely good God predestined to glory those whom he has chosen, and consigned to condemnation those whom he has rejected, but not in such a way that he would justify the one, and consign and condemn the other, without cause. For that would be contrary to the nature of God, who is the common Father of all and no respecter of persons, and who would have all men to be saved and to come to the knowledge of the truth. [. . .] But those who refuse to obey and cooperate with grace and who, therefore, refuse to observe those things that God would have us perform, and who abuse in the service of Satan the free will that they have received from God to perform voluntarily what is good, these are consigned to eternal condemnation. But to say, as the most wicked heretics do [. . .] that God, in predestinating or condemning, did not have regard at all to the works of those predestinated or condemned, we know to be profane and impious. [. . .]

8. *homonymies and sophistries*—tricky, equivocal, or cleverly deceptive methods of reasoning.

· Decree 5 ·

We believe that all things that are, whether visible or invisible, are governed by the providence of God; but although God foreknows evils and permits them, yet in that they are evils, he is neither their contriver nor their author. [. . .]

· Decree 6 ·

We believe that the first man, who was created by God, fell in Paradise, when, disregarding the divine commandment, he yielded to the deceitful counsel of the serpent. And from this the ancestral sin flowed to his posterity, so that none is born after the flesh who does not bear this burden— there is inherent in our members an inclination toward sinning, not sin as such, for such approaches that lack assent and are not put into practice are not sin, because it says that "the imagination of man is intently bent upon evil things from his youth"—and who does not experience its fruits in this present world. [. . .]

· Decree 8 ·

We believe that our Lord Jesus Christ is the only mediator, and that in giving himself as ransom for all he has through his own blood made a reconciliation between God and man, and that, having a care for his own, he is the advocate and the propitiation[9] for our sins. At the same time, in prayers and supplications to him, we say that the saints are intercessors, and above all the undefiled mother of the very God the Word, as well as the holy angels—whom we know to be set over us—the apostles, prophets, martyrs, pure ones, and all whom he has glorified as having served him faithfully. With them we number also the bishops and priests, as standing about the altar of God, and righteous men eminent for virtue. For that we should pray one for another, and that the prayer of the righteous avails much, and that God listens to the saints rather than to those who are steeped in sins—this we learn from the sacred oracles. And not only do we confess that the saints while on their pilgrimage are mediators and intercessors for us with God, but especially after their death, when, all reflective vision being done away, they clearly behold the Holy Trinity, in whose infinite light they know what concerns us. [. . .]

· Decree 10 ·

[. . .] Of this catholic church, because a mortal man cannot universally and perpetually be head, our Lord Jesus Christ himself is head, and himself holding the rudder is at the helm in the governing of the church, through the holy fathers. And therefore, over particular churches that are

---

9. *propitiation*—atonement or salvation.

real churches and consist of real members, the Holy Spirit has appointed bishops as leaders and shepherds who are, not in an improper sense of the word but properly, authorities and heads; they look, not to a mortal man but to the author and finisher of our salvation, and refer to him what they do in their capacity as heads.

But among their other impieties the Calvinists have fancied this also: that the simple priest and the high priest are perhaps the same; that there is no necessity for high priests; that the church may be governed by a group of priests; and that not a high priest only, but also a priest is able to ordain a priest, and a number of priests to ordain a high priest. They affirm in lofty language that the Eastern church assents to this wicked notion, for which purpose the tenth chapter was written by Kyrillos. Therefore we explicitly declare, according to the mind that has obtained from the beginning in the Eastern church: That the dignity of the bishop is so necessary in the church that without him neither church nor Christian could either be or be spoken of. Having been deemed worthy of being a bishop as a successor of the apostles, and having received in continuous succession by the laying on of hands and the invocation of the all-Holy Spirit the grace that is given to him from the Lord of binding and loosing, he is a living image of God on earth; and by a most ample participation of the operation of the Holy Spirit, who is the chief functionary, he is a fountain of all the sacraments of the catholic church, through which we obtain salvation. And he is, we maintain, as necessary to the church as breath is to man, or the sun to the world. [. . .]

And that this great mystery and dignity of the episcopate has come down to us by a continued succession is manifest. For the Lord has promised to be with us always; although he is with us by other means of grace and divine operations, yet it is in a more eminent manner, through the bishop as chief functionary, that he makes us his own and dwells with us, and through the divine sacraments is united with us. Of these the bishop is the first minister and chief functionary, through the Holy Spirit, and he does not permit us to fall into heresy. [. . .]

And the one having received the dignity of the priesthood from the bishop, can only perform holy baptism and the sacrament of unction,[10] minister sacrificially the unbloody sacrifice,[11] and impart to the people the all-holy body and blood of our Lord Jesus Christ, anoint the baptized with the holy myrrh,[12] crown Orthodox couples who are entering into holy matrimony in accordance with the law, pray for the sick, and that all men may be saved and come to the knowledge of the truth, and especially

10. *unction*—anointing the ill with holy oil.

11. *unbloody sacrifice*—the Eucharist.

12. *anoint the baptized with holy myrrh*—the sacrament of chrismation, in which the priest anoints a believer with chrism, or holy oil.

for the remission and forgiveness of the sins of the faithful, living and dead. [. . .] And the ordinations of all orders and degrees in the church are proper to him; and in a primary and highest sense he binds and looses and his sentence is approved by God, as the Lord has promised. And he preaches the sacred Gospel and contends for the Orthodox faith; and those who refuse to hear he casts out of the church as heathens and publicans, and he puts heretics under excommunication and anathema, and lays down his own life for the sheep. [. . .]

· Decree 12 ·

We believe that the catholic church is taught by the Holy Spirit. For he is the true Paraclete,[13] whom Christ sends from the Father, to teach the truth and to drive away darkness from the minds of the faithful. The teaching of the Holy Spirit, however, does not illuminate the church without means, but through the holy fathers and leaders of the catholic church. For as all scripture is, and is called, the word of the Holy Spirit, not that it was spoken directly by him, but that it was spoken by him through the apostles and prophets; so also the church is indeed taught by the life-giving Spirit, but through the medium of the holy fathers and doctors (whose rule is acknowledged to be the holy ecumenical councils). And therefore we are not only persuaded, but we confess as true and undoubtedly certain, that it is impossible for the catholic church to err, or to be deceived at all, or ever to choose falsehood instead of truth. For the all-Holy Spirit, continually operating through the faithful ministry of the holy fathers and leaders, delivers the church from error of every kind.

· Decree 13 ·

We believe that a man is not simply justified through faith alone, but through faith that works through love, that is to say, through faith and works. But the notion that faith, fulfilling the function of a hand, lays hold on the righteousness that is in Christ and applies it to us for salvation, we know to be far from all true piety. For faith thus understood would be possible in all, and so no one could miss salvation, which is obviously false. But on the contrary, we rather believe that it is not the correlative of faith, but the faith that is in us, which, through works, justifies us with Christ. But we regard works not as witnesses certifying our calling, but as being fruits in themselves, through which faith becomes efficacious, and as in themselves meriting, through the divine promise, that each of the faithful may receive what is done through his own body, whether it be good or bad.

13. *Paraclete*—Comforter.

• Decree 14 •

We believe that man in falling by his transgression became comparable and similar to the beasts; that is, he was utterly undone and fell from his perfection and impassibility,[14] yet did not lose the nature and power that he had received from the supremely good God. For otherwise he would not be rational, and consequently not a human being; but he still has the same nature in which he was created, and the same power of his nature, that is free will, living and operating, so that by nature he is able to choose and do what is good, and to avoid and hate what is evil. For it is absurd to say that the nature that was created good by him who is supremely good lacks the power of doing good, for this would be to make that nature evil—and what could be more impious than that? [. . .] [I]t is also manifest that the good that a man may do cannot be sin, for it is impossible that what is good can be evil. Nevertheless, [. . . good work] does not contribute to salvation by itself, without faith. For it is incomplete and totally powerless. It is incomplete, because without the knowledge and the performance of the great and holy precepts it cannot attain to deification.[15] [. . .]

A man, therefore, before he is regenerated,[16] is able by nature to incline to what is good and to choose and work mortal good; but this is not directed to blessedness, for a natural action has a natural end, not a divine and blessed one. But for the regenerated to do spiritual good—for the works of the believer, being contributory to salvation and wrought by supernatural grace, are properly called "spiritual"—the guidance and provenience of grace is necessary [. . .]

• Decree 15 •

We believe that there are in the church sacraments of the Gospel, and that they are seven in number. For a lesser or a greater number of the sacraments we do not have in the church, because any number of the sacraments other than seven is the product of heretical madness. And the seven of them were instituted in the holy Gospel and are gathered from it, like the other dogmas of the catholic faith.

For in the first place our Lord instituted baptism by the words, "Go you and make disciples of all the nations, baptizing them in the name of the Father and of the Son and of the Holy Spirit"; and by the words, "He that believes and is baptized shall be saved, but he that believes not shall be damned."

14. *impassibility*—state of being incapable of suffering or feeling pain.

15. *deification*—see "Eastern Trends in Christian Theology" above and the discussion on theosis.

16. *regenerated*—spiritually reborn.

And that of confirmation,[17] that is to say, of the holy myrrh or holy chrism, by the words, "But you—tarry you in the city of Jerusalem, until you be endued with power from on high." [. . .]

And the priesthood by the words, "This do for my memorial"; and by the words, "Whatsoever you shall bind and loose upon the earth shall be bound and loosed in the heavens."

And the unbloody sacrifice by the words, "Take eat: this is my body"; and "Drink you all of it: this is my blood of the New Testament"; and by the words, "Except you eat the flesh of the Son of man and drink his blood, you have not life in yourselves."

And marriage, when, having recited the things that had been spoken of it in the Old Testament, he, as it were, set his seal on them by the words, "Those whom God has joined together, let not man put asunder"; and this the divine apostle also calls "a great sacrament."

And penance,[18] with which is joined sacramental confession, by the words, "Whoever's sins you remit, they are remitted to them; and whoever's sins you retain, they are retained"; and by the words, "Except you repent, you shall all likewise perish."

And lastly, the holy oil or sacrament of unction is spoken of in Mark, and is expressly witnessed to by the Lord's brother.

The sacraments consist of something natural, and of something supernatural. And they are not bare signs of the promise of God, for then they would not differ from circumcision: what could be worse than such a notion? We confess that they are, of necessity, efficacious means of grace to those who receive them. But we reject, as alien to Christian doctrine, the notion that the integrity of the sacrament depends upon its reception. [. . .] Moreover, we reject as something abominable and pernicious the notion that when faith is weak, the integrity of the sacrament is impaired. For heretics who abjure their heresy and join the catholic church are received by the church even though they received their valid baptism with weakness of faith. Therefore, when they afterward become possessed of the perfect faith, they are not re-baptized. [. . .]

· Decree 17 ·

We believe that the all-holy sacrament of the sacred Eucharist, which above we have enumerated fourth in order, is that which our Lord delivered in the night in which he gave himself up for the life of the world. [. . .]

17. *confirmation*—usually called "chrismation" in the Orthodox churches. The priest confirms the believer by making the sign of the cross with holy oil on his or her forehead immediately after baptism.

18. *penance*—the confession of sins to a priest, often followed by some pious action prescribed by the priest.

In the celebration of this sacrament we believe that the Lord Jesus Christ is present, not typologically, nor figuratively, nor by superabundant grace, as in the other sacraments, nor by a bare presence, as some of the fathers have said concerning baptism, nor by impanation,[19] so that the divinity of the Word would be united hypostatically[20] to the bread of the Eucharist that is set forth, as the followers of Luther most ignorantly and wretchedly suppose; but truly and really, so that after the consecration of the bread and of the wine, the bread is transmuted, transubstantiated, converted, and transformed into the true body itself of the Lord, which was born in Bethlehem of Mary the ever-virgin and Theotokos.[21] [. . .]

Further we believe that after the consecration of the bread and of the wine, there no longer remains the substance of the bread and of the wine, but the very body and blood of the Lord, under the species and form of bread and wine, that is to say, under the accidents[22] of the bread and the wine.

Further, that the all-pure body itself and blood of the Lord is imparted, in the same manner and under both kinds to priests and to laity, and enters into the mouths and stomachs of the communicants, whether pious or impious. Nevertheless, they convey remission of sins and life eternal to the pious and worthy, but to the impious and unworthy they involve condemnation and eternal punishment. [. . .]

Further, that the body itself of the Lord and the blood that are in the sacrament of the Eucharist ought to be honored in the highest manner, and adored with latreia;[23] for the adoration of the Holy Trinity and the adoration of the body and blood of the Lord are one and the same.

Further, that it is a true and propitiatory sacrifice[24] offered for all the faithful, living and dead, and for the benefit of all, as is set forth expressly in the prayers of the sacrament delivered to the church by the apostles, in accordance with the command they received from the Lord.

Further, that before its use, immediately after the consecration, and after its use, what is reserved[25] in the sacred vessels for the Communion

19. *impanation*—a belief that Christ's material body and blood are *united* with the substance of the elements *without a change* in the nature of the elements.

20. *united hypostatically*—united with a hypostasis of God. See "Trinitarian Debates" for a discussion of hypostases.

21. *Theotokos*—God-bearer: the Virgin Mary.

22. *accidents*—properties of a thing not essential to its nature.

23. *latreia*—the highest form of worship, reserved for the Godhead alone.

24. *propitiatory sacrifice*—a sacrifice that satisfies or appeases God's demand for justice.

25. *what is reserved*—portions of the eucharistic bread and wine to be distributed to those unable to attend the liturgy in person, for example, the sick or the lame.

of those who are about to depart this life is the true body of the Lord, and not in the least different from it, so that before its use after the consecration, in its use, and after its use, it is in all respects the true body of the Lord.

Further, the catholic church teaches that this sacrament of the holy Eucharist is not carried out by anyone other than an Orthodox priest, and one who has received the priesthood from an Orthodox and legitimate bishop. [. . .]

· Decree 18 ·

Question 1. Ought the divine scriptures be read in the vernacular by all Christians?

Answer. No. For that all scripture is divinely inspired and profitable we know, and it is of such necessity that without it, it is impossible to be Orthodox at all. Nevertheless it should not be read by everyone, but only by those who with fitting research have inquired into the deep things of the Spirit and who know in what manner the divine scripture ought to be searched, taught, and read. But to those who are not prepared this way, or who cannot distinguish, or who understand what is contained in scripture only in a literal way or in any other way contrary to Orthodoxy, the catholic church, knowing by experience the mischief arising from this, forbids them to read it. [. . .] For prohibiting unprepared persons from reading all of sacred scripture is the same as requiring infants to abstain from solid food. [. . .]

Question 3. Which books do you call holy scripture?

Answer. Following the canon of the catholic church, we call holy scripture all those books that Kyrillos collected from the Synod of Laodicea[26] and enumerated, adding to them those that he foolishly and ignorantly, or rather maliciously, called "apocryphal,"[27] namely: Tobit, Judith, six chapters of Esther in addition to the ten, the other book of Esdras, Baruch, the Song of the Three Children contained in the third chapter of Daniel, the History of Susannah, the History of Bel and the Dragon, the Wisdom of Solomon, the Wisdom of Sirach, and the three books of the Maccabees. For we judge these also to be genuine parts of scripture together with the other books of holy scripture. For the catholic church, which has handed down by tradition the divine and holy Gospels and the other books of scripture, has undoubtedly delivered these also as parts of scripture; and the denial of these is the rejection of those. [. . .]

Question 4. How should we think of the holy icons and of the worship of the saints?

26. *Synod of Laodicea*—a small synod held ca. 363–364, which specified the "canon" or list of true scripture.

27. *apocryphal*—scripture that most Protestants do not recognize as valid.

Answer. The saints being intercessors and being confessed by the catholic church as such, as has been said in the eighth chapter, it is time to say that we honor them as friends of God and as those who pray for us to the God of all. And the honor we pay them is twofold. According to one manner, which we call "hyperdouleia,"[28] we honor the Mother of God the Word. For although the Theotokos is indeed the servant of the only God, yet she is also the Mother of God, as having given birth according to the flesh to one of the Trinity. Therefore she is also hymned as being beyond compare, above all angels as well as above all saints; and therefore we also pay her the worship of hyperdouleia. But according to the other manner, which we call "douleia," we worship, or rather honor, the holy angels, apostles, prophets, martyrs—in short, all the saints.

Moreover, the worship of icons is honor, not adoration, even though the swarm of the heretics mistakenly equates honor with adoration. Therefore we worship and honor the wood of the precious cross, on which our savior underwent his world-saving passion, the most blessed manger at Bethlehem, through which we have been delivered from irrationality, the place of the skull,[29] the life-giving sepulcher, and the other holy objects of worship, as the church has handed down by tradition [. . .], likewise the holy Gospels and the sacred vessels with which the unbloody sacrifice is performed. And by annual commemorations and popular festivals and sacred edifices and offerings we respect and honor the saints.

And then we worship and honor and kiss the icons of our Lord Jesus Christ, of the most holy Theotokos, of all the saints, yes, and of the holy angels, as they appeared to some of the forefathers and prophets. We also represent the all-Holy Spirit as he appeared, in the form of a dove.

And if some say that we commit idolatry in honoring the saints, the icons of the saints, and the other things, we regard this as foolish and frivolous. [. . .]

28. *hyperdouleia*—veneration paid specifically to Mary. *Hyperdouleia* is a lesser type of veneration than *latreia* (reserved for the Godhead alone) but a higher type than *douleia*, the veneration paid to saints and icons.

29. *place of the skull*—Golgotha, where Christ was crucified.

Popular Piety and Popular Practices

D ebates about the degree to which native pagan practices "influenced," "enhanced," "corrupted," "broadened," or "stunted" Russian Orthodoxy swirl among scholars of Russian cultural studies.

Whatever the particular conclusions (and there are many), nearly all scholars can agree with Nikolay Andreyev that "Christianity in Russia was not transplanted into an uncultured soil, into a wild desert, but into a powerful [pagan] community which, though scattered and illiterate, had its own customs, art, and religion and which, in some sectors, had long maintained contacts with other civilizations."[1] This community could not, of course, simply ingest Christianity immediately or entirely. The historian Georgy Florovsky suggested that Byzantium offered pagan Russia "too much at once—an enormous richness of cultural material, which simply could not be absorbed at once."[2] Russia could become Orthodox only over a long span of time.

There can be no question that remnants of pagan practice persisted alongside Orthodox Christian practices well into the twentieth century. But what such practices indicate about Christian belief in Russia remains the subject of much deliberation. Disagreements begin over terminology. What, exactly, was Russian paganism? Andreyev de-

1. Nikolay Andreyev, "Pagan and Christian Elements in Old Russia," *Slavic Review* 21 No. 1 (1962): 18.
2. Georges [Georgy] Florovsky, "The Problem of Old Russian Culture," *Slavic Review* 21 No. 1 (1962): 13.

spaired of ever adequately characterizing pre-Christian belief: "The absence of native, contemporary documentary evidence on the Slavs of pre-Christian Russia makes it necessary to exercise great caution in seeking to establish the character of this indigenous, organic, primitive, yet tenacious and distinctive civilization."[3]

Still, some things are clear. The early Slavs had, in Andreyev's words, an "essentially pantheistic conception of the world," recognizing numerous deities and the magical powers of "Moist Mother Earth."[4] We know something of ancient folklore, and scholarship on the subject is still expanding.[5] We also know that the church of ancient Rus' and Muscovy struggled with varying degrees of success to eliminate pagan practices: we have evidence of resistance and uprisings by pagan priests against the new Christian faith, and we know that Christianity penetrated rural regions more slowly than it did urban areas.

A number of scholars have characterized the coexistence or intermingling of Christian and pagan practices and beliefs as *dvoeverie,* that is, "double belief" or "dual faith." Stella Rock conducted a survey of the various ways historians have used this term: Evgeny Golubinsky argued that in adopting "Christianity and not renouncing paganism the mass of Russian people had become double-believing in the precise and literal sense of the world"; George Vernadsky defined *dvoeverie* as the preservation of paganism "under a thin veneer of Christian rights"; and John Fennell, one of the leading authorities on the early Russian church, wrote that

> as far as the history of the spread of Christianity in Russia is concerned, perhaps the most insidious aspect of the old beliefs and ways of life is the curious association of paganism with Christianity. The so-called "double-faith"—the simultaneous adherence to both Christianity and heathen relics—is evidenced by many of the church's writings, not only in the period under consideration, but also deep into the seventeenth, and even as late as the nineteenth century.[6]

3. Andreyev, 16.

4. Ibid., 17.

5. See, for example, Felix Oinas, *Essays on Russian Folklore and Mythology* (Columbus, OH: Slavica, 1984); Myroslava Znayenko, *The Gods of the Ancient Slavs* (Columbus, OH: Slavica, 1980); Elizabeth Warner, *Russian Myths* (Austin: University of Texas Press, 2002).

6. All quoted in Stella Rock, "What's in a Word?: A Historical Study of the Concept *Dvoeverie,*" *Canadian-American Slavic Studies* 35 No. 1 (2001): 19.

Some historians, on the other hand, eschew the word *dvoeverie* altogether, arguing that it represents an unwarranted judgment as to what constitutes true or "pure" Christianity. Others maintain that we should not speak of a dual faith among Christians who felt no duality or conflict about their personal beliefs, however eclectic.

This section seeks not to resolve the debate about *dvoeverie,* but simply to present some examples of popular beliefs and practices by Russians who considered themselves Orthodox Christians. We include examples of how ordinary Russians behaved, thought, and lived their faith.

Parish Issues a Certificate of Election for a New Priest (1684)

"Documents on Church Self-Government in Northern Russia, 1657–1697," in *A Source Book for Russian History from Early Times to 1917,* ed. George Vernadsky (New Haven, CT: Yale University Press, 1972), 1:253–54. Used by permission of Yale University Press.

The next two texts address a mundane issue—the practice of electing and paying rural priests and elders—while shedding some light on the qualities parishioners sought in their job candidates.

We, the parishioners of the village of Kozmodem'iansk, the [. . .] crown peasants of the great sovereign[7] [. . .] and all the parishioners of the parish of the Church of Saints Kosmas and Damian. [. . .] By the will of God, our spiritual father the priest Nester Vasilev has become a widower; his wife has departed this life, and he has left for the Monastery of Saint Nikolai in Vykksin'ia; and we, the parishioners, taking counsel among ourselves at the communal assembly, have chosen the priest Samson Mikhailov for the church of the uncovetous doctors and miracle workers Kosmas and Damian [. . .] and we, the parishioners, have all chosen him, the priest Samson Mikhailov, because he is a good and gentle man, does not engage in any knavery,[8] is not a drunkard, [and] shuns any evil doing; and we, the people of the commune, have made him, the priest Samson Mikhailov, our choice. And the election [document] was written in accordance with the will of the parishioners, by the church clerk-psalmist. [. . .]

7. *crown peasants of the great sovereign*—peasants belonging to the state.
8. *knavery*—dishonesty, trickery.

Agreement between Church Elders and a Priest (1686)

"Documents on Church Self-Government," in *A Source Book for Russian
History from Early Times to 1917*, ed. George Vernadsky (New Haven, CT:
Yale University Press, 1972), 1:254. Used by permission of Yale University Press.

[. . .] [The] church elders of the Church of the Holy Prophet Elijah [. . .]
have resolved [to appoint] Matfei, son of Ivan Shergin, to that church.
And he is to be with us in that church, and to labor and officiate, and
he is not to fail to hold services in the church. And we have agreed upon
a salary for the priest Matfei of half a chetverik[9] of rye and the same
amount of oats, and each year he is to mow himself the lower hayfields
on the Striga River from the meadow set aside for the church. [. . .] And
he is to visit the parish sick with every appropriate ministration, without
laziness. And he, Matfei, is to live in the church enclosure; and we have
resolved to erect a new dwelling [for him]. To this effect we, the elders
and parishioners, have given him a certificate of election. [. . .]

Village Priests' Reports on Religious
Practices of the Peasantry (1853)

"Peasant Rituals," trans. Carol Apollonio Flath, in *Russian Women, 1698–
1917: Experience and Expression, an Anthology of Sources*, ed. Robin Bisha,
Jehanne Gheith, Christine Holden, and William Wagner (Bloomington: Indiana
University Press, 2002), 236–41. Used by permission of Indiana University
Press. Some explanatory notes draw from notes in this edition.

**Here a parish priest describes what he considers remnants of pagan
practices in his parish—practices he dismisses as superstition.**

When a village is threatened with an epidemic (for example, the recent cholera), several old maids—elderly, unmarried women known for
their Christian way of life—will meet at night and walk together in a
circle around the village, carrying an icon and lighted candles in their
hands and singing religious songs. Some of them walk behind with a
plow, plowing the earth in the absolute certainty that no plague can cross
the line they make. At the stroke of midnight, one of the girls will steal
up to the bell tower and begin to ring the bell, sounding the alarm. The

9. *half a chetverik*—approximately thirteen liters.

frightened villagers come running out of their houses, looking around in all directions to see if there's a fire somewhere; seeing nothing, they run to the church, and, meanwhile, the girl slips away unnoticed. They say this is directed at the witch who inflicts people with the deadly plague, to scare her so that she won't dare come near the village.

During a cattle plague it is customary to hold a public prayer service out in a field. All the livestock are herded through a deep, specially dug ditch, with a wood fire burning at its entrance. [. . .]

The local people are so blinded by superstition that they attribute even divine punishments to magic spells cast by witches and sorcerers. For example, the cattle plague in 1847 was attributed to the evil spells cast by dogs and pigs that were believed to be werewolves, and so during the plague several dogs and a pig were destroyed. And there were so many tales during the cholera of witches, werewolves, and sorcerers who the people believed were causing people to die! In fact, to this very day some of the local villagers still deny that the cholera was sent down by God as a punishment for the people's sins; the majority continues stubbornly to believe that it was a spell cast by evil witches and sorcerers.

· Christening Customs ·

The parents of a newborn baby choose the godparents from among their relatives and friends. They choose people who don't have children themselves or who have many, or, leaving the choice to God's will, go outside on the day of the christening and approach the first person they see, begging him to be the godparent, persisting in the certainty that this person was sent by God and that the baby's life may very well depend on him. The christening follows church ritual. After the holy sacraments the godfather drops a piece of wax with some hair from the baby into the font and watches to see whether it will sink; if the wax sinks, it means that the baby will die; if it doesn't, then it will live. Experience shows that the wax never sinks, but babies die very often; nevertheless the superstition persists to this very day. [. . .]

I feel it necessary to note that the peasants don't wash the new baby for six whole weeks after the christening, until the time comes for the mother to undergo the forty-day or purification prayer—so as not to cause the baby's mouth to "bloom," i.e., to develop milk-blisters. It's hard to imagine the terrible state of uncleanliness in which the baby is kept during this time, and the bad smell that results.

· Wedding Rituals ·

On the day of the wedding ceremony the princess[10] gets up early, sits on the bench at the door of her house, and starts wailing again: "Dear

10. *princess*—bride.

father NN [so-and-so] and dear mother NN, did you have a deep, peaceful sleep? Me, poor orphan that I am, I didn't sleep all night long: I spent the whole dark night thinking bitter thoughts." If the ceremony is taking place on a Sunday or holiday, the prince[11] and princess arrive at the church for matins;[12] the prince wears a white sheepskin coat and a blue armiak,[13] open in the front; the wedding kerchief he has tied around his arm distinguishes him from all the other men; it remains hanging on his arm throughout the wedding ceremony. The princess wears a fur coat, white or covered with nankeen[14] or woolen cloth. In addition to the usual scarf worn over her hair, her head is covered by a long, broad white veil made of thin homespun linen or other fine cloth; the bride hides her face behind it from shame throughout the service. In church, the prince and princess listen to the prayer to the savior and the Mother of God. It is worth noting that throughout the entire prayer service and wedding ceremony the princess keeps her right hand wrapped in the long sleeve of her blouse, so that she will not have to do without and will live in prosperity. The prince goes straight home from the church, while the princess, wailing loudly, visits her family graves. She stays at the cemetery for a long time, wailing and lamenting all her deceased relatives; she invites them to her banquet and asks them all for their blessing for her new life, saying, "Dear NN, I don't want gold or silver from you; I ask for your blessing as I go under the golden crown, under the silver[15] to live with strangers." She wails the same refrain for the second relative, the third, etc., until she's addressed all her deceased relatives. A large crowd of women always stands and listens. Then she goes home, where she is met by her friends; the princess, wailing, tells them they will no longer see her virginal beauty. Finally the bride goes inside to await the arrival of the prince and the wedding party.

The prince comes for the bride in a kibitka[16] drawn by a troika,[17] fitted with numerous bells of different sizes, accompanied by the whole wedding party and bringing a barrel of beer. The guests sit down for a long dinner; those who drink alcohol get drunk; everyone partakes except the prince and princess, who do not eat or drink anything. After dinner the parents bless the princess: the father takes her icon and puts it on top of

---

11. *prince*—groom.

12. *matins*—a liturgy conducted at night; usually set to end at daybreak.

13. *armiak*—cloth coat.

14. *nankeen*—yellowish cotton cloth.

15. *under the golden crown, under the silver*—in Orthodox wedding ceremonies the priest places a crown on the head of the bride and the groom. Sometimes the groom's crown is made of gold and the bride's is made of silver.

16. *kibitka*—wagon or sled with a rounded cover or hood.

17. *troika*—a sleigh or carriage drawn by a team of three horses.

a loaf of bread sprinkled with salt; the princess bows three times before
the icon and keeps her head bowed, and her father, holding the icon with
the bread and salt, makes three circles with it over her head; then the
princess kisses the icon, bows down to the floor, and in tears kisses her
father, who is also weeping, three times. Then her mother takes her turn,
blessing the bride with the icon in the same manner. Then she is blessed
by her godfather and godmother, each using their own icons. All these
icons will enter the household of the groom. During the blessing of the
bride, the best man serves the beer brought by the groom to all the people
standing outside, called the pozoriane.[18] After she has received everyone's
blessing, the princess, weeping and wailing and covered by her veil, leaves
her parents' home; the prince seats her in the kibitka, and all her closest
friends gather around, wailing over her at the top of their voices. The
groom drives the horses himself. Before they start off, the prince strikes
the gateposts several times with his whip to make sure that his future wife
will not miss her old home. The whole way home the best men ride along
ahead of the prince, and those riding in the wedding party in front and
behind sing loudly to let people know how well they were treated at the
dinner. On their way out of the village, the wedding party stops, the best
man goes back to the bride's house, gives a low bow from the prince and
invites all the guests to come to his house, "the whole household except
for the four walls." At that time the bride's friends say their good-byes
to her. The party stops often along the way, and anyone who wants to
drinks the spirits and beer brought along for the trip. Finally the procession arrives at the church, except for those who are too drunk, who go
straight to the groom's house.

When they arrive, the prince and princess enter the church. The wedding follows the usual procedure. When the time comes to stand on the
carpet,[19] the bride and groom try to step on it at the same time, for superstition has it that the one who steps first on the carpet will run things
in their life. After the ceremony, the members of the wedding party ask
the newlyweds: who is subordinate to whom? Instead of an answer, the
princess bows down at the prince's feet and then kisses him, holding his
head with her hands behind the ears: among the peasants this is considered the most sincere and, as they say, the warmest kiss: not everyone
is kissed this way by the princess—only her closest relatives. Then the
newlyweds are led to the refectory or onto the church porch, and the
princess is "encircled," that is, her hair is fixed into the style for married
women, two braids with a handful of flax woven in and a volosnik[20] and

18. *pozoriane*—witnesses.

19. *carpet*—a carpet brought to the ceremony by the bride.

20. *volosnik*—cap made of cloth.

soroka[21] attached. After that the newlyweds are given a mirror, which they look into together, admiring each other. Finally, the bride is covered again with the same veil, and they leave the church; the prince seats the princess in the carriage, and they all set off for the groom's house, singing loudly.

When the newlyweds arrive home from the church, the father and mother of the bridegroom greet them with an icon and bread and salt. They bless them again, in the same way as when they were being sent off to the altar. Wise parents at this time admonish their children to love God, to obey the authorities, to honor their elders, and to take care of them, their old parents. After the blessings, the best man seats the newlyweds down on a fur coat, helps them up, seats them down, and raises them up again, and seats them again a third time. He has them sit on a fur coat, rather than on the bare bench, so that they will not have to do without, and will live in prosperity. [. . .]

· Funeral Customs ·

All the close relatives of the deceased come to the funeral. Women and girls wear white kerchiefs as a sign of their grief. When the deceased is carried out of the house, the women walk behind, wailing and keening loudly.[22] In the church they encircle the coffin, laying their heads on the sides of the coffin, and continue wailing. They are silent during the burial service, but when it's over, they again begin to wail, which they continue until the grave is filled in; then they go home and again wail loudly there. There are two funeral banquets for every deceased person: one on the day of the funeral and one six weeks afterward.[23] A special meal is served, which concludes with oat kisel[24] with honey. If the deceased drank alcohol, the memorial dinner includes spirits and beer; but if he didn't, it is not served. After dinner the relatives spend a long time wailing over the deceased. [. . .]

21. *soroka*—headdress worn only by married women.

22. *keening loudly*—peasant women have lamented the dead since pre-Christian times. Flath notes that the practice's association with paganism disturbed some in the church.

23. *six weeks afterward*—Flath notes that in the Russian church prayers are offered for the deceased on the third, ninth, and fortieth days after death; the prayers on the fortieth day are particularly important, because on that day the fate of the deceased before judgment day is said to be determined.

24. *oat kisel*—a delicacy made from soured oat gelatin.

Reports on Peasant Action against Witches (1879)

"Agrafena Ignateva" and "Maria Markova," trans. Christine Worobec, in
*Russian Women, 1698–1917: Experience and Expression, an Anthology
of Sources,* ed. Robin Bisha, Jehanne Gheith, Christine Holden, and
William Wagner (Bloomington: Indiana University Press, 2002),
262–65. Used by permission of Indiana University Press. Some
explanatory notes draw from notes in this edition.

Christine Worobec, who translated the next text, notes that many
Russian peasants believed in witches and witches' ability to in-
jure people and animals with words, spells, and potions. Although
witches could be either male or female, women accounted for close to
three-quarters of those charged with witchcraft and sorcery between
1861 and 1917. This ratio differed markedly from the ratio in early
Muscovy—roughly seven men for every three women.

Whatever the cause of this shift (Worobec suggests "a growing identification of women and their sexuality" as "potentially dangerous
to the patriarchal society in which peasants lived"), peasants—even
those who considered themselves good Orthodox Christians—took
seriously the possibility of witches in their midst. Russia's criminal
code prohibited violence against suspected witches, but peasants often ignored the code. It was difficult for courts to identify those who
harmed or killed suspected witches; peasants protected each other,
and sometimes entire communities claimed responsibility for killing a
witch so that no one person could be prosecuted.

The following accounts come from a St. Petersburg newspaper, the
Government Herald.[25]

· Agrafena Ignateva ·

On 4 February 1879 in the village Vrachevo, [. . .] the fifty-year-old
soldier's widow Agrafena Ignateva, who since she was a young woman
had been considered to be a sorceress who had the ability to hex people,
was burned alive in her hut. For her part, Ignateva, not believing the
premise that she was a sorceress, however, did not even try to dissuade
the peasants of this, using the fear that she invoked to live at someone
else's expense. The conviction that Ignateva was a sorceress found support in several cases of nervous illnesses that struck peasant women in

25. *Pravitelstvennyi viestnik* No. 230 (1879): 87–89.

the same place where Ignateva lived. Around Epiphany[26] 1879 Ignateva came to the peasant Kuzmin's home and asked for cottage cheese, but [the family] refused to give her any, and quickly thereafter his daughter, who during her fits shouted that she had been bewitched by Ignateva, fell ill. The peasant woman Maria Ivanova of the village Perednikovo also suffered from the same illness. Finally, at the end of January 1879 in the village Vrachevo the daughter of the peasant woman Ekaterina Ivanova Zaitseva, whose blood sister had earlier died of the same illness and cried out before she died that she had been bewitched by Ignateva, became ill. Since Ivanova shouted that she had been bewitched by Ignateva, her husband, retired Private Zaitsev, filed a complaint with a constable who, several days before the burning of Ignateva, traveled to Vrachevo to undertake an investigation. The peasant Nikiforov asked the peasants to save his wife from Ignateva, who was allegedly about to bewitch her, just as the ill Ekaterina Ivanova had shouted.

They locked Ignateva up in her hut, boarded up the windows, and set [the hut] on fire. Three of the participants were sentenced to a church penance, while the others were acquitted.

· Maria Markova ·

On 15 December 1895 the Kashinsky circuit court and participating jurors heard a case concerning a mistaken sorceress:

The wife of the peasant Peter Briukhanov developed a typical case of "grand hysteria,"[27] the cause of which, according to popular superstition, involved spoiling.[28] The mother-in-law was suspected of being the source of the spell. Once, on the first day of Easter in the presence of his mother and neighbors, Peter Briukhanov gave his wife "holy water"[29] and asked her who bewitched her. "Your mother," answered Briukhanov's wife, and at the sight of her mother-in-law standing before her, her face suddenly became transformed, she jumped as though lifted up by her hair, sang something, and with convulsive movements lunged at the seventy-year-old woman, threw her to the ground, [and] began to drag her by the hair and to strike her all over her body, demanding that she "break the spell." Her husband joined her, and the two of them began to kick the old woman everywhere. All those present looked on without saying a word;

26. *Epiphany*—holiday commemorating the baptism of Jesus by John the Baptist.

27. *grand hysteria*—severe fits and a loss of consciousness.

28. *spoiling*—bewitchment resulting from a spell or hex cast by a witch or sorcerer.

29. *holy water*—said to cause paroxysms and force demons to identify the witch or sorcerer who planted them inside their victims.

when the old man-father tried to defend his wife, one of the peasants sat on his knees and would not let him get up, while another held the door. In the end, the peasant Vinogradov suggested that they throw the old woman into a cellar so that she could exhume the spell, and with that goal in mind he brought a rope, tied it around her neck, and dragged her to the cellar, into which he, together with others, threw her, after which they gave her a tool so that she could dig up the spell. Finally, when the old woman Maria lost all her strength, they left her in peace. Meanwhile, a crowd from neighboring villages, which by now had learned a sorceress was being beaten in Sinitsy, had gathered. One of the newcomers advised Peter Briukhanov to heat up an iron bar so that he could brand the witch, for which purpose he had already set up a bonfire in the yard, but by that time Maria had fallen from the mound of earth on which she had been sitting and died.

Briukhanov's wife, who had been having strong hysterical fits the whole time, danced, grabbed incense, and yelled, "Now they are dispersing, dispersing"[30] (i.e., they are breaking the spell). All of those persons enlisted as defendants, not negating the fact that a crime had been committed, maintained that they themselves, with the exception of the young Briukhanova, had not beaten the old woman and had not intended for her to lose her life, but had simply wanted her to reverse the spell, which, in their opinion, she had actually cast. All of them, in their own words, had been "as if bewitched," as a result of which they had lost all reason.

During the juridical investigation it was established that rumors that the mother-in-law had bewitched Briukhanov's wife had circulated in the village all winter; in the neighboring village of Gorokhovo a hexed woman also appeared. Rumor ascribed this spell to the same Maria Markova (the mother-in-law). According to popular belief, the person whose name the ill person calls out is the one who "spoiled" her. It is important to note that Olga Briukhanova was subjected to a juridical-medical examination in a [. . .] hospital and was pronounced to have committed the crime in a state of delirium. The expert, the district doctor Kovalev, gave his opinion that a strong fit of grand hysteria is infectious for those present, so that the accused, being normal and healthy people, in all probability must have found themselves in a situation of unconsciousness and hardly knew what they were doing.

The assistant prosecutor, evidently a surgeon by profession, incidentally said the following: the ignorance of the accused does not excuse them, [and] the jurors should "do a surgical operation" and cut off the unhealthy organisms.

The counsel for the defense, having set forth the circumstances of the case in detail, pointed out how slowly and reluctantly Peter Briukhanov

30. *they are dispersing*—the demons are abandoning her body.

came to be convinced that his mother was a sorceress and [that he] had to resort to all the methods available to him of verifying this. When he was convinced that Maria Markova was no longer his mother, but instead a sorceress, a pernicious person, an evil being, it was necessary to struggle with her in order to save his suffering wife.

On a joyous holiday, on a Sunday of goodness and love, a dark source, "a devil," appears particularly subversive, and in the name of goodness it is necessary to destroy evil. Thus, there was nothing evil in the mood of the accused. They found themselves in an essentially defensive position and saved the life of their neighbor with those means that appeared to them to be the most rational. Therefore, they did not have ill intent, which should be the one thing punished. One-hundred-million[-strong] Russia poses the following question to the judges: What should be done with these people who committed a crime out of ignorance? Is a "surgical operation" really necessary? Perhaps begin with education in such a way that they can dissect the brain and put a book there? No, they place it [the book] in the hands and act not with a knife but with words. Now, when the Russian people's disease of darkness and ignorance is pointed out from the heights of the throne, then the ways of healing that disease are pointed out: school and education. It is impossible to resort to shackles together with this. To punish them—that means hitting a person when he is down, for darkness has tangled up these unfortunate people's arms and legs.

The defendants were sentenced to hard labor. Thus, new perspectives have been added to the experience of suffering. From the heart we hope that this distinctive case, weighed down by the darkness of the middle ages, is understood as the obscurantism[31] of the apostles and publicly fought with the diffusion of popular education.

A Critique of the Rural Clergy (1858)

Reprinted from I. S. Belliustin, *Description of the Clergy in Rural Russia: The Memoir of a Nineteenth-Century Priest,* translated by Gregory L. Freeze, pp. 88–93, 124–25, 173–78. Copyright © 1985 by Cornell University. Used by permission of the publisher, Cornell University Press.

This document, written by Ioann Belliustin, a rural priest, offers a scathing critique of the Russian church. The translator, Gregory Freeze, writes that soon after

Belliustin's *Description of the Clergy in Rural Russia* appeared in French bookstalls in 1858, it became a sensation in Russia. It was

---

31. *obscurantism*—opposition to knowledge or enlightenment.

a book without precedent: a rural priest in Russia had dared to denounce his superiors in print, exposed all the seamy sides of the ecclesiastical establishment, and summoned the state to impose reform on the church. For most laymen, even those closely associated with the church, it was their first inside view of the church and its clergy. And what they found in Belliustin's slim volume was a shocking exposé of an institution in such disarray and so racked by evil and injustice that it simply could not perform its high mission to the world. On Belliustin's canvas the bishops appeared tyrannical and cruel, ecclesiastical administration venal and incompetent, seminaries ineffectual and misdirected, priests destitute and demoralized. Not surprisingly, government authorities prohibited public sale and circulation of the book—an act of repression that, naturally enough, guaranteed the widest possible interest and circulation.[32]

Indeed, Belliustin's book described major problems. Parish priests in Russia possessed shockingly little education. In the mid-eighteenth century most could claim only a "seminary" education, which referred not to graduate schools in theology, but to elementary schools for the children of priests. Belliustin argued that such schooling was woefully inadequate.

Unlike priests and pastors in Western Europe, Russian clergy did not receive state salaries or "benefices," that is, appointments with property and incomes. Instead, priests raised some of their own food and relied on "emoluments," voluntary gifts from parishioners in return for performing rites such as confessions, marriages, and burials. This system, notes Freeze, "could scarcely have been less satisfactory." It "provided too little support; agriculture diverted the priest from his proper religious duties and lowered his social status; as the emoluments were voluntary and of unspecified amount, they generated incessant conflict with parishioners and left the priest highly dependent on their good will, and hence reluctant to challenge their moral foibles and deviation from Orthodox canons and convictions."[33]

This is a bitter document by a bitter man. But while hyperbolic, Belliustin touched on serious challenges facing the rural church, that is, the church known by most of the Russian populace.

32. Gregory Freeze, ed. and trans., *Description of the Clergy in Rural Russia: The Memoir of a Nineteenth-Century Priest* (Ithaca: Cornell University Press, 1985), 13–14.

33. Freeze, 26–27.

• Seminary Education •

The chief figure in the seminary, the person who exercises the greatest influence on the pupils, is the rector. He is always a monk, a choice that defies explanation: the principal overseer and director of the education of youth, the majority of whom are preparing to become village priests, is someone who has renounced the world forever, with all its concerns and demands—that is, someone who (at least ideally) is dead to all that is alive in this vale of tears called earth. He invariably holds a master's degree; in other words, he is learned, even a most learned man. But is such abstruse learning of any use in real life? [. . .] Where did he—this man with a master's degree or a doctorate in theology—learn about daily life, knowledge of which comes solely through experience and remains inaccessible to pure reason? Not behind the walls of a theological academy or in some monastery (of which he is the chief administrator): even if he wants to know the realities of life, he simply has no opportunity to do so. [. . .] It would be one thing if the majority of youths were preparing for an ascetic life; in that case it would make sense to appoint a monk as rector. But here the youths are preparing for battle with the flesh, with the entrancing power of the prince of darkness,[34] and with the world alongside. What can the rector's lessons (very learned, but purely theoretical) teach them about true, reliable means to wage this battle successfully?

No, education of future priests should be left to the control of a priest, who is not so much learned as experienced in life, having himself encountered all that awaits the pupils later in their onerous sphere of service. Rather than having him explain all the scholastic subtleties of theology, have him explain the behavior of human passions—diverse, infinitely variable, often strikingly apparent, still more often barely detectable and visible. Have him show the youths how to combat these passions! [. . .]

Take, for example, theology—the queen of learning, the most important field of all human knowledge, the foundation of our education and life. With cold indifference the professor reads his lecture (some sort of abstract from his lecture notes at the academy, or a garbled translation from some German Lutheran theologian); the students listen with the same cold indifference and can hardly wait till it is over. The professor orders them to learn it; everything now depends on how well they memorize it. Thus only the students' memory is put to work; the teachers give no thought to seeing that the great teachings of salvation move the student's soul, penetrate deeply into his heart, and become his very flesh and blood. What is the result? The pupils regard theology just as any other subject—that is, as an onerous burden, from which they would do anything to be free. They remember what they have memorized only while

34. *prince of darkness*—Satan.

they are still at the seminary; after they have lived for a year or two in the parish, they have forgotten everything: they cannot satisfactorily explain a single dogma, and from the entire course of theology they have only a dim recollection that X gave lectures on something or other. [. . .] As a result, the pupil who heard in a morning lecture that something is forbidden does it that very evening. If he is caught, they hasten to punish him, never troubling to make him conscious of the baseness of his conduct, never explaining to him all the ruinous consequences of such behavior. Hence the boy who is punished regrets not that he did something iniquitous, only that he did not know how to conceal it. He becomes used to every form of lying, cunning, and deception. [. . .]

From the bishop to the lowliest seminary inspector, all have just one concern: to see that the pupil before them trembles. They never give the slightest thought to winning their pupil's trust, love, and childish obedience so that he may open his soul to them, with total sincerity, as though to his own parents. As a result, every prank, if the culprit is caught, entails punishment. It is unheard of for the seminary authorities to consider and weigh the import of the deed, to determine whether it was intentional or not, whether the cause is a corrupted heart or the excesses of inexperienced youth, and whether accordingly one should order physical punishment, be content with a strict reprimand in his peers' presence, or have a fatherly talk with the boy in his office. "Punish them all without mercy, so they will all be fearful"—that is the heart of seminary administration. [. . .]

· Finances ·

Abolish dishonest exactions from parishioners, let there be no monetary deals between them and the priest, and you will restore peace between them. Then the parishioners will look with trust and love upon their pastor, and will listen to his every word with reverence. I will offer an example of what it means to give a priest proper support, and I hope that our all-wise bishops who oppose clerical salaries will not object. I shall quote the words of an intelligent person who has conducted research on the Chuvash people.[35] Earlier, when the priests took emoluments from them, the Chuvash were more pagan than Christian, and despised the priests with all their hearts. Recently, however, their relations with priests changed completely and in the most favorable fashion. What caused this miracle? It was this: the priest was given a salary from the state treasury and also was assured punctual delivery of support in kind and thereby became fully independent of his flock. Hence the priest no longer had to indulge the weaknesses of his spiritual children and to overlook their

---

35. *Chuvash people*—descendants of Tatars and Bulgars who lived in Kazan province (east-central European Russia).

misdeeds; and the flock has no cause to be indignant about levies or to complain of avarice. The consequence of these mutual relations between them is now beginning to manifest itself in respect from the flock, in their obedience, in their readiness to perform those demands by the priest that are grounded in religion.

The very same thing that earlier existed among the Chuvash is found in villages all across Russia: people detest the priest precisely because of his levies. Despising the priest, they are ill disposed toward his very service and look with hostility upon religion itself. [. . .]

Do authorities wish to correct this deplorable state of affairs? There is but one means: provide the clergy with proper material support. [. . .]

Ivan Pryzhov Ridicules Holy Fools (1865)

Ivan Pryzhov, 26 *Moskovskikh prorokov, iurodivykh, dur i durakov i drugie trudy po ruskii istorii i ethograffii* (St. Petersburg: Ezro, 1996), 53–54, 57–59. Translated by Bryn Geffert. CC BY-SA.

While many rural and urban believers revered holy foolishness,[36] some clergy and laypeople questioned the practice, finding it ridiculous at best and corrupt or profane at worst. The radical writer Ivan Pryzhov argued that holy foolishness bore no connection to Christianity: it smacked of paganism and served as a means for beggars and charlatans to panhandle under false pretenses. Determined to expose holy fools as hypocrites and charlatans, Pryzhov disguised himself as a peasant and accompanied a group of holy fools on a pilgrimage from Moscow to Kiev. "I put on a peasant shirt," he wrote, "and joined a horde of bigots (some hundred and fifty of them, including little girls who were later sold off for sexual exploitation). I began to wander from one monastery to another. I saw incredible examples of drunkenness, blasphemy, the selling off of the innocents for sex, fanatic ranting, singing, praying, hysterics, the reading of scriptures and pagan incantations."[37]

Here are three profiles that Pryzhov sketched of holy fools.

• Feodosy •

He is from the peasantry of the Dmitrovsky district of Moscow province. He previously lived in the Maidenfield, in the merchant Ganeshiny's

36. See "Holy Fools" above.

37. Quoted in Ewa Thompson, *Understanding Russia: The Holy Fool in Russian Culture* (Lanham: University Press of America, 1987), 7.

factory, and then, after finding idiocy quite profitable, started to play the holy fool. [. . .] Feodosy walks barefoot, wears iron chains, and prophesies. He has a family, and his daughter—a young girl—visits him from time to time to collect the money he has gathered.

• Peter Ustiuzhsky •

Not a big man, thirty years old, with a light-brown beard and hair down to his shoulders. He wears a novice's half-caftan, fastened with a belt. You might meet him on the Moscow streets, on which he always walks with a skip: that's why among the hypocrites he is known as "the runner." He lives at a well-known merchant's, a lover of all prophets and prophetesses. Petrusha[38] especially loves good honeycombs, rich, sweet pirogi,[39] flower tea, soaked apples, jam of all types, unpressed caviar,[40] bliny,[41] omelets, and young housemaids. [. . .] Petrusha adopts one of his holy names when visiting a home where a housemaid is present, and believers attribute holy-foolishness to him. One of his special talents is his ability to eat an entire watermelon in one sitting, as if it were nothing. Upon spying a melon, he begins to shout, "Temptation, temptation! Great temptation." And then, holding the melon with his knees—a knife in his hand—he works away on it until only the rind remains. The same thing happens upon spying a beetroot with unpressed caviar. "Temptation," he shouts, "temptation." "My soul demands it. My soul desires it!" And he grasps the beetroot with his knees and eats the caviar until not a single grain remains.

• Father Andrei •

A certain Petersburg native is known in Moscow as "Father Andrei." He studied, according to his stories, at the St. Petersburg Academy, but was dismissed before completing his studies. He then lived in various monasteries, including a number in Moscow. He was investigated and jailed for various escapades. He continued along these lines [. . .] and began to live the life of a holy fool. Earlier he walked barefoot wearing a white hat; but having made some money, he bought himself various suits for various occasions. In the house of a rich merchant-woman and on church holidays he appears dressed as a novice, wearing a belt and a calotte[42] on his head. In the home of a rich lady he wears a frock-coat,

---

38. *Petrusha*—a diminutive for Peter.
39. *pirogi*—dumplings containing fruit, meat, cheese, cabbage, eggs, etc.
40. *unpressed caviar*—a high grade of caviar.
41. *bliny*—thin pancakes.
42. *calotte*—a skull cap.

a hat, and even a lorgnette.[43] On his strolls he dresses as a merchant or a peasant.

Father Andrei is about forty years old. He is well built, he has good facial features, light-brown hair that is not very long but curly, and a beautiful, thick beard. Although his manners are rough and awkward, he knows how to talk in French with such a soft, ingratiating voice that it gets into your very soul and then into your pocket.

Having joined the society of sanctimonious people—old women and old wenches—he begins to hold forth on death and Hell, on his great trespasses, and calls himself a great sinner. Arriving at the home of one even more pious he slips chains over himself, knowing that he will remain there to spend the night. He arranges his chains so skillfully that invariably somebody will see them. They will prepare him a soft, clean bed, but he will not lie on it, lying instead on the bare floor. [. . .]

Arriving at the home of a rich, sanctimonious woman, he claims to be a noble from a well-known family, and says that he still corresponds with notable figures, both spiritual and secular. He says that he left his parents' house and renounced his inheritance for God's sake, having conceived from infancy a desire to save his soul. That he is a great, begging ascetic, is—for Christ's sake—voluntary rather than accidental.

But when he happens to fall in with a group of young merchant women and salesmen—then the picture changes. Then Father Andrei becomes a boon companion, and talks not about Heaven and Hell, but about his different adventures. His stories, each more scandalous than the other, flow unceasingly and inexhaustibly, rousing his listeners to laughter, guffaws, and applause. Produce some vodka and he will drink and sing a rollicking song. If there is a guitar—"give me the guitar"—then the entire upstanding company strolls about with noise, shouts, songs, and dance. One pious merchant while visiting his salesman found the honored Father Andrei amidst the revelry—yes, even on Friday[44]—as the salesman pretended to place a plate of sausage before Father Andrei.

"What will you do with that, Father Andrei?" asked the dumbfounded admirer of the holy fox.

Father Andrei, not at all disconcerted, answered: "Have you really not read in the Prologue[45] that godly saints eat sausage?"

43. *lorgnette*—a pair of glasses attached to a short handle. Here a *lorgnette* is a preposterous affectation.

44. *even on Friday*—Orthodox Christians are to fast on Wednesdays and Fridays, avoiding meat, fish, eggs, dairy products, olive oil, and wine. The carousing described here would be especially unseemly on a Friday.

45. *Prologue*—a collection of saints' lives.

Another time a lady found him in a very intimate position with her maid. "What kind of dirty tricks are you playing, my dear fellow," she said, clasping her hands in distress.

"Mother Matrena Ivanovna," replied the old fox. I don't play dirty tricks, but I do seduce. [. . .]

Anthropological Account of Religious Practices among the Peasantry (1906)

Olga Semyonova Tian-Shanskaia, *Village Life in Late Tsarist Russia*,
ed. and trans. David Ransel (Bloomington: Indiana University, 1993),
16–18, 90–92, 133–38. Used by permission of Indiana University Press.

The Russian anthropologist Olga Semyonova Tian-Shanskaia lived among peasants for four years between 1898 and 1902, with the goal of writing a "realistic" portrait of the peasantry, a group alternately reviled and idealized—but rarely understood—by Russia's educated classes. Her study was not published until 1914, seven years after her death.

Following are some of Tian-Shanskaia's observations about the peasantry's religious life and beliefs. These observations (like much of her book) are somewhat patronizing: she finds peasants uncouth, superstitious, and hardly Orthodox. But despite the condescending tone, Tian-Shanskaia provides useful insights into the free intermingling of the sacred and the profane in everyday life, and the remnants of pagan beliefs in the peasants' worldview. Her section on peasant views of priests accords nicely with Belliustin's criticisms above.

• Christening Ceremonies •

The christening[46] normally takes place about eleven o'clock in the morning or twelve noon. After the ceremony, the parents [or grandparents] of the newborn invite the godparents to their house for the christening dinner, as well as the parents of the new mother, her sisters, and sometimes her brother. Vodka is served immediately. The average peasant provides, depending on the harvest, from one bottle up to five pints of vodka and even more, if he is the type that does not pass up an occasion to get drunk and, at the same time, happens to have extra money to spend on liquor. The hosts offer drinks first to the godparents, and only after that to the rest of the guests. [. . .] Guests place copper money and small silver coins on a plate as gifts for the new mother. Normally, only the

46. *christening*—baptizing infants.

godparents give money, though sometimes the maternal grandfather, in a fit of generosity, will also place a coin on the plate.

The midwife, while she is serving bread and cake, also places her saucer on the table; the guests fill it with a few two-kopeck silver pieces, and on rare occasions someone will drop in a five-kopeck piece. The guests stay at the table for two or three hours talking about their affairs, the harvesting, the crops, and the sowing, or they gossip about the neighbors. When the vodka is plentiful, everyone gets drunk. But songs are not sung, as this is not appropriate at a christening dinner. The new mother is also in attendance, but, because the christening usually takes place the day after the delivery, she stays removed from the crowd, resting on a bench in the back of the room. The newborn wails. The guests joke around. When the baby makes too much noise, they say [to the mother]: "Hey, you little cow, where did you hide your teats?" The sisters of the new mother sometimes leave the table and go over to the mother to redo the baby's swaddling clothes. When the guests leave, the father of the newborn, the grandparents, and the midwife show them to the door, bowing all the while. [. . .]

The midwife's assistance is sometimes sought in treating a sick baby. Most often she is called on to treat "hernia" and recurrent crying. For the treatment of hernia, the midwife mixes horse dung, strained through a cloth, with mother's milk and administers this potion to the infant. Crying is the result of the "evil eye," and the midwife exorcises it in three sessions—two at dusk, and one at dawn. For this she goes out into a field with the baby, faces the sun, and bowing to it says: "God bless us. The sunset, summer lightning, fair maid, evening, morning, day, night, midday, midnight, hour, minute! Take the crying from Ivan[47] and give him sleep and health. Amen." The incantation is repeated three times. In return for this ceremony or for the treatment, the midwife receives payment in bread or grain. Diarrhea in children is treated with sacramental wine bought at the church for five kopecks and given to the sick child in drops. [. . .]

· Love and Marriage ·

A woman who seeks to charm a man into making love to her washes the menstrual blood off her shift and secretly places the blood—or, more accurately, water with traces of the blood in it—in the kvass[48] or tea that she offers to the object of her desire.

Lovers pledge fidelity by making an oath on the holy sacraments. They say, for example: "May I forever be denied the sacraments if I fail to

47. *Ivan*—The generic name Tian-Shanskaia used for children.

48. *kvass*—a weak alcoholic drink made from fermented bread. A staple of the peasant diet.

marry you." They may also pledge their troth to one another by a vow to "moist mother earth," and occasionally they eat some soil to affirm the oath. But the strongest and most inviolable oath is one made on the holy sacraments.

At the wedding ceremony, the following superstitions are common:

When the groom arrives to take the bride to the church and pays his way, as they say, through the entryway to the main room of the house, he must be preceded into the room by a blood relative of the bride, lest as [an unaccompanied] "stranger" he bring trouble and discord to the bride's family.

The best man watches the behavior of the horses before the departure of the couple. If the horses are standing with their heads down, it means the couple will live unhappily. If the horses are in good spirits but quiet, the couple will live in peace. If the horses are violent, the newlyweds will live in discord.

The bride and the groom are seated on oats. This is supposed to bring wealth into the family.

If the husband begins to undo his wife's hair himself after the wedding ceremony, this too will ensure accord in family life.

Returning from the church, the young wife, on entering the house, grabs the lintel with both hands so that "the husband will love her."

When the mother-in-law shows the couple to the table, no one should pass between the husband and wife. Otherwise they will live in discord.

Sorcerers and witches are feared at the time of the wedding, for it is easiest to put a curse on the couple when they are in the church or returning home after the ceremony. In the church a spell can be cast "through the wind" onto the couple's backs. When newlyweds enter the house, it is not difficult to toss in their path a piece of string tied into a knot with a spell on it. The effects of such a curse may be lack of affection between the husband and wife, illness, lack of appetite, and the like.

In former times, the father of an "unchaste" bride had to wear a yoke on the morning following the wedding after the discovery of his daughter's shame. The former partner of an "unchaste" woman may spread a bast[49] mat on the church's porch as the newlyweds exit after the ceremony. [. . .]

· Payments to the Priest ·

Wedding: six rubles cash, three bottles of vodka (fifty-five kopecks per bottle), two pounds of pretzels, a chicken, bread, and pies. For lighting of the chandelier and other candles in the church, about two rubles. This provides a "first-class wedding."

49. *bast*—a strong, woody fiber.

Baptism: fifty kopecks, plus bread.

Funeral: three rubles (but if candle holders and a high-quality shroud are used, the price could go as high as eight rubles). Funeral for a child: seventy-five kopecks.

Office for the dead: ten kopecks.

Special Mass: two rubles.

Confession: from five to twenty kopecks (as you wish).

Extreme unction:[50] one and a half rubles (with candles).

Prayers requested by the commune for rain: three or four rubles.

Cleansing ritual against mice: thirty to fifty kopecks. If a mouse falls into a tub of pickles, sauerkraut, or pickled apples, the woman of the house will nearly always summon the priest to perform a cleansing ritual. The mouse is plucked from the tub, and the priest proceeds to say a prayer over the tub, pass a cross over it three times, and then bite into a pickle or apple or try some of the sauerkraut. After this, the contents of the tub are again regarded as clean. (A mouse, to the peasants' way of thinking, is "foul" and "polluting.") [. . .]

Communal prayer for Easter: one ruble. The priest makes the rounds of his parishioners with a public prayer (that is, a collection) five times a year. At Easter, he receives forty-five kopecks, bread, and a pie from each household and an egg from each individual. At Christmas, he gets fifteen kopecks and a pie; at Epiphany,[51] twenty-five kopecks, bread, and a pie; on the tsarist holy day, twenty kopecks, bread, and a pie; and at St. Nicholas Day in the spring, fifteen kopecks and a pie. [. . .]

Some priests simply go right up and take bread off the shelf in a peasant home, saying: "Well, I guess you baked that bread for me, didn't you?" This is the reason the peasants hide their bread from the priest's prying eyes.

When a peasant owes a debt to the clergy, the priest puts pressure on him to pay as the opportunity presents itself, especially at weddings: "Pay me what you owe, and then I'll do the wedding; otherwise I won't do it." And, indeed, he will refuse to do it. In one village in which the priest is adamant about debts, I know several instances in which his refusal to perform a marriage ceremony has led to cohabitation by unwed couples. In some villages, the clergy organizes obligatory memorial services (every Saturday), for which they exact one ruble a year per household. For entering a marriage in the official records of vital events, the priest takes two and a half rubles; this is paid by the bride. The groom pays for the wedding itself.

---

50. *Extreme unction*—a sacrament in which the priest prays for spiritual or physical healing and anoints the critically ill believer with oil.

51. *Epiphany*—holiday commemorating the baptism of Jesus by John the Baptist.

Peasants consider a priest to be a sponger: "He just stands there, reads a prayer, and you have to give him a fifty-kopeck piece."

As for witchcraft and goblins, werewolves, and the like, they are believed in least by the very persons who are considered to be sorcerers and witches, the peasants who do cures by reciting incantations and such. "Witchcraft" is a fairly lucrative occupation, and it is amusing to observe how a clever witch "acts out her role" in the village. I wish I could listen in when two "witches" were having a conversation and did not have to pretend in front of each other.

We have a witch like that in our village, a really audacious one, and it has occurred to me more than once that she might look upon the parish priest as her colleague, a fellow professional.

· General Religious Beliefs ·

When the tsar was ill, the peasants asked me what he was suffering from, inquiring with some interest but also with complete equanimity. "You see, there he is the tsar and all; no one escapes illness. Of course, they have to go and call in the doctors." (A clear note of mistrust toward doctors can be heard in this statement.) "Hear tell he's not in Piter[52] but at his country estate; if he dies there, won't they be taking him, just as they did with his father, into Piter for burial?" "They said Mass for the tsar—the priest was saying that they prayed for the tsar." All this, I repeat, is said with complete composure in the course of the peasants' daily chores. They speak with much greater animation about some wedding scandal in a nearby village. The tsar is far away—"at the other end of the earth," off in a fog.

I have sometimes thought that a belief in the tsar, a belief that he is here in existence somewhere, ought to lend support to the peasants' belief in God. For a peasant the tsar is as far away as God, and his existence is beyond question; so the existence of God, too, ought to seem more certain than it does to us [educated people].

The peasant God is something material, very much so, in fact. He is the giver of rain, of drought, health, and sickness. The tsar is a provider in case of need perhaps, the defender of our borders, of our land, which feeds the peasant. Among the mass of peasants, there is nothing mystical about their relationship to the tsar or to God, just as there is nothing mystical about their idea of an afterlife. They simply give no thought to an afterlife, just as they give no thought to the coming year. It is amazing how essentially irreligious they are! It is only the old people when their health is failing who exhibit a confused fear in the face

52. *Piter*—St. Petersburg.

of "the life beyond the grave." Here we see an ordinary association of their physical pain with what they assume will be the physical sufferings of Hell. Can they really be considered Russian Orthodox? Not at all. They are confused, helpless, and terrified, and have no idea of what to do "to gain salvation." "Who knows," they say, "maybe the Freemasons[53] or the Molokane[54] have a better way to achieve salvation!" How timid, uncertain, and full of doubt is this statement, uttered by gasping and coughing old folks!

Both Heaven and Hell are understood purely in material terms. In Hell people suffer physically for their sins, and in Heaven their goodness is rewarded obviously with apples (although the Molokane sect believes that Heaven is a place where people sing hymns to God). You only have to recall the usual formula in folktale references to Heaven: "and he found himself in a garden of Eden; the trees were leafy and green and heavy with apples." The apple is the favorite peasant delicacy. People associate the idea of apples with something that does not demand the kind of heavy labor that growing grain does. Real Paradise is a place where people do not have to sow and reap by the sweat of their brows.

It is said that our people cannot imagine a person "without God." Perhaps it is so. I have heard peasants pose the question about many upper-class people who do not go to church: "What faith do they practice?" "Don't they have their God?" The [sectarians known as] flagellants have "their God." [In reference to people with a good standard of living, they might say:] "Look how wealthy they are; he must give them that." The word "give" is the crux of the matter, it seems to me. Every person needs his or her God as a personal benefactor.

It is in the notions associated with the land, with moist mother earth, that you find the mystical side of the peasants. Here you see the residue of their ancient, separate worldview, which alas is much more deeply felt and poetic than our vaunted Russian Orthodoxy. Here are also the affecting "radiant sun," "bright moon," "valiant charger-faithful steed," plus vivid and touching images of communion with nature, human sorrow, and orphanhood. It is not God whom the orphan girl asks to resurrect her parents so that they can give her their blessing as she goes off to be married, but instead moist mother earth to whom she appeals to raise her mother from the grave. And, of course, Orthodoxy does not conform

---

53. *Freemasons*—a secretive fraternal society, popular in Russia from the 1700s into the early 1900s, devoted to (sometimes quasi-spiritual) free thinking. Rulers and peasants alike distrusted Freemasons, around whom conspiracy theories constantly swirled.

54. *Molokane*—literally "milk-drinkers," a religious sect that refused to recognize civil authority.

especially well to the peasant soul. And what is it that the peasant lacks in this regard? An awareness of his sinfulness is inborn in him. There is also a "spiritual thirst" (which you see expressed at least in the church schisms), but he has not one iota, and nowhere to obtain it, of any kind of "platonic" attachments or "platonic" interests. [. . .]

[As for the peasants' ideas about who is just and who will attain salvation,] whether it is the poor people or the rich people, he will say that in most cases "the just" are the old people, and definitely not the rich. Yet it is harder for these just people to win salvation than it is for the rich. Merchants, for example, can always bequeath their money to the church or leave funds at a number of monasteries for prayers to be said in their memory, and in this manner "save their souls" and enter into Heaven. In regard to life on earth, the poor "just" people are, of course, better.

The peasants hold to the notion that the last judgment will take three days. On the first day, the Lord will judge the monks and priests, on the second, the nobility and merchants, and on the third, the peasants. (Antichrist will be born on the fourth day. He will lure the people with promises of "food, clothing, and shoes.") In general, peasants are impressed most by what is written in the Gospels about the last judgment, and their thoughts dwell mainly on that. "O," they say, "how terrifying it will be!" [. . .]

Orthodoxy under Ottoman Rule

By the 1800s most of the Balkans had lived under Ottoman rule for centuries. Bulgaria fell to the Ottoman Turks in 1371. Serbia capitulated in 1389. Constantinople succumbed in 1453. Athens held out five years longer, but Ottoman forces overran the city in 1458. Some Greeks managed to bunker down from bases in the Peloponnese until 1460, and Venetians and Genoese defended a few Greek islands a bit longer. But by 1500 the Turks occupied most of the Greek mainland and the Greek Islands.

Orthodox Christians in Greece and in Constantinople feared and despised their Islamic conquerors. Still, as the historian Richard Clogg notes, many Orthodox Christians found Ottoman rule "preferable to accepting the pretensions of the papacy, the price Western Christendom had sought to exact in return for military assistance to ward off the Turkish threat."[1]

Life for Christians could be difficult in the Ottoman state. They enjoyed fewer professional opportunities than did Muslims. Christians could not serve in the military, and they paid a special tax for this mandatory exemption. Although legal cases between exclusively Christian litigants could be tried in courts run by Orthodox authorities (see below), judges in state courts always accepted the testimony of Muslims over that of Christians. Christian men could not marry Muslim women (although Muslim men could marry non-Muslim

---

1. Richard Clogg, "Greece," in *New Encyclopaedia Britannica* (Chicago: Britannica, 2005). This introduction borrows heavily from Clogg.

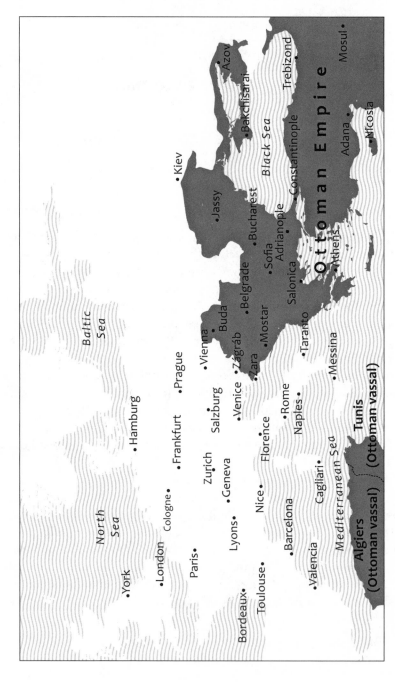

Figure 43. Ottoman Empire, 1683

women). Any Christian who converted to Islam and then converted back to Christianity faced a death sentence.

The Ottoman state required Christian families to turn over their smartest and most handsome boys at regular intervals to serve in the Janissary corps, an elite band of army troops and civil servants. Since Christians could not serve in the military, Janissaries were forced to convert to Islam. Such children enjoyed a good life—indeed, we have evidence of Muslim families pretending their children were Christians so they could enter the Janissary corps. Still, forcible conscription and conversion was . . . forced.

Despite these burdens, and as already noted, Greek Christians enjoyed a good deal of freedom, at least in comparison to rights afforded non-Christians in some Christian countries. Ottomans organized conquered peoples by religious groups, or "millets." Muslims formed the ruling millet, but Orthodox millets, Jewish millets, and Roman Catholic millets all oversaw the affairs of their respective confessions. Greek Christians could worship as they wished as long as they did not try to convert Muslims. Steven Runciman notes that as long as the members of each millet "paid their taxes and did not cause riots or indulge in treasonable activity, they were, at least in theory, left in peace."[2]

If, however, Orthodox Christians did not pay taxes or showed signs of political opposition, Ottoman authorities responded swiftly and violently. In 1821 the Turks executed the patriarch of Constantinople, Gregorios V, for failing to quell an uprising, *even though Gregorios had denounced the uprising.* "In the eyes of the Ottomans," writes Runciman, "Gregorios had signally failed to carry out his fundamental obligation, that of ensuring that the Orthodox flock remained loyal subjects of the sultan."[3]

While Gregorios would not have agreed, it is possible to argue that the patriarchate of Constantinople actually gained power under Ottoman rule. The Ottoman sultan granted patriarchs authority in both religious and civil matters. The powers of ecclesiastical courts expanded significantly under the Turks, and they adjudicated all manner of issues—civil and religious—affecting the Christian population.

With such power, particularly power bestowed according to the whims of a "foreign" state, came corruption. The Ottomans demanded

---

2. Steven Runciman, *The Great Church in Captivity: A Study of the Patriarchate of Constantinople from the Eve of the Turkish Conquest to the Greek War of Independence* (New York: Cambridge University Press, 1968), 78.

3. Ibid.

bribes in return for installing new patriarchs. Turnover in the patriarchate was high, since each new patriarch meant new revenue for the Ottoman state. It was not unusual for a single patriarch to be elected and deposed multiple times: an Armenian historian in the 1700s suggested that the Greeks changed their patriarchs more often than they changed their shirts. In fact the Turks demanded bribes for ecclesiastical appointments at all levels. Clerics, in turn, had to extract funds from their parishioners to pay the bribes demanded by Ottoman overlords. As a result, parishioners tended to view their clergy as greedy, venal, and more concerned with staying in the good graces of the Turks than with ministering to their flocks.

Christians in the Ottoman Empire dreamed of liberation. Some looked to Russia in the north, and various prophecies promised that Russian troops would someday ride to the rescue. From the 1700s onward the Russian state thought constantly about how it might push the Ottomans out of the Balkans and assert Russian influence in the region.

Let us pause here for a digression and retracing of steps. We've already noted that the political history of the Russian church is in part a history of the church's quest for greater autonomy and independence from the church in Constantinople. The Tatar occupation of Russia from 1223 to 1480 isolated Russian church leaders from Constantinople and consequently weakened Greek control over the Russian church. Greek capitulations at the Council of Ferrara-Florence in 1439 made the Russians suspicious of Constantinople's orthodoxy and its claims of leadership in the Eastern world. When the Turks captured Constantinople in 1453, some in Russia suggested that the defeat was divine payback for Greek apostasy.

The fall of Constantinople thus constituted an important milestone in the Russian church's attempt to position itself as both the defender of the true faith and the protector of the Orthodox world, that is, to position Moscow as the "Third Rome," the successor to the now-fallen "Second Rome" of Constantinople. Eastern Christians increasingly looked north to Russia rather than east to Constantinople for leadership.

But Greeks in Constantinople resented these usurpers to the north: we Greeks, they reasoned, constitute the historic bastion of the faith; we are responsible for the dissemination of Christianity to the once-pagan Slavs. The Slavs are Johnny-come-latelies who still require instruction and guidance from us. The patriarchate of Constantinople, not the patriarchate of Moscow, should hold primacy of honor in the

Eastern Orthodox world. (Constantinople listed the Russian patriarchate as fifth, not first, in order of primacy.)

After the Jerusalem patriarchate fell to the Turks in 1517, close relations developed between the patriarchate of Jerusalem and the patriarchate of Moscow, which Jerusalem regarded as Palestine's best hope for liberation from the Islamic occupiers. The Russian foreign office, long eager to extend Russia's influence into Palestine, viewed the Jerusalem patriarchate as a bulwark against Western religious influence in the East. Moscow cultivated two like-minded and powerful Jerusalem patriarchs—Ioakim (1674–1690) and Dositheos II (1690–1707)—who, like colleagues in Moscow, opposed Western diplomatic, religious, and cultural overtures. Dositheos sought Moscow's help in resisting Roman Catholic efforts to exert control over holy places in Jerusalem. When the Ottoman sultan in 1689 turned control of the holy places over to Roman Catholics, Dositheos tried to persuade Moscow to declare war on Turkey. Two years later he even sent Moscow a war plan.

Russia's interest in Palestine coexisted with another interest, namely warm-water ports that did not freeze during Russian winters. In the quest for such ports Russia launched four wars against Turkey during the 1700s, hoping to win control of the Black Sea. The patriarchs in Constantinople usually resented such adventurism: Russian attacks angered the sultan and threatened the privileges they had worked so hard to cultivate within the Ottoman Empire. Formal relations between Constantinople and Russia ceased almost entirely in the 1700s.

But unofficial contact continued. Christians from the Ottoman Empire embarked on pilgrimages to Russia, and Russian Christians flocked to Bethlehem, Nazareth, Jordan, and holy places throughout Ottoman-controlled Palestine. Representatives of all Russian classes—nobles, merchants, and peasants—dreamed of treading the same ground trod by Jesus. Genuine piety provided a powerful reason to embark on a pilgrimage, as did the knowledge that alms could be solicited en route: wily adventurers could compile tidy sums. The Russian church and state supported pilgrims, both because they believed in the spiritual value of pilgrimage and because state officials and simple pilgrims alike wanted Russia—the most powerful state in the Orthodox world—to control Palestine and Constantinople.

The Ottoman Empire during this period experienced a slow but steady decline, and by the late 1800s it was flailing. The Russo-Turkish War of 1877–1878 threatened the once-mighty empire with

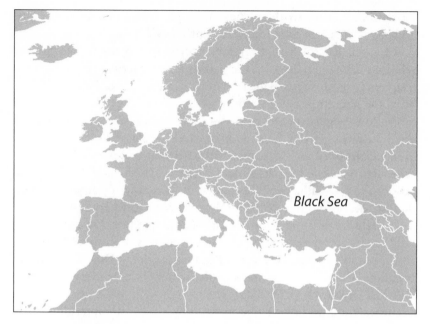

Figure 44. Black Sea

total collapse. This war began when Russia and Serbia came to the aid of anti-Ottoman rebels in Bosnia-Herzegovina and Bulgaria. Although the Russians suffered heavy losses, they won some important battles—victories that alarmed Britain and Austria-Hungary. For while neither Britain nor Austria-Hungary possessed any sympathy for the Ottoman Empire, they agreed that the only thing worse than Islamic control of the Balkans was Russian expansion into the Balkans. In Britain's calculations, the decline of the Ottoman Empire in this strategic region must not be accompanied by the rise of Russia. So, as Russian troops advanced toward Constantinople, the British navy dispatched a fleet to prevent those troops from taking the city. The tactic worked: Russia failed to "liberate" the Second Rome.

Religion made this complicated diplomatic scenario even more complex. Yes, the churches of Russia, Britain, and Austria all argued that Christians in the Balkans should be free from Islamic rule; the diplomats of the Christian powers ostensibly agreed. But such agreement was offset by an even stronger desire to ensure that one's Christian rivals not benefit in this region at the expense of one's own state. If, for example, you were a British diplomat, you naturally sought to guarantee that the vacuum created by the dying Ottoman Empire not be filled by your Christian competitors: Russia and Austria-Hungary. Such concern for international stability—a "balance of power" in diplomatic terms—consistently trumped religious solidarity. Thus the suspicions of the great powers toward one another ensured that the Ottoman Empire—the "sick man of Europe"—survived until the First World War.

While Great Britain, Austria-Hungary, and Russia concerned themselves with balance-of-power politics, the Greeks had a simpler concern: throwing off the "Ottoman yoke," that is, winning independence from an empire now on its last legs. Nationalism, Enlightenment philosophy, and revolutionary fervor from France began trickling into Greece during the late 1700s, a trickle that turned into a flood by the early 1800s. The European Enlightenment, of course, found much to admire in Greece's classical past. Reams of books on the language, literature, and history of ancient Greece appeared during the fifty years before the Greek Revolution of 1821. Such literature bolstered Greece's sense of its own importance and increased the resolve of public intellectuals to gain independence.

But while such ideas burned brightly within the Greek intelligentsia, Greeks who enjoyed positions of power in the Ottoman state had no desire to bite the hand that fed them. Highly placed clerics, wealthy Greek merchants, and Greek officials appointed to administer regions within the Ottoman Empire all had a vested interest in maintaining Ottoman rule. The supreme irony here is that powerful figures in the Orthodox churches found themselves defending an Islamic state against parishioners who wanted to overthrow that state.

The Christian states of Britain, Prussia, Austria-Hungary, and Russia all opposed revolution in Greece: Britain claimed, somewhat disingenuously, to oppose in principle intervention in the internal affairs of sovereign states, while the deeply conservative—and, in many respects, reactionary—governments of Prussia, Austria-Hungary, and Russia lived in fear of revolution in any form. Calls by Greek revolutionaries to their "Christian brethren" thus fell largely on deaf ears. Russia's leaders did vacillate somewhat, torn between a genuine desire to liberate their fellow Orthodox believers and the Russian state's passionate opposition to revolution. But in the end, Russia chose stability over the interests of Greek Christians, and Tsar Alexander (1801–1825) denounced the Greek revolutionaries.

Treaty of Küçük Kaynarca (1774)

"Treaty of Peace (Küçük Kaynarca)," in *Diplomacy in the Near
and Middle East, a Documentary Record,* ed. J. C. Hurwitz
(New York: Van Nostrand, 1956), 54–61.

War broke out between Turkey and Russia in 1768 when Turkey
demanded that the Russian empress Catherine the Great cease her
meddling in Poland's affairs—a favorite activity that eventually led to
Russia's annexation of Poland. When Russian troops pursued Polish
forces into Ukraine and then into part of Ottoman territory, the Ottoman sultan declared war on Russia.

The war proved a disaster for the Ottomans. The Russian navy
annihilated the Ottoman fleet. Emboldened by Russia's success,
Christian subjects of the Ottomans in Egypt and Syria rebelled. Faced
with chaos, Turkey sued for peace in the Bulgarian town of Küçük
Kaynarca.

The terms of the treaty were humiliating for the Turks: Russia's
southern frontier moved farther south; the Ottomans promised independence to the strategic Crimean peninsula in the northern Black
Sea (an "independence" that in reality meant Russian control of the
Crimea); and Russia gained the right to maintain a fleet in the Black
Sea—a right it had sought for decades. Finally, and most relevant to
our study, the sultan granted Russia rights over Christian subjects
throughout the Balkans. As is evident in excerpts from the treaty below, the phrasing of such rights was vague, and Russia and Turkey
each read the treaty to mean different things. From the perspectives
of Russia and of some neutral observers, the treaty gave Russia—
the self-proclaimed protector of Orthodoxy—the ability to meddle in
Turkey's internal affairs any time "Christian interests" called for such
meddling.

[. . .]

• Article VII •

The sublime porte[4] promises to protect constantly the Christian religion and its churches, and it also allows the ministers of the imperial

---

4. *sublime porte*—the court of the Ottoman Empire. This was the term of
choice in diplomatic circles.

Figure 45. Crimea

court of Russia to make, upon all occasions, representations [. . .] on
behalf of its officiating ministers [. . .]

· Article VIII ·

The subjects of the Russian Empire, as well as laymen and ecclesiastics,
shall have full liberty and permission to visit the holy city of Jerusalem,
and other places deserving of attention. No charatsch,[5] contribution,
duty, or other tax, shall be exacted from those pilgrims and travelers by
anyone whomever, either at Jerusalem or elsewhere, or on the road; but
they shall be provided with such passports and firmans[6] as are given to
the subjects of the other friendly powers. During their sojourn in the Ottoman Empire, they shall not suffer the least wrong or injury; but, on the
contrary, shall be under the strictest protection of the laws.

· Article XIV ·

After the manner of the other powers, permission is given to the high
court of Russia, in addition to the chapel built in the minister's residence,
to erect in one of the quarters of Galata, in the street called Bey Oglu, a

5. *charatsch*—tax or tribute.
6. *firmans*—Ottoman license or passport.

public church of the Greek ritual,[7] which shall always be under the protection of the ministers of that empire, and secure from all coercion and outrage. [. . .]

· Article XVII ·

[. . .] [T]he Christian religion shall not be exposed to the least oppression any more than its churches, and that no obstacle shall be opposed to the erection or repair of them; and also that the officiating ministers shall neither be oppressed nor insulted. [. . .]

· Article XXV ·

All the prisoners of war and slaves in the two empires, men and women, of whatever rank and dignity they may be, with the exception of those who, in the empire of Russia, shall have voluntarily quitted Islam in order to embrace the Christian religion, or in the Ottoman Empire have voluntarily abandoned Christianity in order to embrace the Islamic faith, shall be, immediately [. . .] set at liberty on either side [. . .]

Complaints about Corruption and Oppression in the Church (1796)

S. I. Asdrakhas, "Corruption and Oppression in the Church," in *The Movement for Greek Independence, 1770–1821: A Collection of Documents*, ed. and trans. Richard Clogg (New York: Barnes & Noble, 1976), 65–66, reproduced with permission of Palgrave Macmillan. First published 1976 by The Macmillan Press Ltd., London and Basingstoke. Published in the U.S.A. 1976 by Harper & Row Publishers, Inc., Barnes & Noble Import Division.

Ottoman officials demanded bribes—"gifts" in the euphemistic parlance of the time—to secure clerical appointments. In addition to raising money for bribes, new priests also had to assume any debts accrued by the previous incumbent. "Seeking help" from villagers in the diocese was the only way to pay these debts. Screeds against such practices emerged with some regularity during the late 1700s. The following complaint is from 1796.

Those who in this century rise to office in the hierarchy are slaves and servants either of the patriarch or of the higher clergy [. . .] [they] slave for their superiors with great patience, in the hope of becoming the suc-

7. *Greek ritual*—Eastern Orthodox ritual.

cessors of their own superior or to become bishops of another diocese. And when the chief priest of a diocese dies, immediately the lobbying begins in force, some going to the patriarch, some going to the senior clergy, some to the notables and their wives, and often to the magnates,[8] and of the many one is lucky and receives the office. But as such as he succeeds, many expenses follow him, five, ten, fifteen thousand grosia.[9] Some of these expenses are occasioned by gifts to the go-betweens, some to the Porte,[10] some to the higher clergy, all with I.O.U.s. And if perhaps the diocese also has old debts from the previous incumbents, he promises [repayment of] all these, with 15 percent [interest] at least—and there is not a diocese that does not have debts of 10 or 20 thousand grosia. This new bishop, then, without having 50 grosia of his own, falls into an abyss of debt. He comes to the diocese and has no other way of repaying his debts and of holding the high office. [. . .] And no one dares to oppose him in the customary ecclesiastical revenues or gifts, those from ecclesiastics, priests and monasteries, as those from the laity. And with this power, immediately he arrives in the diocese, he begins to seek from the villages help for his new high priestly office of from 50 to 100 grosia, from the monasteries of from 100 to 200 grosia, from the priests, some 10, some 15 grosia and so on, all excessive amounts. The poor cannot resist, fearful of excommunications, curses and exclusion from church, the notables are ashamed of the daily coffee and pipes and gifts. The ağas[11] do not object, for he says to them: "It is the custom, as my predecessor took it, so do I want it."

Patriarch Anthimos of Jerusalem Demands Allegiance to the Ottomans (1798)

Patriarch Anthimos of Jerusalem, "Submission to the Powers That Be," in *The Movement for Greek Independence, 1770–1821: A Collection of Documents*, ed. and trans. Richard Clogg (New York: Barnes & Noble, 1976), 56–62, reproduced with permission of Palgrave Macmillan. First published 1976 by The Macmillan Press Ltd., London and Basingstoke. Published in the U.S.A. 1976 by Harper & Row Publishers, Inc., Barnes & Noble Import Division.

Patriarch Anthimos of Jerusalem, a city under Ottoman control since 1517, enjoyed the authority granted him by his Ottoman overlords. In the following document Anthimos argues that God instituted

8. *magnates*—wealthy and influential nobility.
9. *grosia*—Greek currency.
10. *Porte*—the court of the Ottoman Empire; the seat of government.
11. *ağas*—Ottoman governors or officers.

the Ottoman Empire according to his divine will and that Ottoman rule in fact *preserves* the Orthodox faith. Hence, according to Anthimos, democracy and notions of "liberty" are the work of the devil.

[. . .] See how clearly our Lord, boundless in mercy and all-wise, has undertaken to guard once more the unsullied holy and Orthodox faith of us, the pious, and to save all mankind. He raised out of nothing this powerful empire of the Ottomans, in the place of our Roman [Byzantine] Empire, which had begun, in a certain way, to cause to deviate from the beliefs of the Orthodox faith, and he raised up the Empire of the Ottomans higher than any other kingdom so as to show without doubt that it came about by divine will, and not by the power of man, and to assure all the faithful that in this way he deigned to bring about a great mystery, namely salvation to his chosen people.

The all-mighty Lord, then, has placed over us this high kingdom, "for there is no power but of God," so as to be to the people of the West a bridle, to us the people of the East a means of salvation. For this reason he puts into the heart of the sultan of these Ottomans an inclination to keep free the religious beliefs of our Orthodox faith [. . .] even to the point of occasionally chastising Christians who deviate from their faith [. . .]

The church of Christ has all the freedom that it has under Orthodox sovereigns of the same faith in the building of churches, as from generation to generation many splendid churches in different provinces and places have been built with the permission of the mighty empire. [. . .] And let no one think that, because the building of many churches is sometimes hindered, freedom of Christian worship is thereby curtailed. For shame! [. . .]

Brothers, do not be led astray from the path of salvation; but as you have always with bravery and steadfastness trampled underfoot the wiles of the devil, so now also close your ears and give no hearing to these newly-appearing hopes of liberty "for now is salvation nearer to us." And be very certain that their boastings and teachings, as we have been able to understand them, and from what we know in practice of the nations that have received them, that they are not only the direct contradiction of the written word of the scriptures and the holy apostles, which enjoins us to subject ourselves to the superior powers, not only to those who are just but also to those that are perverse, that we may have tribulation in this world, and keep our minds pure for the Lord; they are, I say, not only the contradiction of Holy Writ, but they do not bring about any transitory good in the present life, as they guilefully promise, in order to lead you astray and to strip you of all riches in Heaven and earth. [. . .]

Everywhere this illusory system of the diabolical one has led to poverty, murder, damage, rapine, complete ungodliness, spiritual destruction and vain repentance.

The teachings of these new libertines, Christian brethren, are deceitful. And beware: guard steadfastly your ancestral faith and, as followers of Jesus Christ, resolutely give your obedience to the civil government, which grants you that which alone is necessary to the present life, and what is more valuable than anything, does not present any obstacle or damage to your spiritual salvation. "For what is a man profited, if he gain the whole world, and lose or forfeit his own self?" [. . .]

[In a democracy] the powerful will dominate the weak, the healthy the sick, and the wise will deceive the ignorant. What order can then remain in such a government, and what morality, when the passions rule? What safety is there for the citizens, when rapine prevails? [. . .]

You should understand, brethren, that true freedom cannot exist in a good government without faith in God. And for this reason, the holy apostles, the immovable pillars of the godliness of our faith, who were enlightened by God, thus preached to the world, thus they and their successors behaved. These same things the church of Christ received from them and guarded steadfastly.

And when we see with such clarity that this new system of liberty is none other than a confusion and overturning of good government, a path leading to destruction or, simply speaking, a new ambush of the evil devil to lead astray the abandoned Orthodox Christians, are we not going to be judged worthy of all condemnation if we give the slightest hearing to these sly and deceptive teachings? [. . .]

No, Christians! Let us have steadfastness and prudence, let us not lose the unfading crowns of eternal blessedness for a false and non-existent liberty in this present life. Let us not deprive ourselves of the inexpressible rewards. [. . .]

Strengthen yourselves then, brethren, in the Lord and in the greatness of his strength, take on the panoply of God so that you can resist the machinations of the devil. [. . .]

English Chaplain Recounts the Conversion of a Muslim (1819)

Richard Clogg, "A Little-Known Orthodox Neo-Martyr, Athanasius of Smyrna (1819)," *Eastern Churches Review* 5 (1973): 34–35.

The Ottoman Empire explicitly forbade Orthodox believers—and everyone else, for that matter—from trying to convert Muslims to

another faith. The penalty for a Muslim who did convert was death. Here, an English chaplain ministering on the west coast of modern Turkey recounts the consequences of one such conversion.

[. . .] Athanasius, a young man of about four and twenty years of age, in deportment and appearance as handsome as a cedar of Libanus,[12] in constancy to the Christian religion as firm as Stephen,[13] as ready as Ridley and Latimer[14] to seal the faith with his blood, was the son of a boatman who carried on a small carrying trade in the archipelago. [. . .] Having served two or three masters he fell into the service of a Turk in decent circumstances and something above the common rank. The master was pleased with the conduct of his servant and to reward his fidelity, influenced also by the general inclination of converting another of a different faith, often proposed with great offers and temptations to elevate him from the degrading bondage of a Greek to the privileges of a Turk, which can be done only by taking the exterior mark of a disciple of Muhammad with the renunciation of Christianity in the presence of the meccamay, who is the Ottoman bishop and judge. Every temptation and importunity was humbly and manfully resisted till one fatal festival night when Satan moved his tongue, the words of abjuration once spoken the deed is done! Next morning made the man a Turk!

He remained with his master about a twelve-month, suffering no doubt many pangs of conscience for the horrid deed and having no alternative but to die, as he could not live, a Christian. Thus circumstanced, and no doubt, urged by his own people, he resolved to sacrifice his life as an atonement for the crime. With this intention he quitted the Turk and went on a pilgrimage to Mount Athos,[15] covered with convents filled with monks and friars; here he remained some months receiving instructions and preparing for death. On the expiration of his pilgrimage he quitted Mount Athos with the congratulations of the whole body on the prospect of his becoming a distinguished saint. He arrived at Smyrna in the habit of a caloyer, a Greek monk, and went immediately, with the approbation of the Greeks, to the meccamay's, declaring his resolution to die a Christian rather than live an apostate, a Turk.

12. *cedar of Libanus*—a kind of cedar tree frequently mentioned in the Bible.

13. *Stephen*—recognized by tradition as the first Christian martyr.

14. *Ridley and Latimer*—Protestants Nicholas Ridley and Hugh Latimer, two of the so-called Oxford Martyrs burned at the stake by Queen Mary's order in 1555.

15. *Mt. Athos*—the peninsula on the northeastern coast of Greece that has been home for many centuries to dozens of Orthodox monasteries and sketes.

The judge wished to persuade the Turks that he was mad and to save his life, but he persisted in publicly abjuring Mahomedanism[16] and asserting his readiness to die, upon which he was confined in a dungeon and tortured, which he endured with the greatest firmness and patience. The Greeks were afraid that, during his confinement, the tortures and extravagant promises and allurements of the Turks would shake his resolution, and actually sent a violently fanatical priest to strengthen him to suffer death. On the day of his execution Athanasius was led out of prison with his hands tied behind, he walked firmly to the square, a very public place, before the large mosque: he was there again offered his life with riches, women, lands and houses, if he would remain a Turk, but nothing could tempt him to save his life. At last a Turkish blacksmith was ordered by the captain of the guard to strike his head off, but as a last attempt to induce the sufferer to live a Turk, the executioner was desired to cut a little of the skin of his neck that he might feel the edge of the sword; this last attempt having failed of success, and Athanasius on his knees on the ground declaring with a calm and resigned countenance that he was born with Jesus and would die with Jesus, the horrid deed was finished with a single blow.

The Turkish guard instantly threw buckets of water upon the neck of the corpse and dissevered head, to prevent the multitude of expecting Greeks from dipping their handkerchiefs in his blood, to keep as a memorial of the great event. The body lay guarded and exposed for three days, the breast and stomach toward the ground, the head placed between the legs on the anus. It was afterwards given up to the Greeks and buried in the principal churchyard. Dearly purchased Christian burial!!! In such a circumstance it is difficult to say who are the most culpable, the Turks or the Greeks? The Turks are savages always ready to shed the blood of a Christian. But how abominable that a church, a Christian church, should refuse mercy to a fallen member! O when will the days come that will open the eyes of these people. [. . .]

16. *Mahomedanism*—Islam.

The Greek Revolution and
Orthodox Nationalism

In 1815, six years before Greek revolutionaries launched a war against the Turks to throw off the "Ottoman yoke," the Christian leaders of Russia, Austria, and Prussia—having recently defeated Napoleon—formed a "Holy Alliance," agreeing, in their words, "to consider themselves all as members of one and the same Christian nation [...] delegated by Providence to govern three branches of the One family, namely Austria, Prussia and Russia, thus confessing that the Christian world of which they and their people form a part has in reality no other sovereign than Him to whom power alone really belongs."[1]

Tsar Alexander I of Russia (1801–1825) envisioned the alliance as a means of promoting Christian virtues in political life.[2] Reformers throughout Europe and Greek revolutionaries in particular invested great hope in this document, believing that a Holy Alliance of "Christian princes" would come to their aid in a revolution against the Muslim Turks.

In reality, the alliance proved to be a reactionary body whose primary accomplishment was the preservation of autocratic governments and the status quo. David Brewer notes "an inherent and disabling contradiction in the principles of the Holy Alliance when applied to the Greek situation: the Alliance's commitment to uphold the Chris-

---

1. "Congress Treaty of Vienna, 1815," in *The Great European Treaties of the Nineteenth Century*, ed. Sir Augustus Oakes and R. B. Mowat (Oxford: Clarendon, 1930), 35.

2. David Brewer, *The Greek War of Independence* (New York: Overlook, 2001), 136.

tian religion argued in favor of supporting the Greek revolutionaries, but its commitment to uphold established governments meant support for the sultan."[3] Much to the Greek revolutionaries' sorrow, the great powers' commitment to established governments trumped their commitment to the idea of a Christian state. Commitments to autocracy trumped commitments to Orthodox Christianity. None of the three powers supported the Greek revolution.

What follows is an unsuccessful appeal to the great powers written by the new proto-Greek government, founded after Greek revolutionaries drove the Turks from much of the Greek peninsula. Note the appeals both to Enlightenment principles ("liberty," "justice," freedom from "oppression") and to Christianity ("mysteries of Christ" and defense of "the righteous").

The Greek Government to the Christian Powers of Europe (1822)

"Declaration to the Christian Powers," in J. L. Comstock, *History of the Greek Revolution Compiled from Official Documents of the Greek Government* (New York: W. W. Reed, 1828), 501–3.

The great struggle in which the Greek nation is engaged has occupied Europe as it will the pens of historians. From the first moment, all hearts, imbued with honor and sensibility, applauded these words—"Greece is fighting for liberty." A prey to the most humiliating and severe oppression, she excited the pity of the whole civilized world. Humanity loudly claimed the deliverance of her benefactress. Justice, prostrate before the throne of the most high, accused those who profaned the mysteries of Christ, plundered all property, and caused the tears of the widow and the orphan to flow. [. . .]

The Greeks were serving foreign masters, inexorable tyrants, insatiable tigers! No compact bound them to the foreign power, which in the madness of its pride, claimed to rule them by mere brute force forever. [. . .] An execrable administration was sucking the last drop of blood from the veins of the political body. The complaints of the oppressed expired before they reached the sublime Porte.[4] [. . .] Already a conversion to Mahometanism[5] appeared their sole safeguard to the wretched

3. Ibid.
4. *Porte*—seat of the Ottoman government.
5. *Mahometanism*—Islam.

population; and what would have become of the sacred claims that the Gospel has acquired to the pious gratitude of the Greeks? Would Europe have wished to see the consummation of this gigantic act of apostasy? Would she, though proud of a Christian Holy Alliance, have sanctioned afresh the triumph of the Arabian code over Christianity, of barbarism over civilization?

We did right in taking up arms, if it was only to fall with honor. [. . .] It is thus that the Greeks have chosen the desperate alternative of perishing or of being delivered. And they would in fact have perished, if providence had not hitherto vouchsafed the miracle of our successes. For the last thirteen months, God has aided the work of the righteous. They see the all-powerful hand, which created this harmonious system of worlds, laid heavily on both nations and kings, repairing the ravages of time, and distributing the compensations of ages. Greece, abandoned by the rest of the earth, with the volume of her past splendor, and her woes, and her rights, in her hand—Greece will still pursue her arduous career. Her cities sacked, her villages burnt, her population decimated, her fields ravaged, bear witness to her proud determination. Crushed by numbers, she will yet wash out her defeats in her blood. What will be the feelings of Europe toward her? [. . .] The Greeks aim at peace combined with independence, and at the political fruits of civilization. They protest beforehand against any violation of their rights, so lately purchased by the most heroic sacrifices. In a word, humanity, religion, interest, all plead in their favor. It is for the powers of Christendom to decide on this occasion, what legacy they propose bequeathing to history, and to posterity.

Although the patriarch of Constantinople, solidly under the thumb of the Ottoman state, condemned the Greek revolution, many clerics in Greece supported it. In fact some Greeks trace the outbreak of their revolution to 25 March 1821, when the Greek metropolitan Germanos supposedly bestowed his blessing on the Greek national flag (a blue cross on a white background) while declaring a national uprising. In 1821 we thus witness the strange phenomenon of a metropolitan rallying his flock to a revolution explicitly condemned by the patriarch to whom he was subject. After Greece won its independence, the new nation proclaimed the church in Greece in 1833 to be "autocephalous"[6]—independent from Constantinople.

The Greek revolution marked the first of several successful revolutions in the Balkans against the Ottomans, all of which elicited

---

6. *autocephalous*—an autocephalous church is a church whose head bishop or governing body does not report to another bishop. It is, in other words, independent from some outside or higher body.

Figure 46. Bulgaria, Greece, Romania, and Serbia

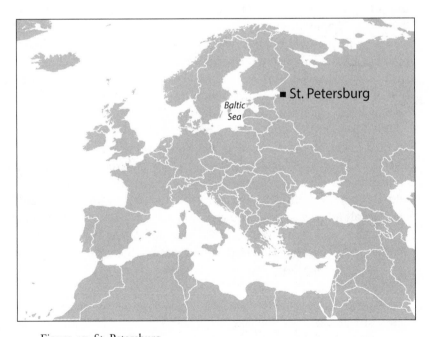

Figure 47. St. Petersburg

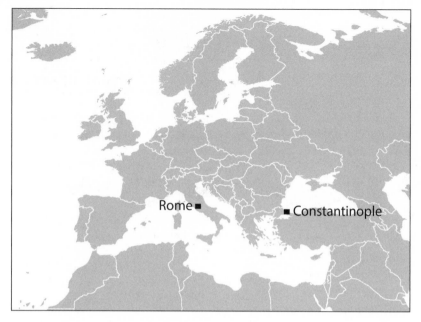

Figure 48. Rome and Constantinople

support from local clerics subject to the antirevolutionary patriarch of Constantinople. In each case local church leaders found themselves aligned with political revolutionaries in defiance of Constantinople. In Serbia, clerics supported uprisings against the Turks, preaching patriotic sermons and exhorting parishioners to arms. When Serbia won its independence in 1832, the church, with the support of the new Serbian state, declared itself "autonomous."[7]

Links between revolutionary activity and patriotic Christianity emerged in region after region in the Balkans. In fact the Romanian church declared itself autocephalous in 1865—thirteen years *before* Romania achieved independence from the Ottomans in 1878.

In Bulgaria, a multiethnic region populated by both Greeks and Slavs, revolutionary sentiment manifested itself in messier forms. The patriarchate of Constantinople had long appointed Greek bishops (not Bulgarian bishops) to oversee dioceses in Bulgaria. These bish-

7. *autonomous*—the head of an autonomous church is appointed by the patriarch of another church, but the autonomous church governs itself. The Serbian church later declared itself "autocephalous" in 1879 after the large nations of Europe recognized Serbia as an independent nation.

ops, to nobody's surprise, proved unwilling to endorse the formation of a Bulgarian national church. To their minds, a national church was fine for their own Greek homeland, but not for Bulgaria. (The fact that Greek bishops often refused to allow their parishioners to worship in the Bulgarian vernacular hardly endeared them to the Bulgarian populace.)

Tensions between Greeks and Bulgarians intensified in the 1820s through the 1860s, when Bulgarians began to insist that Bulgarian bishops rather than Greek bishops oversee their dioceses. Such sentiment, driven in part by an emergent nationalism, fit well with calls for political independence. Bulgarian bishops resented the Ottoman Empire not only as a foreign *political* power, but also as a foreign *religious* power, since it controlled the patriarchate of Constantinople, which appointed unwelcome Greek bishops to oversee Bulgarian churches. By the end of the 1860s Bulgarian bishoprics had expelled, to the fury of the patriarchate of Constantinople (whose members were mostly Greek), most Greek bishops from Bulgaria.

The Ottoman Empire, sensing an opportunity to assuage revolutionary ferment and demands for Bulgarian independence, took advantage of the anti-Greek sentiment: the sultan issued a decree creating an autonomous Bulgarian exarchate—a Bulgarian church still formally subject to the patriarchate of Constantinople but effectively independent. The Greeks and the patriarch of Constantinople were livid. The patriarch of Constantinople summoned his co-patriarchs from Alexandria and Jerusalem to a gathering in Constantinople, and they condemned the Bulgarians as guilty of "phyletism," namely the sin of mixing nationalistic principles with religious principles. The Bulgarian church thus found itself in schism with Constantinople, a schism not resolved until 1945, when Constantinople finally capitulated and recognized Bulgarian autocephaly.

In the 1800s it became difficult to disentangle religious principles from nationalistic political aims. Local bishops framed independence movements as God's work; revolutionary leaders portrayed Christianity as a bulwark of nationalism; local churches condemned a "foreign" patriarchate of Constantinople subject to foreign Muslim Turks. Political and religious leaders in newly independent nations spoke a great deal less about the universal church of Christ than about national churches. In short, the fall of the Ottoman Empire led not to the reunification of the Eastern Orthodox world, but in important respects to the splintering of that world. We will revisit the question of Orthodoxy and nationalism again (see "Orthodox Nationalism and Fundamentalism").

New Thinking and Church Reform

T he 1800s were a tumultuous time in Russia, when intellectu-als, especially in Moscow and St. Petersburg, continually asked themselves, Что делать? (*Chto delat'*? What is to be done?) about Russia's myriad problems: serfdom, poverty, illiteracy, hunger, economic backwardness, and autocratic government.

Social and intellectual histories of Russia in the latter half of the 1800s often focus on members of the "intelligentsia," that is, edu-cated people, usually of financial means and often from the nobility, who took Russia's problems to heart and criticized those institutions (the government, the church, the educational system, etc.) that they considered responsible. Although "intelligentsia" is broad enough to encompass those of all political persuasions who argued for change, particularly change in government, the term often functioned as short-hand for "liberals": democrats, socialists, communists, anarchists, and even pacifists.

This section focuses on those who advocated change and who were accused of liberalism by more conservative elements in the church.

Leo Tolstoy, Critique of Dogmatic Theology (1891)

Leo Tolstoy, "Critique of Dogmatic Theology," in *Complete Works of Count Tolstoy*, trans. Leo Wiener (Boston: Dana Estes & Company, 1904), 13:93–451.

After finishing his most mature novel, *Anna Karenina* (1877), the great Russian writer Leo Tolstoy experienced a spiritual crisis and began to question whether his life or work had any meaning. How did the peasants on his estate find contentment when he could not? Perhaps, he surmised, happiness could be found in their simple lives. Tolstoy began dressing in peasant garb, working alongside peasants in the field, eating their plain food, and worshipping with them.

He discovered, however, that he could not accept the teachings of the peasants' Orthodox faith. Orthodox doctrine struck him as contradictory, nonsensical, and even immoral. He taught himself Hebrew (he already knew Greek) so he could study scriptures in the original language, and he concluded that the church had departed radically from Jesus's central message of love and humility, while introducing a host of superstitious teachings and bizarre theology. The church, in other words, had replaced Christ's original message—true Christianity—with an institutionalized and corrupt set of doctrines.

For many years Tolstoy abandoned his fiction and began churning out religious studies. One of these, *Critique of Dogmatic Theology,* is a searing attack on fundamental doctrines of the church. In *Critique* Tolstoy employs a technique he used to great effect in his fiction— *ostranenie*—perhaps best translated as "de-familiarization" or "making strange." The goal is to present common things or beliefs in unfamiliar ways, forcing readers to confront them in a new light.

In the following excerpt Tolstoy offers an ostensibly straightforward, neutral, and factual summary of Orthodox theology, but he uses nontraditional theological language—language that is unmistakably glib—to encourage readers to consider Orthodox theology anew, and to find it strange and preposterous.

[...] A man asks what this world is in which he finds himself. He asks what the meaning of his existence is and what he is to be guided by in that freedom which he feels within himself. He asks all that, and God through the lips of the church established by him replies:

Do you want to know what this world is? Here it is:

There is a God, one, omniscient, all-good, almighty. This God is a simple spirit, but he has will and reason. This God is one and yet three. [...]

This trine God has existed eternally one in three, and suddenly it occurred to him to create the world and to create it from nothing with his thought, will, and word. [...]

Man was created good and absolutely perfect. His whole duty lay in this, that he should not eat the forbidden apple, and God not only had created him perfect, but also aided him in every way possible, teaching, amusing, and visiting him in the garden.

But Adam nonetheless ate the forbidden apple, and for that the good God wreaked revenge on Adam and drove him out of the garden, cursing him, the whole earth, and all the descendants of Adam.

All that is not to be understood in any transferred, but in a direct sense, as having actually occurred. [. . .]

God rules over the bad and good angels, and over the bad and good men. The angels help God to rule the world. There are angels who are attached to kingdoms, to nations, and to men, and omniscient, almighty, and all-good God, who has created them all, cast down forever legions of evil angels, and all men after Adam, but has not ceased caring for them in a natural and even in a supernatural manner. This supernatural manner of his care consists in this: that when five thousand years had passed, he found a means for paying himself for Adam's sin, whom he himself had made such as he was. This means consisted in this: that among the persons of the Trinity one is the Son. He, that person, has always been the Son. So this Son issued from a virgin, without impairing her virginity; he entered into the Virgin Mary as her husband, the Holy Ghost, and came out as a Son, Jesus Christ, and this Son was called Jesus, and he was God, and man, and a person of the Trinity.

This God-man has saved men. This is the way he saved them. He was a prophet, a high priest, and a king. As a prophet, he gave a new law; as a high priest he sacrificed himself by dying on the cross; and as a king he performed miracles and went down into Hell, let out from it all the righteous, and destroyed sin, and the curse and death in men.

But this means, however strong it was, did not save all men. Legions of legions of devils remained devils, and men must know how to take advantage of that salvation.

In order to take advantage of this means, a man must become sanctified, but only the church may sanctify, and the church is all those people who say about themselves that certain men have laid their hands on them, men upon whom other men have laid hands, and so forth, upon whom hands were laid by the disciples of the God Jesus himself, upon whom hands were laid by God the Son, the Savior, himself. When God himself laid his hands upon them, he blew, and with that blowing he gave to them, and to those to whom they would transmit it, the power to sanctify men, and that very sanctification is necessary in order to be saved.

What sanctifies man and saves him is grace, that means, the divine power which in a certain form is transmitted by the church. In order that this grace should be efficacious, it is necessary for the man who wishes to be sanctified to believe that he is being sanctified. He may even not believe entirely: he must obey the church and, above all, not contradict it, and then grace will pass into him. [. . .] This grace is transmitted by the church by various manipulations and by the pronunciation of certain words, which are called sacraments.

There are seven such manipulations:[1]

1. Baptism. When the hierarch [official] of the church has bathed a person in the proper way, that person becomes cleansed from sin, above all, from Adam's original sin, so that if an unbathed infant dies, it will perish as being filled with sin.

2. If he anoints that person with oil, the Holy Ghost enters into him.

3. If the person eats bread and wine under certain conditions and with the conviction that he is eating the body and blood of God, he becomes pure from sin and receives everlasting life. (In general there is a lot of grace about this sacrament and, as soon and as quickly as possible after it has been performed, a person must pray, and then the prayer will be heard according to the grace.)

4. When the priest has listened to that person's sins, he will say certain words, and the sins are gone.

5. When seven popes anoint a person with oil, his bodily and spiritual diseases will be cured.

6. When the wreaths are put on the bridal pair, the gift of the Holy Ghost will enter them.

7. When the hands are laid on, the Holy Ghost will enter. [. . .]

In these manipulations lies that means for salvation, which God has invented. He who believes that he is sanctified and purified, and will receive eternal life, is actually sanctified and purified and will receive eternal life. All those who believe in that will receive their retribution, at first a private retribution, soon after death, and later a general one, after the end of the world. The private retribution will consist in this, that they will be glorified in Heaven and on earth. On earth their relics and images will be honored with incense and tapers, and in Heaven they will be with Christ in glory. But before attaining that, they will pass through aerial spaces, where they will be stopped and questioned by angels and devils, who will contend with each other on their account, and those for whom the defense of the angels shall be stronger than the accusation of the devils will go to Paradise, and those whom the devils shall win will go to eternal torment, into Hell. [. . .]

To my question as to what sense my life will have in this life, the answer will be as follows:

1. *seven such manipulations*—here Tolstoy lists the seven sacraments: (1) baptism, (2) chrismation, (3) Eucharist, (4) confession, (5) unction, (6) marriage, and (7) ordination.

God, by his arbitrary will, created a strange world; a wild God, half-man, half-monster, created the world as he wanted it, and he kept saying that it was good, that everything was good, and that man was good. But it all turned out bad. Man fell under a curse, and his whole posterity was cursed, but God continued to make men in the wombs of their mothers, though he knew that all of them, or many, would perish. After he had invented a means for saving them, everything was as of old, and even worse, because while, as the church says, men like Abraham and Jacob could save themselves by their good lives, I am now certainly going to perish, if I was born a Jew, or a Buddhist, and accidentally do not come in contact with the sanctifying action of the church, and I shall be eternally tormented by the devils; more than that—if I am among the number of the fortunate, but have the misfortune to regard the demands of my reason as legitimate and do not renounce them, in order to believe the church, I perish just the same. [. . .]

According to this teaching the meaning of my life is an absolute absurdity, much worse than what presented itself to me by the light of my reason. [. . .]

From all the moral applications of the dogmas there results but this: save yourself by faith; you cannot understand what you are commanded to believe—say that you believe, crush out with all the powers of your soul the necessity of light and truth, say that you believe, and do what results from faith. [. . .]

The Russian Holy Synod Condemns Tolstoy (1901)

"Opredielenie Sviatieishago Synoda," *Tserkovnyia viedomosti* No. 8 (24 February 1901): 45–47. Translated by Bryn Geffert. CC BY-SA.

The Russian Orthodox Church struggled to respond to Tolstoy's gleefully heretical assertions, hoping for many years to entice him back into the fold. After all, as Pål Kolstø notes, Tolstoy made a "strenuous effort to live and believe like an Orthodox faithful" between 1877 and 1879, and he exhibited a penchant for "spectacular spiritual volte-faces earlier in his life." It "could not be excluded that an additional metanoia[2] might bring him to his senses."[3] But Tolstoy did not have one final volte-face in him.

The bishop of Tula gathered reports from Tolstoy's village priest about Tolstoy's work and passed them on to superiors in St. Peters-

---

2. *metanoia*—repentance or reorientation.

3. Pål Kolstø, "A Mass for a Heretic? The Controversy over Lev Tolstoy's Burial," *Slavic Review* 60 No. 1 (2001): 75.

burg. On 25 February 1901 the Holy Synod released a statement condemning Tolstoy's heresy and ordered that it be read from the Uspensky cathedral in St. Petersburg and then in all Russian churches. Although not technically an excommunication, it was widely interpreted as just that.

Tolstoy died nine years later, in 1910. At the funeral between seven thousand and eight thousand people—none of them priests—escorted his coffin. It was, as one of Tolstoy's biographers points out, "the first public burial in Russia since the conversion of St. Vladimir which was not attended by the rites of the church."[4]

Decision of the Holy Synod, 20–22 February 1901, No. 557, An Epistle to the Loyal Offspring of the Orthodox Greek Church Regarding Count Leo Tolstoy.

The Holy Synod—in its care for the children of the Orthodox church, safeguarding them from pernicious temptation, and seeking the salvation of those who have gone astray—has issued this judgment regarding Count Leo Tolstoy and his false, anti-Christian and anti-church teaching, and has deemed it timely to issue this notification in the *Tserkovnyia viedomosti*[5] regarding this offense against the peace of the church:

With God's mercy,

The Holy, All-Russian Synod: To the faithful offspring of the Orthodox Greek Catholic church.

May it please God.

"I urge you, brothers, to keep an eye on those who cause dissentions and offenses in opposition to the teaching we have learned; avoid them." (Romans 16:17).

The church of Christ has suffered abuse and attacks from numerous heretics and false teachers who have attempted to overthrow her and shake the essentials of her foundations, firmly established upon faith in Christ, the Son of the living God. But according to God's promise, all the strength of Hell cannot overcome the holy church, which will remain invincible for all time. In our day, with God's consent, a new, false teacher has appeared, Count Leo Tolstoy. A writer known around the world—Russian by birth, Orthodox by baptism and upbringing—Count Tolstoy—enticed by his proud intellect—audaciously rose against God and against his Christ and against his holy property, manifestly renouncing everything instilled and taught by his mother—the Orthodox church; he devoted his literary work and God-given talent to disseminating teaching amongst the people against Christ and the church, destroying in the

4. A. N. Wilson, *Tolstoy: A Biography* (New York: Norton, 1988), 517.
5. *Tserkovnyia viedomosti*—Church Bulletin.

hearts and minds of the people the paternal faith—the Orthodox faith—which established the universe, and in which we live and by which we are saved, and by which until now holy Rus' was firmly supported. In his works and his letters—the majority of which he and his pupils circulate in broad daylight, particularly within the borders of our dear fatherland—he preaches the overthrow of all dogmas of the Orthodox church and the very essence of the Christian faith with the zeal of a fanatic; he rejects a personal, living God—creator of and provider for the universe—within the glorious, Holy Trinity; he denies the Lord Jesus Christ—the God-man, redeemer and savior of the world—suffering for the sake of our salvation and for the resurrection of the dead; he denies the immaculate conception of Christ the Lord, the virgin birth, and the sinless birth of the Mother of God, the Virgin Mary; he does not recognize life after death and the resurrection; he denies all sacraments of the church and their grace-giving effects as realized through the Holy Spirit; he curses the Orthodox people's holy articles of faith; he has not shuddered to subject the supreme sacrament—the holy Eucharist—to mockery. To the horror and temptation of the entire Orthodox world, in everything Count Leo Tolstoy continually preaches—in word and in print, not hidden but clear to all—he has torn himself from all communion with the Orthodox church. His former attempts at clarification were not crowned with success. Therefore the church does not consider him a member and cannot consider him a member as long as he fails to recant and to reestablish relations with her. Now we testify to this before the entire church, for those in good standing and for the clarification of those who have gone astray, and especially for the clarification of Count Tolstoy. Many of those close to him—preachers of the faith—contemplate with sorrow that he remains without faith in God and our Lord savior at the end of his days, having turned away from the blessings and prayers of the church and from all communion with her.

Therefore, we testify to his fall from the church while praying that he will give himself to God in repentance and knowledge of the truth (2 Timothy 2:25). Not desiring a sinful death, we pray, merciful God, listen and forgive, and turn him back to your holy church. Amen.

Sergei Bulgakov on the Russian Intelligentsia (1909)

Sergei Bulgakov, "Heroism and Asceticism: Reflections on the Religious Nature of the Russian Intelligentsia," trans. Marian Schwartz, in *Landmarks: A Collection of Essays on the Russian Intelligentsia, 1909,* ed. Nikolai Berdyaev et al. (New York: Karz Howard, 1977), 19–27, 34–37, 44–47, 49.

The latter part of the 1800s and the early part of the 1900s were years of revolutionary ferment in Russia, decades during which an

increasingly secular body of thinkers and political actors—inspired by liberalism, socialism, Marxism, positivism, nihilism, agnosticism, atheism, humanism, and many other "-isms"—promoted solutions to Russia's problems that envisioned little to no role for the church. The church, in turn, tended to condemn all calls for political reform that did not promote the primacy of autocracy and the church's role within autocracy. A major reason for this reactionary stance, of course, was the church's subjugation to the state through the Holy Synod. As an arm of the government, the church could not extend support to those who opposed government policy.

Still, individual clerics and theologians, particularly those who focused on Christianity's social message, sometimes found themselves in sympathy with the intelligentsia. One such *intelligent,* disliked by the conservative hierarchy but embraced by more radical Christians, was Sergei Bulgakov. Although his father served as a priest, Bulgakov found himself drawn to Marxism, a materialistic, economic philosophy focused on class relations and the control of "capital" or money. Karl Marx insisted that all societies progress through certain stages of economic development, leading to an inevitable socialist revolution in which the working classes seize the means of production. Bulgakov later eschewed Marxist ideology and returned to the church, but he retained his commitment to social issues and argued for a just and representative system of government.

In 1909—four years after the Russian Revolution of 1905, which forced the tsar to accept a constitution and an elective, legislative body —Bulgakov and a number of well-known religious philosophers published a collection of essays titled *Signposts* (*Vekhi*). While sensitive to the need for significant change in Russia, Bulgakov and his friends criticized the antireligious ideals so prevalent among the revolutionary intelligentsia. Bulgakov and company argued that the intelligentsia— while admirably denouncing the police state, resisting censorship, calling for democracy, demanding social justice, and dreaming of a prosperous society—had nevertheless become spiritually "bankrupt," estranged from the Christian ideals that should animate social reform. This critique spawned a lively debate among Russia's educated classes. *Signposts* became one of the most popular books of the early 1900s: it was reprinted five times during its first year.

· I ·

[. . .] The Russian intelligentsia's character was shaped by two basic factors, one external and the other internal, to speak in general terms. The first was the merciless and unremitting pressure applied by the police, which could have crushed and completely destroyed a group with a weaker spirit. The fact that the intelligentsia remained alive and vigorous even under this pressure bears witness at least to its extraordinary courage and viability. The intelligentsia's isolation from real life, imposed upon it by the whole atmosphere of the old regime,[6] intensified that "underground" mentality that was part of its innate character in any case. Isolation numbed its spirit, supporting and to a certain extent justifying its political obsession (the "Hannibal's vow"[7] of struggle against autocracy), and hampering normal spiritual development. [. . .]

The second, subjective factor that determined the character of our intelligentsia is its special world-view and the spiritual outlook that accompanies it. This essay will be wholly devoted to a characterization and critique of that world-view. [. . .]

· II ·

Following Dostoevsky,[8] it has frequently been noted that the Russian intelligentsia's spiritual make-up contains elements of religiosity that sometimes even approximate Christianity. The intelligentsia's historical predicament was primarily responsible for fostering these traits: on the one hand, government persecution gave it a feeling of martyrdom and confessorship, while forcible isolation from life, on the other, produced dreaminess, occasional starry-eyed idealism, utopianism, and, in general, an inadequate sense of reality. [. . .]

A certain otherworldliness, an eschatological[9] dream of the city of God and the future reign of justice (under various socialist pseudonyms), and a striving for the salvation of mankind—if not from sin, then from suffering—are, as we know, the immutable and distinctive peculiarities of the Russian intelligentsia. Anguish at the disharmony of life and a yearning to overcome it distinguish the foremost *intelligent* writers (Gleb

---

6. *old regime*—regimes of the tsars.

7. *Hannibal's vow*—Hannibal of Carthage (d. ca. 183 BCE) was a great military leader; this is a reference to his supposed vow of eternal enmity toward Rome, sworn with his hand upon the entrails of a ritual sacrifice.

8. *Dostoevsky*—Feodor Dostoevsky (1821–1881), a Russian novelist whose work cleverly and savagely criticizes revolutionary thought and revolutionary thinkers.

9. *eschatological*—related to eschatology, the study of the end of history or the "end times."

Uspensky, Garshin).[10] It may be that in this striving for the future city, beside which earthly reality pales, the intelligentsia has preserved in their most recognizable form some features of its lost life in the church. While I listened to the stormy speeches of the atheistic left bloc in the second State Duma,[11] how often I heard—remarkably—echoes of the psychology of Orthodoxy, as the effects of the members' spiritual indoctrination by it were suddenly revealed.

In general, the spiritual habits instilled by the church explain a number of the Russian intelligentsia's best qualities, but it loses them the more it departs from the church. Among them are a certain puritanism, rigorous morals, a distinctive asceticism, and a general strictness of personal life. [. . .] In the spiritual make-up of the most outstanding figures of the Russian Revolution we can discern Christian traits that they absorbed, sometimes without knowledge or desire, from their surroundings, from family and nurse, from a spiritual atmosphere steeped in church life. But since this merely obscures the real opposition between the Christian temperament and that of the *intelligent,* it is important to point out that these traits are superficial, borrowed, and in a certain sense atavistic.[12] They disappear with the weakening of former Christian habits, revealing the full-blown image of the *intelligent.* That image made its most forceful appearance during the Revolution, when it sloughed off the very last vestiges of Christianity.

The Russian intelligentsia, especially in earlier generations, was also distinguished by a feeling of guilt toward the people, a kind of "social repentance," not before God, of course, but before the "people" or the "proletariat."[13] Although there is a touch of lordliness in the historical origins of these sentiments of the "repentant nobleman" or the "classless *intelligent,*" they do leave a mark of special profundity and suffering on the intelligentsia's countenance. Another apparently religious trait is the intelligentsia's self-sacrifice, the constant readiness of its best representatives to make any sacrifices and even to seek them. Whatever its psychological motivation, the readiness for sacrifice reinforces that

10. *Gleb Uspensky, Garshin*—Gleb Uspensky (1843–1902) was a writer known for his essays on the peasantry; he spent the last ten years of his life in a mental institution before committing suicide. Vsevolod Garshin (1855–1888) was a writer known particularly for his stories set in lunatic asylums.

11. *second State Duma*—Bulgakov was a member in 1907 of the second Russian Duma (the new legislative body), whose membership was known for its radicalism. Bulgakov caucused with the Kadets (liberals) but considered himself a Christian Socialist.

12. *atavistic*—something ancient or dated; a throwback.

13. *proletariat*—the exploited, laboring classes.

otherworldliness that makes the intelligentsia's outlook so foreign to bourgeois philistinism[14] and gives it distinctive religious features.

And yet, despite all these qualities, it is common knowledge that there is no intelligentsia more atheistic than the Russian. Atheism is the common faith into which all who enter the bosom of the humanistic intelligentsia church are baptized, not only those who come from the educated class but those who come from the people as well. [. . .] Just as every social group elaborates its own customs and special creeds, the Russian intelligentsia's traditional atheism has come to be taken for granted—it is considered a mark of bad taste even to talk about it. In the eyes of our intelligentsia a certain level of education and enlightenment is synonymous with indifference to religion or rejection of it. [. . .]

The most striking feature of Russian atheism is its dogmatism, the religious frivolity, one might say, with which it is accepted. Until recently, Russian "educated" society simply ignored the problem of religion and did not understand its vital and exceptional importance. For the most part it was interested in religion only insofar as the religious problem involved politics or the propagation of atheism. In matters of religion our intelligentsia is conspicuously ignorant. This is not an indictment, for there is, perhaps, sufficient historical justification for this ignorance, but a diagnosis of the intelligentsia's spiritual condition. As far as religion is concerned, our intelligentsia simply has not emerged from adolescence. [. . .]

The best proof of this contention is the historical origin of Russian atheism. We assimilated it from the West, and not without reason it became the first article in the creed of our "Westernism." We accepted it as the last word in Western civilization. [. . .] Western civilization is a tree deeply rooted in history, with many branches; we chose only one, without knowing or wishing to know any of the others, fully confident that we were grafting onto ourselves the most authentic European civilization. [. . .]

Nowadays we tend to lose sight of the fact that Western European culture has religious roots and is at least half built on the religious foundations laid down by the Middle Ages and the Reformation. Whatever our view of Reformation dogma and of Protestantism in general, we cannot deny that the Reformation stimulated a tremendous religious upsurge throughout the Western world, even in the areas that remained true to Catholicism but were forced to renew themselves in order to combat

14. *bourgeois philistinism*—"bourgeois" is a Marxist term for those who control capital (money) and thus own the "means of production." A philistine is an anti-intellectual or dolt. "Bourgeois philistinism" is, then, a Marxist's snarky dismissal of ideas embraced by wealthy idiots.

their enemies. In this sense, a new European personality was born in the Reformation, and this origin left its mark. Political freedom, freedom of conscience, and the rights of man and the citizen were also proclaimed by the Reformation (in England). Recent investigations are shedding light on the significance of Protestantism, especially in the Reformed Church, Calvinism, and Puritanism, for economic development, for it molded individuals fit to become the leaders of a developing national economy. Modern learning, and especially philosophy, also developed primarily in Protestant areas. [. . .]

Our intelligentsia's Westernism was restricted to the superficial assimilation of the latest political and social ideas. Moreover, they were adopted in conjunction with the most extreme and caustic forms of Enlightenment philosophy. The intelligentsia made this choice itself, and Western civilization as an organic whole is essentially not responsible for it. [. . .]

In any event, this broke the continuity of Russia's intellectual development, and the breach has made our country sick in spirit.

· III ·

The intelligentsia rejects Christianity and its standards and appears to accept atheism. In fact, instead of atheism it adopts the dogmas of the religion of man-Godhood, in one or another of the variants produced by the Western European Enlightenment, and then turns this religion into idolatry. The basic tenet common to all the variants is belief in the natural perfection of man and in infinite progress. The latter is to be effected by human forces, but at the same time it is viewed in mechanistic terms. Since all evil is explained by the external defects of human society, and consequently there is neither personal guilt nor personal responsibility, it follows that the whole problem of social reorganization is to overcome these external defects—by means of external reforms, of course. Denying the existence of providence and of any pre-eternal plan working itself out in history, man puts himself in place of providence and sees himself as his own savior. A mechanistic, sometimes crudely materialistic conception of the historical process, which reduces it to the play of spontaneous forces (as in economic materialism), manifestly contradicts this image of man, but it develops nonetheless; man remains the sole rational, conscious agent, his own providence. [. . .]

Here the religion of man-Godhood and its essence, self-worship, were adopted not only with youthful ardor but with adolescent ignorance of life and its forces, and they assumed almost frenzied forms. Thus inspired, our intelligentsia felt called upon to play the role of providence to its own country. It was conscious of its position as the sole bearer of light and European education in this land where everything, it felt, was lost in impenetrable darkness and seemed so barbaric and alien. The intelligentsia saw itself as Russia's spiritual guardian and determined to save her, as best it could and as best it knew how. [. . .]

. V .

The special character of intelligentsia heroism will become clearer if we contrast it with the opposite spiritual type, Christian heroism—or, more precisely, Christian asceticism, for in Christianity the hero is the ascetic. The basic difference between them is not so much external as internal and religious. The hero puts himself in the role of providence, and by this spiritual usurpation he assigns himself a responsibility greater than he can bear and tasks that are beyond the reach of men. The Christian ascetic believes in God the provider, without whose will not a hair falls from the head. In his eyes both history and a single human life are a realization of God's plan, and even though he does not comprehend it in its individual details he humbles himself before it in an act of faith. This frees him at once from heroic posturing and pretensions. He concentrates his attention on his true task, his real obligations, and their strict, absolute fulfillment. [. . .]

The shift of attention to oneself and one's obligations, the emancipation from a false image of oneself as the unacknowledged savior of the world and from the pride that inevitably goes with it, heals the soul and fills it with a sense of wholesome Christian humility. In his Pushkin speech,[15] Dostoevsky called the Russian intelligentsia to this act of spiritual self-renunciation, to the sacrifice of its proud *intelligent*'s ego in the name of a higher sanctity. "Humble yourself, proud man, and first of all subdue your pride . . . If you will conquer yourself, if you will humble yourself, you shall become free as you never imagined, and you shall begin a great work and make others free, and you shall see happiness, for your life will be full. . . ."

No word is more unpopular with intelligenty[16] than "humility," and few concepts have been more misunderstood and distorted, or fallen such easy prey to intelligentsia demagogy. Its hostility to this concept is perhaps the best testimony to the intelligentsia's spiritual nature and betrays its arrogant heroism resting on self-worship. [. . .]

But this is not what creates the deepest gulf between the intelligentsia and the people,[17] for it is really only a derivative distinction; the fundamental difference between them is their attitude to religion. The people's world-view and spiritual outlook are determined by the Christian faith.

15. *Pushkin speech*—Feodor Dostoevsky delivered this famous speech in 1880 at the unveiling of a monument to Russia's greatest poet, Aleksandr Pushkin.

16. *intelligenty*—plural of *intelligent*.

17. *the people*—the uneducated; those not members of the intelligentsia.

However great the distance between ideal and reality, however "dark" and unenlightened our people may be, their ideal is Christ and his teaching, and their standard is Christian asceticism. What has the whole history of our people been, if not asceticism: oppressed first by the Tatars[18] and then by the Muscovite and Petersburg state, bearing the centuries-old historical burden of standing watch to safeguard Western civilization from the savage peoples and the sands of Asia, in this cruel climate, with its everlasting famines, cold, and sufferings. If our people have been able to bear all these afflictions while still preserving their spiritual forces, and come through alive though crippled, it is only because their faith and the ideals of Christian asceticism gave them a source of spiritual strength, a well-spring of national health and vitality. [. . .]

The intelligentsia usually gloats over the numerous evils of church life, which we have no desire either to minimize or to deny (although the intelligentsia neither knows nor understands any of the positive sides of church life). But does the intelligentsia really have the right to criticize when it remains indifferent to religion or rejects it on principle, seeing in religion only darkness and idiocy?

A church intelligentsia combining true Christianity with a clear and enlightened understanding of cultural and historical tasks (which contemporary churchmen so often lack), were one to arise, would meet an urgent historical and national need. And even if it had to suffer in its turn the persecution and oppression that the intelligentsia endures for the sake of atheistic ideals, this would have enormous historical and religio-moral significance and would find a very special response in the people's soul. [. . .]

· VII ·

[. . .] The intelligentsia rejected Christ; it turned away from his countenance and cast his image from its heart; it deprived itself of the inner light of life, and together with its country it is paying for this betrayal, this religious suicide. [. . .] Although it has renounced Christ, it bears his seal on its heart and burns with an unconscious longing for him, not knowing how to slake its spiritual thirst. And this bewildering anxiety, this unearthly dream of unearthly justice, leaves its special mark on the intelligentsia and makes it strange, frenzied and unbalanced, as though possessed. It is like the beautiful Shulamite[19] who had lost her lover: on her bed at night, in the streets and broad ways, she sought him whom her soul loved; she asked the watchmen that go about the city if they had

18. *Tatars*—Mongols who controlled much of Rus' from the 1200s to the 1400s.

19. *Shulamite*—unnamed woman in the Song of Songs.

seen her beloved, but instead of answering they only smote and wounded her. (Song of Songs, 3:1–3, 5:7.) And meanwhile, the beloved,[20] the one for whom its soul yearns, is near. He stands and knocks at that heart, that proud, recalcitrant intelligentsia heart . . . Will his knock someday be heard? . . .

20. *the beloved*—Christ.

PART IV

Revolutions and Reevaluations

Russian Revolution

Karl Marx famously called religion the "opium of the people," a force that anesthetizes the working classes, keeps them content with the status quo, and prevents them from realizing their true plight and need to free themselves from the tyranny of capitalism.

Marx had little interest in theology and no desire to construct theological critiques. For him the problem of religion was simple: religion is corrupt because it stems from corrupt societies. Religion is not an ultimate truth or an aspect of divine law or reality. Rather, it is a human construct, part of society's "superstructure," that is, those ideas that grow out of the "infrastructure" created by the ruling classes, be they capitalist, monarchical, or feudal. Religion is, therefore, a cynical tool of the ruling classes, a fiction the oppressed do not recognize as fiction. The people will abandon religion, Marx argued, once the capitalist infrastructure is overthrown and a new, just infrastructure assumes its place.

Vladimir Lenin, the Marxist revolutionary who led the Bolshevik party to power in Russia in 1917, took Marx's characterization of religion to heart. Religion, Lenin argued, is part of the superstructure indicative of Russia's corruption. The creation of a just society—led by the working-class proletariat (or at least the Bolshevik party governing on behalf of the proletariat)—would cause religion to dry up and wither away. Neither Marx nor Lenin argued that religion ought to be banned in a socialist society. In fact Lenin even welcomed religious believers into the Bolshevik party. But both believed firmly that religion was oppressive and ultimately irrelevant.

Lenin took active measures to make religion irrelevant. Upon assuming power in late 1917, he quickly signed a decree establishing strict separation of church and state. The state would have no official religion: "Every citizen can practice any religion he wishes, or not practice one at all." Civil marriages were permitted for the first time ever. Religion could not be taught in schools, even in most private schools. Neither the church nor religious societies could own property. On 13 January 1918, with the stroke of a pen, all church property became property of the state.

The Bolshevik Revolution came at a time that should have been one of immense hope for the church. The section "New Thinking and Church Reform" examined forces of religious renewal in Russia and the return of some members of the secular intelligentsia to the arms of the church. In August 1917 (i.e., during the seven-month period between the fall of the tsar in February and the Bolshevik seizure of power in October) a great council of church representatives, or *sobor,* from throughout the Russian Empire abolished the Holy Synod (established by Peter the Great), reestablished the patriarchate, and elected the first Russian patriarch since the early 1700s. The *sobor* promised to make the church more democratic, more attuned to social problems, more sensitive to the plight of the peasantry, and more attentive to education.

The Bolshevik decrees below thus not only removed the church from its honored place in Russian society, but dashed hopes for reform that had been building for years. The newly elected Patriarch Tikhon denounced the Bolsheviks in scathing terms.

When civil war broke out shortly after the Bolshevik Revolution, most in the church sided with the "Whites"—an odd conglomeration of royalist, democratic, and ultraconservative forces that fought the Bolshevik "Reds." The church experienced terrible persecution during and after the civil war. Red troops imprisoned and executed clergy and laity. The Soviet regime closed churches, confiscated valuables (ostensibly to raise money for famine relief), and kept the new patriarch under house arrest until he signed an oath of loyalty to the Soviet regime.

The church's plight only worsened after Lenin's death in 1924. Between 1929 and 1933 Joseph Stalin closed at least half the churches that survived the revolution. Many Russians fell away from the church. Still, in 1937, 57 percent of those aged sixteen or older declared themselves believers.

Persecution eased only with the outbreak of the Second World War, when Stalin decided the church might prove valuable in bolstering morale and fostering nationalistic sentiment against German forces. By then the church leadership was snuggly in the pocket of the Soviet state. With no court of appeal, the church had, in effect, no legal existence apart from the state. Metropolitan Sergei (who became *Patri-*

arch Sergei with Stalin's blessing in 1943) declared that all Russian Orthodox Christians bore a duty to support the Soviet regime. He denied that Christians in Russia faced any persecution. And he delivered a full-throated defense of the Soviet cause in World War II, aka the "Great Patriotic War." We do not yet know the full story of collaboration between church leaders and Soviet officials. And scholars disagree about who bears primary responsibility for rapprochement between church and state. It is clear, however, that the Second World War gave the Russian church a new lease on life. It is also clear that the church compromised itself badly and that a number of its leaders worked for the Committee for State Security, or KGB.

Although most believers abhorred the Soviets' treatment of the church, not all sympathized entirely with the church. Before the revolution parishioners and even intellectuals frequently complained about the large sums funneled to support the church: its ecclesiastical academies, its journals, and its well-living leaders. Sheila Fitzpatrick notes that many peasants viewed priests as "idle, greedy, and drunken."[1]

This section does not focus on the grisly stories of arrests and executions, which are well documented elsewhere. It focuses instead on the church's attempts to make sense of the new Soviet state. Here we see a church, formerly considered the bedrock of the nation, now struggling to find its place in a secular and atheistic state.

A note about dates: until the revolution Russia followed the old Julian calendar rather than the Gregorian calendar used in the West. As a result, the Bolsheviks' "October Revolution" occurred in November according to Western reckoning. Introductions to the following documents use Western dates.

Holy Sobor's Encyclical to the Russian People (13 November 1917)

James Cunningham, *The Gates of Hell: The Great Sobor of the Orthodox Church, 1917–1918*, ed. Keith and Grace Dyrud (Minneapolis: University of Minnesota Press, 2002), 156–59. Used by permission of Modern Greek Studies, University of Minnesota.

The church *sobor,* or council, convened in 1917 to consider a number of reforms. It issued the following statement seven days after the Bolsheviks seized power.

1. Sheila Fitzpatrick, *Stalin's Peasants* (New York: Oxford University Press, 1994), 35.

Grace and peace be to you from God the Father and our Lord Jesus Christ (Galatians 1:3).

Although great calamities have already befallen our motherland, the cup of divine wrath is still being poured out on us. We can expect that because of new transgressions, his righteous anger will increase further. To our already existing calamities has been added civil war, which is enveloping the Russian land. On the one hand the soldiers and people are deceived by every promise of earthly goods and swift peace,[2] while on the other our land is crimsoned with the blood of brothers. Russian guns and cannons now are not trained on the enemy,[3] but on Russian cities, not sparing even defenseless women and children. Those directing the slaughter pay small attention to that matter. There has been a completely sacrilegious attack on the Orthodox faith, on the entire Orthodox people, and their history. Russian arms have fired on the most revered holy sites of Russia, on the holy Moscow Kremlin[4] in which its ancient cathedrals stand, where the sacred miracle-working icons, and the relics of the holy saints—the heritage of Russia—are preserved. [. . .]

The Orthodox people have looked with horror on what has transpired. Our descendants will stigmatize that malicious envy with rage and repugnance. We are covered with shame before the whole world. We cannot hold up our heads because of humiliation and grief. Jeremiah's words have truly been fulfilled on us: "You have made us garbage and refuse among the nations . . . Terror and the pit have befallen us, desolation and destruction" (Lamentations 3:45–47).

By whose hands have these horrifying events been accomplished? Alas, by our own Russian soldiers,[5] the very soldiers whom we prayerfully honored as Christ-loving, who until just recently demonstrated great feats of valor, humility, and piety. [. . .] Instead of the new social order promised by false teachers there is bloody conflict; instead of peace and the brotherhood of peoples there is the babble of tongues and bitter hatred among brothers. People, having forgotten God, fall on one another like raging wolves. There appears to be a general darkening of conscience and reason. The responsibility in this affair does not lie equally with all who participated. We believe that many of them, perhaps the majority, are simple and unsophisticated people, confused, deluded, and suborned, not knowing what they were doing. The responsibility lies with those who deceived them and led them. "Woe to the world because of scandal.

2. *swift peace*—Bolsheviks' pledge to withdraw Russian troops from the First World War.

3. *enemy*—the German army on Russia's western front.

4. *Kremlin*—the walled inner city of Moscow.

5. *Russian soldiers*—the Bolsheviks won the allegiance of many battle-weary troops.

If there need be scandal, woe to that man through whom it comes" (Matthew 18:7). [. . .]

There can be no earthly kingdom governed on the basis of atheism; it would perish from internal strife and partisan disorder. Accordingly, the Russian state has been disrupted by atheism. Before our very eyes the just judgment of God is being visited on those who have abandoned their sacred heritage. [. . .]

For those who view the essential basis of their power as lying in the supremacy of one class over all the people,[6] the motherland and its sacred places do not exist. They remain traitors to their motherland who perpetrate an unheard of treachery on Russia and its true allies. To our misfortune there still has not appeared a power that is truly of the people, one which would merit the blessing of the Orthodox church. And it will not appear in the Russian land, so long as we do not turn to him, without whom all labor is in vain, with painful prayers and tearful repentance.

The Holy Sobor calls on the whole Russian church to undertake prayerful repentance for the great sin of those of its sons who, having fallen into temptation, and through ignorance, gave into fratricide and sacrilegious destruction of the holy sites of the people. We accept what was done by them as a sin of the whole people and we will beg the Lord for forgiveness. [. . .]

Let God arise again and scatter his enemies, and may all who abhor him flee from his face.

Draft Bill of Rights for the Russian Church (15 November 1917)

James Cunningham, *The Gates of Hell: The Great Sobor of the Orthodox Church, 1917–1918*, ed. Keith and Grace Dyrud (Minneapolis: University of Minnesota Press, 2002), 171–73. Used by permission of Modern Greek Studies, University of Minnesota.

In the summer of 1917, a church *sobor,* eager to establish clear rights and prerogatives for the church under a new government, drafted a "Bill of Rights," which, the *sobor* hoped, a constituent assembly would adopt in November. The *sobor* approved this bill ten days before the assembly was to convene. Given the uncertainties of the time, this text can be read either as naive optimism or as a final, desperate effort to stake a claim in the new state. In either case, it

---

6. *one class over all the people*—the Bolsheviks called for a "dictatorship of the proletariat," the rule of the working class.

reflects the Russian church's ambitious sense of its role within Russian society. While the Bill of Rights does not in any sense summon Byzantine notions of *symphonia,* the grand vision of church and state working together in harmonious accord, it nevertheless envisions a lofty set of privileges for the church. It is difficult to imagine a vision more at odds with political realities.

1. In the Russian state the Orthodox church, comprising part of the ecumenical church, occupies the premier, legal, public position in relation to other religious denominations, since it is the transcending *sviatyne*[7] of the overwhelming majority of the people. [. . .]

5. The government acknowledges the hierarchy of the church and the laws of the church as they are defined by the church. [. . .]

7. The head of government, the minister of denominations, the assistant minister of denominations, the minister of public education, and the assistant minister of public education will be Orthodox Christians. [. . .]

9. The Orthodox calendar[8] will be recognized as the calendar of the government.

10. The twelve major feasts, Sundays, and days especially revered by the Orthodox church shall be legal holidays observed by the government.

11. The government will guarantee the free profession and preaching of the Orthodox faith and the right to publicly celebrate liturgies. The government will criminally prosecute

  a) abuse or revilement of clergy or servants of the church.
  b) defilement of places of worship and religious veneration.
  c) force or threats designed to effect abandonment of Orthodoxy.

12. Abandonment of Orthodoxy will not be permitted until the age of maturity established for marriage. Earlier abandonment will be permitted only at the request of parents who themselves have left Orthodoxy. Children who have achieved the age of nine will give their personal consent to the abandonment of Orthodoxy. [. . .]

14. Orthodox solemnization of marriage will be recognized as having the force of law.

15. Ecclesiastical divorce or annulment of marriage will be recognized as having the force of law.

7. *sviatyne*—holy place. In other words, the state church is the embodiment of holiness for the nation.

8. *Orthodox calendar*—the old Julian calendar, abandoned by most Western countries.

16. Orthodox canon law shall prevail in legal questions arising from mixed marriages. [. . .]

19. State and private schools will provide education consonant with the spirit of the Orthodox church for pupils of Orthodox parentage. Instruction in religion will be obligatory for them in primary, secondary, and higher educational institutions. Religious instruction in state schools will be underwritten by subventions from the treasury.

20. The religious requirements of the personnel of the army and navy will be guaranteed by the government. Each military unit will have an Orthodox chaplain. [. . .]

24. The Orthodox church shall receive from the state treasury an annual appropriation for its needs computed by a special estimate. A regular financial report on the use of funds will be submitted on a general basis. [. . .]

Bolshevik Decree on Church, State, and Schools (23 January 1918)

Nikita Struve, *Christians in Contemporary Russia* (New York: Charles Scribner's Sons, 1967), 378–79. Copyright © 1967 The Harvill Press. Reprinted by permission of Cengage Learning.

Elections to the anticipated Constituent Assembly occurred ten days later, on 25 November 1917. The Bolsheviks did not fare well, gaining only 25 percent of the vote. When the assembly convened on 18 January 1918, the church prayed that the assembly would include the rights enumerated above in the final constitution. It was not to be. Bolshevik delegates, unhappy with their failure to win a number of demands, walked out; the next day troops loyal to the Bolsheviks dissolved the assembly. Six days later the Bolshevik Council of People's Commissars issued the following decree: the antithesis of what the church *sobor* had envisioned.

1. The church is separated from the state.

2. Within the territory of the republic, it is forbidden to promulgate any laws or local decrees that would hamper or limit freedom of conscience or establish advantages or privileges on the basis of the confessional membership of citizens.

3. Every citizen can practice any religion he wishes, or not practice one at all. All loss of rights resulting from the practice of any faith or the

non-practice of a faith, is repealed. *N.B.* All indication of religious membership or non-membership of citizens is deleted from all official acts.

4. The activities of any state or other public, legal or social bodies will not be accompanied by any religious rites or ceremonies.

5. The free practice of religious rites is guaranteed in as far as it does not interfere with public order and is not accompanied by any attempt on the rights of the citizens of the Soviet Republic. Local authorities will be empowered to take all necessary measures in these cases, to protect public order and security. [. . .]

7. Religious oath taking or swearing is annulled. Where necessary, only a solemn promise will be given.

8. Marriage acts will only be drawn up by the civil authorities—by marriage and birth registration offices.

9. Schools are separated from the church. The teaching of religious doctrines in all state and public as well as any private educational establishments where general subjects are taught is prohibited. Citizens may teach and be taught religion privately. [. . .]

12. No ecclesiastical or religious society has the right to possess property. It does not enjoy any legal rights.

All the possessions of ecclesiastical and religious societies existing in Russia are declared to be national property. The buildings and objects specially intended for use in services, are made over, by special decree of the local or central state authority, for the free use of the aforesaid religious societies.

Soviet Propaganda

TEXTS

Although Soviet tactics to combat religion varied over time, the ideology that underlay these different approaches remained relatively consistent. *The Atheist's Handbook,* published during the time Nikita Khrushchev was in office (1953–1964), nicely outlined the official Soviet line on religion. The excerpts here attempt to explain why religious belief persisted despite Soviet efforts to eradicate it.

Soviet Line on Religion under Khrushchev (1959)

The Atheist's Handbook: USSR (Washington, DC: U.S. Joint Publications Research Service, 1961), 199–204, 211–14. Translation of *Sputnik Ateista* (Moscow, 1959).

As a result of the victory of socialism in our country, the exploiter classes that spread and supported religion and religious and ecclesiastical organizations were destroyed. In this way, the social roots of religion were undermined. As a result of the cultural revolution that has taken place in our country and the spread of scientific atheist propaganda, the overwhelming majority of the population of the Soviet Union has made a complete break with religion and has adopted the position of atheism.[1] A certain number of citizens, however, while breaking with religion still do not have a firm scientific outlook and philosophy; hence they are

---

1. *overwhelming majority* . . . —a gross exaggeration.

wavering. Furthermore, a considerable number of the population retains its religious beliefs of various types and doctrines.

How can the retention of religious beliefs in a socialist society be explained?

One of the most important reasons for the tenacity of religious beliefs in the USSR is the psychological lag of men behind the development of their everyday life. The general law of the evolution of a society is that first the material conditions change, and then in conformity with this there are changes in the thinking of the people, their manners and morals, customs, and philosophy. This law maintains its force even in a socialist society. Ideas, concepts, views, and notions may persist in men's minds because of customs and traditions even when the material conditions that engendered them have disappeared; religion is specially equipped so to do. Once it has appeared, religion always retains a certain supply of ideas inherited from past times since in all areas of ideology, traditions are often a great conservative force.

Another reason for the retention of religious beliefs in a socialist society is the one-sidedness and subjectivism in conceptions of the surrounding world (the gnosiological[2] roots of religion). In cognizing objective reality, man is abstracted from individual phenomena and objects and creates in his own mind general conceptions and general ideas: man in general, a house in general, a tree in general, a society in general, etc. Abstractions are a necessary and very important element in the cognition of objective reality; they reflect the most general and essential properties of the objects and phenomena of the world around us. However, in the process of cognition there is a possibility of divorcing abstract ideas from real objects and phenomena, whose reflection the given abstract ideas are.

Having divorced ideas from reality, man may imagine them as standing above the world around him and endow them with supernatural properties. In this way, religious-minded persons come to the idea of God, angels, saints, the evil spirit, etc.

To a considerable degree, the retention of religious beliefs in the Soviet Union is abetted by the insufficient knowledge by some Soviet citizens of the basic laws or the development of nature and society. Despite the fact that an enormous amount of cultural and educational work has been done in our country, a certain portion of the population of the USSR still does not have correct scientific ideas about certain parts of the world around us. This lack of knowledge is fertile soil for religious ideology.

Another factor influencing the retention of religion is the great influence exerted by the simple practice of the religious life on the individual believer. The process of exercising religious rites enkindles the human imagination, intensifies the emotions, and creates a religious frame of

2. *gnosiological*—cognitive.

mind. A person enters a church; he is struck by the unique architecture of the building, the luxuriously painted iconostasis,[3] the skillfully done pictures of the mythical gods and saints; he is captivated by the church music and chant; he is intoxicated by the smell of incense; the peal of the church-bell affects him; the prayers, preaching, confession, and other forms of active religion exert an influence over him. The religious rites, supplemented by the reading of holy books, which are scarcely intelligible to the hearer, act on his psyche and drive him into a religious ecstasy.

One of the reasons for the tenacity of religious prejudices and superstitions is the presence of the hostile capitalist system. The world capitalist and world socialist systems have begun a historic competition with each other. In the course of this competition the absolute superiority of socialism is being displayed, which is spreading far and wide. However, the dying, obsolete, and disintegrating capitalist world in its last agony is furiously fighting against the countries of the socialist camp. In this struggle it is using all means and methods to prolong its supremacy, to halt and, if possible, to destroy the victorious march of socialism and prevent the growth of the socialist revolution. The attempt to revive religious beliefs in our country is one of the forms of the struggle of the bourgeois ideology against the socialist ideology. Bourgeois propaganda is trying by all means and through the most varied channels to support and cultivate religious prejudices and superstitions among the Soviet people and to incite them to religious fanaticism. Recently, several bourgeois radio stations have begun to broadcast Masses and various church rituals, biblical legends about the creation and existence of the world, etc.

Religious survivals were greatly revived during World War II. The enormous front that stretched for 3,000 kilometers took many human lives every day, and thousands of families were visited by bereavement. Alarm about the fate of friends and relatives inevitably engendered a desire to help in some way, in some way to prevent a possible misfortune. The enormous battles that unfolded on the fields of World War II frightened some people, and they were not able to understand quickly or correctly what was happening. And a person who has ceased to understand the world around him correctly—its threatening events and phenomena—becomes a victim of prejudices and falls under the influence of religious people and beliefs. [. . .]

The predominant philosophy in our society is Marxism-Leninism, which is in direct contradiction to religion. While Marxism-Leninism teaches that besides the material world, which develops according to its own inherent inner laws, there is no other world, religion maintains that the world was created by God and is directed by him. "The ways of

3. *iconostasis*—a wall, covered in icons, that separates the nave of an Orthodox church (where congregants worship) from the sanctuary of that church (which only the priest may enter). The altar stands in the sanctuary.

the Lord are inscrutable," maintains religion. The world can be known, proves dialectical materialism,[4] and this is brilliantly confirmed by the achievements of Soviet scientists in the area of science and technology.

The strength and vitality of the scientific philosophy consists in the fact that by revealing the laws of evolution, it arms men with the knowledge of ways to transform the world.

While religion maintains that the class division of society is eternal and man is helpless to change the social order that supposedly was established by God, Marxism-Leninism teaches that with knowledge of the laws of social evolution, human society can be altered after social oppression and exploitation of the workers have been eliminated. The correctness of Marxist-Leninist teaching is brilliantly confirmed by the experiences of the socialist countries that have freed themselves forever from the fetters of capitalist slavery.

The clergy of all religions maintain that man's happiness is only possible "in Heaven." The Marxist-Leninist philosophy proves and the practice of social evolution in socialist countries confirms that man himself is capable of creating on earth a just social system where everything is created for human happiness. [. . .]

SUBSTITUTION CEREMONIES

The cultural historian René Fülöp-Miller suggested in the 1920s that the "furious hostility with which the 'scientific materialism' of the Russians confronts all religion is one of the surest proofs that Bolshevism itself may perhaps be treated as a sort of religion."[5]

Those working to eliminate religious rites often created secular equivalents, equivalents that bore their own religious character. Bolshevism celebrated secularism to be sure, but secularism with messianic overtones.

The *Komsomol*—the youth wing of the communist party—challenged religious organizations for the time and devotion of Soviet youth. Factories sponsored activities to keep workers out of church; schools sponsored plays; and music guilds sponsored song contests. These "revolutionary counter-celebrations"—processions, plays, songs, competitions, musical performances, lectures, caroling, games, marches, charitable work—all shared characteristics of the religious ceremonies they hoped to supplant.

4. *dialectical materialism*—the fundamental tenets of Marxism.

5. René Fülöp-Miller, *The Mind and Face of Bolshevism* (New York: G. P. Putnam's Sons, 1927), 71–72.

Following are texts from five ceremonies, all explicitly intended to replace common religious ceremonies.

Red Baptism (1923)

Jennifer McDowell, "Soviet Civil Ceremonies," *Journal for the Scientific Study of Religion* 13 No. 3 (1974): 267–68.
Used by permission of John Wiley & Sons.

We cover you not with a cross, not with water and prayer—the inheritance of slavery and darkness, but with our red banner of struggle and labor, pierced by bullets and torn by bayonets . . . We bid the parents of the newborn child: bring up your child to be a devoted fighter for the liberation of the toilers of the entire world, an advocate of science and labor, an enemy of darkness and ignorance, [an ardent defender of the power of the Soviets] [. . .] To the patron of the newborn child, Comrade Kliukovkina, we give these instructions: as far as possible, aid and assist the parents in their educational work and in their concerns for the future heiress of our general cause. [The workers, having signed this document, turn to the child with the words]: With joy we greet you in the face of your future, in the name of which we have given hundreds of thousands of lives, in the name of which we are all prepared to die. When your reason has been strengthened, read through these lines, realize these ideas, dash into the ranks of fighters, liquidate the remnants of slavery and suffering, in which humanity has been for centuries.

Red Wedding (n.d.)

Jennifer McDowell, "Soviet Civil Ceremonies," *Journal for the Scientific Study of Religion* 13 No. 3 (1974): 268.
Used by permission of John Wiley & Sons.

Today, the day of the formation of your family, we hope that you will live your life together well, that you will live it in such a fashion that you, Mikhail, and you, Nadezhda, and your future children will always be faithful to the support of Soviet power. You love one another. And love is a flame. Let there not be in your life a destructive fire. Let love be a guiding star for you, a bonfire which warms the wayfarer. Support this life-giving flame by respect and care for one another.

A Komsomol Christmas Carol (ca. 1922–1923)

Jennifer McDowell, "Soviet Civil Ceremonies," *Journal for the
Scientific Study of Religion* 13 No. 3 (1974): 267 n1.
Used by permission of John Wiley & Sons.

Your Komsomol Christmas[6]
Restoring to the world the light of reason
Serving the worker's revolution,
Blooming under the five-pointed star,
We greet you, sun of the commune,
We see you on the heights of the future,
Russian Komsomol, glory to you!

Passport Ceremony (n.d.)

Jennifer McDowell, "Soviet Civil Ceremonies," *Journal for the
Scientific Study of Religion* 13 No. 3 (1974): 274.
Used by permission of John Wiley & Sons.

Our young comrade!
Today you have received a passport[7] . . . years will pass and much of that which you will have experienced and seen will be forgotten, but this day will remain forever in your memory, in your heart. You are young now, full of strength, you have so much energy, so much audacious daring! And life is so beautiful! And you and your friends are faced with making it still more beautiful. Step through life boldly, be a genuine human being, love your native land, be faithful to the Communist Party and to your people. Carry through your entire life a thirst for knowledge, for creative endeavors. Sometimes it will not be easy for you, perhaps very difficult. But be courageous, do not give way to momentary weakness. Know: a decisive human being will always find a way out of a difficult situation. Let the bright sun of reason always light up your path, let your good deeds warm and gratify people, and may work always bring joy to you.

6. *Your Komsomol Christmas*—this carol, sung by Komsomol members who traveled caroling from door to door, is a parody of the following carol: "Thy nativity, O Christ our God / Hath arisen upon the world as the light of wisdom / For at it, they who worshipped the stars / Were, by a star, / Taught to adore you, the sun of righteousness / And to know you, the Orient from on high. / O Lord, Glory to you."

7. *passport*—all Soviet citizens required passports to travel within the country.

Oath on Induction into the Worker-Peasant Red Army (1918)

Mass Culture in Soviet Russia: Tales, Poems, Songs, Movies, Plays, and Folklore, 1917–1953, ed. James von Geldern and Richard Stites (Bloomington: Indiana University Press, 1995), 15.

Leon Trotsky, people's commissar of army and navy affairs, wrote this oath the year he assumed command of the armed forces. It echoes oaths administered upon entry into the prerevolutionary tsarist army, but unlike those oaths, it makes no mention of "Almighty God," it does not reference "his Holy Gospel," and the oath-taker does not promise to "kiss the words and cross of my Savior." Trotsky instead directs the oath-taker's attention to "the power of the worker-peasant government," the new source of morality and fealty.[8]

1. I, son of the laboring people, citizen of the Soviet Republic, assume the title of warrior in the worker-peasant army.

2. Before the laboring classes of Russia and the entire world, I accept the obligation to carry this title with honor, to study the art of war conscientiously, and to guard national and military property from spoil and plunder as if it were the apple of my eye.

3. I accept the obligation to observe revolutionary discipline and unquestioningly carry out all orders of my commanders, who have been invested with their rank by the power of the worker-peasant government.

4. I accept the obligation to restrain myself and my comrades from all conduct that might debase the dignity of citizens of the Soviet Republic, and to direct all my thoughts and actions to the great cause of liberating the laboring masses.

5. I accept the obligation to answer every summons of the worker-peasant government to defend the Soviet Republic from all danger and the threats of all enemies, and to spare neither my strength nor my very life in the battle for the Russian Soviet Republic, for the cause of socialism and the brotherhood of peoples.

6. If I should with malicious intent go back on this my solemn vow, then let my fate be universal contempt and let the righteous hand of revolutionary law chastise me.

8. Prisiaga v Russkoi imperatorskoi armii," in "Voennaia prisiaga," *Vikipedia* [sic], https://ru.wikipedia.org/wiki/Военная_присяга, accessed 14 August 2015.

Church under Stalin

Joseph Stalin's regime (1920s to 1952) persecuted the Russian Orthodox Church relentlessly. Russia had some fifty-four thousand church parishes in 1917; by 1939 this number had fallen to a mere several hundred. More than one hundred thousand bishops, priests, monks, and nuns were shot during 1937 and 1938 alone.[1]

Persecution of the church, however, ceased almost entirely after 1943, when Stalin enlisted its support in the war of "Holy Russia" against Nazi Germany. That same year Stalin permitted the election of a patriarchate. After the war, Orthodoxy in Russia experienced something of a rebirth. The patriarchate reopened theological schools, and thousands of churches, once empty and derelict, began to hold services again. By 1959 active churches numbered nearly twenty-five thousand.

The price, however, was steep. The church became in many respects an agent of the state. Many clerics (numbers remain a matter of conjecture) secretly worked for Soviet security and spy agencies. Church leaders adopted a fawning, almost sycophantic attitude toward Soviet leaders. One such example is a speech from 1949, delivered by Patriarch Aleksei I (1945–1970) in celebration of Stalin's seventieth birthday.[2]

---

1. See section 35, "Church under Stalin," in the online supplement.

2. See document 35.6, "Solzhenitsyn Accuses the Church of Complicity," in the online supplement for one response to such rhetoric.

Patriarch Aleksei Celebrates Stalin's Seventieth Birthday (21 December 1949)

Aleksei, "Sviateishego Patriarkha Moskovskogo i vseia Rusi Aleksiia
v Bogoiavlenskom Patriarshem Sobore pered molebnom po sluchaiu
semidesiatiletiia Iosifa Vissarionovicha Stalina," in *Aleksii, Patriarkh Mokovskii
i Vseia Rusi: slova rechi, poslaniia, obrashcheniia, stati* (Moskva: Moskovskoi
Patriarkhii, 1954), 2:173–74. Translated by Bryn Geffert. CC BY-SA.

Today our country celebrates the seventieth birthday of its leader, Iosif
[Joseph] Stalin.

Expressions of love, greetings, good wishes, and recognitions of his
great contributions to the homeland—of all that is morally right and
all that represents the ideals of striving humanity—come rushing to him
from all corners of the earth.

The entire world acknowledges him as the leader, not only of the Soviet State, but of all working people. He is first in line among promoters
and defenders of peace among the peoples all around the world.

[. . .] [There is no] need to remind you that—thanks to his brilliant
leadership—our glorious army in the hour of the gravest trial ever to
befall our fatherland, defeated the powerful and evil enemy that attacked
it, and our homeland emerged from that crucible of testing stronger, more
glorious, and more powerful than ever.

Anyone personally acquainted with our leader is astounded by the
charm of his personality. He conquers his company with his considerate attitude toward everything, with his affection, with his extraordinary
knowledge of everything, with the strength and wisdom of his words,
and with the quick and favorable resolution of every question and thing
submitted to him.

We, the people of the church, should thank him especially for his sympathetic treatment of our church's needs. In the civic sphere he resolves
every church question favorably for the church. In him our holy church
has a loyal defender.

As is typical for us, we gather today in our churches in great numbers so that we, with believers and people of the church, may participate
through prayer in this celebration of a day momentous both for him and
for all of us. We ask God for continued blessings on his great service to
the fatherland and the people, and for success in all his good initiatives.

Yes, God will grant him many years of health and prosperity to stand
at the helm of our homeland's governance. And God will prosper our
country under his wise leadership over many, many years of joy and happiness for our people.

Amen.

Orthodoxy and Ecumenism

B etween November 1917 and March 1921 more than one million people fled Russia and Bolshevik persecution; Russian Orthodox Christians dispersed throughout Europe. The Russian Historical Archive estimates that between 635,000 and 755,000 unassimilated Russians lived in Europe by 1923. Some took refuge with friends and relatives. Some became homeless. Nicolas (Nikolai) Zernov, a Russian émigré whose work appears below, described his fellow travelers as "lonely, misunderstood and destitute," feeling "helpless and unwelcome in Europe." Russian Orthodoxy lacked a tradition of large-scale relief efforts, and funds simply did not exist to support the poverty-stricken. Less than 10 percent of Russian priests made it out of the country, leaving Russian émigrés largely without spiritual leadership.

Many émigrés looked to the Church of England and the British government for relief. Orthodox churches in the Balkans sought Britain's financial and political support during the chaos following the First World War. Serbian Orthodox came to know British life well when they studied in English universities. The French government offered aid to Russians in Paris. So did the American oil baron John D. Rockefeller. Christians throughout Europe donated to various funds. The Young Men's Christian Association (YMCA) became a major source of aid.

Westerners who supported relief efforts took an interest in learning more about the Orthodox believers they helped. Several official and unofficial organizations in the Church of England investigated the possibility of intercommunion between the churches. Some even talked of reunification. Orthodox believers, living among Roman Catholics and virtually every major branch of Protestantism, now found themselves—many for the first time and often uncomfortably—forced to define their relationship to the rest of Christendom. Isolation was no longer a reality or a possibility.

The Russian emigration coincided with a burgeoning ecumenical movement, which reached its zenith between the First and Second World Wars. Many Christians during the 1920s believed that the various branches of the Christian church stood on the verge of reunification. In 1927 luminaries from Orthodox, Anglican, and numerous Protestant confessions arrived in Lausanne, Switzerland, from all corners of the globe for a conference on "Faith and Order," designed to reconcile theological differences and lay the groundwork for church reunion.

But the ecumenical movement proved challenging for the Eastern churches. Orthodox believers soon found themselves at odds with each other regarding Orthodoxy's proper attitude toward other Christian confessions. In the early 1920s the ecumenical patriarch in Constantinople bent over backwards to cultivate ties with Western churches: he was shocked by the denunciations these overtures elicited from Orthodox colleagues.

Russian émigrés who settled in France, where exiled academic theologians founded the Orthodox Theological Institute in Paris, generally welcomed ecumenical discussions. Some faculty members at the institute played leading roles in Lausanne and at a second conference in Edinburgh, Scotland, in 1937. Politically and theologically conservative Russian émigrés, on the other hand, who established their own synod in Serbia, tended to eschew ecumenism, considering the movement anti-Orthodox at best and the work of the Antichrist at worst. Greeks, Bulgarians, Romanians, Serbs, and representatives of the ecumenical patriarchate often found themselves feuding with one another—unable to present a united front that could effectively negotiate with the huge body of Protestants interested in dialog. (The Roman Catholic Church simply forbade its members from participating in ecumenical conferences.)

The readings in this section are from Orthodox theologians, clergy, and laity trying to make sense of the ecumenical movement and Orthodoxy's place within it. The significance of the texts, however, extends far beyond ecumenical concerns: the ecumenical movement forced the Orthodox churches to confront fundamental questions about

Christianity and the church of Christ. What, exactly, is the Orthodox Church? Where do the boundaries of the church lie, and do they encompass Christians who belong to other confessions? Can Christians who do not belong to the Orthodox Church be saved? Should Orthodox churches identify themselves with the nations in which they reside, or is Orthodoxy, by definition, pan-national or even extranational or antinational? What about the Roman Catholic Church? Is there hope for reunion with the See of Peter? Are divisions within Christendom entirely the fault of Protestants or Roman Catholics, or does Orthodoxy bear some of the blame? Is there, ultimately, any hope for a reunited church?

Sergei Bulgakov Defines the Church (1927)

Sergius Bulgakow, "The Church's Ministry," in *The Orthodox Church in the Ecumenical Movement: Documents and Statements, 1925–1975,* ed. Constantin Patelos (Geneva: World Council of Churches, 1978): 166–71. Used by permission of The World Council of Churches.

Few characters in twentieth-century Orthodoxy are more interesting than Sergei Bulgakov, whom we encountered above. A committed Marxist as a young man, Bulgakov grew disenchanted with the secular intelligentsia, gradually found his way back to the church, and emerged in the 1920s and 1930s as an original and controversial theologian. He also became a dedicated advocate for the reunion of all Christian churches. The following text, taken from a speech Bulgakov delivered to the ecumenical conference in Lausanne, Switzerland, constitutes his attempt to define "the church" and to engage other churches—particularly Protestant churches—that do not employ priests or bishops. This essay reflects Bulgakov's commitment to the church's hierarchy and the key role Orthodox clergy play in conveying grace and charismatic gifts. But Bulgakov's commitment to the hierarchy coincided with a belief that the church must operate in harmony with "every organism" of its body, a belief that troubled Bulgakov's more conservative colleagues, who placed more emphasis on the independent rights and prerogatives of church leaders.

The church is Christ's body, in which there are many members, differing from each other and yet indispensable to the body, and in that sense each has the same value. They are many: the body is one. This we learn from St. Paul (1 Corinthians 12), who reveals to us the fundamentals of the church's hierarchy; for the church has a hierarchy and its constitution is hierarchical, and yet it is an organism rather than an organization, a mystical unity rather than a juridical institution. This does not run contrary to the fact that some sides of the church's life are clothed in legal form, and express themselves alike in canon law and also in common, public and private law. [. . .]

Russian theology expresses the fundamental essence of church unity in a word for which no other language has an equivalent. *Sobornost* connotes alike the catholicity[1] of the church—the integral totality of its being—and its spiritual character as the oneness of its members in faith and love; its outer aspect, as at all points resting on the freely-chosen unanimity of its members; and lastly its ecumenical character, which links it to all nations and subordinates to it all local churches. It is the conception of *sobornost,* summing up as it does the organic nature of the church, which underlies the doctrine of the hierarchy in the Orthodox system. Every member of the spiritual organism has his part in the life of the whole [. . .]

The laity, no less than the clergy, has its place and value in the church as a whole. The status of the layman is not negative, it is not merely a non-clerical status, but is rather a special order, imparted in confirmation. [. . .]

Priesthood within the church is related inseparably to the laity, and the relationship is not merely that of ruler to subject: it is also a relation of mutual help and of unity within the *sobornost.* The priest requires the cooperation of the laity in the administration of the sacraments, and the laity take their share in service and sacrament through singing, responses and prayers. [. . .]

[. . .] Still, the episcopate has the right to use its power and authority in the defense and proclamation of the truths acknowledged by the church, and this is what the bishops, in local and ecumenical councils, have done, when speaking in the name of the church and expressing not their individual views but the faith of the whole Christian people, with their expressed or implied assent. The presence of representatives of the whole church, clergy and laity, at local councils, gives visible expression to this assent.

[. . .] Only one ministry is withheld entirely from the laity, that of the mysteries—the celebration of the holy Eucharist and the other sacraments. No human consent or election can confer this power upon men, even though an act of election is a preliminary condition of ordination. The divine power of Christ alone, given to the apostles and transmitted

1. *catholicity*—comprehensiveness or freedom from exclusiveness or narrowness.

by apostolic succession,[2] can confer it. The hands laid by the bishop upon the head of an ordinand[3] are the hands of the apostles. It is Christ himself, our supreme bishop, who ordains his ministers. [. . .]

[. . .] The charismatic authority of the episcopate is not an idea but a fact, before which we must bow in gratitude to God, humbling ourselves beneath his holy will. This authority alone conserves and fortifies the fullness of charismatic life in the church, and restores to the right path such groups as have strayed outside church unity into isolation.

The task of reunion remains merely abstract unless it is approached by way of intellectual interchange and the discussion of principles. As an idea, it requires an incarnation: as a problem, it demands to be realized. The union of Christians cannot be brought about otherwise than by a sharing of the same cup at the holy table[4] and by the ministry of a priesthood that is an integral unity and indubitably charismatic.

At the present time we find that the apostolic succession is broken and set aside in some quarters,[5] while in others it has lost its evidential clearness through the historical complications of the Reformation and the Western schism; while in all these quarters there is a historical reaction against the Roman clerical system, although the papacy has not violated the apostolic succession.

The Orthodox priesthood of the Eastern church has preserved all its vigor and charismatic purity, and that church embraces in love all who seek it, expecting from them no juridical submission but rather brotherly love. When it is God's pleasure to accomplish that work of reunion to which our prayers look forward, may all be kindled with the longing for one undoubted charismatic priesthood that will rebuild what has perished and complete what is doubtful, in such modes as the love of the church and the grace of the Holy Spirit shall reveal. In that day the eyes of all will turn toward our mother, the Orthodox Eastern church, and toward its charismatic episcopate, for that healing of infirmities and renewal of exhausted energies of which a prayer in our ordinal speaks.

2. *apostolic succession*—the doctrine, common to both the Roman Catholic Church and the Eastern Orthodox churches, asserting that authority for ministry in the church passes down from the original apostles, through successive generations of bishops, only when bishops consecrate other bishops by the "laying on of hands." Most Eastern Orthodox believe that ministries not conferred through apostolic succession are either invalid or inadequate.

3. *ordinand*—one being ordained.

4. *sharing of the same cup at the holy table*—jointly partaking in the Eucharist, that is, drinking wine together from the same cup.

5. *some quarters*—that is, within Protestant denominations.

This is the road that the reunion of the church must follow: the whole past history of the church, no less than its present condition, makes this clear. And from this point of view our present gathering is symbolic; Christians from all over the world are here, and the only absentees are the representatives of the Roman hierarchy, which conceives of union as involving submission to the absolute power of the pope. But here you behold, present among you, bishops and ministers of the Orthodox church, and by their voice that church summons all men toward oneness in faith, in love, and in sacramental grace, in the words which come before the creed in the liturgy of the holy Eucharist: "Let us love one another, unto the confession, with one heart and soul, of the same faith."

Nicolas Zernov on Barriers to Reunion with Western Churches (1928)

Nicholas Zernoff, "Psychological Barriers to Reunion," *Journal of the Fellowship of St. Alban and St. Sergius* No. 2 (September 1928): 22–25.

Nikolai (Nicolas, to his English-speaking friends) Zernov fled Russia with his family in 1921. He spent four years in Serbia, where he came to detest the conservative, royalist Russian émigrés who settled there and occupied themselves with dreams of restoring the Russian tsar to power, while criticizing the very idea of serious discussions with non-Orthodox Christians. Arriving in England in 1928 with a shaky command of English, Zernov enrolled in Oxford University at age thirty, earned a doctorate in near-record time, and quickly found himself at the center of ecumenical discussions. He spent much of his early professional life traveling around England, teaching English laity and clergy about Eastern Orthodoxy while working tirelessly for a number of ecumenical organizations. He wrote the essay excerpted below the year he enrolled at Oxford, and it reflects the wide-eyed optimism of a young man convinced that centuries-old divisions could be overcome if only Christians would adopt positive and generous mindsets. The eminent theologian and co-ecumenist Georgy Florovsky[6] felt little fondness for Zernov, considering him naive and lacking in serious theological training and ability.

6. See document 39.1, "Georgy Florovsky on Limits of the Church," and document 39.3, "Florovsky on Historical Commonalities," both in the online supplement.

408   *Revolutions and Reevaluations*

[. . .] I think one can subdivide [barriers to church reunion] into two principal groups: dogmatic and psychological. The first are, of course, the fundamental barriers to reunion. [. . .] But I think that these at-first-sight-serious differences, in reality, will be comparatively easily overcome and will not be the stone against which we shall be dashed. [. . .] [I]t is much more difficult to overcome psychological differences that stand between us, and they frequently seem to be the more considerable the less they are dogmatically founded, or founded merely on church ignorance. These psychological barriers are both varied and numerous and I shall only consider those I have met in practice. [. . .]

1. *National pride,*[7] *failure to grasp the ecumenical nature of the church.* Both Russians and English possess a high degree of national pride, which is particularly clearly demonstrated in church life. The church is the favored property of the nation; the best forces of the nation are given to it. But, as a result of this, the conception of the ecumenical nature of Christianity is lost. The necessity of feeling ourselves within her as members of the one Christian society is forgotten. This strong, national love of the church is perhaps the love that is most difficult to overcome. Christianity does not destroy nationalities; on the contrary it discloses national consciousness, and we realize this well; but quite often we fail to notice how nationalistic principles in the church come to obscure within us our ecumenical consciousness. [. . .]

2. *Church "restfulness"—lack of knowledge about each other.* [. . .] In practice the overwhelming majority of the Russian Orthodox population lived outside any contact with non-Orthodox Christianity. [. . .] The average Russian Orthodox received complete spiritual satisfaction in the bosom of his mother church and had no direct urge to be interested in or wish for a reunion with Anglicanism. For the average Russian or for the average Englishman—Anglicanism and Orthodoxy were mutually almost non-existent values. The years of the [First] World War, and for Russians especially of the Revolution, undermined this church exclusiveness. Russian church people in their struggle with militant atheism bearing an international character, came to realize their loneliness and felt the importance of a fellowship between Christian nations. [. . .]

3. *The third obstacle—our differences of culture.* To Russian Orthodox people Western culture always seemed heretical and hostile to Orthodoxy. Nothing good could come to the Orthodox from the West. [. . .] All the Orthodox East, including Russia, inherited from Byzantium on the one hand a feeling of cultural superiority in relation to the barbaric West—for Orthodoxy is the direct heir of the most noble Hellenic culture. [. . .] This

7. *National pride*—here Zernov has in mind the nationalistic monarchists from Russia who settled in Serbia.

feeling, even now, doubtlessly lives in the Russian church consciousness. We are accustomed both to look down on Western Christians and at the same time to fear them, and we are not at all used to encountering sincerity and true friendship in the West. This attitude has been cultivated for centuries and only extensive and carefully planned work can do away with the prejudice. While on the side of the English there exits another though very similar feeling. The East is represented as possessing a lower kind of culture, which has become set in some primitive form of development, behind the times, from which there is nothing to learn and which one cannot consider as equal to Western culture. [. . .]

4. [. . .] The whole Orthodox church in the course of centuries recognized only the eastern ceremonial[8] developed in the Constantinople patriarchate. All other ceremonials gradually dropped out of use in the Orthodox church. They were retained and developed only either in heretical eastern communities, or in the West amongst Roman Catholics. Orthodoxy loves ceremonial, comprehends deeply its mystical strength, its significance for the religious life of the believers. [. . .] We Orthodox frequently find it difficult to imagine the possibility of a true unity in fundamentals with freedom and diversity in details. It is difficult for us to imagine, for example, a clean-shaven Orthodox priest, a Western Orthodox Mass—only quite recently did these ideas began to penetrate into the masses of believers. [. . .] [T]o the majority of Russians an Anglican church in communion with Orthodoxy would, quite involuntarily, be thought of in terms of customary Russian forms—with an iconostasis[9] in churches, with the Liturgy of St. John Chrysostom, with priests wearing beards and long hair, etc. This is, of course, a very great failure to understand the structure of the ecumenical church. [. . .]

For the reunion of the churches to be attained, it is necessary, on the one hand, for the Anglicans to cultivate and develop a consciousness of the church as of a visible body, and for the Orthodox, on the other, a better understanding of that which is eternal and unchangeable in the church and of that which can be freely changed in different epochs and by different nations. [. . .]

[. . .] Only a disinterested love of the church, only a fiery desire to see the words of our Lord Jesus Christ fulfilled "That they all may be one"— can serve as lawful incentives in this great work. It calls for many efforts and sacrifices on our part; it will again and again confront us with the tragic depth of strife and lack of understanding, which always enfeebles

---

8. *eastern ceremonial*—the Eastern liturgy and forms of worship.

9. *iconostasis*—a wall, covered in icons, that separates the nave of an Orthodox church (where congregants worship) from the sanctuary of that church (which only the priest may enter). The altar stands in the sanctuary.

Christian mankind: but we must not lose heart at this if we have the faith that in working for the reunion of the churches we are fulfilling God's will. [. . .]

Archbishop Serafim Condemns the Ecumenical Movement (1948)

Archbishop Serafim, "Should the Russian Orthodox Church Participate in the Ecumenical Movement?" *Major Portions of the Proceedings of the Conference of the Heads of the Autocephalous Orthodox Churches Held in Moscow, July, 1948*, ed. Paul Anderson, trans. O. F. Clarke (Paris: YMCA Press, 1948), 209–19.

The Russian archbishop Serafim delivered the following speech at a 1948 gathering in Moscow of Orthodox leaders from Eastern Bloc countries. Orthodox clerics from other nations refused to attend, believing that the gathering, which was sanctioned by the Soviet government (the proceedings opened with a salute to Joseph Stalin), could not be taken seriously. Here we find a denunciation of the ecumenical movement in terms still used by some quarters of Eastern Orthodoxy.

[. . .] Up till now the Orthodox church in Russia has not joined the ecumenical movement. It is likewise desirable that in the future it should have nothing in common with this movement owing to the considerations that follow.

The Russian Orthodox church is asked to take part in the ecumenical conference as one among a multitude of church organizations, each conceived as a church. But we Orthodox Christians confess that—in the strict sense of the word—one can describe a church only as one community of true-believing Christians, established by God himself for our salvation. But to describe every heretical society as a church implies that one lacks a correct conception of the church, and tramples our faith's dogma of the church, as articulated in the ninth article of the Nicene Creed.[10] [. . .]

[The] ecumenical point of view diverges completely from the Orthodox approach. [. . .] Our church never considered that heretics were part of the body of Christ. And how is it possible to regard this ecumenical point of view as Orthodox when the ecumenical councils always anathema-

10. *ninth article of the Nicene Creed*—this article refers to "*one* [emphasis added] holy catholic and apostolic church."

tized heretics, that is, excommunicated them from the church? It appears that the ecumenists in their teaching about the church do not recognize the authority of the ecumenical councils. [. . .]

However strange it may seem, the ecumenists [. . .] assign to this apostolic church all the so-called "Christian churches" that have no apostolic origin or succession. They regard all heretical confessions as belonging to the apostolic church, in spite of the fact that Paul, the greatest of the apostles, distinguishes all heretics from the Orthodox church and anathematizes them: "But though we, or an angel from Heaven, should preach to you any Gospel other than that which we preached to you, let him be anathema" (Galatians 1:8).

But most of all, Orthodox ecumenists sin against the ninth article of the Nicene Creed and its description of the church as holy, when they include heretics in the holy church. The church is called holy because she is the distributor of the grace of the Holy Spirit, which she imparts to the faithful in the sacrament of chrismation[11] when baptism is administered. [. . .]

But the Protestants cannot possess this blessing [of chrismation], which is most precious to us, this quickening grace of the Holy Spirit with its holiness, for they have no sacrament of chrismation. In baptism, as is apparent from the "Orthodox confession," we are only purified from sins; we die to the life of the flesh and we are reborn of the Holy Spirit for a new and holy life. The latter is made possible for us only with the help of that grace we receive in the sacrament of chrismation. [. . .]

[. . .] Members of the Orthodox church, while being sinners—however great their sins—can always through the sacrament of confession and with the help of efficacious and saving grace become saints, that is, attain a true and perfect holiness through grace. But for heretics, either individually or in whole groups and organizations, this holiness will never be inherent, for in heretics the grace of the sacrament of chrismation and the grace of confession do not work. Heretics can become saints only after repentance, or by renouncing their heresies and reuniting with the Orthodox church. Only then can non-Orthodox Christians be included in the holy church of Christ.

The disobedience of Orthodox ecumenists leads them to announce that "the dividing walls between the churches do not extend up to Heaven, to the head who is Christ, but descend to the very heart of the church, to the Holy Spirit."

But these dividing walls—namely the divisions between the Orthodox church and heretics—began to arise during the ecumenical councils. They arose to preserve the Orthodox faith from perdition through an intermingling with destructive heresies. These divisions arose to fulfill the words

11. *chrismation*—anointing with oil.

of Christ: "Think you that I am come to give peace on earth? Nay, but rather division" (Luke 12:18). [...]

The tenth rule of the apostles states, "If anyone will pray with those who have been excommunicated from the church, even if this be only in a house, the same shall be excommunicated himself." While the forty-fifth apostolic rule says, "A bishop or a priest, or even a deacon, if he has only prayed with the heretics, shall be excommunicated. But if he allows them to act in some manner as ministers of the church—he shall 'be deposed.'" [...] Such a statement, however, in no way contradicts the spirit of Christian love and tolerance, which is characteristic of the Orthodox church, because there is a great difference between tolerating those who have strayed from the faith [...] and living with them in external civil fellowship, and in entering into religious contact with them without making any difference. The latter would imply that we are not only not striving to convert them to Orthodoxy, but that we are actually ourselves uncertain in our faith.

[...] What fruits will our church receive from participating in these ecumenical conferences? Only bad fruits, of course.

[...] [Protestant propaganda] has as its aim the union of Orthodoxy with Protestantism and the annihilation of the Orthodox church. Making use of its tremendous resources, Protestants spread their propaganda through the press and publish books and papers. In doing this they not only "smear" our veneration of icons, our rites, and Orthodoxy in general, but they also argue against the Bible, against its portrayal of the creation of the world by God in six days; they have a negative attitude toward biblical accounts of some miracles. As a result of such propaganda a multitude of various sects such as Adventists, Baptists, Methodists, Pentecostals, Evangelicals, etc., is springing up in Orthodox countries. [...]

Ecumenism at present cannot celebrate victory for it does not include all the Orthodox churches within its ecumenical, universal ring.

Let us not grant it victory! Remembering its essence and its aims, let us completely renounce the ecumenical movement, for here is a retreat from the Orthodox faith, a betrayal of and treason toward Christ, which we must avoid at all costs, so that we may fulfill the words of St. Seraphim, "Woe be to him who retreats even an iota from the holy ecumenical councils." [...]

Women's Ordination

Q uestions about the ordination of women have roiled Roman Catholicism and Protestantism over the past century. Most but not all Protestant denominations now ordain female pastors. The pope and virtually all cardinals in the Roman Catholic Church, however, maintain a firm stance against women's ordination, although the question is one of fierce debate among the laity and, to a lesser extent, nuns and priests.

The question of women's ordination has received far less attention in the Eastern Orthodox Church. Although a few Orthodox theologians have raised the issue in recent decades, the debate has not gained much traction. Still, Eastern Orthodoxy has not entirely ignored the issue, thanks in large part to the issue's prominence at ecumenical gatherings.

Gennadios Limouris against Ordaining Women (1988)

Gennadios Limouris, "Orthodox Reactions to Non-Orthodox Positions in Support of the Ordination of Women," in *The Place of the Woman in the Orthodox Church and the Question of the Ordination of Women* (Istanbul: Ecumenical Patriarchate, 1988), 265–85. Used by permission of the Ecumenical Patriarchate of Constantinople.

Constantly dogged by questions about women's ordination at international symposia, the ecumenical patriarch summoned Orthodox theologians and church leaders to Istanbul in 1986 to produce a unified response.

For many Christians today the possibility of conferring the priesthood upon women has become an essential item in what they call the "liberation of women." [. . .]

The movement for women's liberation came primarily from the United States in the early 1960s and had a profound effect on the realm of religion. Shortly after the movement began, feminists decided that sexism had penetrated the church throughout Christian history and judged Christian denominations as patently unfair to women. Women began to scrutinize the structures of the Christian denominations, including their beliefs and theology, and concluded that all of Christendom had been trained by male chauvinism.

Feminists also noted that men usually made up the "power stratum" of the churches; men, and only men, were usually ordained to be pastors, priests or bishops. In addition, God was constantly addressed in "masculine" terms (Father, Son and Holy Spirit—he), thus alienating women from God, while men could more easily be associated with him. Also, women—for the most part—were relegated to less important positions and tasks in church gatherings. [. . .]

The priest, as St. John Chrysostom affirms, is primarily the "iconic representation of Christ, the groom of the bride—not the bride of the bride." The priest is ontologically[1] bound, as an iconic symbol, to the incarnate Logos.[2] He does not merely represent Christ's function as "teacher" and "king" to the community. To say it otherwise would be to misunderstand the priesthood in terms of its functional dimension only. The priest, rather, is a living icon of the bridegroom and truly acts in the place of Christ (*vice Christi*). While the priest may preach, counsel, direct others, and do works of mercy, his performance of these ministries is unique, primarily because of his sacramental priesthood by which he is the father of a Eucharistic community. [. . .]

Even to discuss the lack of participation of women in the ordained priesthood as an "exclusion" implies that they are somehow "included." The woman is simply not a father, her "very womanhood precludes it since she cannot possibly be a husband and father." According to Orthodox theology, to speak of an ordained female Christian priesthood is a contradiction in terms. It is a theoretical issue for discussion without any theological basis, since the woman cannot symbolize Christ's masculine ontological relationship with the church, his bride, or his eternal sonship to the eternal Father.

The Orthodox church affirms that manhood and womanhood are not interchangeable. [. . .]

---

1. *ontologically*—by his very nature or existence.
2. *incarnate Logos*—Christ.

To an Orthodox Christian today it seems not so much ironic as tragic that, at a time when Christians everywhere are praying for church unity, we should see a new chasm opening up to create new divisions. And in Orthodox eyes, at any rate, it is a chasm of horrifying dimensions. "The ordination of women to the priesthood" amounts for us to a radical and irreparable mutilation of faith, the rejection of the explicit teaching of holy scripture, and "constitutes a threat of an irreversible and irreparable act that, if it becomes reality, will produce a new, and this time . . . final division among Christians." Another Orthodox voice should say that "the acceptance of women priests involves a fundamental and radical rejection of the very substance of the biblical and Christian understanding of God and creation . . . " These may seem to be strong words for non-Orthodox Christians, but this has been the reality of the Orthodox church for many centuries and still is today. [. . .]

A French-speaking Swiss Reformed theologian, Jean-Jacques von Allmen, writes: "The New Testament, in spite of the chance for the total renewal that it provides for women as well as for men, never testifies that a woman could be, in a public and authorized way, representative of Christ. To no woman does Jesus say, 'He who hears you, hears me.' To no woman does he entrust the ministry of public preaching. To no woman does he give the command to baptize or to preside at the Communion of his body and blood. To no woman does he commit his flock."

We are confronted here with the question of our obedience to Christ: Are we as Christians obliged to remain faithful to his example or not? Do we accept "the givenness" and finality of the revelation in Jesus, and do we believe in the apostolic character of the church? Do we wish to belong to the same church as that which Christ founded? The church today claims to be "apostolic." This means that its faith is based upon the testimony of Christ's eyewitnesses, its ministry of Christ and that it is defined in terms of the unique, unrepeatable act of God, accomplished in Christ once . . . No new revelation can complete or replace what Jesus Christ did "when the fullness of the time finally came" (Galatians 4:4). [. . .]

Here, then, is the first and fundamental argument that the Orthodox church employs. Faced by the unanimous and unvarying practice of the church throughout the ages and up to our own time, we, living in the twentieth century, have no authority to alter the basic patterns of Christian faith and life. Our appeal as Orthodox is not to holy scripture alone nor to the holy tradition alone, but to both at once.

We do not appeal simply to the fact that Christ chose only men to be apostles, but to the fact that for more than twenty centuries Christ's body, the church, has never ordained anyone except men to the priesthood and episcopate. Our appeal is addressed to the total life of the church over two thousand years—and not only to what was said, but also to what was done. [. . .]

Sometimes it is claimed that the appeal to tradition is nothing more than an argument from silence, and therefore lacking in cogency. Indeed, it is not correct to say that until our own days the matter was passed over in silence. On the contrary, it was often discussed in the early church. The apostolic church order, as we have seen, states directly that women are not to officiate at the Eucharist. A hundred years earlier, Tertullian (d. ca. 225) was equally definite: "It is not permitted for a woman to speak in church, not yet to teach, nor to anoint, nor to make the offering, nor to claim for herself any office performed by men or any priestly ministry." The apostolic constitutions (late 300s) discuss the ministry of women in some detail, and in the same terms as Tertullian. Women are neither to preach nor to baptize, and *a fortiori* it is implied that they do not celebrate the Eucharist. The reason given points specifically to the faithfulness of Christ's example—he never entrusted such tasks to women, although he could easily have done so; thus the church has no power to commission for work of this kind.

Nor did the question of women priests remain merely hypothetical in the early history of the church. Various heretical groups in the second and fourth centuries had women as priests and bishops: the Gnostic Marcosians, for example, and the Montanists, and the Colyridians.[3] When referring to these last, St. Epiphanius[4] examines at length the possibility of women priests. "Since the beginning of time," he states, "a woman has never served God as priest."

After so many generations, Christians cannot now start to ordain women to the priesthood for the first time. Such, then, is St. Epiphanius' conclusion concerning women and the ministerial priesthood: "God never appointed to this ministry a single woman on earth." The ordination of women to priesthood is an innovation, without any sound basis whatsoever in holy tradition.

The evidence is explicit and unanimous, and there is nothing further to be said. [...]

---

3. *Marcosians . . . Montanists . . . Colyridians*—founded by a woman, the Marcosian sect (200s and 300s) allowed women to administer the Eucharist and to prophecy. Montanists (late 100s) permitted both men and women to preside over worship services. Colyridians (known to exist in the 300s) apparently worshipped the Virgin Mary as a goddess.

4. *St. Epiphanius*—(early 300s–403) known as a staunch defender of Orthodoxy.

Constantinos Yakarinis in Favor of Ordaining Women (1999)

Constantinos Yakarinis, "The Priesthood of Women: A Look at
Patristic Teaching," in *Orthodox Women Speak: Discerning the "Signs
of the Times,"* ed. Kyriaki Karidoyanes FitzGerald (Brookline, MA:
Holy Cross Orthodox Press, 1999), 167–75. Used by permission
of Holy Cross Orthodox Press, Brookline, Massachusetts.

Constantinos Yakarinis, a professor of education at the University of Athens, delivered the address excerpted below at a conference hosted in 1996 and 1997 by the World Council of Churches, the ecumenical patriarchate, and the patriarchate of Antioch. Although Yakarinis promised not to take a stance on the question of whether women should be ordained, his speech made clear his receptiveness to the idea. Note that, much like Limouris, he relies heavily on tradition but derives much different conclusions from that tradition than did theologians and church leaders at Istanbul in 1986.

The ordination of women is certainly one of the most controversial issues in the Christian world today. [. . .]

When we try as Christians to resolve these disagreements, we immediately face the question of which criteria should be used to decide them. Do we appeal simply to the words of the Bible? Or to the authority of two millennia of tradition embodied in the church? Or to the working of the Holy Spirit in the church today? Or to our God-given powers of reasoning about such matters? And if we appeal to more than one of these criteria, which if any are to have priority? For all Christians, these are theological questions.

The priesthood of women has had a long history. It arose as a serious issue in the Christian community for the first time during the period of Gnosticism and Montanism.[5] It was revived in the divided Christian church eighteen hundred years later. A century after that, the question still has a dynamic in the life of the church that threatens to undermine all efforts to restore church unity. [. . .]

My research has been based exclusively on the patristic and dogmatic teaching of the Orthodox church. I should make absolutely clear at the outset that I am not going to answer the question, "Should women be

---

5. *Montanism*—Montanists (late 100s) permitted both men and women to preside over worship services.

accepted into the priestly office or not?" I believe that a decision on such a disputed fundamental issue belongs to the church. Consequently, any disagreement on it can be overcome only after long and exhaustive theological research. What is needed is theological common ground, and I believe my research can contribute positively to this quest.

[. . .] In this examination it emerged clearly that the critical point of the dispute is the "male character" of the incarnated God-Logos.[6] [. . .]

• The Mystery of the Incarnation •

[. . .] The incarnate Word[7] is the founder of the kingdom of God, the reason of our salvation and our eschatological hope. What does the Orthodox church believe and teach about incarnation according to the dogma of Chalcedon,[8] which is the cornerstone of the church?

Because both sides, for and against, focus on the male character of Christ, we must take the fact of God's incarnation as our starting point, basing this theologically on the dogma of Chalcedon. In other words, the answer to the problem is connected directly with the human nature of Christ, because the male character of his incarnation is at the heart of the problem.

The patristic understanding of the elements of the human nature of the incarnate Logos was summarized succinctly by John of Damascus: "all the attributes of the first Adam, save only his sin, these attributes being body and the intelligent and rational soul." According to biblical anthropology, Adam's human nature consisted of the following elements and properties:

—The image and likeness of God. [. . .] According to John of Damascus, "'after his image' clearly refers to the side of his nature that consists of mind and free will, whereas 'after his likeness' means likeness in virtue, so far as that is possible." Such an understanding implies that biological elements or characteristics are absent from the image and likeness, and that the image is only one for both sexes, male and female. [. . .]

—The first Adam—one and undivided human being and nature—has been "torn" into forms of existence, male and female. This distinction

---

6. *God-Logos*—Christ.

7. *incarnate Word*—Christ.

8. *dogma of Chalcedon*—theological statements formulated at the fourth ecumenical Council of Chalcedon in 451. The council issued what many (although not all) Eastern churches consider to be the definitive statement on the incarnation, that is, an understanding of Christ as both perfect God and perfect man—fully divine and fully human. See section 2, "Chalcedon and Non-Chalcedonian Churches," in the online supplement for a discussion of those who rejected the Council of Chalcedon.

was added provisionally at the end in order to enable the human being as created to survive in the conditions after the fall.[9]

—One of the most important divine properties was the ability of the human person to exercise a form of leadership and power over the creation. The grammatical form of the verb *archetosan* is plural. This means that both sexes have received from the creator the authority in equal terms to exercise sovereignty over the creation. This demonstrates in a clear and convincing way their equality as human beings and bearers to the same degree of the special properties, qualities and abilities assigned to both of them. [. . .]

Let us now take a synoptic look at the patristic teaching on what the God-Logos actually assumed, in regard to his human nature, in his incarnation.

1. According to John of Damascus, "'the nature of the word' means neither the subsistence alone, nor 'the common nature of the subsistence,' but 'the common nature viewed as a whole in the subsistence of the word'"—in other words, body and soul. Human nature as a whole, both male and female, has been assumed by the incarnate Logos. If Christ as human being had belonged to the divided or "torn" human nature, he would not have been able to offer any healing to the human race, because he himself would have needed healing—and the female would have been excluded from his salvation.

It should be noted that the perfection of the human being does not exist in Adam or Eve, nor in the Virgin Mary, nor in John the Baptist, but only in the incarnate Word, who is the archetype of humanity, the image of perfection of all human beings, male and female.

2. Theologically, his conception by the Virgin Mary and from the Holy Spirit, not from man's sperm, is interpreted as abolishing the division into male and female, because in himself Christ has "recapitulated" humanity and creation.

3. The male character of his becoming human has been taken on "in order that his individuality (*idiotes*) might endure" even on the level of his humanity, thus proving how genuinely he is co-essential (*homoousios*) with our human nature. Thus his being male attests to a relationship, just as his hypostasis[10] as "Son of God" does. Furthermore, his male character indicates that we were given by grace what God has by nature.

4. There are two reasons for saying that the male character of his incarnation has nothing to do with any concept of human sexuality. First,

9. *after the fall*—after Adam and Eve sinned and distanced themselves from God.

10. *hypostasis*— the "person" or manifestation of the Son in the Godhead. See "Trinitarian Debates" for a discussion of hypostases.

he has taken on himself the pre-fall nature of the first man, who at that stage had no awareness of his biological differentiation as male or of his sexual functioning—remembering here that the division into male and female was to serve the post-fall conditions of the human race, while the incarnate Logos assumed the human nature without sin.

Second, the human nature of Jesus Christ has no previous existence. The human nature Christ assumed in the womb of the Holy Virgin was not a complement of his mother's humanity in the way that the first Eve assumed the nature of Adam in order to be his complement. Christ's human nature was unique, because it came to existence from the pure blood and holy flesh of the Holy Virgin and from the Holy Spirit. So, the incarnated Logos became the *aparche tou phyramatos,* "the beginning of a new essence," the second or new Adam, which means the one and undivided human being. [. . .]

6. The first Adam was created "in the image and likeness" of God, but in the case of the incarnation, the aforesaid elements are not dynamic properties in the God-man, but are fulfilled reality, since the Lord himself was made man in order to make man God. The Lord did not raise "the previously fallen image" in his God-man hypostasis, but united it to his own by grace. This is a new element, which did not exist in the human nature of the first Adam, because in the context of incarnation there is a substantial difference: we move from "in the image" to the "image," which is the Son of God. [. . .]

The traditional view that priesthood belongs exclusively to men because the incarnate Logos was a male human being reduces the archetype of all human beings to the level of a *natural resemblance*. This is understandable in terms of our sexuality, which is characterized by polarity, conflict, and passion and related to the situation after the fall. But patristic teaching is more than clear on this point. Jesus Christ united humanity, and the difference between male and female has been taken away by the Spirit in a mysterious way. [. . .]

The sacrifice on the holy cross is a sacrifice of the God-man, not of his maleness. Therefore the male character of his humanity cannot be used as a criterion for excluding women from the priesthood, because this would completely contradict the dogma of Chalcedon. There is no dogmatic decision that would justify such an exception based on the distinction of sexes: the only reasons for doing so are connected with the human weakness for understanding and living the mystery of the divine economy,[11] because, according to Maximus the Confessor, "[Christ] is seen and understood by many people as flesh and not as Logos, although truly he is Logos."

11. *divine economy*—all of God's plans for and actions in the world.

Of course, it cannot be denied that some fathers[12] rejected female ordination as emphatically as possible, basing their claim that a woman is unsuited to ministerial orders on the fact of her subordination to the man—particularly if one takes into consideration God's intervention to define the structure of human relationships, fixing the duties and rights of male and female, so that by definition woman is seen as incapable of receiving the divine grace that would empower her to perform the duties of the ministry.

Our human weakness has been aggravated by negative historic conditions such as social stratification, the domineering role of men, the disadvantageous position of women. Interpersonal relations between the two sexes throughout history have been kept in a climate of conflict and division. The tradition of the church as an expression of how we live our faith is formed in the reality of its historical context. The church has grown up and organized itself in the realm of history: it is not an extraterrestrial community. So it is not surprising that it has been influenced to a certain extent by the dominant patriarchal structures and ideas of the Greco-Roman world in which Christianity emerged. The church has always struggled to get rid of any form of sin. Only in this context can the survival of such elements of division as the exclusion of women from priesthood be understood.

[. . .] As the church struggles to make the kingdom of God a reality, the first thing to be overcome is every form of division. John Chrysostom specifically says: "See the dignity of the church, the angelic condition! No distinction there, 'neither male nor female.' I would that the churches were such now!" [. . .]

12. *fathers*—referring to church fathers, that is, theologians of the early church.

Orthodox Nationalism and Fundamentalism

We've discussed the emergence of religious nationalism in Russia, including the curious support for such nationalism under the atheistic Joseph Stalin. We noted as well the emergence during the 1800s of religious nationalism in the Balkans, particularly in the formation of state churches in Serbia, Romania, and Bulgaria. (See "The Greek Revolution and Orthodox Nationalism," above.)

The trend established in the 1800s—national churches emerging after the collapse of an empire—continued into the 1900s with the fall of the Russian Empire. Russia's disastrous performance in the First World War led to the overthrow of the Russian tsar, a weak provisional communist government, and then a nascent communist government unable to hold the empire together. The former imperial territories of Finland, Estonia, Latvia, and Lithuania all achieved independence, and each established an autonomous church.

The church in Albania declared itself autocephalous in 1922. And three national churches formed in the 1800s—those of Serbia, Romania, and Bulgaria—each created their own patriarchates in the 1900s: Serbia in 1920, Romania in 1925, and Bulgaria in 1953. Such moves reflected aspirations of those countries to claim larger roles within the Eastern Orthodox world.

All of these churches faced persecution when communist forces seized control of their respective states after the Second World War. Yet in no Eastern state did the oppressed national church cease to think of itself as the embodiment of its respective nation. All national churches in the Eastern Bloc of communist nations cooperated with their atheistic states to the degree they deemed necessary (and debates about what constituted "necessary" will rage for decades). Yet all continued to imagine their states as Christian nations and their churches as the rightful source of identity for these nations.

The collapse of communism throughout Eastern Europe in 1989 and 1990 led to a revitalization of Christianity in nations once governed by atheistic bodies; it led as well to new and often strident expressions of religious nationalism. Unfortunately, we cannot do this phenomenon justice here—entire books have been (and still need to be) written on the topic. Instead, we limit ourselves to a few words about Russia, the giant among Eastern Orthodox countries, whose recent struggles with religious identity have assumed an outsized significance.

Aleksei Ridiger, a cleric with close ties to the KGB, became patriarch of Moscow as Aleksei II (1990–2008) just one year before the dissolution of the Soviet Union. The new post-Soviet Russian state, shaky and uncertain, badly wanted the church's support. But debates, which continue today, arose immediately about what, if any, support the church owed the state, and what, if any, the state owed the church.

These debates occurred within what had become a highly secular society, one in which religion played only a small public role. Alexander Agadjanian has observed that the fall of the Soviet Union moved religion from "a secret form of 'inner immigration'" and "private refuge" to a central force in the now "empty public space." Yet religion had to compete with other forces—globalization, postmodern relativism, and consumerism—to fill this empty space. Russian interest in religion thus emerged at the same time that Russia seemed "to be rapidly moving toward a fully secularized society in the Western sense." Hence

> Russia was exposed simultaneously to two developments that appear to be theoretical opposites: secularization and religious revival. Both trends had particular causes. The liberal idea of building a civil society and a European democracy required absolute religious neutrality, new multicultural approaches, and a sort of technocratic naiveté refusing any kind of ideological programming. . . . At the same time, religion was perceived as fresh spiritual and emotional compensation for the shocking breakup of the social system, as well as a repository of cultural arguments, collective memories, and the symbolic strength needed to build new national, group, and individual identities.[1]

1. Alexander Agadjanian, "Public Religion and the Quest for National Ideology: Russia's Media Discourse," *Journal for the Scientific Study of Religion* 40 No. 3 (2001): 351–52.

Revolutions and Reevaluations

Patriarch Aleksei II worked hard to place Orthodoxy squarely in the center of Russian life. During the last years of the Soviet Union he successfully demanded more freedoms for the church, and once the Soviet Union dissolved he vastly increased the church's visibility and influence. He negotiated the return of church property. He sought the state's patronage and secured financial support, which led many to question the degree to which church and state relied on each other. All the new political parties that arose during 1990–1991 either declared their adherence to or at least indicated great respect for the Orthodox Church.[2]

But what role can the church now play in a more secular Russia? Where does the church fit in an industrialized and multicultural society? The secularism and pluralism of modern Russia signal a threat to some Orthodox believers, and this threat helps explain the rise in the past few decades of nationalistic or "fundamentalist" Orthodoxy.

Alexander Verkhovsky describes Orthodox fundamentalism as the dream of restoring a prerevolutionary "golden age" in Russia, with a "full-fledged autocracy," restrictions on the rights of foreigners and foreign confessions, an official state church, a "rejection of the concepts of democracy and human rights (in particular as far as freedom of conscience is concerned)," and "the compulsory imposition of 'Orthodox values' in everyday life, culture and even the economy."[3] Such fundamentalism has manifested itself in various ways: in the successful movement, culminating in 2000, to canonize Tsar Nicholas II, who was murdered by the Bolsheviks; in anti-Semitic literature sold in kiosks and bookstalls in some Orthodox churches; in frantic warnings from abbots and other church officials about taxpayer identification numbers functioning as the "seal of the Antichrist"; in widespread warnings about the dangers of globalization; and in calls from parishes to resist Western missionaries.

2. Thomas Parland, "Christian Orthodoxy and Russian Nationalism," in *Questioning the Secular State: The Worldwide Resurgence of Religion in Politics* (New York: St. Martin's Press, 1996), 124.

3. Alexander Verkhovsky, "The Orthodox in the Russian Ultranationalist Movements," trans. Walter Sawatsky, *Religion in Eastern Europe* 22 No. 3 (2002): 21; Alexander Verkhovsky, "The Role of the Russian Orthodox Church in Nationalist, Xenophobic and Antiwestern Tendencies in Russia Today: Not Nationalism, but Fundamentalism," *Religion, State & Society* 30 No. 4 (2002), 334.

Patriarch Aleksei II largely succeeded in marginalizing liberal and reformist wings of the church. Partly because of his lobbying, the Russian Duma (parliament) in 1997 passed a law, "On Freedom of Conscience and Religious Associations," that, though declaring Russia a secular state, recognized "the special role of the Orthodox church in the history of Russia [and] the formation and development of its spirituality and culture." This statute makes it difficult for foreign missionaries to enter the country, and it mandates that all non-Orthodox confessions desiring legal status prove that they have already been registered legally for at least fifteen years.[4]

Patriarch Kirill (2009–) regularly rails against Western confessions and the West itself. The world's problems, in Kirill's estimation, stem largely from the Enlightenment, which "declared man, born free from sin, to be the center of the universe"; "the French Revolution introduced this paradigm into political logic." The Protestant Reformation, another "tragedy," arose from a "rejection of the absolute authority of the church in interpreting holy scriptures."[5] And he continues, "The principal question raised, is whether the secular liberal humanistic model of the structure of the state, society and international relations is entitled to a global monopoly."[6]

Kirill faults "almost the entire Western world" for adopting "the pose of 'teaching the East about life.'" He worries that "European integration" will become "just an expansion of the authority of Western institutions and norms."[7] To Kirill's mind the Russian Orthodox Church is as much "the main living bearer of the 'identity code of Russian civilization'"[8] as it is the body of Christ.

4. *On the Freedom of Conscience and Religious Associations*, Federal Law No. 125-FZ of 26 September 1997 (Legislation Online), accessed 8 August 2015, http://legislationline.org/download/action/download/id/4379/file/RF_Freedom _of_Conscience_Law_1997_am2008_en.pdf.

5. Metropolitan Kirill, "No Freedom without Moral Responsibility," *Russian Social Science Review* 47 No. 4 (2006): 53.

6. Metropolitan Kirill, "The Future of Europe and the Eastern Christian Tradition," *Sourozh* no. 91 (2003): 24.

7. Ibid., 21–22.

8. Ibid., 22.

Moscow Bishops on the Church, the Nation, and Globalization (2000)

Moscow Patriarchate, Department for External Church Relations, "The Basis of the Social Concept," http://www.mospat.ru/en/documents/social-concepts.

In 2000 the Moscow patriarchate convened a conference of bishops to produce a statement addressing issues such as globalization, secularization, and church-state relations. This document, "The Basis of the Social Concept," now constitutes the "official position of the Moscow patriarchate on relations with the state and secular society." Kirill, then metropolitan of Smolensk and Kaliningrad and now the patriarch of Moscow, supervised the proceedings.

The document is complex and sometimes inconsistent. It argues that the church is "universal and therefore supernatural." It references the Apostle Paul's contention that "there is no distinction between Jew and Greek" (Romans 10:12) and that God is the God of both Jews and Gentiles (Romans 3:29). But it also makes a strong case for national identity and Christian patriotism, bluntly asserting that "the Christian is called to preserve and develop national culture."

It argues that the church is universal—a single organism composed of members with a common faith in Christ—but also a collection of "national churches." Christians should avoid "aggressive nationalism, xenophobia, national exclusiveness and inter-ethnic enmity," but they should also identify themselves with their "people," their "birth," and their "nation."

The document concludes by lamenting the spread of a uniform, transnational or globalized, secular culture, and it calls on the church and Orthodox Christians to oppose the spread of "a world order that places the human personality, darkened by sin, in the center of everything."

The Moscow patriarchate declined to grant us permission to reprint the document, so we include only short excerpts here.

Orthodox Christians, aware of being citizens of the heavenly homeland, should not forget about their earthly homeland. [. . .]

Among saints venerated by the Orthodox church, many became famous for the love of their earthly homeland and faithfulness to it. [. . .]

In all times the church has called upon her children to love their homeland on earth and not to spare their lives to protect it if it was threatened. The Russian church on many occasions gave her blessing to the people for them to take part in liberation wars. [. . .] [As St. Filaret of Moscow said,][9] "If you avoid dying for the honor and freedom of the fatherland, you will die a criminal or a slave; die for the faith and the fatherland and you will be granted life and a crown in Heaven." [. . .]

The Orthodox Christian is called to love his fatherland. [. . .] This love is one of the ways of fulfilling God's commandment to love [. . .] one's family, fellow-tribesmen and fellow-citizens.

The patriotism of the Orthodox Christian should be active. It is manifested when he defends his fatherland against an enemy, [. . .] [and] works for the good of the motherland. [. . .] The Christian is called to preserve and develop national culture and people's self-awareness. [. . .]

God blesses the state as an essential element of life in the world distorted by sin. [. . .]

The state is aware as a rule that earthly well-being is unthinkable without respect for certain moral norms. [. . .] Therefore, the tasks and work of the church and the state may coincide not only in seeking purely earthly welfare, but also in the fulfillment of the salvific mission of the church. [. . .]

Spiritual and Social Problems of Globalism (2001)

Revised translation of Alexander Verkhovsky's translation in "The Role of the Russian Orthodox Church in Nationalist, Xenophobic and Antiwestern Tendencies in Russia Today: Not Nationalism but Fundamentalism," *Religion, State, and Society* 30 No. 4 (2002): 342.

In 2001 the St. Petersburg Theological Academy—the alma mater of many high officials in the Russian church and arguably Russia's leading seminary—sponsored a conference on "the spiritual and social problems of globalization." The conference and the academy's head, Konstantin Gorianov, produced the document excerpted here.

1. The ideology of globalization stands in opposition to the Christian world outlook; it is incompatible with [that outlook]; through efforts of the world elite it takes root and is propagandized in secular society and in the church, and it expresses [the world elites'] interests. Globalization becomes

9. *St. Filaret of Moscow*—metropolitan of Moscow (1826–1867). At the time of this pronouncement—in 1813, that is, during Russia's war against Napoleon—Filaret served as an inspector at the St. Petersburg Seminary.

an embodiment of the utopian idea of mondialism[10] about the creation of a unitary, supranational and rigidly controlled community on Earth. [. . .]

3. Mondialists reject and do not recognize the historical calling of Russia as a country preserving the Orthodox faith, culture, and traditions. Yet such values are important for the whole world.

4. Changes in the traditional system of values; the destruction of national culture, Christian morals, and senses; the primitivization of people's thinking; universal work to accustom people to the "voluntary-compulsory" acceptance of digital identifiers[11] (personal codes), thus replacing a human name in all state-public relationships—such are the current and primary manifestations of the globalization process in the Russian Federation. [. . .]

Zhanna Bichevskaya, "We Are Russians" (2006)

"My russkie!," music and lyrics by Gennady Ponomarev, sung by Zhanna Bichevskaya, YouTube, https://www.youtube.com/watch?v=NpO81OnoLUg. Translated by Bryn Geffert.

Zhanna Bichevskaya (1944–) made her name in Russian popular music by researching, arranging, and popularizing Russia folk songs. She became something of a hero among folk enthusiasts, particularly high school and college students, who, given a guitar and a campfire, sang her songs late into the night.

In the late 1980s and early 1990s Bichevskaya became a devout Orthodox believer. Her public appearances ceased almost entirely, and her work began to adopt strident nationalistic and religious overtones.

Bichevskaya and her associates produced a video to accompany her famous (or infamous) song "We Are Russians." This combustible mix of nationalistic and religious sentiment contains a hodgepodge of images: the Russian flag; Russian victims of atrocities; Orthodox processions; Patriarch Aleksei II; Napoleon and his troops as depicted in the movie *War and Peace;* evil Germans from *Aleksandr Nevsky,* a film about Teutonic invasions; and images of the Russian military (fighter planes, ships, tanks, and troops), which could be mistaken for part of an armed-forces recruiting video.

---

10. *mondialism*—universalism.

11. *digital identifiers*—tax identification codes. Fundamentalists in the church began warning in 1998 that new taxpayer identification numbers represented the "mark of the beast" or the "seal of the Antichrist."

The version of this video that aired on a St. Petersburg television station in 2006 included clips from the Hollywood movie *Independence Day* of Los Angeles burning and the U.S. Capitol exploding.[12] U.S. diplomatic officials filed a protest, and these images were removed from later versions, including the YouTube version referenced here. Still, "We Are Russians" represents an extreme version of religious nationalism, which views Orthodoxy as supportive of and dependent on Russian military might.

The video may be found on YouTube (youtube.com) by searching "Zhanna Bichevskaya We Are Russians," or "Жанна Бичевская Мы Русские."

> We were formed for the glory of Christ.
> The monstrous enemy cannot devour us;
> They struck with a crescent[13] and attacked with stars,[14]
> But our banner is and will be the cross.
>
> *Refrain:*
> The narrow paths lead us to Christ.
> We know death, persecution, and captivity.
> We are Russians, we are Russians, we are Russians,
> We nevertheless rise up from our knees.
> We are Russians, we are Russians, we are Russians,
> We nevertheless rise up from our knees.
>
> Vowing allegiance to the tsar, we kiss the cross.
> Treachery laid low the Russian race.
> Scattered around the world, we are outcasts
> Like God's former, chosen people.
>
> *Refrain*
> Lacerating wounds scar the body of Russia,
> But the light of Christ shines clearly ahead.
> And if the foul ones attack us,
> We go forth into battle with a cross on our chests.
>
> *Refrain*
> Discussions with our enemy have ended.
> We again summon ourselves to heroic deeds of sorrow.

12. "Piterskoe televidenie vzryvaet kapitolii: i kommentiruet protest Americanskikh diplomatov," *Novaia Gazeta* (21 September 2006).

13. *struck us with a crescent*—reference to Islamic invasions.

14. *stars*—Bichevskaya concocts a verb (translated here as "attacked") from the Russian word for stars, which rhymes with the word for "baptize." She thus suggests attempts by communist authorities to replace the cross, the symbol of the Christian faith, with the communist star.

Russia, Ukraine, and Belarus—
Three tribes of Slavic heroes.

Refrain
A crimson peal fills the world,
A Russian dawn portends victory.
And we, having risen with crosses and icons,
Proceed to crown the Russian tsar.

Refrain
Indeed, angels sound the assembly for the last battle:
For the faith, for the tsar, but not for cowardice!
Through *soborny*,[15] penitence, and prayer
God will revive Holy Rus'.

Refrain:
The narrow paths lead us to Christ,
We know death, persecution, and captivity.
We are Russians, we are Russians, we are Russians,
We nevertheless rise up from our knees.
We are Russians, we are Russians, we are Russians,
We nevertheless rise up from our knees.

15. *soborny*—uniquely Russian Orthodox word denoting mystical unity within the church.

Recommended Reading

PREFACE

Kallistos, Bishop of Diokleia. *The Orthodox Church,* new ed. New York: Penguin, 1993. 358 pp.

McGuckin, John Anthony. *The Orthodox Church: An Introduction to Its History, Doctrine, and Spiritual Culture.* Malden, MA: Wiley-Blackwell, 2010. 457 pp.

Meyendorff, John. *The Byzantine Legacy in the Orthodox Church.* Crestwood, NY: St. Vladimir's Seminary Press, 1982. 268 pp.

———. *The Orthodox Church: Its Past and Its Role in the World Today,* 3rd ed. Crestwood, NY: St. Vladimir's Seminary Press, 1981. 343 pp.

Schmemann, Alexander. *The Historical Road of Eastern Orthodoxy.* Crestwood, NY: St. Vladimir's Seminary Press, 1977. 343 pp.

Zernov, Nicolas. *Eastern Christendom: A Study of the Origin and Development of the Eastern Orthodox Church.* New York: G. P. Putnam's Sons, 1961. 326 pp.

BEGINNINGS, SCRIPTURE, AND PATRISTICS

Beckwith, Roger T. *The Old Testament Canon of the New Testament Church and Its Background in Early Judaism.* Grand Rapids, MI: Eerdmans, 1986. 528 pp.

Childs, Bravard W. *The New Testament Canon: An Introduction.* Philadelphia: Fortress, 1985. 572 pp.

Cross, Frank Leslie. *The Early Christian Fathers.* London: Duckworth, 1960. 218 pp.

Harvey, Susan Ashbrook, and David G. Hunter, eds. *The Oxford Handbook of Early Christian Studies.* New York: Oxford University Press, 2008. 1020 pp.

McGuckin, John Anthony. *The Westminster Handbook to Patristic Theology.* Louisville, KY: Westminster John Knox, 2004. 367 pp.

Metzger, Bruce M. *The Canon of the New Testament: Its Origin, Development, and Significance.* New York: Oxford University Press, 1987. 326 pp.

Moule, Charles Francis Digby. *The Birth of the New Testament,* 3rd ed. San Francisco: Harper & Row, 1981. 382 pp.

Souter, Alexander. *The Text and Canon of the New Testament,* 2nd ed. London: Duckworth, 1954. 236 pp.

Young, Frances M., Lewis Ayres, and Andrew Louth, eds. *The Cambridge History of Early Christian Literature.* Cambridge: Cambridge University Press, 2004. 538 pp.

NEW SECT

Corwin, Virginia. *St. Ignatius and Christianity in Antioch.* New Haven, CT: Yale University Press, 1960. 293 pp.

Richardson, Cyril Charles. *The Christianity of Ignatius of Antioch.* New York: Columbia University Press, 1935. 120 pp.

Sherwin-White, Adrian Nicholas. *The Letters of Pliny: A Historical and Social Commentary.* New York: Oxford University Press, 1966. 808 pp.

NEW CHURCH—CONSTANTINE AND CONSTANTINOPLE

Aföldi, Andreas. *The Conversion of Constantine and Pagan Rome.* Oxford: Clarendon, 1948. 140 pp.

Jones, Arnold Hugh Martin. *Constantine and the Conversion of Europe.* London: English Universities Press, 1948. 271 pp.

MacMullen, Ramsay. *Constantine.* New York: Dial, 1969. 363 pp.

Talbot-Rice, David. *Constantinople from Byzantium to Istanbul.* New York: Stein and Day, 1965. 214 pp.

INCARNATIONAL THEOLOGY AND ARIAN CONTROVERSIES

Barnes, Timothy David. *Athanasius and Constantius: Theology and Politics in the Constantinian Empire.* Cambridge, MA: Harvard University Press, 1993. 343 pp.

Gregg, Robert C., ed. *Arianism: Historical and Theological Reassessments.* Eugene, OR: Wipf & Stock, 1985. 380 pp.

Gregg, Robert C., and Dennis Groh. *Early Arianism: A View of Salvation.* Philadelphia: Fortress, 1981. 209 pp.

Gwatkin, Henry Melvill. *The Arian Controversy.* New York: Longmans, Green, 1898. 176 pp.

Hanson, Richard Patrick Crosland. *The Search for the Christian Doctrine of God: The Arian Controversy, 318–381.* Edinburgh: T & T Clark, 1988.

Williams, Rowan. *Arius: Heresy and Tradition,* rev. ed. Grand Rapids, MI: W. B. Eerdmans, 2002. 378 pp.

REACTION

Athanassiadi, Polymnia. *Julian and Hellenism: An Intellectual Biography.* Oxford: Clarendon, 1981. 245 pp.

Bowersock, Glen Warren. *Julian the Apostate.* Cambridge, MA: Harvard University Press, 1978. 135 pp.

Browning, Robert. *The Emperor Julian.* London: Weidenfeld and Nicolson, 1975. 256 pp.

Ricciotti, Giuseppe. *Julian the Apostate.* Milwaukee: Bruce Publishing, 1960. 275 pp.

Smith, Rowland. *Julian's Gods: Religion and Philosophy in the Thought and Action of Julian the Apostate.* New York: Routledge, 1995. 300 pp.

TRINITARIAN DEBATES

Ayres, Lewis. *Nicaea and Its Legacy: An Approach to Fourth-Century Trinitarian Theology.* New York: Oxford University Press, 2009. 475 pp.

Beeley, Christopher. *Gregory of Nazianzus on the Trinity and the Knowledge of God: In Your Light We See Light.* New York: Oxford University Press, 2008. 396 pp.

———. *The Unity of Christ: Continuity and Conflict in Patristic Tradition.* New Haven, CT: Yale University Press, 2012. 391 pp.

Hildebrand, Stephen M. *The Trinitarian Theology of Basil of Caesarea: A Synthesis of Greek Thought and Biblical Truth.* Washington, DC: Catholic University Press of America, 2007. 254 pp.

Meredith, Anthony. *The Cappadocians.* Crestwood, NY: St. Vladimir's Seminary Press, 1995. 129 pp.

———. *Gregory of Nyssa.* New York: Routledge, 1999. 166 pp.

PRIESTS AND BISHOPS

Dix, Gregory. *Jurisdiction in the Early Church, Episcopal and Papal.* London: Church Literature Association, 1975. 124 pp.

Hatch, Edwin. *The Organization of the Early Christian Churches: Eight Lectures Delivered before the University of Oxford in the Year 1880.* London: Rivingtons, 1881. 216 pp.

Lane Fox, Robin. *Pagans and Christians.* New York: Knopf, 1987. 799 pp. See pp. 493–545.

Liebeschuetz, John Hugo Wolfgang Gideon. *Barbarians and Bishops: Army, Church, and State in the Age of Arcadius and Chrysostom.* New York: Oxford University Press, 1990. 312 pp.

Mitchell, Margaret Mary. *The Heavenly Trumpet: John Chrysostom and the Art of Pauline Interpretation.* Louisville, KY: Westminster John Knox, 2000. 563 pp.

Stone, Darwell. *Episcopacy and Valid Orders in the Primitive Church: A Statement of Evidence,* 2nd ed. New York: Longmans, Green, 1926. 62 pp.

EARLY MONASTICISM

Brakke, David. *Athanasius and the Politics of Asceticism.* New York: Oxford University Press, 1995. 356 pp.

Burton-Christie, Douglas. *The Word in the Desert: Scripture and the Quest for Holiness in Early Christian Monasticism.* New York: Oxford University Press, 1993. 336 pp.

Chitty, Derwas James. *The Desert a City: An Introduction to the Study of Egyptian and Palestinian Monasticism under the Christian Empire.* Oxford: Blackwell, 1966. 222 pp.

Décarreaux, Jean. *Monks and Civilization from the Barbarian Invasions to the Reign of Charlemagne.* London: Allen & Unwin, 1964. 397 pp.

Hussey, J. M. "Byzantine Monasticism," *History* 24 No. 93 (1939): 56–62.

Lacarrière, Jacques. *Men Possessed by God: The Story of the Desert Monks of Ancient Christendom.* Garden City, NY: Doubleday, 1964. 237 pp.

Rousseau, Philip. *Pachomius: The Making of a Community in Fourth-Century Egypt.* Berkeley: University of California Press, 1985. 217 pp.

CHRISTIANITY AND THE BYZANTINE STATE

Downey, Glanville. *Constantinople in the Age of Justinian.* Norman: University of Oklahoma Press, 1960. 131 pp.

Every, George. *The Byzantine Patriarchate, 451–1204,* 2nd ed. rev. London: S.P.C.K., 1962. 204 pp.

Hussey, Joan Mervyn. *The Orthodox Church in the Byzantine Empire.* Oxford: Clarendon, 1986. 408 pp.

Runciman, Steven. *The Byzantine Theocracy.* New York: Cambridge University Press, 1977. 197 pp.

HOLY FOOLS

Ivanov, Sergei Arkad'evich. *Holy Fools in Byzantium and Beyond.* New York: Oxford University Press, 2006. 479 pp.

Krueger, Derek. *Symeon the Holy Fool: Leontius's Life and the Late Antique City.* Berkeley: University of California Press, 1996. 196 pp.

Saward, John. *Perfect Fools: Folly for Christ's Sake in Catholic and Orthodox Spirituality.* New York: Oxford University Press, 1980. 247 pp.

EASTERN TRENDS IN CHRISTIAN THEOLOGY

Lossky, Vladimir. *The Mystical Theology of the Eastern Church.* Crestwood, NY: St. Vladimir's Seminary Press, 1976. 252 pp.

———. *Orthodox Theology: An Introduction.* Crestwood, NY: St. Vladimir's Seminary Press, 1978. 137 pp.

Meyendorff, John. *Byzantine Theology: Historical Trends and Doctrinal Themes,* 2nd ed. New York: Fordham University Press, 1983. 243 pp.

Pelikan, Jaroslav. *The Spirit of Eastern Christendom (600–1700).* Chicago: University of Chicago Press, 1974. 329 pp.

MARRIAGE AND WOMEN IN THE EARLY CHURCH

Brown, Peter. *The Body and Society: Men, Women, and Sexual Renunciation in Early Christianity.* New York: Columbia University Press, 1988. 504 pp.

Hunter, David. *Marriage in the Early Church.* Minneapolis: Fortress, 1992. 157 pp.

MacHaffie, Barbara. *Her Story: Women in Christian Tradition.* Philadelphia: Fortress, 1986. 183 pp. See pp. 1–48.

Meyendorff, John. *Marriage: An Orthodox Perspective,* 2nd ed. Crestwood, NY: St. Vladimir's Seminary Press, 1975. 131 pp.

Salisbury, *Church Fathers, Independent Virgins.* London: Verso, 1991. 168 pp.

HOLY WOMEN

Talbot, Alice-Mary, ed. *Holy Women of Byzantium: Ten Saints Lives in English Translation.* Washington, DC: Dumbarton Oaks, 1996. 351 pp.

HOLY OBJECTS

Freeman, Charles. *Holy Bones, Holy Dust: How Relics Shaped the History of Medieval Europe.* New Haven, CT: Yale University Press, 2011. 306 pp.

Greene, Robert. *Bodies like Bright Stars: Saints and Relics in Orthodox Russia.* DeKalb: Northern Illinois University Press, 2010. 299 pp.

Meinardus, Otto Friedrich August. "A Study of the Relics of Saints of the Greek Orthodox Church," *Oriens Christianus* 54 (1970): 130–279.

Wortley, John. *Studies on the Cult of Relics in Byzantium up to 1204.* Farnham: Ashgate, 2009. 278 pp.

MISSIONS TO THE NORTH: BALKANS AND RUS'

Duichev, Ivan, ed. *Kiril and Methodius: Founders of Slavonic Writing: A Collection of Sources and Critical Studies,* trans. Spass Nikolov. Boulder, CO: East European Monographs, 1985. 335 pp.

Dvornik, Francis. *Byzantine Missions among the Slavs: SS. Constantine-Cyril and Methodius.* New Brunswick, NJ: Rutgers University Press, 1970. 484 pp.

Fennell, John. *A History of the Russian Church to 1448.* New York: Longman, 1995. 266 pp.

Obolensky, Dimitri. *The Byzantine Commonwealth: Eastern Europe, 500–1453.* New York: Praeger, 1971. 445 pp. See pp. 136–53.

Poppe, Andrzej. "How the Conversion of Rus' Was Understood in the Eleventh Century," *Harvard Ukrainian Studies* 11 No. 3/4 (1987): 287–302.

———. "Two Concepts of the Conversion of Rus' in Kievan Writings," *Harvard Ukrainian Studies* 12/13 (1988/1989): 488–504.

Sevcenko, Ihor. "The Christianization of Kievan Rus'," *Polish Review* 5 No. 4 (1960): 29–35.

Vlasto, A. P. *The Entry of the Slavs into Christendom: An Introduction to the Medieval History of the Slavs.* Cambridge: Cambridge University Press, 1970. 435 pp.

ICONOCLASTIC CONTROVERSY

Besançon, Alain. *The Forbidden Image: An Intellectual History of Iconoclasm,* trans. Jane Marie Todd. Chicago: University of Chicago Press, 2000. 448 pp.

Brown, Peter. "A Dark-Age Crisis: Aspects of the Iconoclastic Controversy," *English Historical Review* 88 No. 346 (1973): 1–34.

Gero, Stephen. *Byzantine Iconoclasm during the Reign of Constantine V with Particular Attention to the Oriental Sources.* Louvain: Corpus SCO, 1977. 191 pp.

———. *Byzantine Iconoclasm during the Reign of Leo III with Particular Attention to the Oriental Sources.* Louvain: Secrétariat du Corpus SCO, 1973. 220 pp.

HESYCHASM

Lossky, Vladimir. *The Vision of God,* trans. Asheleigh Moorhouse. Crestwood, NY: St. Vladimir's Seminary Press, 1983. 175 pp.

Meyendorff, John. *A Study of Gregory Palamas,* trans. George Lawrence. Crestwood, NY: St. Vladimir's Seminary Press, 2010. 245 pp.

GREAT SCHISM

Congar, Yves. *After Nine Hundred Years: The Background of the Schism between the Eastern and Western Churches.* New York: Fordham University Press, 1959. 150 pp.

Pelikan, Jaroslav. *The Spirit of Eastern Christendom (600–1700).* Chicago: University of Chicago Press, 1974. 329 pp. See pp. 170–83.

Runciman, Steven. *The Eastern Schism: A Study of the Papacy and the Eastern Churches during the XIth and XIIth Centuries.* Oxford: Clarendon, 1963. 189 pp.

Claims of the Roman See

Chapman, John. *Studies on the Early Papacy.* London: Sheed & Ward, 1928. 238 pp.

Fortescue, Adrian, and Alcuin Reid. *The Early Papacy to the Synod of Chalcedon in 451,* 4th ed. San Francisco: Ignatius Press, 2008. 121 pp.

Morris, Colin. *The Papal Monarchy: The Western Church from 1050 to 1250.* New York: Oxford University Press, 1989. 673 pp.

Noble, Thomas F. X. *The Republic of St. Peter: The Birth of the Papal State, 680–825.* Philadelphia: University of Pennsylvania Press, 1984. 374 pp.

Papadakis, Aristeides, and John Meyendorff. *The Christian East and the Rise of the Papacy: The Church AD 1071–1453.* Crestwood, NY: St. Vladimir's Seminary Press, 1994. 424 pp.

Ullmann, Walter. *The Growth of Papal Government in the Middle Ages,* 3rd ed. London: Methuen, 1970. 496 pp.

Filioque

Ffoulkes, Edmund. *An Historical Account of the Addition of the Words "Filioque" to the Creed of the West.* London: Rivingtons, 1867. 32 pp.

Nichols, Aidan. "The Photian Schism and the 'Filioque,'" in *Rome and the Eastern Churches: A Study in Schism,* 2nd ed. San Francisco: Ignatius Press, 2010, chap. 7.

Pelikan, Jaroslav. *The Spirit of Eastern Christendom (600–1700).* Chicago: University of Chicago Press, 1974. 329 pp. See pp. 183–98.

Charlemagne and the Pope Assert Themselves

Bullough, Donald. *The Age of Charlemagne,* 2nd ed. London: Elek, 1973. 212 pp.

McKitterick, Rosamond. *The Frankish Church and the Carolingian Reforms, 789–895.* London: Royal Historical Society, 1977. 236 pp.

Wallace-Hadrill, John Michael. *The Frankish Church.* New York: Oxford University Press, 1983. 463 pp.

Anathemas of 1054

Gilchrist, J. T. "Cardinal Humbert of Silva-Candida," *Annuale Mediaevale* 3 (1962): 29–42.

Hussey, Joan Mervyn. *The Orthodox Church in the Byzantine Empire.* Oxford: Clarendon, 1986. See pp. 129–38.

Ryan, J. Joseph. "Cardinal Humbert *De s. Romana ecclesia:* Relics of Roman-Byzantine Relations, 1053–1054," *Medieval Studies* 20 (1958): 206–38.

Smith, Mahlon H. *And Taking Bread . . . : Cerularius and the Azyme Controversy of 1054.* Paris: Beauchesne, 1978. 188 pp.

Fourth Crusade

Phillips, Jonathan. *The Fourth Crusade and the Sack of Constantinople.* New York: Penguin, 2005.

———. *Holy Warriors: A Modern History of the Crusades.* New York: Random House, 2009. 464 pp.

Riley-Smith, Jonathan. *The Crusades: A Short History.* New Haven, CT: Yale University Press, 1987. 302 pp.

———, ed. *The Oxford Illustrated History of the Crusades.* New York: Oxford University Press, 1995. 436 pp.

Tyerman, Christopher. *God's War: A New History of the Crusades.* Cambridge, MA: Belknap Press of Harvard University Press, 2006. 1023 pp.

Council of Ferrara-Florence

Gill, Joseph. *The Council of Florence.* Cambridge: Cambridge University Press, 1959. 452 pp.

———. *Personalities of the Council of Florence and Other Essays.* Oxford: Blackwell, 1964. 297 pp.

Hussey, Joan Mervyn. *The Orthodox Church in the Byzantine Empire.* Oxford: Clarendon, 1986. See pp. 267–86.

Fall of Constantinople

Crowley, Roger. *Constantinople: The Last Great Siege, 1453.* London: Faber and Faber, 2005. 304 pp.

Runciman, Steven. *The Fall of Constantinople, 1453.* Cambridge: Cambridge University Press, 1965. 256 pp.

RISE OF ISLAM AND TURKISH EXPANSION

Busse, Herbert. *Islam, Judaism, and Christianity: Theological and Historical Affiliations,* trans. Allison Brown. Princeton, NJ: Markus Wiener, 1998. 207 pp.

Daniel, Norman. *The Arabs and Mediaeval Europe,* 2nd ed. New York: Longman, 1979. 285 pp.

———. *Islam and the West: The Making of an Image.* Edinburgh: Edinburgh University Press, 1960. 443 pp.

Kedar, B. Z. *Crusade and Mission: European Approaches toward the Muslims.* Princeton, NJ: Princeton University Press, 1984. 246 pp.

Southern, Richard William. *Western Views of Islam in the Middle Ages.* Cambridge, MA: Harvard University Press, 1962. 114 pp.

RISE OF THE MOSCOW PATRIARCHATE

Lobachev, Valerii, and Vladimir Pravotorov. *A Millennium of Russian Orthodoxy,* trans. Mikhail Nikolsky. Moscow: Novosti Press Agency, 1988. 116 pp.

Poe, Marshall. "Moscow, the Third Rome: The Origins and Transformations of a 'Pivotal Moment,'" *Jahrbucher fur Geschichte Osteuropas* 49 No. 3 (2001): 412–29.

BYZANTINE RITE CATHOLICS

Groen, Bert, and William van den Bercken, eds. *Four Hundred Years: Union of Brest (1596–1996): A Critical Re-evaluation.* Leuven: Peeters, 1998. 269 pp.

Gudziak, Borys. *Crisis and Reform: The Kyivan Metropolitanate, the Patriarchate of Constantinople, and the Genesis of the Union of Brest.* Cambridge, MA: Ukrainian Research Institute, Harvard University, 1998. 489 pp.

Halecki, Oskar. *From Florence to Brest (1439–1596),* 2nd ed. Hamden, CT: Archon Books, 1968. 456 pp.

PETER THE GREAT'S REORIENTATION OF RUSSIAN ORTHODOXY

Cracraft, James. *The Church Reform of Peter the Great.* Stanford, CA: Stanford University Press, 1971. 336 pp.

———. *The Revolution of Peter the Great.* Cambridge, MA: Harvard University Press, 2003. 192 pp.

ENGAGING THE WEST THROUGH CREEDS

Pelikan, Jaroslav. "The Eastern Orthodox Quest for Confessional Identity: Where Does Orthodoxy Confess What It Believes and Teaches?," *Modern Greek Studies Yearbook* 14/15 (1998/1999): 21–36.

POPULAR PIETY AND POPULAR PRACTICES

Belliustin, Ioann. *Description of the Clergy in Rural Russia: The Memoir of a Nineteenth-Century Priest,* ed. and trans. Gregory Freeze. Ithaca, NY: Cornell University Press, 1973. 214 pp.

Freeze, Gregory. *The Parish Clergy in Nineteenth-Century Russia: Crisis, Reform, Counter-reform.* Princeton, NJ: Princeton University Press, 1983. 507 pp.

———. *The Russian Levites: Parish Clergy in the Eighteenth Century.* Cambridge: Cambridge University Press, 1977. 325 pp.

Heretz, Leonid. *Russia on the Eve of Modernity: Popular Religion and Traditional Culture under the Last Tsars.* New York: Cambridge University Press, 2008. 280 pp.

Levin, Eve. "Dvoeverie and Popular Religion," in *Seeking God: The Recovery of Religious Identity in Orthodox Russian, Ukraine, and Georgia,* ed. Stephen K. Batalden. DeKalb: Northern Illinois University Press, 1993, 29–52.

Semenova-Tian-Shanskaia, Ol'ga Petrovna. *Village Life in Late Tsarist Russia,* ed. and trans. David Ransel. Bloomington: Indiana University Press, 1993. 175 pp.

Steinberg, Mark D., and Heather J. Coleman, eds. *Sacred Stories: Religion and Spirituality in Modern Russia.* Bloomington: Indiana University Press, 2007. 420 pp.

Worth, Dean S. "Religion: Russian Orthodoxy," in *The Cambridge Companion to Modern Russian Culture,* ed. Nicholas Rzhevsky. New York: Cambridge University Press, 2012, 38–56.

ORTHODOXY UNDER OTTOMAN RULE

Braude, Benjamin, and Bernard Lewis, eds. *Christians and Jews in the Ottoman Empire: The Functioning of a Plural Society.* New York: Holmes & Meier, 1982. 2 vols.

Frazee, Charles. *Catholics and Sultans: The Church and the Ottoman Empire 1453–1923*. New York: Cambridge University Press, 1983. 388 pp.

Runciman, Seven. *The Great Church in Captivity: A Study of the Patriarchate of Constantinople from the Eve of the Turkish Conquest to the Greek War of Independence*. Cambridge: Cambridge University Press, 1985. 454 pp.

THE GREEK REVOLUTION AND ORTHODOX NATIONALISM

Brewer, David. *The Greek War of Independence: The Struggle for Freedom from Ottoman Oppression and the Birth of the Modern Greek Nation*. Woodstock, NY: Overlook, 2001. 393 pp.

Prousis, Theophilus Christopher. *Russian Society and the Greek Revolution*. DeKalb: Northern Illinois University Press, 1994. 259 pp.

NEW THINKING AND CHURCH REFORM

Aizlewood, Robin, and Ruth Coates, eds. *Landmarks Revisited: The Vekhi Symposium 100 Years On*. Brighton, MA: Scholars Press, 2013. 321 pp.

Boot, Alexander. *God and Man according to Tolstoy*. New York: Palgrave Macmillan, 2009. 254 pp.

Byrnes, Robert F. *Pobedonostsev: His Life and Thought*. Bloomington: Indiana University Press, 1968. 495 pp.

Cunningham, James. *The Gates of Hell: The Great Sobor of the Russian Orthodox Church, 1917–1918*, ed. Keith Dyrud and Grace Dyrud. Minneapolis: University of Minnesota Press, 2002. 524 pp.

———. *A Vanquished Hope: The Movement for Church Renewal in Russia, 1905–1906*. Crestwood, NY: St. Vladimir's Seminary Press, 1981. 384 pp.

Evtuhov, Catherine. *The Cross & the Sickle: Sergei Bulgakov and the Fate of Russian Religious Philosophy*. Ithaca, NY: Cornell University Press, 1997. 278 pp.

Gustafson, Richard. *Leo Tolstoy. Resident and Stranger: A Study in Fiction and Theology*. Princeton, NJ: Princeton University Press, 1986. 480 pp.

Sutton, Jonathan. *The Religious Philosophy of Vladimir Solovyov*. New York: St. Martin's Press, 1988. 247 pp.

Zernov, Nicolas. *Three Russian Prophets: Khomiakov, Dostoevsky, Soloviev*, 3rd ed. Gulf Breeze, FL: Academic International Press, 1973. 171 pp.

RUSSIAN REVOLUTION

Fletcher, William C. *The Russian Church Underground, 1917–1970.* New York: Oxford University Press, 1971. 314 pp.

Pospielovsky, Dimitry. *The Russian Church under the Soviet Regime, 1917–1982.* Crestwood, NY: St. Vladimir's Seminary Press, 1984. 2 vols.

SOVIET PROPAGANDA

Texts

Pospielovsky, Dimitry. *A History of Soviet Atheism in Theory and Practice, and the Believer.* New York: St. Martin's, 1987–88. 3 vols.

Powell, David E. *Antireligious Propaganda in the Soviet Union: A Study in Mass Persuasion.* Cambridge, MA: MIT Press, 1975. 306 pp.

Substitution Ceremonies

McDowell, Jennifer. "Soviet Civil Ceremonies," *Journal for the Scientific Study of Religion* 13 No. 3 (1974): 267–68.

CHURCH UNDER STALIN

Chumachenko, Tat'iana, and Edward Roslof. *Church and State in Soviet Russia: Russian Orthodoxy from World War II to the Khrushchev Years.* Armonk, NY: M. E. Sharpe, 2002. 234 pp.

Fireside, Harvey. *Icon and Swastika: The Russian Orthodox Church under Nazi and Soviet Control.* Cambridge, MA: Harvard University Press, 1971. 242 pp.

Fletcher, William C. *The Russian Church Underground, 1917–1970.* New York: Oxford University Press, 1971. 314 pp.

———. *A Study in Survival: The Church in Russia 1927–1943.* New York: Macmillan, 1965. 168 pp.

Pospielovsky, Dimitry. *The Russian Church under the Soviet Regime, 1917–1982.* Crestwood, NY: St. Vladimir's Seminary Press, 1984. 2 vols.

ORTHODOXY AND ECUMENISM

Geffert, Bryn. *Eastern Orthodox and Anglicans: Diplomacy, Theology, and the Politics of Interwar Ecumenism.* South Bend, IN: Notre Dame University Press, 2010. 501 pp.

Patelos, Constantin, ed. *The Orthodox Church in the Ecumenical Movement: Documents and Statements, 1902–1975.* Geneva: World Council of Churches, 1978. 360 pp.

WOMEN'S ORDINATION

Behr-Sigel, Elisabeth. *The Ordination of Women in the Orthodox Church.* Geneva: World Council of Churches, 2000. 96 pp.
Kallistos, Bishop of Diokleia, and Thomas Hopko. *Women and the Priesthood.* Crestwood, NY: St. Vladimir's Seminary Press, 1983. 190 pp.

ORTHODOX NATIONALISM AND FUNDAMENTALISM

Agadjanian, Alexander. "Public Religion and the Quest for National Ideology: Russia's Media Discourse," *Journal for the Scientific Study of Religion* 40 No. 3 (2001): 351–52.
Parland, Thomas. "Christian Orthodoxy and Russian Nationalism," in *Questioning the Secular State: The Worldwide Resurgence of Religion in Politics.* New York: St. Martin's Press, 1996, 117–39.
Verkhovsky, Alexander. "The Orthodox in the Russian Ultranationalist Movements," trans. Walter Sawatsky, *Religion in Eastern Europe* 22 No. 3 (2002): 18–36.
———. "The Role of the Russian Orthodox Church in Nationalist, Xenophobic and Antiwestern Tendencies in Russia Today: Not Nationalism, but Fundamentalism," *Religion, State & Society* 30 No. 4 (2002), 333–45.

Illustration Credits

All illustrations are courtesy of Bryn Geffert, except as noted below.

Figure 1. Bryn Geffert, with reference to "Orthodoxy by Country," 2010, Wikimedia Commons, http://en.wikipedia.org/wiki/File: Orthodoxy_by_Country.svg.

Figure 3. Rachel Gucker and Bryn Geffert, with reference to R. R. Palmer, Rand McNally *Atlas of World History* (Chicago: Rand McNally, 1995), 42–43.

Figure 4. Rachel Gucker and Bryn Geffert, with reference to Henry Chadwick and G. R. Evans, *Atlas of the Christian Church* (New York: Facts on File, 1987), 25.

Figure 10. Rachel Gucker and Bryn Geffert, with reference to Frederik van der Meer and Christine Mohrmann, *Atlas of the Early Christian World* (London: Nelson, 1958), 29.

Figure 11. Rachel Gucker and Bryn Geffert, with reference to Frederik van der Meer and Christine Mohrmann, *Atlas of the Early Christian World* (London: Nelson, 1958), 30.

Figure 15. Bryn Geffert, adapted from SeikoEn, "East Slavic Tribes Peoples 8th 9th Century," 2010, Wikimedia Commons, http://en.wikipedia .org/wiki/File:East_Slavic_tribes_peoples_8th_9th_century.jpg.

Figure 16. Rachel Gucker and Bryn Geffert, with reference to Henry Chadwick and G. R. Evans, *Atlas of the Christian Church* (New York: Facts on File, 1987), 44–45.

Figure 17. Bryn Geffert, adapted from Tankred, "Great Moravia Svatopluk," 2007, Wikimedia Commons, http://en.wikipedia.org/ wiki/File:Great_moravia_svatopluk.png.

Figure 18. Bryn Geffert, adapted from Max Naylor, "Viking Expansion," 2007, Wikimedia Commons, http://en.wikipedia.org/wiki/File:Viking_Expansion.svg.

Figure 20. Rachel Gucker and Bryn Geffert, with reference to Martin Gilbert, *Routledge Atlas of Russian History,* 4th ed. (New York: Routledge, 2007), 15.

Figure 22. Passage from the Gospel of Mark in the Zograf Codex. "Zografskoe evangelie (kirillitsa)/Evangelie ot Marka," n.d., Vikiteka, https://ru.wikisource.org/wiki/Зографское_евангелие_(кириллица)/Евангелие_от_Марка.

Figure 23. Bryn Geffert, adapted from "Location map of Mount Athos (Greece)," Wikimedia Commons, http://commons.wikimedia.org/wiki/File:Location_map_of_MountAthos (Greece).svg, and "Blank map of Europe," Wikimedia Commons, http://commons.wikimedia.org/wiki/File:Blank_map_of_Europe.svg.

Figure 24. Bryn Geffert, adapted from Cassowary, "Great Schism 1054," 2010, Wikimedia Commons, http://commons.wikimedia.org/wiki/File:Great_Schism_1054.svg.

Figure 25. Bryn Geffert, adapted from Mandrak, "Map of the Roman Empire at the Death of Theodosius, Divided in Two Parts," 2009, http://commons.wikimedia.org/wiki/File:Partition_of_the_Roman_Empire_in_395_AD.png.

Figure 26. Bryn Geffert, adapted from Tataryn77, "Justinian555AD," Wikimedia Commons, https://commons.wikimedia.org/wiki/File:Justinian555AD.png.

Figure 27. Cronholm144, "Coat of Arms of the Vatican City," 2007, Wikimedia Commons, http://en.wikipedia.org/wiki/File:Coat_of_arms_of_the_Vatican_City.svg.

Figure 29. Rachel Gucker and Bryn Geffert, with reference to Thomas Cussans, *The Times Atlas of European History* (New York: HarperCollins, 1994), 62.

Figure 30. Rachel Gucker and Bryn Geffert, with reference to Jonathan Riley-Smith, *Atlas of the Crusades* (New York: Facts on File, 1991), 29.

Figure 32. Rachel Gucker and Bryn Geffert, with reference to Charles Anderson, *Augsburg Historical Atlas of Christianity in the Middle Ages and Reformation* (Minneapolis: Augsburg, 1967), 14.

Figure 33. Rachel Gucker and Bryn Geffert, with reference to Charles Anderson, *Augsburg Historical Atlas of Christianity in the Middle Ages and Reformation* (Minneapolis: Augsburg, 1967), 23.

Figure 34. Rachel Gucker and Bryn Geffert, with reference to *The Times Atlas of European History* (New York: HarperCollins, 1994), 100–101.

Figure 35. Bryn Geffert, adapted from Gabagool, "Kievan Rus 1000," Wikimedia Commons, 2009, http://en.wikipedia.org/wiki/File: KievanRus1000.png.

Figure 36. Bryn Geffert, adapted from Gabagool, "Moscow 1500," Wikipedia Commons, 2009, http://en.wikipedia.org/wiki/File: Moscow1500.png.

Figure 37. Bryn Geffert, adapted from "Polish Lithuanian Commonwealth at its maximum extent," 2007, Wikimedia Commons, http:// en.wikipedia.org/wiki/File:Polish-Lithuanian_Commonwealth_at _its_maximum_extent.svg.

Figure 38. Rachel Gucker and Bryn Geffert, with reference to Martin Gilbert, *Routledge Atlas of Russian History,* 4th ed. (New York: Routledge, 2007), 24.

Figure 39. Bryn Geffert, with reference to Barbara Skinner, *The Western Front of the Eastern Church: Uniate and Orthodox Conflict in 18th-Century Poland, Ukraine, Belarus, and Russia* (DeKalb: Northern Illinois University Press, 2009), xiii.

Figure 42. Rachel Gucker and Bryn Geffert, with reference to Charles Anderson, *Augsburg Historical Atlas of Christianity in the Middle Ages and Reformation* (Minneapolis: Augsburg, 1967), 57.

Figure 43. Rachel Gucker and Bryn Geffert, with reference to Thomas Cussans, *The Times Atlas of European History* (New York: Harper-Collins, 1994), 130.